A World History
of the Seas

A World History of the Seas

From Harbour to Horizon

MICHAEL NORTH

Translated by

Pamela Selwyn

BLOOMSBURY ACADEMIC

LONDON • NEW YORK • OXFORD • NEW DELHI • SYDNEY

BLOOMSBURY ACADEMIC
Bloomsbury Publishing Plc
50 Bedford Square, London, WC1B 3DP, UK
1385 Broadway, New York, NY 10018, USA
29 Earlsfort Terrace, Dublin 2, Ireland

BLOOMSBURY, BLOOMSBURY ACADEMIC and the Diana logo are trademarks
of Bloomsbury Publishing Plc

First published in 2016 in Germany as Zwischen Hafen und Horizont.
Weltgeschichte der Meere by Verlag C.H. Beck

First published in Great Britain 2022

English translation © Pamela E. Selwyn 2022
German edition © Velag C.H. Beck oHG München 2016

Michael North has asserted his right under the Copyright, Designs and Patents Act,
1988, to be identified as Author of this work.

For legal purposes the Acknowledgements on pp. xiii–xiv constitute an extension
of this copyright page.

Cover design: Terry Woodley
Cover image © Ocean waves, Katsushika Hokusai. FineArt/Alamy Stock Photo

A catalogue record for this book is available from the British Library.

A catalog record for this book is available from the Library of Congress.

ISBN: HB: 978-1-3501-4544-3
            PB: 978-1-3501-4543-6
      ePDF: 978-1-3501-4546-7
    eBook: 978-1-3501-4545-0

Typeset by Integra Software Services Pvt. Ltd.
Printed and bound in Great Britain

To find out more about our authors and books visit www.bloomsbury.com
and sign up for our newsletters.

For Christopher

Contents

Illustrations

Maps

Preface

In the autumn of 2016, C. H. Beck published *Zwischen Hafen und Horizont. Weltgeschichte der Meere*. The book was well received and won the prize of the German Foundation of Maritime History. Translations into Estonian and Arabic followed. I am grateful to Bloomsbury Academic, and especially to Maddie Holder, for making the English-language edition a reality. Working on this edition has enabled me to incorporate the fruits of recent research and even to add new chapters to the book.

The translation was supported by the University of Greifswald's International Graduate Program 'Baltic Borderlands'. If the book is as readable in English as it was in German, it is the work of my long-standing translator Pamela Selwyn, and I would like to thank her here again. It is always a pleasure to work with her.

The book gained much from the critical comments of various colleagues. Peter Borschberg (Singapore) read the whole translation and provided a wealth of advice which has improved the manuscript. Rainer F. Buschmann (Ojai), Ranabir Chakravarti (New Delhi/Kolkata), Salvatore Ciriacono (Venice/Padua), Jeroen Dewulf (Berkeley) and John W.I. Lee (Santa Barbara) offered valuable suggestions on the Pacific, the Indian Ocean, the early modern Mediterranean, the Atlantic and the seas in Antiquity. In Greifswald, Lasse Seebeck researched new literature, and Vivien Popken updated the bibliography. Karla Hartmann, Martin Hildebrandt and Julian Hildebrandt compiled the index. I owe a special debt of gratitude to Doreen Wollbrecht and Hielke van Nieuwenhuize, who dedicated themselves with great commitment to the final production of the manuscript.

Acknowledgements

I have spent many years studying the Baltic Sea, which has expanded my view of other seas. The Vikings, after all, already connected the Baltic with the Black Sea, the North Sea and the North Atlantic. Accordingly, I found it both worthwhile and necessary to explore the connection between the seas. This perspective was inspired by my own research project 'The Sea as Realm of Memory', which I am conducting in Greifswald together with the universities of Lund and Tartu as part of the international research training group 'Baltic Borderlands'. Those who – like merchants and sailors – leave their home seas for the world's oceans cannot do so without a safe harbour and above all not without the hosts across the globe who make international research possible. At the same time, we need colleagues who can shed new light on our own insights. In writing this book, I accordingly relied upon the collaboration of many people. First of all, I would like to mention Renate Pieper in Graz and Peter Borschberg in Singapore, who read large segments of the manuscript and provided comments and corrections. I would like to thank them along with my Greifswald colleagues Bernard van Wickevoort Crommelin, Alexander Drost and Robert Riemer, whose comments significantly enriched the manuscript. Astrid Erll in Frankfurt has my warmest thanks for the wealth of suggestions.

I am also grateful to the many individual helpers who read shorter passages of the text and responded to questions of detail. I would like to thank my students in Greifswald, who allowed me to test early versions of this book in my lectures. Beyond Greifswald, thanks are owed to the many friends across the world who provided a fertile working atmosphere during my shorter or longer visits. They include, in particular, my colleagues at the University of California at Santa Barbara, who are too numerous to list here. I would also like to mention Peter Arnade, David Chappell and Barbara Watson-Andaya in Hawaii, Kristoffer Neville in Riverside, Thomas DaCosta Kaufmann in Princeton, Maryanne Kowaleski in New York and Richard Unger in Vancouver. My exchanges with Sun Lixin in Beijing, Akiko Sugiyama and António Vasconcelos de Saldanha in Macao and Miki Sugiura, Yoriko Kobayashi-Sato, Toshiaki Tamaki and Yuta Kikuchi in Japan are always refreshing. Ranabir Chakravarti in Delhi has assisted me for many years now. In Europe, I continue to benefit from conversations with Wim Blockmans, Erik Aerts and Herman Van der Wee in

Belgium, Cátia Antunes, Filipa Ribeiro da Silva, Leonard Blussé and Pieter Emmer in the Netherlands, Olga Katsiardi-Hering and Gelina Harlaftis in Greece, Salvatore Ciriacono and Luciano Pezzolo in Italy, Amélia Polónia in Porto, Bartolomé Yun-Casalilla in Seville, Maria Fusaro in Exeter and Jari Ojala in Jyväskylä.

Stefan von der Lahr and his assistant Andrea Morgan at my German publisher C. H. Beck ensured that the book would be readable and attractively produced. As always, the details of book production fell to the staff of the Chair of Modern History of the University of Greifswald. Jörn Sander, Lasse Seebeck, Jan Oliver Giese, Erik Ladenthin, Sven Ristau, Friederike Schmidt, Stefan Lukas and Martin Hildebrandt researched, tracked down and reviewed the vast literature. Jörg Driesner located and transcribed source material in Jakarta. Hielke van Nieuwenhuize gathered original sources and literature in Dutch libraries and archives and accompanied the manuscript through its various stages. The manuscript was formatted by Lasse Seebeck and Doreen Wollbrecht. The latter also did the final editing together with Robert Riemer and Hielke van Nieuwenhuize, with the support of Gero von Roedern and Jörn Sander. I owe them all my deepest gratitude.

Greifswald, summer 2016
Michael North

Introduction

In his poem 'The Sea is History', the Caribbean poet Derek Walcott places the sea at the heart of history: 'Where are your monuments, your battles, martyrs? Where is your tribal memory? Sirs, in that grey vault. The sea. The sea has locked them up. The sea is History'.[1] The sea contains and preserves the memories that lie in its bed, like the sailors, slaves, fishermen and treasure, until people bring them back to light. It is the historian's task to revive or keep alive these memories. The sea thus presents the historian with both a task and a challenge.[2]

Three-quarters of the earth's surface is covered by water. It thus seems something of a misnomer to call our planet the earth rather than the seas or the waters.[3] Many disciplines, especially historical ones, have rediscovered the sea. Historians of science, for instance, have been studying the science of navigation, that is, the long road to determining longitude and latitude.[4] Literary scholars explore conceptions and representations of the sea.[5] Social historians focus on dock workers, sailors and pirates,[6] while economic historians turn their attention to global trade and shipping. Finally, environmental historians deal with the environmental history of the seas, with tsunamis and ecological changes such as pollution and warming. Given the increased interest in global history, the seas and oceans have become a topic of enquiry in new ways today and a new historical thalassology is emerging.[7]

This sheds a different light on ideas of the sea conveyed by art, literature and philosophy. Here, the image of unwelcome wildness, terror and the irrational still dominates the Western, European perspective,[8] while in other parts of the world, for example, the islands of the Pacific or southeast Asia, the sea is perceived as a familiar element.[9]

The sea challenges humankind in a variety of ways. The power of water demands adaptation and reflection by those who live from the sea, and those affected by its nature. Living by the sea, living from the sea and living with the sea generate a panoply of notions and practices whose study could lead to an altered way of looking at the relationship between land and sea.

The present volume explores the various roles that the sea has played in history against this backdrop.[10] First and foremost, we think of the exchange of material and immaterial goods via the sea as well as migration by groups of persons. Here the seas at once connected and separated, and people who did not cross the seas themselves still felt the consequences of contact. Confrontations with the sea also shaped human societies. Since time immemorial, the sea has offered vital resources, whether they lay on the sea floor, swam in the water or moved along its surface in the form of ships. For that reason, states sought to appropriate the seas by laying claim to ships' treasures and passages while also ensuring their safety.

People and societies accordingly assigned to the sea different roles: as a source of livelihood, means of transport, theatre of war and site of longing and memory.[11] This book will also address how society and the arts perceived, imagined and constructed the seas.

Studies on the seas are still influenced by the vision of Fernand Braudel, whose *La Méditerranée et le monde méditerranéen à l'epoque de Philippe II* was the first book to present a maritime region over the centuries and its natural conditions as a unified entity in which human beings were at the mercy of nature.[12] Inspired by Braudel, various historians have constructed other seas following his Mediterranean model,[13] but have gradually realized that it is not possible or sensible to fully apply his paradigms to the Indian Ocean,[14] the Pacific[15] or the Atlantic.[16] In recent years, even the so-called Atlantic System has come under scrutiny, since the term suggests a coherent Atlantic, merely reflects imperial history and leaves the inland populations out of the picture.[17] Moreover, a viewpoint that understands the sea as a closed system ignores global and regional connections. The networks that form around one of the seas have always led to connections with others. This offers new perspectives for global history.

I follow John Parry here, who already noted in his 1974 *The Discovery of the Sea*, 'All the seas of the world are one [...] they are all connected with one another. All seas, except in the areas of circumpolar ice, are navigable.'[18] In the meantime, global warming has changed this as well, and it is now possible to traverse the polar seas travelling to the east or west.

When we write a history of the seas, it is one of connections and comparisons, as in global history more generally.[19] The focus is on the people who created these connections, as well as the goods and ideas that were transported from one world to another. The advantage of such an altered perspective is that we no longer look at the sea from the national viewpoints of the littoral states but take into account the connectivity of the seas.

In this context, the book deals with Jewish, Arabic, Chinese, Tamil and many other maritime networks and highlights cross-regional linkages on the world's oceans and seas. Thus, I will try to pay more attention to 'non-Western agents' in maritime history. Even after the arrival of the Europeans in several oceans, local actors resisted, cooperated and creatively accommodated to the new opportunities.[20]

The maritime networks will be treated first in the chapters on the individual seas and oceans, which explore both the connections among the seas and their imaginations. Two final systematic chapters address the sea's agency, its role as resource and humankind's changing relationship to the ocean environment. This will help us to understand the impact of the sea on human history and how people have changed, and continue to change and even endanger, the ocean environment.

Notes

1   D. Walcott, *The Star-Apple Kingdom*, 4th edn (New York, 1986), 364, 366.

2   S. E. Larson, 'Sea, Identity and Literature', *1616. Anuario de Literatura Comparada* 2 (2012): 171–88; J. C. Tung, 'The Sea Is History. Reading Derek Walcott through a Melancolic Lens', BA thesis, Mount Holyoke College 2006, 52–3.

3   C. Schmitt, *Land und Meer. Eine weltgeschichtliche Betrachtung* (Leipzig, 1942); R. Carson, *The Sea around Us* (New York, 1951).

4   D. Sobel, *Longitude. The True Story of a Lone Genius Who Solved the Greatest Scientific Problem of His Time* (New York, 2007).

5   B. Klein and G. Mackenthun (eds.), *Sea Changes. Historicizing the Ocean* (New York, 2004).

6   M. Rediker, *Outlaws of the Atlantic. Sailors, Pirates, and Motley Crews in the Age of Sail* (Boston, MA, 2014).

7   J. H. Bentley, R. Bridenthal and K. Wigen (eds.), *Seascapes. Maritime Histories, Littoral Cultures, and Transoceanic Exchanges* (Honolulu, 2007); P. Horden and N. Purcell, 'The Mediterranean and "the New Thalassology"', *American History Review* 111 (2006): 722–40; A. Games, 'Atlantic History. Definitions, Challenges, Opportunities', *American History Review* 111 (2006): 741–57; M. K. Matsuda, 'The Pacific', *American History Review* 111 (2006): 758–80; P. N. Miller (ed.), *The Sea. Thalassography and Historiography* (Ann Arbor, 2013); D. Abulafia, *The Boundless Sea: A Human History of the Oceans* (London, 2019); H. M. Rozwadowski, *Vast Expanses. A History of the Oceans* (London, 2018); D. Armitage, A. Bashford and S. Sivasundaram (eds.), *Oceanic Histories* (Cambridge, New York, Melbourne, New Delhi, Singapore, 2018); R. F. Buschmann and L. Nolde (eds.), *The World's Oceans. Geography, History, and Environment* (Santa Barbara, CA, 2018).

8   Larsen, 'Sea, Identity and Literature', 171–88; J. Mack, *The Sea. A Cultural History* (London, 2011); H. Blumenberg, *Schiffbruch mit Zuschauer. Paradigma einer Daseinsmetapher* (Frankfurt/M., 2011).

9   A. Calder, J. Lamb and B. Orr (eds.), *Voyages and Beaches. Pacific Encounters, 1769–1840* (Honolulu, 1999).

10   For mediaeval England, see R. Gorski, 'Roles of the Sea. Views from the Shore', in Gorski (ed.), *Roles of the Sea in Medieval England* (Woodbridge, 2012), 1–24.

11   P. E. Steinberg, *The Social Construction of the Ocean* (Cambridge, 2001), 8–38.

12   F. Braudel, *La Méditerranée et le monde méditeranéen à l'époque de Philippe II* (Paris, 1949); English: *The Mediterranean and the Mediterranean World in the Age of Philip II*, trans. S. Reynolds, 2 vols (London, 1972–73). Also critical are P. Horden and N. Purcell, *The Corrupting Sea. A Study of Mediterranean History* (Oxford, 2000); and D. Abulafia, *The Great Sea. A Human History of the Mediterranean* (Oxford, 2011).

13   K. N. Chaudhuri, *Asia before Europe. Economy and Civilisation of the Indian Ocean from the Rise of Islam to 1750* (Cambridge, 1990); M. N. Pearson, *The Indian Ocean* (London, 2006); A. Schottenhammer (ed.), *The East Asian 'Mediterranean'. Maritime Crossroads of Culture, Commerce and Human Migration* (Wiesbaden, 2008); P. Butel, *Histoire de l'Atlantique, de l'Antiquité à nos jours* (Paris, 2012); C. King, *The Black Sea. A History* (Oxford, 2004).

14   H. Sutherland, 'Southeast Asian History and the Mediterranean Analogy', *Journal of Southeast Asian Studies* 34, no. 1 (2003): 1–20; F. Gipouloux, *La Méditerranée asiatique. Villes portuaires et réseaux marchands en Chine, au Japon et en Asie du Sud-Est, XVIe-XXIe siècle* (Paris, 2009); D. Lombard, 'Une autre "Méditerranée" dans le Sud-est Asiatique', *Hérodote* 28 (1998): 184–93; M. Haneda (ed.), *Asian Port Cities, 1600–1800. Local and Foreign Cultural Interactions* (Singapore, 2009); R. Ptak, *Die maritime Seidenstraße. Küstenräume, Seefahrt und Handel in vorkolonialer Zeit* (Munich, 2007); Schottenhammer, *The East Asian 'Mediterranean'*; R. B. Wong, 'Entre monde et nation: les régions braudeliénnes en Asie', *Annales* 66, no. 1 (2001): 9–16.

15   D. Armitage and A. Bashford (eds.), *Pacific Histories. Ocean, Land, People* (New York, 2014); M. K. Matsuda, *Pacific Worlds. A History of Seas, Peoples, and Cultures*, 3rd edn (Cambridge, 2014).

16   B. Bailyn, *Atlantic History. Concept and Contours* (Cambridge, MA and London, 2005); J. P. Greene and P. D. Morgan (eds.), *Atlantic History. A Critical Appraisal* (Oxford, 2009); D. Armitage and M. J. Braddick (eds.), *The British Atlantic World, 1500–1800*, 2nd edn (Basingstoke and New York, 2009); P. A. Coclanis (ed.), *The Atlantic Economy during the Seventeenth and Eighteenth Centuries. Organization, Operation, Practice, and Personnel* (Columbia, SC, 2005).

17   J. P. Greene and P. D. Morgan, 'Introduction: The Present State of Atlantic History', in Greene and Morgan (eds.), *Atlantic History*, 5–7.

18   J. Parry, *The Discovery of the Sea* (New York, 1974), xi.

19   P. O'Brien, 'Historiographical Traditions and Modern Imperatives for the Restoration of Global History', *Journal of Global History* 1 (2006): 3–39, 4; C. A. Bayly, *The Birth of the Modern World 1780–1914. Global Connections and*

Comparisons (Oxford, 2004); J. Osterhammel, *Transformation of the World. A Global History of the Nineteenth Century* (Princeton and Oxford, 2014). See also W. Reinhard (ed.), *Empires and Encounters. 1350–1750* (Cambridge, MA, 2015); M. Berg (ed.), *Writing the History of the Global. Challenges for the 21st Century* (Oxford, 2013).

20 N. Thomas, *Islanders. The Pacific in the Age of Empire* (New Haven and London, 2010), 2–4.

1

Bridging the Sea

World literature owes its earliest awareness of the sea and the dangers of seafaring to Homer and his protagonist Odysseus:

> When we had left that island and no other land appeared, but only sky and sea, then verily the son of Cronos set a black cloud above the hollow ship, and the sea grew dark beneath it. She ran on for no long time, for straightway came the shrieking West Wind, blowing with a furious tempest, and the blast of the wind snapped both the fore-stays of the mast, so that the mast fell backward and all its tackling was strewn in the bilge. On the stern of the ship the mast struck the head of the pilot and crushed all the bones of his skull together, and like a diver he fell from the deck and his proud spirit left his bones.[1]

This sea, the Mediterranean, had been discovered several millennia before (ninth to eighth century BCE), when hunters, gatherers and farmers from Asia Minor settled the islands of Cyprus and Crete. From there the farmers also reached the Greek mainland, most notably Thessaly. Evidence of intensive maritime trade remains limited, however, with the exception of obsidian tools from the island of Melos and the shells that became popular as adornment.[2]

The beginnings: Phoenicians and Greeks

Scholars have noted an intensification of exchange in the second millennium BCE, when people travelled voluntarily or as captives and goods were transported between the coasts and islands of the (eastern) Mediterranean. Political centres such as Avaris, 'Venice on the Nile', Ugarit in present-day Syria and Knossos on Crete stimulated long-distance trade. The Bronze Age ship from Uluburun discovered in 1982 thus carried not just copper and tin but also glass from Egypt and many precious amber objects from the Baltic, whose magical properties were prized in the Mediterranean region.[3]

Inhabitants of the Cyclades played an important role as intermediaries, who made contact with other islands and the coastal mainland in their canoes. One innovation was the introduction of a sailing ship – familiar to us from seals – with a lower keel, which could travel more quickly over long distances and transport more cargo. In the *Odyssey* Homer describes such a craft setting sail:

> And Telemachus called to his men, and bade them lay hold of the tackling, and they hearkened to his call. The mast of fir they raised and set in the hollow socket, and made it fast with fore-stays, and hauled up the white sail with twisted thongs of ox- hide. So the wind filled the belly of the sail, and the dark wave sang loudly about the stem of the ship as she went, and she sped over the wave accomplishing her way.[4]

For a long time, the new ships stimulated shipping and trade as well as the establishment of ports. In the second millennium BCE, the centre of these activities was initially Minoan Crete, which was named after its storied king and occupied a favourable position between the Aegean, Anatolia and Egypt. Palace settlements such as Knossos, Malia and Phaistos were erected along its coasts. Archaeological evidence shows that overseas goods brought to Knossos included copper from present-day South Russia, lapis lazuli from

FIGURE 1 *Ship procession: Fresco from the Bronze Age in the Minoan town Akrotiri, Santorini, Greece. © Wikipedia Commons.*

Central Asia, silver from Attica and gold and ivory from Egypt. The goods were transported to Anatolia or Egypt along the traditional routes and then shipped to Crete. In exchange, Crete offered woollen fabrics, wine and olive oil as well as essential oils and medicinal herbs and wood, for which there was demand in Egypt.

The palace city of Mycenae on the Peloponnese was located at the intersection of the western and eastern Mediterranean. From here there was easy access to the Gulf of Argos and Crete; similarly, one could reach the Adriatic via the Gulf of Corinth and the Aegean via the Saronic Gulf. We accordingly find Mycenaean ceramics in both the West and the East. Apart from painted ceramics, the Mycenaeans exported weapons and in exchange imported copper and tin, the components of the bronze used to make weapons. The copper came from Attica, and tin was transported from the Iberian Peninsula by a Mycenaean fleet.[5]

Mycenae is also associated with the heroes of the *Iliad* and the *Odyssey*, who could rightly claim to have travelled the entire known world of their day. After returning from the victorious siege of Troy, Menelaus could boast

> For of a truth after many woes and wide wanderings I brought my wealth home in my ships and came in the eighth year. Over Cyprus and Phoenicia I wandered, and Egypt, and I came to the Ethiopians and the Sidonians and the Erembians, and to Libya.[6]

Historically, however, the Greeks were preceded as maritime people by the Phoenicians (Gr. *Phoinikes*), whom Homer disdained for their business sense. Their name came from the purple dye obtained from the *Murex* mollusc found along the coast of the Eastern Mediterranean, one of the commodities in which they traded. Phoenicia, which corresponded roughly to present-day Lebanon, had a number of commercial centres, for example, Ugarit in the north (destroyed *c.* 1190 BCE), Byblos and Sidon. Apart from Tyrian purple, the main export was native cedar, which the Egyptians in particular used for shipbuilding. A papyrus in a Moscow collection, for example, recounts the journey of the priest Wenamun, who around 1075 BCE was sent from the temple of Amon in Thebes (Upper Egypt) to acquire cedarwood for the ship of the god Amon.

This account and other Egyptian sources provide insight into trade in Byblos as well as the goods used to pay for cedarwood: gold and silver vessels, linen clothing, papyrus rolls, cowhides, ropes, lentils and fish. Cyprus was colonized from Tyre, another Phoenician centre, which was of interest particularly for its deposits of copper. Other Phoenician trading posts followed in Sicily, Sardinia and North Africa, where Carthage would develop as a new centre.[7]

Around 800 BCE, the Phoenicians advanced into the Atlantic through the Straits of Gibraltar and founded an outpost in Gadir (Cádiz) on an island on the Atlantic coast. From there, Phoenician settlements spread eastwards along the coast. The Phoenicians lived from agriculture and fishing as well as trade. At times they competed with the Etruscans, who shipped wine from their main settlements in central Italy to present-day southern France.

South of the Straits of Gibraltar, the Phoenicians settled the West African coast, where the trade in ivory, ostrich eggs, exotic animals and slaves beckoned. These emporia were later integrated into the Carthaginian network.[8]

The Phoenician presence is evident from sacred sites and cultural commonalities. The Phoenicians venerated Melkart, the principal deity of Tyre, who protected shipping and foreign outposts, and erected shrines to the god in the Mediterranean world and Gadir as well as on Cyprus. The graves of native Iberians also contain Phoenician figurines, which suggests the spread of similar practices or beliefs among local elites.[9] Decorative metal drinking vessels manufactured in various 'Phoenician' workshops in Crete, Anatolia or Iberia also indicate Phoenician influence on ways of life more generally.[10]

The Phoenicians also mediated contacts between the 'early Greeks' and the Mediterranean world, as is evident from funerary objects. The alphabet, without which Homer's textualization of the old stories and songs would have been impossible, was also developed by the Phoenicians and adapted by the Greeks.[11]

Around the middle of the eighth century BCE, the Greeks began to advance almost simultaneously into the western Mediterranean world. Many cities such as Ampurias (Emporion), Marseille (Massalia), Nice (Nikaia), Antibes (Antipolis), Naples (Neapolis), Reggio (Rhegion), Syracuse (Syrakusai), Taormina (Tauromenion) and Palermo (Panormos) owe their Greek names to this process of colonization.

Sicily and southern Italy in particular were settled far more densely than elsewhere and thus known as *Magna Graecia*. The settlers brought their political institutions as well as their deities and cults. One of the first settlements, which has been well studied by archaeologists, is Pithekussai on Ischia, whose iron ore deposits made it attractive. In 700 BCE the town had 4,000 inhabitants who originally came from Etruria, Sardinia, Phoenicia, North Africa and the Greek motherland.[12]

The search for metals finally took the Greeks to the southern coast of the Black Sea. Soon they presumably also arrived at the great rivers of the Eurasian steppes. The Black Sea region was rich in fish and wood for shipbuilding, and also offered a low population density.

The journey to the Black Sea crossed a psychological boundary beyond which the Amazons and Hades were not far distant. Crimea was home to the Tauri, who had sacrificed Iphigenia to Artemis, and to the east, in the Caucasus, Prometheus had been chained to a rock until he was freed by Herakles. It was, however, above all the city-states of the Ionian coast, which, like Miletos, profited from trade (cereals, metals, fish) with the region around the Black Sea and controlled the passage through the Dardanelles and Bosporus. The colonies of Sinope on the south coast, Dioskurias near present-day Sukhumi at the foot of the Caucasus, Pantikapaion (present-day Kerch) at the entrance to the Sea of Azov and Olbia at the mouth of the Bug River opened up trade with the hinterland. According to Plato, putting his words in Socrates' mouth, in the fifth century BCE Greek settlements spread out like 'ants or frogs about a pond', with sailing ships travelling along the coasts and canoes along the rivers. The Black Sea colonies occupied an

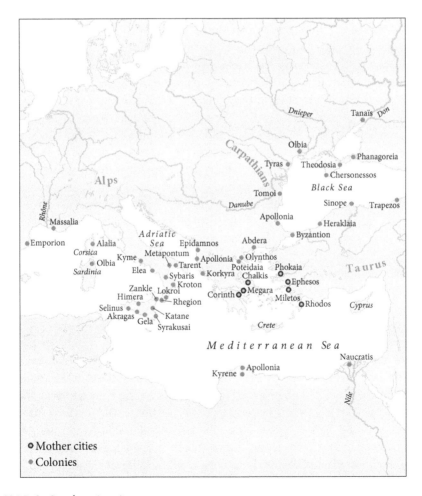

MAP 1 *Greek emigration*

important place in the Greek economy. If the winds were favourable, one could sail from the Sea of Azov to the island of Rhodes in nine days and supply the Ionian cities and the Greek mainland with vital cereals – if Sparta was not blocking the Dardanelles. Fish was also available in large quantities and was preserved with local salt.[13] In first century BCE Rome, salt fish from the Black Sea was considered a delicacy. Exotic animals like pheasants, which were brought from there to Greece and Italy where they were bred, were also highly prized.[14]

Thalassocracies: Athens, Alexandria, Carthage and Rome

The Greek word *thalassokratia* refers to a maritime power; however, this was not a simple sea power, but the establishment of a realm that linked territories scattered across the waters with the aid of ships, thereby creating a particular political space. Thucydides uses the words θαλασσοκρατεῖν and θαλασσοκράτωρ in reference to the Athenian fleet and its naval supremacy as well as 'to the Peloponnesians, for whom the rule of the sea was an unnerving and insecure novelty'.[15] Athens, which had risen out of the Persian wars, and where maritime and terrestrial interests went hand-in-hand, was naturally a thalassocracy. Thus, in the fifth century BCE the Athenians expanded their territory, occupying land in Euboea and using it for food production. Moreover, rule over the Aegean islands allowed Athenian citizens and officeholders to make careers as administrative specialists or acquire additional land holdings. Over time, the Athenians even tried unsuccessfully to incorporate Syracuse in Sicily.[16]

The Athenian system of alliances, the so-called Delian League, also points to the strong significance of organizing politics and war through the sea. The Delian League was a product of the Persian Wars, which began with the occupation of the kingdom of Lydia in Asia Minor. In this enterprise, the Persian fleet could rely on Phoenician mariners and ships. When the Ionian cities rebelled, the Persians invaded again. The revolt was soon put down and ended with parts of Miletos being burnt to the ground (493 BCE). Punitive expeditions on the Greek mainland followed, but attempts by a small Persian force to land at Marathon were surprisingly beaten back. The next Persian invasion in 480 BCE could only be held back briefly at Thermopylae. Now, however, the equipping of the naval forces propagated by the politician Themistocles showed its first successes. The Athenians vanquished the Persian fleet at Salamis and again at Mykale (Mycale) in 479 BCE. Athenian warships played a key role in the lasting Persian withdrawal.

Athens claimed all the glory and founded the Delian League as a defensive alliance to protect the Greek cities and Aegean islands in the long term. The members of the alliance owed a fixed sum – after all, the oarsmen had to be paid – and also participated directly in the shared fleet with warships and sailors. Smaller islands and towns not in a position to do so could make monetary payments instead. Athens played the leading role and used it to discipline their allies and build up a maritime empire. Achieving economic unity played a key role here. It was attained by standardizing coins, weights and measures to conform to those used in Athens. In this way, a unified economic area arose, although some cities or islands repeatedly sought to escape it. When the island of Thasos abandoned the alliance, a naval blockade in 465–463 BCE brought it back into line.

The Athenians managed to maintain their naval supremacy even during the Peloponnesian War, although on land they were inferior to their main enemies, the Spartans. Neutral islands such as Melos were dragged into the war and forced into the coalition by the Athenians. After the Spartan fleet under the command of Lysander defeated the Athenians at Aigospotamoi in the Dardanelles, the Athenian was replaced by the Spartan thalassocracy.[17] In 377 BCE, Athens made another attempt to re-establish its command of the seas with the help of a second maritime league. Although the Athenians rejected the imperial practices of the Delian League, this second league was short-lived.[18]

In the meantime, the rise of Macedon had permanently altered the political and economic map of the eastern Mediterranean. Alexander did not stop at the Black Sea but aimed to conquer the Persian Empire and ended at the shores of the Indian Ocean. When Alexander reached the Indus River by the land route, he had a fleet built, which brought part of his troops, under the command of his friend Niarchos, down the Indus, across the Arabian Sea and Persian Gulf and up the Tigris.

After Alexander's death in 323 BCE his empire disintegrated into rival kingdoms: the Antigonids in the Aegean, the Seleucids in the eastern Mediterranean and the Ptolemies in Egypt. In Egypt, the ruling class was Greek, the army Macedonian. Despite rural Egyptian resistance, Greek culture proved attractive to many inhabitants of the new Ptolemaic capital Alexandria, including the city's Jewish population. The Lighthouse of Alexandria, celebrated as the 'Seventh Wonder of the World', thus also symbolized the Ptolemaic city's role as the 'lighthouse of Mediterranean culture'.[19]

Mediterranean trade formed the basis for Alexandria's economic and cultural supremacy, with Carthage in the west and Rhodes in the east as important trading partners. Rhodes, whose harbour with its Colossus boasted another wonder of the world, had taken the opportunity of the decline of Athens to establish itself as a centre of shipping. Ships from Rhodes brought grain from Egypt to the north and took wine in the opposite direction, as is evident from the many amphora found in Alexandria, the Aegean and Black Sea and also Carthage and Sicily.[20]

After 275 BCE Ptolemy II laid out a new port on the western shore of the Red Sea, which he named after his mother Berenice. The port was intended mainly for shipping African war elephants to Egypt, after the Seleucid empire had imposed a blockade on the delivery of Indian war elephants.[21]

The regional power in the western Mediterranean was Carthage, which further developed the legacy of the Phoenicians, established outposts in Sicily and placed them under its protection. When Carthage attempted to establish a thalassocracy and conquer Sicily, however, the North African city's interests collided with the Greek and later Roman sphere of influence. Syracuse and Carthage finally agreed to the partitioning of Sicily, with the west being controlled by Carthage and the east by Syracuse. Rome's interests, in contrast, initially lay in Etruria, whose cities it integrated into its Roman sphere of influence.

It was only the invasion of King Pyrrhus I, whose aid against Rome the Greek city of Tarentum sought and who brought southern Italy and Sicily under his control despite heavy losses (so-called Pyrrhic victories), that brought southern Italy to Rome's attention. Although Rome and Carthage at times joined forces against Pyrrhus, they soon became enemies in the Sicilian theatre of war. This led to the First Punic War (264–241 BCE), in which the Romans allied with the Greek cities fought not just on land but also at sea against the Carthaginian ships, which they boarded using the famous corvus, dispensing with the Greek tactic of ramming. In the peace treaty of 241 BCE, Carthage promised to pay reparations and to evacuate Sicily, which became a Roman province in 227 BCE. Sardinia and Corsica also became Roman, so that Carthage subsequently had to shift its activities further west.

Hannibal's expansion on the Iberian Peninsula instigated the Second Punic War (218–201 BCE), in which Hannibal marched from Hispania to Italy over the western Alps, but despite spectacular military successes he could not assert himself in the long term. After Scipio's victory over the Punic army at Zama (202 BCE), the peace treaty limited the military potential and radius of action of Carthage, which henceforth was allowed to maintain only ten warships. In the years that followed, Spain, which Hannibal had ruled for a time, and, after the destruction of Carthage in the Third Punic War, North Africa as well were integrated into the Roman Empire. The Greek city of Corinth, which had also resisted Roman expansion, shared the same fate.[22] The result was a Roman or Roman-dominated Mediterranean region. Octavian's victory over the Egyptian fleet commanded by Mark Antony at the naval battle of Actium (31 BCE) concluded this process. Octavian established a permanent fleet with bases in Misenum on the Gulf of

Naples and Ravenna on the Adriatic. With time, additional fleets arose in Egypt, Syria, North Africa, on the Black Sea and the Rhine and Danube rivers. For the first and only time, a thalassocracy encompassed the entire Mediterranean, which the Romans therefore dubbed *Mare Nostrum* (our sea).[23]

To be sure, the existence of the Roman Empire was not based solely on supremacy at sea, but without access to the Mediterranean its appearance and form would have been very different. With military and political control, Rome was also able to open up trade. Victories brought spoils and money to Rome, which the Roman elites used to buy landed estates (*latifundia*). At the same time, the wars affected the population, making agricultural labourers scarce.[24] For that reason, the *latifundia* were worked by slaves captured in Carthage, Greece or other lands on the Mediterranean coasts. If cities did not surrender in time their populations were enslaved. This was allegedly the fate of 55,000 people from Carthage (146 BCE) and 150,000 from the Greek region of Epirus (167 BCE). Caesar's campaigns swelled the ranks of slaves, especially from Gaul (58–50 BCE). Another source was the slave markets on the Aegean. After these had dried up following Pompey's successful campaign against the pirates (67 BCE), slaves had to be procured from the border regions of the Roman Empire. At the same time, the slave population in Roman households and on the estates rose through reproduction. House slaves did have career opportunities, managing the estates, teaching children Greek or being sent to other parts of the world as agents by their masters.[25]

It was not only the landless population of Italy that flocked to the Roman metropolis; inhabitants of the provinces also sought their fortunes in the capital. This led to the emergence of neighbourhoods inhabited by Greeks, Syrians, Africans and Iberians, and Greek, the dominant language of the eastern Mediterranean, was spoken in Rome as well.[26]

Wheat, wine and precious stones

Roman trade, like Mediterranean trade more generally, no longer concentrated solely on luxury goods. On the contrary, the bulk goods wheat and wine linked Rome with the provinces. Rulers used the grain, which came first from Sicily and Sardinia and later from North Africa and Egypt, to secure provisions for Rome, since they had to keep their population happy with bread and circuses.

Wine transport also played a considerable role, which would have been impossible without the mass production of amphoras and jugs. The mid-first century BCE shipwreck at Madrague de Giens near the port town of Hyères, for instance, carried some 400 tonnes of cargo, including 6,000–7,000 wine amphoras. It is estimated that some 40 million amphoras of Italian wine were transported to Gaul over the century, which corresponds to annual wine imports and consumption of 100,000 hectolitres. The Gallic thirst for wine was legendary and was considered a lucrative business for Italian merchants. Apart from wine, the remains of other ships reveal olive oil from Apulia and dyestuffs whose exporters can be reconstructed in some cases from the names on amphora shards.[27]

The Mediterranean's Roman period was characterized by a number of different ship types, which can be distinguished by size, cargo and sailing routes. There were small coastal ships with a tonnage ranging from 2.5 to 10, while ships with a capacity of 50 tonnes were used for longer distances. The construction of these flat-bottomed boats reflects the transport of wine. The ships that transported amphoras and building materials or even obelisks were larger (200–500 tonnes). Wheat exports from Alexandria, Egypt, to Rome also required large ships. They had two masts, one for the mainsail and one for the headsail. Heavy ballast lowered the ship's centre of gravity. In addition, bilge pumps were introduced to keep ships carrying cereals as dry as possible.[28]

Inland trade was linked to maritime trade, for example, in Roman Germania, where merchants were active on both sides of the border. Roman luxury goods were prized by the Germanic tribal elites, while Roman merchants in turn bought up slaves. Moreover, the mouth of the Rhine allowed for the distribution of Roman goods along the coasts. From there they must have been able to travel farther north via Germanic networks. Thus, bronze and glass objects of Roman origin can be found in large quantities in present-day Norway.[29]

In the Mediterranean, the expansion of the Roman Empire and the construction boom of the Roman imperial period (first to third centuries) generated a need for luxury goods and decorative materials. Greek statues were in demand along with glass and metal objects from the eastern Mediterranean. The wealthy elites also required silk, perfume and other goods from the coasts of the Indian Ocean, as well as exotic birds, papyrus and medicine from Alexandria. The import of pepper and Indian spikenard (an aromatic plant) was also organized through Alexandria and Berenice on the Red Sea. This is confirmed by excavations in Berenice, where 7.5 kg of peppercorns were found in a waste pit. A Roman could have covered his wheat requirements for two whole years with the proceeds from this amount of pepper. Emeralds and diamonds found in archaeological sites also point to the trade in precious stones. Foodstuffs for the local population and Roman soldiers in the region, especially fish oil and olive oil, as well as ship's provisions were also traded. Merchants such as the famous Nikanor of Koptos maintained a number of agents on the Red Sea who organized trade and transport.

A papyrus from the mid-second century CE that survives in Vienna deals with one transport of such Indian goods, offering details of the process. The *Hermapollon*, a ship lying at anchor in the Indian port of Muziris, located in coastal Kerala, was to set sail across the Arabian Sea and into the Red Sea to Berenice or Myos Hormos (to the north of Berenice). From there, the cargo, consisting of spikenard oil, ivory and textiles, was to continue by camel to Koptos on the Nile, whence it would be transported by ship to Alexandria. In Alexandria, a tariff of 25 per cent had to be paid on the goods, and only then were they sold and perhaps shipped to Rome.[30]

Handbooks and travel accounts

Perceptions of the sea have focused thus far on the literature of classical antiquity, on the dangers that human beings faced when they went to sea and challenged the gods. The picture changed with the rise and growing necessity of seafaring, and reflected both the dangers and the prospects, weighing the one against the other. The gravestone of an unknown Roman merchant bears the following inscription:

> If you please, stranger, stay awhile and read. I often roamed the great sea with ships, flying along under sails. I reached many countries, but this is my end which the Fates once sang me when I was born. Here I deposed all my sorrows and my labours, I do not fear the stars nor the clouds nor the raging sea, and I am no longer afraid the costs could be higher than the income. Benevolent Trust, I pay thee thanks, most holy goddess. I was weakened by broken luck three times, and you saved me. You are worthy of being wished for by all mortals. Stranger, goodbye, may there be always money to cover your costs, for you have not disregarded this stone and proclaimed its dignity.[31]

Merchants and mariners had the so-called *periploi* to guide their voyages. These seafaring manuals or accounts of voyages described harbours and coastal landmarks which could serve as orientation for seafarers. With time, information on navigation and also on winds and shallows was added. Various manuals, which often survive only in fragments, belong to genre of the *periploi*. One example is the experiences of Arrian[32] in the Black Sea; the most frequently cited of them is the *Periplus Maris Erythraei*. The travel account by the Greek Pytheas of Massalia, who sailed from the Mediterranean to the Atlantic in the fourth century BCE and wrote the description 'On the Ocean', is another example. Unfortunately, the papyrus does not survive, but Pytheas's experiences appear to have been so significant that ancient geographers such as Pliny and Strabo cite him and thus provide information about his voyage. Barry Cunliffe has reconstructed his route from these fragments. It seems likely that Pytheas did not enter the Atlantic through the Straits of Gibraltar but walked overland from Marseille to the mouth of the Garonne river and then had himself transported to the North Sea on ships belonging to various inhabitants of the coast. He may have circumnavigated the British Isles in the process and perhaps travelled as far as Iceland, since he reports on a land called Ultima Thule, six days' journey from the British Isles. Strabo, however, casts doubt on his credibility:

> Concerning Thule our historical information is still more uncertain, on account of its outside position; for Thule, of all the countries that are named, is set farthest north. But that the things which Pytheas has told about Thule, as well as the other places in that part of the world, have indeed been fabricated by him, we have clear evidence from the districts that are known to us, for in most cases he has falsified them, as I have already said before, and hence he is obviously more false concerning the districts which have been placed outside the inhabited world.[33]

Pliny and others, however, seem to have believed Pytheas and disseminated his observations as geographical knowledge. The astronomer and mathematician Geminos of Rhodes, for example, wrote:

> And it seems that Pytheas of Massalia reached these places. At any rate, he says in his treatise *On the Ocean* that 'the barbarians showed us where the Sun goes to sleep; for around these places it happens that the night becomes very short, 2 hours for some, 3 for others, so that, a little while after setting, the Sun rises straightaway.[34]

Pytheas may also have travelled along the North Sea coast to Jutland; at any rate, he writes about the inhabitants and the amber found there, which was prized throughout the Mediterranean.[35]

While Pytheas's manuscript was likely destroyed along with the library at Alexandria, the *Periplus Ponti Euxini* of Flavius, better known as Arrian, survived. This was one part of the account the new Roman prefect of Cappadocia was supposed to send to Emperor Hadrian in 131 CE. The Romans had long left the Black Sea region to its own devices and only developed an interest in the region and brought it under Roman influence after the expansion of the Pontic Empire under King Mithridates. Arrian, who came from Bithynia in Asia Minor, was a Roman citizen and a member of the provincial aristocracy. He

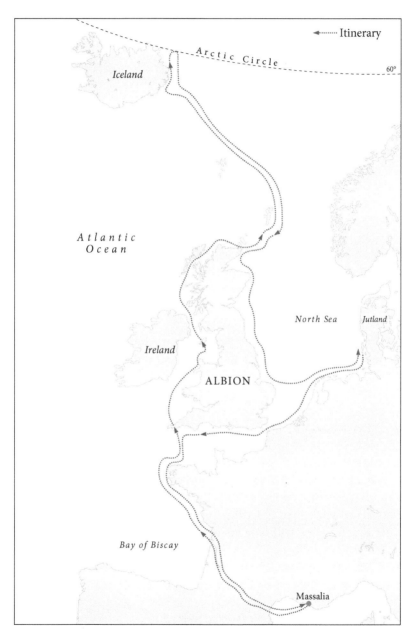

MAP 2 *The travels of Pytheas*

was clearly a skilled general and was connected with the imperial family. His duties included supervising the Roman border region on the eastern Black Sea and the Caucasus. He accordingly reported on his voyage eastwards, which began in Trebizond, the last port under Roman rule. On his voyage he ran into storms, which he described as follows:

> Soon after a cloud suddenly arising burst nearly in an easterly direction from us, and brought on a violent storm of wind, which was entirely contrary to the course that we held, and from the fatal effects of which we had a narrow escape. For it almost instantly produced such a swell of the sea, as to make it appear hollow to the view, and caused a deluge of water to break not only over that part of the ship where the benches of the rowers were placed, but also over the part which is between them and the poop. Our situation was then truly tragic, since as fast as we pumped out the water, so fast did it burst upon us.[36]

Arrian did not allow himself to be put off by the unfortunate weather, however, and visited the old Greek colony of Dioskurias, where he was astonished to find a Roman outpost. He consequently tried to increase the Roman presence in contact with local rulers and gathered intelligence everywhere about the coasts and former trading centres. Apart from his own views and second-hand information, Arrian reported unverified oral and written legends already familiar from Herodotus. Apart from his activities as an administrator, Arrian made a name for himself as an historian who wrote about Alexander the Great as well as Trajan's wars.[37]

The most famous travel manual is the *Periplus Maris Erythraei*, which was written around 50 BCE in Alexandria by an unnamed Greek mariner. The 'Erythraean Sea' here refers to the Indian Ocean, a term first used by Pliny in his *Natural History* (77 CE), which speaks of the *Mare Indicum*, a name that however included the western part now known as the Arabian Sea.[38] The *Periplus* provides glimpses of the harbours, goods and shipping routes of the Indian Ocean and thus, together with Pliny, offers an important source of information on expanding Roman trade in the first century CE:

1 Of the designated harbours of the Erythraean Sea and the ports of trade on it, first comes Egypt's port of Myos Hormos and, beyond it, after a sail of 1800 stades to the right, Berenice. The ports of both are bays of the Red Sea on the edge of Egypt.

2 To the right of these places, immediately beyond Berenice, comes the country of the Barbaroi. The coastal parts are inhabited by Ichthyophagoi ['fish eaters'] living in mean huts built in narrow areas,

hence in scattered groups, while the inland parts are inhabited by Barbaroi and the people beyond them, Agriophagoi ['wild animal eaters'] and Moschophagoi ['shoot eaters'], organized in Chiefdoms. In the interior behind them, in the parts toward the west [is a metropolis called Meroe].[39]

The barbarians (foreigners) the author refers to were the tribes living between the Red Sea coast and the Nile valley, and he distinguishes between the coastal dwellers (fish eaters) and those who lived inland (meat and shoot eaters). The passage in the manuscript that may refer to Meroë is illegible, but Meroë was an ancient capital and a transshipment point near the sixth cataract of the Nile for trade between Egypt and central Africa.[40]

The *Periplus*, like Pliny, also reports that the Graeco-Roman sailors of this period were already familiar with the Etesios and Hippalos winds, which can easily be identified as the southwest monsoons that affect shipping from June to September. Even if the *Periplus* located Scythia in the Indus valley, the work's remarks on trade in certain seaports are consistent with archaeological findings. In particular, it vividly illustrates the flourishing trade in luxury goods between Roman Egypt and the west coast of India.

Disintegration or reintegration?

In *The Making of the Middle Sea*, Cyprian Broodbank notes a protracted process of integration in the Mediterranean that culminated in the second century BCE with the distribution across long distances of shared objects, practices and identities. This is visible above all among the elites, where murals in the Aegean style, carved ivory and decorated gold and silver bowls spread along with rituals, cults and places of worship visited by many population groups. Around 600 BCE shared practices, points of view, tastes, smells and sounds were evident everywhere, along with a similar organization of public life, warfare, sociability and worship.[41]

Proceeding from this presumptive integration, David Abulafia sees a transformation and disintegration of the Roman Empire by 400 CE, if not before. He believes that this was partially owing to Christianity, which had to assert itself alongside the old cults of the gods and Judaism before becoming the state religion at the end of the fourth century. On the other hand, the Great Migration, especially of the Vandals through Spain to North Africa and from there to the northern Mediterranean, fundamentally changed the role of Rome.

In the years that followed, Constantinople, originally founded as a Greek colony in the mid-seventh century BCE, took over Rome's role. The inhabitants of what historians later called the Byzantine Empire referred to themselves as *Romaioi* (Romans). The Empire differed from ancient Rome in that it rested on Hellenistic traditions cultivated in the centres of the Aegean, the Black Sea and the eastern Mediterranean. Another difference was that Constantinople, located on the edge of the Roman Empire, repeatedly had to defend itself against assaults from the steppes. The Byzantine Empire controlled the Bosporus and Black Sea region as well as the eastern Mediterranean and as a centre of Greek Christianity exerted influence far into the Slavic territories in the North and West.[42]

The establishment of West Francia in the mid-ninth century provided an additional stable Christian power bloc. The Byzantine Empire and West Francia reintegrated or reconfigured the Mediterranean or rather its role. While the eastern Mediterranean and the Black Sea were linked to the North and Baltic Sea by the Vikings (Varangians) via Byzantium and the Russian rivers, the western Mediterranean was also connected to the Atlantic and the North Sea via the Rhone delta and the river systems of the West Francia. To the south, the Adriatic linked the Frankish and Byzantine empires, with Venice rising to become a centre of exchange and Italy's other ports establishing contacts with the Muslim world.[43]

Notes

1   Homer, *The Odyssey*, translated A. T. Murray (Cambridge, MA and London 1919), 12.395–430, lines 395–415.

2   B. W. Cunliffe, *Europe between the Oceans. 9000 BC–AD 1000* (New Haven, 2011), 94–9.

3   C. Broodbank, *The Making of the Middle Sea. A History of the Mediterranean from the Beginning to the Emergence of the Classical World* (London, 2013), 373–402, 431–44.

4   Homer, *Odyssey*, 2.415–34.

5   Cunliffe, *Europe between the Oceans*, 185–202; E. Stein-Hölkeskamp, *Das archaische Griechenland. Die Stadt und das Meer* (Munich, 2015), 27–8.

6   Homer, *Odyssey*, 4.75–85.

7   Cunliffe, *Europe between the Oceans*, 240–3; Broodbank, *The Making*, 445–55.

8   Cunliffe, *Europe between the Oceans*, 289–300.

9   C. Bonnet, *Melqart, Cultes et mythes de l'Héraclès tyrien en Méditerranée* (Louvain, 1988).

10   Broodbank, *The Making*, 517.

11   W. Schuller, *Das Erste Europa 1000 v. Chr. – 500 n. Chr.* (Stuttgart, 2004), 44.

12 Schuller, *Das Erste Europa*, 53ff; Stein-Hölkeskamp, *Das archäische Griechenland*, 104.

13 There are some very famous Punic amphora with salted fish, which were found at Corinth. See M. L. Zimmerman Munn, 'Corinthian Trade with the Punic West in the Classical Period', *Corinth. The Centenary 1896–1996* 20 (2003): 195–217, 202.

14 King, *The Black Sea*, 25–33.

15 T. Gardiner, 'Terms for Thalassocracy in Thucydides', *Rheinisches Museum für Philologie,* Neue Folge 112, no. 1 (1969): 16–22, 21.

16 D. Abulafia, 'Thalassocracies', in P. Horden and S. Kinoshita (eds.), *A Companion to Mediterranean History* (Chichester, West Sussex, 2014), 139–53.

17 W. Schuller, *Die Herrschaft der Athener im Ersten Attischen Seebund* (Berlin and New York, 1974); Schuller, *Das erste Europa*, 65–76.

18 M. Dreher, *Hegemon und Symmachoi. Untersuchungen zum Zweiten Athenischen Seebund* (Berlin and New York, 1995).

19 Abulafia, *The Great Sea*, 152.

20 Ibid., 162ff; N. K. Rauh, *Merchants, Sailors and Pirates in the Roman World* (Stroud, 2003).

21 E. A. Alpers, *The Indian Ocean in World History* (Oxford, 2014), 28.

22 Schuller, *Das erste Europa*, 113–21.

23 L. P. Paine, *The Sea and Civilization. A Maritime History of the World* (New York, 2013), 130.

24 N. S. Rosenstein, *Rome at War: Farms, Families, and Death in the Middle Republic. Studies in the History of Greece and Rome* (Chapel Hill, NC, 2004).

25 E. Flaig, *Weltgeschichte der Sklaverei* (Munich, 2009), 56–66.

26 Abulafia, *The Great Sea*, 191ff.

27 Cunliffe, *Europe between the Oceans*, 376ff.

28 R. Gertwagen, 'Nautical Technology', in Horden and Kinoshita (eds.), *Companion to Mediterranean History*, 154–69.

29 Cunliffe, *Europe between the Oceans*, 398.

30 L. Casson, 'New Light on Maritime Loans. P. Vindob G 40822', in R. Chakravarti (ed.), *Trade in Early India* (Oxford and New York, 2001), 228–43. See also R. Tomber, 'From the Roman Red Sea to beyond the Empire: Egyptian Ports and Their Trading Partners', *British Museum Studies in Ancient Egypt and Sudan* 18 (2012): 201–15.

31 Translation from the original text in A. Franzoi, 'Sagezza di mercante (CLE 1533)', *Rivista di Cultura Classica e Medievale* 46 (2004): 257–63. On the aspect of the sea in ancient funerary inscriptions, see also B. Dunsch, '"Why Do We Violate Strange Seas and Sacred Waters?" The Sea as Bridge and Boundary in Greek and Roman Poetry', in M. Grzechnik and H. Hurskainen (eds.), *Beyond the Sea. Reviewing the Manifold Dimensions of Water as Barrier and Bridge* (Cologne, 2015), 38–41.

32 On Arrian, see K. G. Brandis, 'Arrians Periplus Ponti Euxini', *Rheinisches Museum für Philologie* 51 (1896): 109–26.

33 *The Geography of Strabo*, trans. Horace White, vol. II (Cambridge, MA, 1988), 4.5.5.

34 Geminos (Introduction to Phenomena, VI. 9) quoted from J. Evans and J. Lennart Berggren (eds.), *Gemino's Introduction to the Phenomena. A Translation and Study of a Hellenistic Survey of Astronomy* (Princeton and Oxford, 2006), 162.

35 B. Cunliffe, *The Extraordinary Voyage of Pytheas the Greek* (New York, 2002), 141, 148–9.

36 F. Arrianus, *Arrian's Voyage Round the Euxine Sea. Translated, and Accompanied with a Geographical Dissertation, and Maps* (Oxford, 1805), 3.

37 King, *The Black Sea*, 52ff.

38 R. Chakravarti, 'Merchants, Merchandise and Merchantmen in the Western Sea-Board of India (*c.* 500 BCE–1500 CE)', in O. Prakash (ed.), *The Trading World of the Indian Ocean, 1500–1800* (Delhi, 2012), 57–8.

39 L. Casson (ed.), *The Periplus Maris Erythraei* (Princeton, 1989), 51.

40 Ibid., 97–100.

41 Broodbank, *The Making*, 604–5.

42 Abulafia, *The Great Sea*, 213–14, 226–38.

43 Cunliffe, *Europe between the Oceans*, 472ff.

II

North Sea, Baltic Sea and Black Sea:

The Vikings

After antiquity, the Vikings or Northmen were the link between the North Sea, Baltic Sea and Black Sea, and they also ventured as far as the North Atlantic. They first appear in sources from the late eighth century describing raids on monasteries in the British Isles and the estuary of the Loire. The scholar Alcuin, who was active at the court of Charlemagne, for example, lamented the looting of Lindisfarne Abbey (793) in a letter to King Æthelred of Northumbria:

> Lo, it is nearly 350 years that we and our fathers have inhabited this most lovely land, and never before has such terror appeared in Britain as we have now suffered from pagan race, nor was it thought that such an inroad from the sea could be made. Behold, the church of St. Cuthbert spattered with the blood of the priests of God, despoiled of all its ornaments; a place more venerable than all in Britain is given as prey to pagan peoples.[1]

There are various explanations for the sudden appearance of the Vikings. Population pressures and a scarcity of land which forced people to take to the seas have been cited, along with the pugnacious spirit of young men and the greed for easy prey. Leadership positions in the tribal groups (chieftains) had to be won and defended repeatedly. This required not just fortune in war and fame but also an entourage, whose loyalty a successful warrior could only win with a constant stream of booty.

The Frankish kingdom was a worthwhile target, since despite the efforts of Pippin and Charlemagne it was still not internally cohesive, let alone easy to defend everywhere. The prerequisites were ships and nautical knowledge, which the Vikings possessed in abundance. With their seaworthy ships, they could sail or row across the open North and Baltic Seas. They navigated by the sun and stars as well as the currents and the colour of the water. In their large and small ships, the Vikings followed the rivers to the interior, where hardly a port was safe from them.[2]

They profited from the expansion of Frisian trade on the North Sea coast, easily skimming off its riches. Trading centres had been established at Dorestad at the mouth of the Rhine and Domburg on the Walcheren peninsula, where Frisian peasant merchants no longer engaged in shipping solely as a sideline but lived exclusively from trade and the crafts. The Frisians traded with the Franks, Anglo-Saxons and Scandinavians, sailing the North Sea and Atlantic coasts as well as along the Rhine to Cologne, Mainz and Worms. One of their commodities was slaves, whom they sold from the British Isles as well as the Baltic region via Verdun to southern Europe and the Mediterranean. There is evidence of a Frisian merchant who bought a slave in London, who was brought, probably through Dorestad and along the Maas river upstream, to Verdun – the most important slave market – and then further south. There, or in the Mediterranean region itself, the Frisians bought Oriental goods that they then sold further north.[3]

The Frisian trade extended across the Baltic to Hedeby (Haithabu) and Birka, and there was reportedly even a Frisian guild[4] there in the eleventh century. The (Anglo)-Frisian sceatta coins, which were also disseminated in Scandinavia, are witness to the intensive exchange of goods.[5] In the 830s and 840s the Vikings regularly made raids on Dorestad. This alarmed the Frankish Empire, whose kings tried to protect their monasteries and emporiums on the one hand and to include the Viking rulers on the other by supporting some of them against their rivals.

The various invaders formed dominions not just in Scandinavia, but also in the North Sea islands. The Danish kings in particular, who had subjugated chieftains and petty kings from Jutland, at first controlled the neighbouring islands and the passage between the North and Baltic Seas. They extended their influence in the north up to Viken, the region around the Oslo fjord, and in the south up to the Channel coast. The conquest of England was only logical. Around the mid-ninth century the Danes claimed the eastern half of England, and York became the centre of the Danish Viking rulers. They challenged the Norwegians in Ireland, where they had settled the Orkneys, Shetland and Hebrides. The Danish threat to the Frankish empire persisted nonetheless. After the partition of the empire in 843 West Francia suffered particularly from invasions by the Vikings, who sailed or rowed up the rivers and in 845 only spared Paris after being paid tribute of 7,000 pounds of silver. It was not until 870 that protective and defensive measures would prove increasingly successful.

In the years that followed, the Vikings increasingly shifted their focus to the British Isles, where the Anglo-Saxon kings had succeeded for a time in casting off Danish rule. Only in the late tenth and early eleventh centuries did Sweyn Forkbeard and Canute the Great re-establish Danish sovereignty over the Norwegians and the Anglo-Saxons, who in future had to pay tribute to Denmark in precious metals. This so-called *danegeld*, which had predecessors in the taxes levied in Frisia and West Francia, was levied in eight large instalments from 991 to 1040, amounting to 284,647 pounds of silver in all, or nearly 60 million pennies.[6]

The East and the Baltic region offered further opportunities to expand and amass riches. By the eighth century, furs from this region were much sought-after at the Western markets. In subsequent years, the resources of the East would be systematically exploited. This proceeded mainly from Sweden by the Svear, whom the Slavic sources call Rus' or Varangians. The Varangians settled in Staraya Ladoga, some 15 km south of where the Volkhov river empties into Lake Ladoga, on Lake Ilmen and the headwaters of the Dnieper, where they settled along with Slavs, Finno-Ugric peoples and Balts.[7] Via the Don, the Volga or the Caspian Sea they reached the Arab world, where they bargained for or looted large quantities of silver. Arabic sources report as follows on the Varangians:

> With their ships they undertake forays against the Slavs, and upon arriving, take them prisoner and bring them to the capital of the Khazars and to Bolghar, where they put them up for sale. They have no seed fields, but eat only that which they export from the land of the Slavs [...] their employment consists entirely of trade in sable, squirrels and other pelts. They sell these pelts to their customers, and in exchange they receive a small fortune in coins, which they tie to their belts.[8]

Other Arab historians describe raids on the inhabitants of the Caspian Sea region. In 860, a Varangian fleet appeared before Constantinople. Byzantium responded with a politics of embrace, entering into trade agreements with the Varangians. In Kiev on the middle Dnieper, a further Scandinavian outpost among the Slavs, the Byzantines established a trade emporium with a church, whose worship services influenced the pagan Nordic and local Slavic population. The Varangian chieftains surrounded themselves with an entourage of Scandinavians, from which Rurik, the founder of the Old Russian dynasty of the Rurikids, was also descended. Rurik and his son Oleg set up outposts in which they installed their retainers in order to control the country. From them arose the (regional) principalities of Novgorod, Pskov, Polozk (Polotsk) or Rostov. The subsequent rulers of the Kiev Rus', Igor and Olga (Ingvar and Helga), like their retainers, were of Scandinavian origin, but the very name of their son and heir Sviatoslav already suggests a Slavicized dynasty. The warriors recruited from the palace guard in Byzantium were no longer exclusively Scandinavian. Slavs, Balts and Finns entered into a cultural community with the Varangians, as documented by trade agreements between the princes of Kiev and Byzantium. While in 911 alone fifteen envoys of Scandinavian origin negotiated a contract, twenty-six envoys and twenty-eight merchants are already mentioned in 944. Judging by their names, the majority were Scandinavians (forty-seven), but there were also five Baltic Finns or men of Finnish origin, one (Lithuanian) Yotvingian and possibly one Slav. The latter were involved in the trade with Byzantium mainly as boat builders and perhaps as mariners.[9]

The Varangians or Rus' did not, however, limit themselves to trading with and making raids upon Byzantium, but also descended upon the wider Black Sea region, the Caspian Sea and the Sea of Azov. The commodities they traded included slaves, pelts, wax and honey, which they exchanged for silver and silk. Troop payments from Byzantium also flowed to the Rus'.[10] The Khazar empire in particular, which ruled the territory from the Volga to the Crimea, thereby linking the Caspian with the Black Sea, mediated trade between Central Asia and the West. Its emporiums on the Volga and the Don brought together merchants from Europe and Asia. According to Ibn Fadlan, the Vikings regularly went there from the Baltic region to engage in trade. Because the Khazar elite had converted to Judaism, their outposts attracted Jewish merchants from Byzantium and the Arab territories. The Khazar empire was short-lived, however, for the Varangians and the principalities in which their entourage originated were increasingly expanding to the southeast, largely pushing out the Khazars.[11]

While in the east the Vikings reached the Black and Caspian Seas with the aid of coastal and river shipping, west of the British Isles they faced the challenge of navigating the open Atlantic. The Icelandic sagas as well as archaeological finds in Iceland, Greenland and North America confirm this. Contemporary chroniclers report on seafaring and settlement movements on the islands in the North Atlantic. The rich sources show that 'Vikings' from Norway and the British Isles settled in Iceland after 870. This dating arises from a volcanic eruption in 871, since remains of the oldest Icelandic settlements were found directly on top of a layer of volcanic ash. The sagas and chroniclers report that Icelanders embarked for Greenland at the end of the tenth century in order to settle there. There are also accounts of a voyage to North America around the year 1000, which appear to be substantiated by archaeological finds from L'Anse aux Meadows in northern Newfoundland.[12]

People in antiquity already sought the island of Thule in the far north, and Bede (d. 735), who mentions it in his history of the English church, had presumably heard of voyages to Iceland. Around 825, the scholar Dicuil told of Christian priests who had spent a summer on Thule. Irish monks or hermits who felt especially at home in the solitude of the Atlantic probably actually visited Iceland.[13] The first settlers, however, aside from Norwegians, were Gaels from Ireland, Scotland and the Scottish islands. Apart from agriculture their livelihood was clearly based on fishing, since many settlements were located near the richest salmon grounds.

The settlers already included Christians, although Scandinavian paganism still dominated. The social system was notable, with a number of so-called *goden* with religious, administrative and legal functions and large-scale farmers at the top, but there was no king. The chieftains and larger farmers frequently travelled by ship and engaged in trade for their own needs. Weapons, clothing, honey, wheat, wood, wax, tar and canvas were imported, and with time harbours and emporiums arose along the trade routes, the most important of which was Gasar on the Eyjafjörður.[14]

Greenland was settled from Iceland at the end of the tenth century. The settlers were led by Erik the Red, who appears in various sources, according to which he and his father came to Iceland from Norway and left the island for the West because of a murder he had committed. Perhaps the settlers were attracted by fantastic accounts of lands in the West and the riches to be found there. The settlement of Greenland coincided with a warming climate, which offered favourable conditions in the subsequent centuries.

The voyages to North America are described in the *Vinland Sagas*, which tell of journeys from Iceland and Greenland to the American continent around the year 1000. The fact that these sagas only described the voyages well after the fact and in fragments has inspired generations of scholars to offer contradictory hypotheses. Adam of Bremen (d. after 1080) had also heard of Vinland and the wealth of this island, where grapes and wheat reportedly grew, and mentions it in his *History of the Archbishops of Hamburg-Bremen*. One of the *Vinland Sagas*, the Saga of the Greenlanders, mentions Leif and Thorvald, who visited an island to the north of a strait separating the island from the mainland:

Now sailed they thence into the open sea, with a north-east wind, and were two days at sea before they saw land, and they sailed thither and came to an island which lay to the eastward of the land, and went up there, and looked round them in a good weather, and observed that there was dew upon the grass; and it so happened they touched the dew with their hands, and raised the fingers to the mouth, and they thought that they never before tasted any thing so sweet […]. After that they went to the ship, and sailed into a sound, which lay between the island and a ness (promontory), which ran out to the eastward of the land; and then steered westwards past the ness. It was very shallow at ebb tide, and their ship stood up, so that it was far to see from the ship to the water. But so much did they desire to land, that they did not give themselves time to wait until the water again rose under their ship, but ran at once on shore [...]. After this took they counsel, and formed the resolution of remaining there for the winter, and built there large houses [...]. And when the spring came, they got ready, and sailed away, and Leif gave the land a name after its qualities, and called it Vinland.[15]

Following this and other vague descriptions, New England or Newfoundland and the area around the St Lawrence River seem likely locations for this legendary island. Since the sagas were composed long after the events they describe, based on oral tradition, they are not suited to precisely locating the anchorage. Nevertheless, it seems clear that around 1,000 seafarers from Greenland or Iceland embarked on several voyages along the east coast of the North American continent, sailing into the Gulf of St Lawrence and further south. They built camps at various sites, spent several winters or years and also made contact with the native population:

But when spring approached, saw they one morning early, that a number of canoes rowed from the south round the ness; so many, as if the sea was sowen with coal. [...] Karlsefne and his people then raised up the shield,

MAP 3 *Viking voyages in the North Atlantic*

and when they came together, they began to barter; and these people would rather have red cloth [than anything else]; for this they had to offer skins and real furs. They would also purchase swords and spears, but this Karlsefne and Snorri forbad.[16]

Perhaps the Greenlanders were moved to give up their camps by later conflicts with the natives or internal disputes. Although it seems unlikely that the Greenlanders travelled as far south as the sagas suggest, they did sail regularly to Labrador for wood, as we know thanks to an Icelandic chronicle entry for 1347.[17]

The information on voyages and temporary settlements in North America appears to be confirmed by the discovery in the 1960s of remains at L'Anse aux Meadows. Anne and Helge Ingstad immediately identified the site as Leif's Vinland, although it is hard to associate this inhospitable place with wine and grapes.[18] It is more likely that it was a camp or a station for the repair of ships and perhaps for provisioning after the voyage from Greenland, where the seafarers gathered strength for further journeys. One of the needles found there is similar to ones from Dublin, Iceland and Denmark. This suggests that some of the visitors to L'Anse aux Meadows came from Iceland. The discovery of a spindle suggests that women visited L'Anse aux Meadows. Although the archaeologists could find no evidence of a permanent Viking settlement, the saga accounts and settlement finds in L'Anse aux Meadows appear to speak for temporary settlement attempts, which were abandoned after some time, perhaps because the land was already being used by the local population. The returnees then boasted of their adventures in a land flowing with wine and the sagas repeated these stories for posterity.[19]

In Greenland, living conditions seem to have changed to such a degree that population density fell during the late middle ages and the population died out altogether in the course of the fourteenth and fifteenth centuries without any signs – as in Norway or other countries – of plague or other diseases. The causes must be sought elsewhere. Since the Scandinavian settlers in Greenland lived from animal husbandry, hunting and fishing and had to import all their cereals, the interruption to trade and isolation from the motherland, as well as the collapse of agriculture because of the worsening climate, appear to have been responsible for population decline.[20]

Trade routes

Seafarers and traders established the North and Baltic Seas as a trade area and gave it a structure by founding multi-ethnic emporiums. All of the neighbouring countries participated in the long-distance trade, albeit with varying roles. Thus, the Slavs, Kurs, Semigallians and Estonians as well as the Livonians were pirates and traders and, like the Vikings, involved in the exchange of goods between the Muslim world and the Baltic and North Sea. The Old Prussians, in particular, who lived on the Baltic coast of Samland (Sambia Peninsula), possessed a widely sought-after commodity in the guise of amber. The Frisians and Anglo-Saxons from the North Sea benefited from this business along with Arab and Jewish merchants who, like Ibrāhīm ibn Ya'qūb, also wrote about it.

Among the prosperous emporiums were the Viking-dominated Hedeby on the Schlei, the intersection between the North Sea and Baltic trade, Reric on the Bay of Wismar, Wolin on the Oder lagoon and Truso in the Vistula delta, but also Birka on Lake Malar (Mälaren), the island of Gotland and Staraya Ladoga in Russia, which represented the junction between the Baltic and the Black Sea trade. A number of smaller, often only temporarily active stations like Menzlin on the Peene or Ralswiek on Rügen Island coexisted with them and have left behind only archaeological evidence. Thus, funeral customs in the form of ship burials in the case of Menzlin document the presence of Scandinavians alongside the native Slavic population and thereby the multi-ethnic nature of even smaller settlements.

Haithabu (Hedeby) on the Schlei was characterized by a scattered settlement consisting of open hall houses, a port with jetties and palisades and semi-circular ramparts to defend against land assaults. As in other towns, trade took place on the jetties or piers, as suggested by small archaeological finds such as coins and weights. Artisans in Hedeby processed imported raw materials and semi-finished goods. The scope of trade was immense: cloth came from Frisia, and ceramics, glass and weapons from the Rhineland; millstones from the Eifel were probably shipped from Dorestad; while mercury and tin were likely sent from the Iberian Peninsula or England to the Schlei. Scandinavia provided soapstone, whetstone slate and iron, while amber came from the eastern Baltic region. The ethnic composition of the inhabitants was similarly diverse. To judge by their funeral customs, they included Frisians, Saxons, Slavs and Swedes as well as the dominant Danes.[21] Birka on Lake Malar occupied a position in the trade between western Europe across the Baltic comparable to the trading outposts on Lake Ladoga and from there to the Volga Bulgars and the Muslim world. In Birka, a royal official kept order among the local artisans and foreign merchants. The artisans produced for the long-distance trade, but also for the immediate surroundings, which is why Birka can be regarded as an early urban centre. It suffered from the raids of Danish Vikings, however. Around the year 1000, its role in east-west trade was taken over by the island of Gotland, whose farmer-merchants did not settle in Russia like the Svear (Swedes) or Varangians but traded seasonally and then returned to their island. There they hoarded the silver coins they had earned, about one-quarter of the silver in circulation in the entire Baltic region and Russia, which increasingly came from western Europe, especially from German mints.

The more than 800 burial mounds on the southern Baltic coast as well as the sailing ships and a cache of more than 2,000 Arabic coins found there point to the importance of Ralswiek. The chronicles also mention other trading outposts. Thus, we learn of Reric, which can probably be located near Groß Strömkendorf in Wismar Bay, that in the first decade of the ninth century (808) the Danish king Göttrik (Godofried) resettled the local merchants from there to Hedeby.

Adam of Bremen reports of Wolin, another emporium:

It is truly the largest of all cities that Europe has to offer, in which live Slavs and other tribes, Greeks, and barbarians. Even the foreigners from Saxony have received equal settlement rights, although they may not openly profess their Christianity during their stay. They all still remain captive to their pagan heresies; other than that, it would be hard to find another people more honourable and friendly in their way of life and hospitality. The city is full of wares from all the peoples of the north; nothing desirable or rare is unobtainable. Here there is a beacon, which the inhabitants call the Greek fire.[22]

Archaeological discoveries seem to confirm Adam's account: house construction, burial customs and found objects point to the presence of Scandinavian and Frisian traders. Wolin appears to have been so attractive that both the Polish and Danish kings sought to incorporate this emporium under the pretext of combating pirates.

The line between trade and piracy was fluid, especially since human beings represented a valuable commodity. It was presumably Slavic traders who stole the gold jewellery found in Hiddensee and Peenemünde that had been fashioned by goldsmiths in Scandinavia during the tenth century. Regular commodities, in contrast, included cereals, horses, honey and wax as well as furs and amber. Salt was extracted and traded too, as were local and regional manufactured products such as combs.

In order to make quantitative statements about trade volume or shifts in trade routes, we need to consult finds of coins that can be dated precisely. The enormous hoards of coins found in the Baltic region have accordingly attracted the interest of historians. The influx of Arabic dirham coins since the late eighth century, for example, reflects increasing exchange with the Arab world. While most dirhams of this era can be traced to the Old Prussian hinterland of the port of Truso, in the ninth century Arabic coins flowed mainly to Sweden and Gotland, likely as a result of the advance of the Varangians in Russia. Silver coins from the Samanid empire in Central Asia, in turn, were hoarded in larger quantities in northwest Russian trade centres such as Staraya Ladoga, Novgorod, Polozk and Pskov as well as the territory of the Volga Bulgars.

The finds often consist of hacksilver, which, in combination with the scales and weights that are sometimes present, suggests a *Gewichtsgeldwirtschaft*, that is an economy in which silver was valued according to its weight, which may go back to Arab influence.[23] The influx of Arab money to western Europe was less intense; few dirham hoards have been found even in Jutland. This could point to a positive balance of trade between the Baltic and the North Sea region. Perhaps the Arabic silver was re-coined in Hedeby or elsewhere. In the Baltic region as well, however, the influx of Arabic silver slowed in the late tenth century, and in Russia it stopped altogether after 1015.[24] At the same time, the movements of silver reversed.

Because of trade and tribute levies, English pennies were shipped in large quantities from the North Sea region to the Baltic area. Moreover, the mining of new silver deposits in the Harz and the Black Forest, especially the silver of Rammelsberg near Goslar, created the foundation for the minting of denar coins on a mass scale. In exchange for furs, wax, honey and slaves, the so-called Otto-Adelheid pennies minted here as well as other denar coins travelled to Bohemia, Hungary, Poland, Estonia, Russia and above all across the sea to Scandinavia, where they were often hoarded, but presumably also often used as currency. The Swedish hoards from the Viking period, comprising some 80,000 Arabic, 45,000 English and 85,000 German coins, give evidence of regular imports. Since these coins appear comparatively rarely in coin finds in the interior, they came to be known as long-distance trading denars, after their function.[25]

The era of the long-distance trading denar and thus of the influx of these coins to the north and east came to an end in the twelfth and thirteenth centuries, when the need for currency in the interior rose with the founding of cities and the minting of coins by the municipal authorities. The denars became lighter in weight and were no longer valid everywhere, but only in the towns where they were minted. This process also occurred in the Baltic region, where increasingly powerful territorial lords moved the multi-ethnic emporiums to the political administrative centres and integrated them into the regional economy. The trading outposts (Hedeby, Paviken, Staraya Ladoga, Truso, Wolin) became commercial cities (Schleswig, Visby, Novgorod, Danzig/ Gdánsk, Stettin/Szczecin), evidence of urban development on the Baltic Sea.[26]

Swords, jewellery and runestones

Few sources on Viking social structure survive. Large landowners were not only chieftains, but also assumed priestly roles in their districts. These included leading the think (governing assembly) and acting as judges, who administered justice according to customary law upon the advice of the think. These chieftains maintained their own retinue of warriors with whom they went on voyages. They vied with each other for influence and thus over the position of kinglet or king. In Scandinavia, Iceland and Greenland the free peasants, who engaged in agriculture and animal husbandry and held slaves, ranked below the chieftains.[27]

This social stratification is reflected in material culture. The graves of chieftains are striking among both the Vikings and the Slavs. Notable among the burial objects found in the graves of upper-class warriors are the swords, which often came from the Rhineland. The blades consisted of Damascus steel and the artfully worked hilts or pommels point to those who made them. The sword from Liepe near Eberswalde bears the name Hiltipreht, for example, while in other cases the smith Ulfberth is mentioned. Metalworking and communities of smiths also existed in the Baltic region, however.[28] Heroic legends passed down in Nordic poetry and on runestones are associated with the swords. But it was not only swords that conveyed an ideology; upper-class warriors also rode on horseback and wore helmets and chain mail, which made them superior in combat to the foot soldiers.[29]

One component of social life was music, as documented archaeologically by rattles, pipes and flutes made of wood and bone. String instruments and shawms probably came from the Byzantine Empire and the Arab world.[30]

Vikings, Slavs and Balts had similar religious beliefs. Most tribes had a main deity with subordinate gods or even a family of gods. For the Vikings, Odin was the great All-Father, a role that Svantevit played for the Slavs. Both gods were mounted and appeared with a retinue. While according to legend Odin rode the eight-footed steed Sleipnir, the priests of Svantevit tended to the divine white stallion and interpreted the divine will as an oracle using his hoof prints. The Vikings also recognized Njörðr as the god of the sea, whose abode was Nóatún, the ship enclosure.[31]

The rune stones, which however mainly arose in the period of Christianization, document Viking mythology. Some inscriptions contain the kind of orally transmitted poetry later written down in Iceland, which treated gods and heroes. The famous Ardre image stone (no. VIII) on Gotland, for instance, depicts Odin riding with a fallen warrior towards Valhalla. Apart from the world of Viking mythology, the rune stones also give visual evidence of their cultural and social life, since those who commissioned the stones were landowners, generally from families of high social status. The chronology of the rune stones begins with the image stones of the fifth and sixth centuries, which feature rosettes, vortex wheels, longboats with oarsmen, serpents and dragons. Larger stones from the eighth to tenth centuries were divided into horizontal fields showing scenes from the lives of the Vikings and their gods, with representations of manned Viking ships alternating with images of mythical creatures and battles.

FIGURE 2 *Ancient picture stone Ardre VIII. © Wikipedia Commons.*

Frequently, these were memorial stones for fallen warriors, some of them commissioned by women who recorded their inheritance claims in inscriptions dedicated to their dead husbands. The later rune stones with decorative drawings reflect the lives of pagan heroes, sometimes in confrontation with Norse legends and Christianity, where often the cross appears as the only Christian motif with decoratively intertwined ornamental bands. Scholars believe that this labyrinth motif is a borrowing from Homer's epics. Rune stones are scattered from Greenland, England and the Faroe Islands in the west to the Dnieper in the southeast and therefore document the spatial extent of Viking voyages. The significance of journeys across the sea for Vikings is evident from the numerous ship burials and stone ships, which underline the belief that the dead continued to travel in the afterlife.[32]

They are important sources for cultural exchange in the North and Baltic Sea region. In the second half of the twentieth century, archaeologists in particular compiled a variety of material revealing relations between the Baltic region and the Anglo-Irish world, the Orient, the empires of the Bulgars and Khazars on the Volga and the late antique Mediterranean. In this way, European decorative patterns like interlace, foliage or animal elements developed regional versions. While the so-called Viking style drew inspiration from the cultures of Ireland, England and Francia, one finds Scandinavian and Byzantine influences in the Slavic territories. Serpent and animal motifs played a larger role here and long persisted on clothing among the Balts and Finno-Ugric tribes.[33]

In many cases, similar style and ornament in jewellery (bracelets) make it difficult to determine the regional origin of an object. In other cases, the earrings fashioned by Slavic silversmiths in Pomerania document an impact from the Byzantine Empire, which suggests transmission northwards via the Danube region and Great Moravia. We also find this type of earring there, which was further disseminated across the sea to Bornholm and Gotland. Arabic prototypes entered the Baltic region by way of Bolghar, the centre of the Volga Bulgars, and were imitated locally. Other adornments such as the Slavic temple rings remained limited to the Slavic world of the southern Baltic coast. Otherwise, the rings were prized for their silver content, which explains their presence in hoards. The Scandinavian brooches, in contrast, which both adorned clothing and held it together, are found in Scandinavian graves on the southern Baltic coast.[34]

The use and distribution of combs is also a sign of cultural exchange, in this case between the regions on the North and Baltic seas. Influenced by antique models, comb-makers in the Rhineland and Frisia specialized in the manufacture of combs from horn. Initially they were brought to the Baltic area by Frisian merchants, but soon they were being produced in Viking trading outposts like Hedeby, Birka and Staraya Ladoga as well as the southern Baltic coast, so that comb imports ceased. Frisian comb makers presumably settled in the emporiums along with the merchants.[35]

Notes

1   Alcuin, 'Alcuini Epistolae' no. 16, in E. Dümmler (ed.), MGH Epp. 4; English in D. Whitelock (ed.), *English Historical Documents*, vol. I, *c. 500–1042*, 2nd ed. (London, 1979), 842.

2   For a good overview of the various territories settled and ruled by the Vikings, see P. Sawyer (ed.), *The Oxford Illustrated History of the Vikings* (Oxford and New York, 1997).

3 A. Verhulst, 'Der frühmittelalterliche Handel der Niederlande und der Friesenhandel', in K. Düwel and H. Jankuhn (eds.), *Untersuchungen zu Handel und Verkehr der vor- und frühgeschichtlichen Zeit*, vol. 3: *Der Handel des frühen Mittelalters. Bericht über die Kolloquien der Kommission für die Altertumskunde Mittel- und Nordeuropas in den Jahren 1980 bis 1983* (Göttingen, 1985), 385–6.

4 On the Frisian guild in Birka, see O. Mörke, *Die Geschwistermeere. Eine Geschichte des Nord- und Ostseeraums* (Stuttgart, 2015), 54.

5 D. Adamczyk, 'Friesen, Wikinger, Araber. Die Ostseewelt zwischen Dorestad und Samarkand ca. 700–1100', in A. Komlosy, H.-H. Nolte and I. Sooman (eds.), *Ostsee 700–2000. Gesellschaft – Wirtschaft – Kultur* (Vienna, 2008), 32–48.

6 G. Hatz, 'Danegeld', in M. North (ed.), *Von Aktie bis Zoll. Ein historisches Lexikon des Geldes* (Munich, 1995), 78.

7 F. Androshchuk, 'The Vikings in the East', in S. Brink (ed.), *The Viking World* (London, 2009), 517–24.

8 Ahmad Ibn Rustah, 'The Book of Precious Records' [or Things or Objects] (*c.* 903 CE), quoted in M. North, *The Baltic. A History*, trans. Kenneth Kronenberg (Cambridge, MA, 2015), 12.

9 Ibid.

10 D. Adamczyk, *Silber und Macht. Fernhandel, Tribute und die piastische Herrschaftsbildung in nordosteuropäischer Perspektive (800–1100)* (Wiesbaden, 2014), 137–41.

11 King, *The Black Sea*, 73ff.

12 G. Sigurðsson, 'The North Atlantic Expansion', in Brink (ed.), *The Viking World*, 562–70.

13 B. W. Cunliffe, *Facing the Ocean. The Atlantic and Its Peoples, 8000 BC–AD 1500* (Oxford, 2004), 307.

14 J. V. Sigurðsson, 'Iceland', in Brink (ed.), *The Viking World*, 571–8.

15 The Greenland saga is cited here and below from N. L. Beamish, *The Discovery of America by the Northmen, in the Tenth Century* (London, 1841), 61–8.

16 Beamish, *Discovery*, 96.

17 G. Sigurðsson, Introduction, in G. Sigurðsson (ed.), *The Vinland Sagas* (London, 2008), ix–xxxix, xxxvi.

18 H. Ingestad, *The Norse Discovery of America*, vol. 1: *Excavations of a Norse Settlement at L'Anse aux Meadows, Newfoundland 1961–1968* (Oslo, 1985).

19 Sigurðsson, 'North Atlantic Expansion', 568.

20 M. North, *The Expansion of Europe, 1250–1500*, trans. P. Selwyn (Manchester and New York, 2012), 327–8.

21 K. Brandt, M. Müller-Wille and C. Radtke (eds.), *Haithabu und die frühe Stadtentwicklung im nördlichen Europa* (Neumünster, 2002).

22 B. Schmeidler (ed.), *Magistri Adam Bremensis Gesta Hammaburgensis Ecclesiae pontificum* (Hannover and Leipzig, 1917), chapter 22, 79–80.

23 H. Steuer, 'Geldgeschäfte und Hoheitsrechte zwischen Ostseeländern und islamischer Welt', *Zeitschrift für Archäologie* 12 (1978): 255–60, and the same author's 'Gewichtsgeldwirtschaft im frühgeschichtlichen Europa – Feinwaagen und Gewichte als Quellen zur Währungsgeschichte', in K. Düwel (ed.), *Untersuchungen zu Handel und Verkehr der vor- und frühgeschichtlichen Zeit in Mittel- und Nordeuropa*, vol. 4: *Der Handel der Karolinger- und Wikingerzeit* (Göttingen, 1987), 405–527.

24 D. Adamczyk, 'Od dirhemów do fenigów. Reorientacja bałtyckiego systemu handlowego na przełomie X i XI wieku', in I. Panic and J. Sperka (eds.), *Średniowiecze polskie i powszechne* 4 (Katowice, 2007), 15–27; and 'Friesen, Wikinger, Araber', 32–48.

25 G. Hatz, *Handel und Verkehr zwischen dem Deutschen Reich und Schweden in der späten Wikingerzeit* (Stockholm, 1974) and 'Der Handel in der späten Wikingerzeit zwischen Nordeuropa (insbesondere Schweden) und dem Deutschen Reich nach numismatischen Quellen', in Düwel (ed.), *Untersuchungen zu Handel und Verkehr der vor- und frühgeschichtlichen Zeit*, vol. 4: 86–122, and 'Die Münzen von Alt-Lübeck', *Offa* 21/22 (1964/65): 262; I. Leimus, 'Millennium Breakthrough. North Goes West', *Ajalookultuuri ajakiri TUNA,* special issue (2009): 7–34.

26 R. Hammel-Kiesow, 'Novgorod und Lübeck. Siedlungsgefüge zweier Handelsstädte im Vergleich', in N. Angermann and K. Friedland (eds.), *Novgorod. Markt und Kontor der Hanse* (Cologne, 2002), 25–68. See also below, part V 'Metropoles on the North and Baltic Sea', sub-chapter 'The Hanseatic League'.

27 On what follows, see North, *The Baltic*, 9–27.

28 J. Peets, *The Power of Iron. Iron Production and Blacksmithy in Estonia and Neighbouring Areas in Prehistoric Period and the Middle Ages* (Tallinn, 2003).

29 J. Herrmann, *Zwischen Hradschin und Vineta. Frühe Kulturen der Westslawen*, 2nd edn (Leipzig, 1976), 202ff.

30 Ibid., 206ff.

31 J. Herrmann, *Wikinger und Slawen. Zur Frühgeschichte der Ostseevölker* (Berlin, 1982), 24–32. See also H. Janson, 'Pagani and Christiani – Cultural Identity and Exclusion around the Baltic in the Early Middle Ages', in J. Staecker (ed.), *The Reception of Medieval Europe in the Baltic Sea Region, Papers of the XIIth Visby Symposium, held at Gotland University Visby* (Visby, 2009), 171–91.

32 B. Sawyer, *The Viking-Age Rune-Stones. Custom and Commemoration in Early Medieval Scandinavia* (Oxford, 2000); M. Klinge, *Die Ostseewelt* (Helsinki, 1995), 14; R. Bohn, *Gotland*. 5th edn (Kronshagen, 1997), 29–30; N. Price, 'Dying and the Dead. Viking Age Mortuary Behaviour', in Brink (ed.), *The Viking World*, 257–73.

33 Herrmann, *Wikinger und Slawen*, 48ff.

34 Ibid., 44–7.

35 Ibid., 138–42.

III

Red Sea, Arabian Sea, South China Sea:

The Maritime Silk Road

bn Battuta, a scholar and traveller from Tangier, stopped in Aden in 1331 with the intention of sailing along the coast of East Africa. He offered the following description:

> I travelled thence to Aden, the port of Yemen, on the coast of the ocean [...] [I]t has no crops, trees, or water [...]. It is the port of the Indians. [...] Some of the merchants are immensely rich [...]. I took ship at Aden, and after four days at sea reached Zayla [...]. On leaving Zayla we sailed for fifteen days and came to Maqdashah [Mogadishu], which is an enormous town [...]. When a vessel reaches the port, it is met by [...] small boats, in each of which are a number of young men. [...] Each merchant on disembarking goes only to the house of the young man who is his host.[1]

Aden was the centre of trade and shipping between the Red Sea and the Indian Ocean. Its sheltered location provided a suitable anchoring place for the larger ships that arrived from all directions. Apart from Indian and Egyptian merchants, Jewish, Persian and Ethiopian traders were also present in Aden, as other contemporary accounts attest.

Following the triumphal march of Islam in the first half of the seventh century and its expansion into Egypt and Persia, Muslim armies under the Umayyads (661–750) advanced westwards to the Iberian Peninsula and eastwards to the Indus. In the late tenth century, the Fatimids began to set up trade routes between the Red Sea, the Mediterranean and the Indian Ocean.

Muslim merchants travelled south and east in search of luxury goods.[2] In so doing they could refer to the Prophet Mohammed, who had accompanied the caravans from Mecca to Damascus as a merchant's apprentice. The Hajj, the pilgrimage to Mecca, was also associated with trade, inspiring shipping across the Arabian Sea and Red Sea.

Finally, Muslim merchants also reached India and southeast Asia. Here, Brahmanical sects like Saivism, Vaishnavism and Devi cults had displaced Buddhism in the Srivijaya empire (on Sumatra and the coasts of the Malay peninsula) but also on Java as well as Pagan (in present-day Myanmar), Angkor (Cambodia) and Ayutthaya. The north of present-day Vietnam, which was influenced by China, resisted this process. Sanskrit inscriptions and temple foundations document the presence of Indian merchants in the Cham kingdoms of the south. Local rulers attained legitimacy by adopting Hinduism and acquiring mythological genealogies. The religion extended its influence to China, since Chinese traders and pilgrims stopped in Java and Srivijaya and visited India. Srivijaya finally saw itself compelled to enter into a tributary relationship with late Tang and Song dynasty China.[3] Muslim merchants entered this Hindu world in growing numbers in the thirteenth and fourteenth centuries, founding communities and intermarrying with the local population. Islam was promoted by native rulers, although it is worth noting that in southeast Asia, all world religions entered into a symbiosis with local (sea) gods or integrated them into their belief systems. After all, life at sea with its perils such as storms, hidden reefs, sandbars, currents and maelstroms repeatedly confronted even experienced mariners and fishermen with new challenges, which they believed they could master only by appeasing the various sea spirits. While Buddhists venerated the sea goddess Maimekhala, the Chinese made offerings to the goddess Tian Fei, generally known as Mazu. Muslim seafarers in turn believed in the assistance of mythical Sufi masters such as Khidr, the guardian of the seas and rivers.[4]

Arabic became the lingua franca of the Indian Ocean coasts and Islamic law regulated business dealings.[5] Thus on his travels, which took him to China, Ibn Battuta did not need to leave the network of Muslim merchant trading posts.

The preconditions: Winds, ships and navigation

Shipping, and with it trade, in the Indian Ocean was shaped by the monsoons. The word is derived from the Arabic *mawsim*, which means season or seasonal wind. Monsoons were also zones of high air pressure, which caused the air to flow into low-pressure zones thus producing the monsoon winds. Since the air-pressure zones and winds were predictable, once they had understood the system in the first century BCE seafarers could adapt to and use the winds. There is regularly high pressure over continental Asia from November

MAP 4 *The travels of Ibn Battuta*

FIGURE 3 *Relief panel of a ship at Borobudur.* © *Wikipedia Commons.*

to January, so that the winds, the so-called northeast monsoon, blow from southeast Asia in the Indian Ocean towards Africa and from China towards southeast Asia. From April to August the summer or southwest monsoon blows in the opposite direction and speeds sailing ships from East Africa and Arabia towards India, the Malay peninsula and further across the South China Sea to China. The Malay peninsula with its sheltered coasts offered ships the possibility of wintering or waiting for the next favourable winds.[6]

The ships that travelled the Indian Ocean at this time were built without nails and not waterproofed with pitch and tar. Instead, the planks were held together solely by coconut coir ropes. Coconut fibre was accordingly an important commodity in the region. Procuring wood was a problem, since it was always scarce on the Red Sea and the Arabian Sea, and usually had to be transported from India. This led to the spread of Indian shipbuilding techniques. The ships were steered by a stern rudder and had square sails, which were hoisted depending on the wind force. There was little luxury on these ships, which were up to 30 metres long, although cabins for merchants are mentioned by the twelfth and thirteenth centuries, but they were less elaborately appointed than those on Chinese junks.

These ships varied too, however, as Ibn Battuta observed at the beginning of the fourteenth century. The largest junks had crews of up to 1,000 men and featured between three and twelve sails as well as more than four decks.

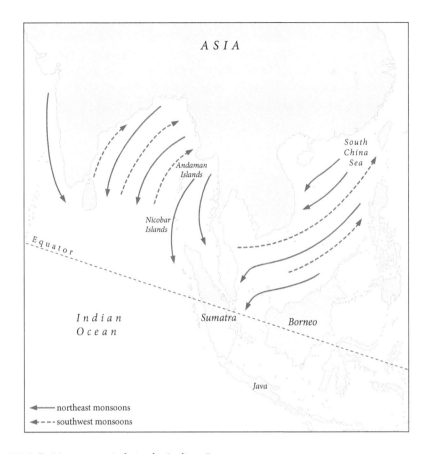

MAP 5 *Monsoon winds in the Indian Ocean*

Unlike the Arab dhows, the sails were attached to the masts with rings, so that the sail surface could be increased or decreased as needed. It was accordingly possible to sail higher into the wind than with square sails. The acquisition of shipbuilding materials did not present a problem, since wood as well as the materials for sails, ropes and caulking was available in China. The ships that sailed in southeast Asia were narrower, with outriggers, as immortalized on reliefs in the temple of Borobodur. They could be used to transport rice from Java to Sumatra but also served as warships.[7]

Aside from the captain, the most important man aboard an Arab ship was the *mu'allim*, the navigator, as the shipping manual of Ibn Mājid suggests. Ibn Mājid had himself been a successful *mu'allim*, who proudly presented his literary abilities in his *Fawa'id*,[8] embellishing the text with infusions of poetry. The *mu'allim* was responsible for the course of the ship and the crew members, who either sailed or rowed the ship and routinely bailed water. The navigator had to recognize shifts in the monsoon winds in order to set sail at the right moment or change course. He also had to steer towards a safe harbour in time, since setting sail too late and catching the full force of the monsoon winds at sea could prove deadly.[9] Navigation was facilitated by the astrolabe, which allowed mariners to determine the latitude of a ship at sea, and the compass, which was borrowed from the Chinese. During the night, beacons on the coast and sea made voyages safer.[10]

Ibn Battuta and Marco Polo:
Merchants and ports

The captain took his instructions from the ship owner, who was usually a merchant. Sanskrit even had the word *nawittaka* for a person whose wealth (*vitta*) derived from his ships (*nau*).[11] We know of most of these merchant ship owners from the letters discovered in 1890 in the *geniza*, a hollow space for storing books and papers, in the Ben-Ezra Synagogue in Cairo. The Geniza letters reflect trade and communications between merchants scattered across the Mediterranean, the Arabian Sea and the Indian Ocean, which helped to constitute a greater maritime region. In 1130, for example, the Jewish merchant Madmun Ben Hassan, the leader of the traders of Aden and a close friend of Abraham Ben Yiju, a Tunisian-Jewish merchant in Mangalore, wrote that he had hired a ship to bring goods and people for him from Aden to Ceylon (Sri Lanka). The vessel, which is later referred to as Madmun's ship, appears repeatedly in the sources. The aforementioned Ben Yiju informed his brother in Fustat (Old Cairo) that he had sent him gifts with this ship. The ship probably sailed for many years between Aden and the Indian coast, and perhaps further westwards.[12]

Muslim merchants increasingly joined Jewish ship owners in this business. One problem was that seafaring was hard to reconcile with the observation of the Sabbath and the associated prohibition on working. For that reason, shipping was not an option for strictly observant Jews, and they sought to direct business from the port cities. The Muslim Karim merchants, who maintained convoys of ships and transported goods and people, took over part of these transactions. Persian and Arab traders had settled on the west coast of India and contributed to the flourishing of trade centres, for example in Gujarat, where the small ports were in regular contact with each other. The southern Malabar Coast was home to both foreign Muslim merchants and Muslims who had integrated into local societies by marriage. Indian ship owners concentrated mainly on the coastal routes and merchants from Gujarat also acted as ship owners. The Geniza letters reveal a range of trade relationships that extended, via various harbours and middlemen, from the Indian Ocean to the Mediterranean. We also know that merchants' wives corresponded with their husbands, although generally only the letters from husbands to wives have survived. This helped to maintain family relationships, even if the couples did not see each other for several years, as in the case of a merchant who arrived in India from Fustat via Aden and traded on the route between Aden and the Malabar Coast. His wife stayed behind in Fustat and waited in vain. To comfort her, he wrote the following in 1204 (perhaps she had threatened him with divorce):

> Now, if this is your wish, I cannot blame you. For the waiting has been long. And I do not know whether the Creator will grant relief immediately so that I can come home, or whether matters will take time, for I cannot come home with nothing. Therefore I resolved to issue a writ which sets you free. Now the matter is in your hand. If you wish separation from me, accept the bill of repudiation and you are free. But if this is not your decision and not your desire, do not lose these long years of waiting.[13]

The merchant tried to raise his wife's spirits. While he admitted to drinking a good deal of alcohol to ease his loneliness, he assured her at the same time that he was not keeping slave girls or visiting brothels. He felt lonely and suffered because they were apart.

Indian literary sources also report on the various groups on the Malabar Coast and their business activities. The wares in demand among the political and military elites included Arabian horses and elephants. While elephants were a rather exceptional commodity, horses and camphor were important trade items on the Indian Ocean. Horses were transported from ports on the Persian Gulf and Red Sea to the west coast of India. Camphor, an essential oil derived from the tree of the same name, arrived on the Indian Subcontinent from southeast Asia and China. Part of the camphor crossed the Arabian Sea to Aden, whence it was transported further west.

The most important products, however, were textiles, especially the cottons that Indian weavers supplied to the markets. The merchants of the subcontinent knew the tastes of the various regions of southeast Asia, where the upper classes demanded costly silks from Gujarat, but the majority preferred cheaper printed cotton fabrics. In exchange they received spices and aromatic woods. Chinese ceramics and coins also reached the Arab world via a number of trade hubs such as Calicut or Aden. Calicut and Quilon also supplied the northwest of India (Gujarat) and the Arab world with pepper from the Malabar Coast as well as cloves and nutmeg from the Moluccas. Like other spices, the black pepper that arrived at the Egyptian markets by way of Aden was distributed from there to the Mediterranean, to Italian ports and cities.

Aromatic agarwood (from Kamrup in Assam) and rhinoceros horn continued to come from the subcontinent. Teakwood and coir were in demand as materials for shipbuilding on the Persian Gulf and Red Sea, where these plants did not grow. Even the Andalusian traveller Ibn Jubayr reports on the large amounts of coir shipped to the Red Sea region. Another important raw material was iron, which was extracted in various forms in India and transported from the Malabar Coast to Aden and points west. But luxury goods and raw materials were not the only commodities sent in exchange across the Arabian Sea; huge quantities of cowry shells were also imported from the Maldives in the Indian Ocean to Bengal, where they were important as currency. The Maldivians received rice from Bengal in exchange.[14]

On the African coast, the most attractive commodities were gold, ivory and slaves as well as wood for building ships and houses. The dhows, which made up the majority of ships on the Indian Ocean, were built of African wood. Since Muslims settled on the African coast and married local women. As Ibn Battuta observed, an Islamic-African society emerged whose representatives in Kilwa gained access to the gold mines in the African interior and transported the precious metal to the port cities.[15] That is why the ships coming from Aden docked in Mogadishu, Mombasa or Kilwa.

Calicut, which was mentioned by Ibn Battuta, was considered the most important harbour. Merchants from China, Sumatra, Ceylon, the Maldives and Yemen all did business there. Muslim traders were present in Ceylon and the southern Coromandel Coast as well, where they met with colleagues from Srivijaya and China as well as the ubiquitous Jewish merchants. Although southeast Asia was shaped by Hinduism and Buddhism, trade heightened the influence of Islam. Moreover, the local princes often supported local or foreign Muslim merchants, even when they undermined the distinctions of the caste system.

But maritime trade was not the only thing to be stabilized. The subjugation of large parts of Asia and Europe by the Mongols, the so-called *Pax mongolica* (c. 1200–1350), made land travel relatively safe as well. This permitted European rulers, travellers and traders to enter into contact and engage in business with the countries occupied by the Golden Horde, and even with China.

Among the many northern Italian merchants trading in China and Asia, the travellers of the Polo family are the best known nowadays. Marco Polo's father Nicolò and his uncle Matteo had already visited China several times between 1250 and 1269 before Marco Polo embarked on his own journey in 1271, which would take him through Selchuk Asia Minor and the empire of the Persian Ilkhans and along the Silk Road to the residence of the Kublai Khan in China. While he entered the service of the khan, his kinsmen worked as merchants and left the Middle Kingdom in 1292.[16] Marco Polo, however, returned home by way of the Indian Ocean, Persian Gulf and Black Sea, reaching Venice in 1295. There he served as a ship's captain in the war against Genoa and was taken prisoner. During his captivity he dictated his fantastic travelogue to a fellow prisoner, who embellished it to such a degree that contemporaries already doubted its authenticity. These doubts are shared by some historians, but the majority believe that Polo could not have derived his detailed knowledge from hearsay alone and that he actually undertook the described journey.

How close the connections were between land and sea routes and how intensively they were used are evident from the spread of the bubonic plague. The pandemic began in 1331/32 in Central Asia and spread from the Genoese trading post of Kaffa in Crimea through trade and shipping in the Black Sea and the Mediterranean. After Constantinople and Cairo, the plague broke out in the Sicilian port city of Messina in October 1347, whence the illness spread to Pisa, Genoa, Venice, Marseille, Barcelona and Florence in 1348. In 1349, the Black Death moved northwards from the southwest coast of England to Scotland, and Hanseatic ships brought the infection to Calais, Bergen, Cologne, Copenhagen, Lübeck and Novgorod.[17]

The Maritime Silk Road

The South China Sea is often regarded as an 'appendage' to the Indian Ocean, to which it is connected by the Straits of Malacca and Singapore as well as the Sunda Strait. It is bounded by the Japanese islands in the northeast and by the Indonesian archipelago in the south and forms a sort of inland sea.

Chinese fishermen and traders generally sailed along two routes: the first led past the Philippines and Moluccas to Java. On the second, the ships passed the coast of South China towards Vietnam and then continued either into the Gulf of Thailand or southwards past the Malay Peninsula and Sumatra to Java.[18] In the fourteenth century, Chinese trade and shipping were divided into three segments: (illegal) private trade, state trade associated with official missions and embassies, and tribute trade with neighbouring countries. The Chinese state tried in vain to prevent smuggling and other illegal mercantile activities but could not protect even their own seafarers and fishermen from attacks by the Japanese pirates known as *wakō*. Trade with the West took on a new quality with the integration of Chinese merchants into existing maritime networks. Muslim Chinese in particular had already left China (Fujian, Guangdong and Yunnan) at the end of the collapse of Mongol rule, a migration further accelerated by the invasion of Ming troops. In this situation, the Indonesian archipelago and the Malay peninsula, where Islam had already made great inroads, seemed natural destinations for Chinese Muslims.[19]

The arrival of immigrants from China signalled an upswing in trade with the West, since they did business and developed contacts with the Muslim merchants of the Indian Ocean and the Arabian Sea from Southeast Asia. Wang Dayuan, for example, who originally hailed from Fujian, travelled the Indian Ocean and the Malay peninsula and reported as follows:

> The Strait is bordered by two hills of the Tanmahsi barbarians which look like dragons' teeth, between them there is a water-way. The soil is poor and paddy fields few. The climate is hot and in the fourth and fifth moons there are heavy rains. The people are addicted to piracy. [...] The natural products of the country are coarse laka-wood and tin. The goods used [by the Chinese] in trading here are red gold, blue satin, cotton prints, Ch'u-chou-fu pourcelain, iron caldrons, and such like things. Neither fine products nor rare objects come from here, all they have is the product of their pillaging of the Ch'uan-chou traders. When [Chinese] junks go to the Western Sea these people let them pass unmolested, but when on the way back they have reached Carimon island then the junk people get out their armour and padded screnes [sic] agains [sic] arrow fire to protect themselves, for, of a certainty, two or three hundred pirate junks will come out to attack them. Sometimes they may have good luck and a favouring wind and they may not catch up with them; if not, then the crews are all butchered and the merchandise made off with in short order.[20]

Wang Dayuan was probably describing the Malay Peninsula here, which used to be known as the Malacca Peninsula. Almost certainly he was speaking of pre-colonial Singapore, which attracted Chinese and Cambodian merchants.[21] It is unclear where exactly the dragon's teeth gate he mentions was located. We do know, however, that Chinese mariners and travellers used Wang's descriptions to guide them on their westward voyages.[22]

While Chinese merchants had long travelled to the West, using the monsoon winds in the Bay of Bengal and the China seas, the maritime Silk Road emerged around the year 1000, linking the South and East China Seas with the West. Aromatic and medicinal substances collectively known as *xiangyao* were prominent among the many import products. They included flowers, myrrh, cloves, nutmeg, mace and sandalwood as well as musk, ambergris and camphor.

Ambergris in particular, one of the many treasures of Southeast Asia, met with lively demand in China. Produced by the digestive system of whales, it floated on the water and was washed onto shore, if it was not extracted from the bodies of dead whales. Ambergris was traded for high prices in China and used to manufacture medicines and perfumes. A wide range of sea turtles could also be found and were used to make tortoiseshell items. The Chinese also ate seaweed and sea snails. Beyond that, the Chinese were mainly interested in pearls. Wang Dayuan emphasized the high quality of pearls from the Sulu Archipelago (Philippines), which were remarkable for their roundness and white colour. Other locations included the Malay Peninsula and especially south-eastern India (around Tuticorin). Pearls symbolized wealth, beauty and supernatural powers and Chinese poets sang their praises. Accordingly, pearl traders from China frequently set forth to negotiate with the local pearl divers. Feathers, for instance from kingfishers, were also very popular. The birds were captured by local tribes in Cambodia, while the bird's nests prized in Chinese cuisine came from Sumatra and Borneo.[23]

For centuries, the most important Chinese export was undoubtedly silk, which was valued by the rulers on the South China Sea as well as by consumers further to the west. In China itself, the coastal regions provided many other areas with silk. Via the tribute system, Chinese silk, which was more highly valued than local textiles, also reached Southeast Asia, where local rulers received it in exchange for gifts and homages to the Chinese emperor.

In the early fifteenth century, Malacca, originally a settlement on the straits, which owed tribute to, or rather belonged to, the kingdom of Siam, evolved into an almost legendary emporium. Apart from its favourable location on a maritime trade route, the conversion to Islam of Malacca's ruling family and elites appears to have increasingly attracted Muslim merchants and seafarers.

Since with the exception of Zheng He's voyages very few Chinese ships sailed west of the Straits of Malacca, and the Indian Ocean constituted a natural and mental barrier for 'normal' Chinese junks, Malacca was a logical place for trade with 'Western' merchants. Moreover, Malacca was located at the intersection of monsoon systems, so that the merchants did not have to wait for the monsoons to change in order to sail from the Gulf of Bengal to the South China Sea. That is why the Arab, Indian and Chinese merchants used Malacca to reduce the turnaround time of their goods. Word of the famed emporium had already reached Europe by the fifteenth century and is mentioned in the accounts of Girolamo da Santo Stefano (Genoa) and Ludovico de Varthema (Bologna). After reaching Calicut, the Portuguese also heard of the renowned trading post, which the governor of Portuguese India Afonso de Albuquerque captured in 1511, driving the sultan into exile. This ushered in a new era for the Europeans.

The Chinese began their maritime expansion in the late thirteenth century. After establishing their rule in the Middle Kingdom, the Mongols discovered seafaring, and Kublai Khan sought to extend his influence to Japan by undertaking two invasions by sea. The first Ming rulers, in contrast, adopted a different strategy from 1368. Since they regarded private trade as a gateway for enemies on the coast, they banned it and expanded state tribute missions instead.

The emperor sent official delegations to Southeast Asia and in return received tribute from envoys from Java, Champa, Siam and Cambodia. Pepper and sappanwood were notable commodities. The pepper came mainly from the Malabar Coast in India, and the amounts the Chinese imported outstripped those arriving at the Mediterranean ports (Venice or Barcelona).[24] The centre for tribute goods was Canton (Guangzhou) on the Pearl River, which therefore attracted not just officials but also merchants.

The Chinese state's involvement in trade and shipping reached a highpoint in the fifteenth century. Maritime expansion is associated with Emperor Yongle and served primarily to solidify the tribute system and with it Chinese power and prestige. To this end, the emperor commissioned the construction of several hundred ships. Between 1405 and 1433, Yongle and his successor sent numerous shipping expeditions to the western Indian Ocean between Malacca and eastern Africa as well as to the southeast and the waters between the Philippines and Timor. These expeditions were commanded by court eunuchs, the most famous of whom today is Zheng He.[25]

Zheng He was born in Kunyang in the province of Yunnan in 1371. His father, who like his grandfather had made the Hajj, the pilgrimage to Mecca, served the Yuan dynasty, which still ruled Yunnan when the Ming dynasty gained the upper hand. Since he resisted the Ming conquest he was killed, and his son was captured and castrated for service as a court eunuch. The expansion of Chinese power on land and at sea coincided with his time at the court of the Ming emperors Hongwu and Yongle. The expansion at sea was entrusted to Zheng He, who was to promote China's position along the old routes, first in the South China Sea and later in the Gulf of Bengal and the Arabian Sea.[26]

The first three voyages (1405–7, 1407–9 and 1409–11) followed the well-known routes already described by Marco Polo over the South China Sea, the Straits of Malacca and across the Indian Ocean to Ceylon and the Malabar Coast, while the fourth voyage (1413–15) took him across the Arabian Sea to Hormuz and on to the east coast of Africa. Apart from gathering tribute, his armada of 27,000 soldiers was supposed to demonstrate military presence (in the Indian Ocean), combating the pirate fleets in Palembang and conducting a war against Ceylon.

Zheng He's fifth voyage of 1417–19 illustrates in detail how these journeys proceeded. The initial aim of the enterprise was to bring home the ambassadors of foreign lands who had paid their respects to the emperor with precious gifts, such as horses, rhinoceroses and elephants. The emperor had presented the envoys not just with silk robes, but also other textiles intended as gifts for the various kings. The list of ports of call included Pahang on the east coast of the Malay Peninsula, Java, Palembang on Sumatra, Malacca, Calicut and Ceylon. Other destinations mentioned are 'Lasa' and Aden on the Arabian Peninsula and Mogadishu, Brava and Malindi in eastern Africa. With the exception of Lasa, all of these places still exist today. The location of Lasa was described as twenty days and nights from Calicut, so it may have been near Aden. Camels, ambergris and frankincense were said to come from there. The gifts offered from Africa and Aden were giraffes, although those in Aden presumably also came from Africa. Perhaps the envoys mentioned in the sources with their gifts were actually traders who engaged in several activities at the same time.[27]

The emperor suddenly suspended further expeditions in 1421 and permanently prohibited them in 1424. There was one brief, sixth voyage in 1421–2 and a final, seventh one in 1431–3, which may have taken Zheng He to Mecca with a smaller group.

Assessments of the purpose and success of the voyages vary. These enterprises show that China was in a position to engage in long-distance trade on a grand scale from the South China Sea across the Indian Ocean to the Arabian Sea and to integrate an increasing number of countries into its tribute system. Accordingly, some historians view the journeys as profitable and advantageous for trade, since China had enough silver and coins to

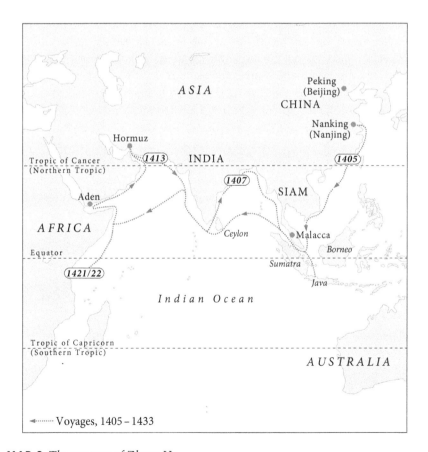

MAP 6 *The voyages of Zheng He*

exchange for Western goods. Others believe that the Chinese squandered valuable resources in order to import Western luxury goods. While the emperor initiated many projects and wars with no concern for the costs, the court bureaucracy eyed these undertakings more critically. In any case, Zheng He's voyages implemented the emperor's decision to expand China's tribute system westwards. This was not, however, calculated to promote Chinese trade, for trading patterns were changing in this period. Merchants of diverse origin acted as individuals rather than according to central state plans, so that the influence of the Chinese fleets remained slight in the long run.

Scholars are still puzzled by China's official abandonment of the sea, especially because it was not forced upon them from outside.[28] Various possible reasons have been suggested. One is the move of the capital from Nanking (Nanjing) to Peking (Beijing) and the establishment of a new centre in the north, another the increased presence on the border to the Mongol empire instead of maritime expansion. Some historians have cited the growing influence of the civilian bureaucracy. In 1436, the construction of large sea-going ships was prohibited, and the number of new small ships reduced. By 1500, only one or two of the original ten warships remained.[29]

Exchange did not simply end, however; it continued via the family networks of the Chinese diaspora, for example in the emerging emporium of Malacca and north Javanese ports,[30] but also through Japanese smugglers and pirates. The Japanese experienced the ocean as a series of connected seas: the South China Sea, the East China Sea, the Yellow Sea, the Sea of Japan. Fishing and other modes of marine exploitation were fundamental to the Japanese economy. This marine exploitation encompassed fishing with trained cormorants as well as the famous diving activities of the Ama. Ama women collected shellfish, octopus, sea urchins, pearls and above all abalone for the Chinese market.[31]

The maritime network of the Ryukyu Islands played an important role in the Sino-Japanese sea trade. Products from South East Asia such as ivory, tin, spices and sappanwood were re-exported from the Ryukyu Islands to China, Japan or Korea. In Japan they were exchanged for gold, swords, *trepang*, shark fins and abalone, the latter being the most precious ingredients in Chinese cuisine.[32]

Moreover, Japanese pirates, so-called *wakō*, profited from the Ming dynasty's restrictive maritime policy. The limits on free trade by Chinese merchants provided new opportunities for pirates. For the *wakō*, as for pirates everywhere, the boundaries between trade and piracy were fluid. Ships' cargos were captured and sold. The *wakō* were especially keen on the luxury objects of the Chinese tribute trade, as the desire for Chinese commodities proliferated in Japan. By adapting and innovating, the Japanese developed their own luxury industry, which found customers all over Asia and also in Europe.[33]

Notes

1 Ibn Battúta. *Travels in Asia and Africa, 1325–1354*, ed. and trans. H. A. R. Gibb (London, 1929), 109–10.

2 Alpers, *The Indian Ocean*, 41; K. R. Hall, *A History of Early Southeast Asia. Maritime Trade and Societal Development, 100–1500* (Plymouth, 2011), 213–4.

3 G. C. Gunn, *History without Borders. The Making of an Asian World Region 1000–1800* (Hongkong, 2011), 37–43.

4 B. Watson Andaya, 'Seas, Oceans and Cosmologies in Southeast Asia', *Journal of Southeast Asian Studies* 48 (2017): 349–71 and 'Rivers, Oceans, and Spirits. Water Cosmologies, Gender, and Religious Change in Southeast Asia,' *TRaNS Trans-Regional and -National Studies of Southeast Asia* 1, no. 2 (2016): 1–25.

5 Alpers, *The Indian Ocean*, 41; Hall, *History of Early Southeast Asia*, 213–4.

6 N. C. Keong, 'At the Crossroads of the Maritime Silk Route', in T. Y. Tan and A. Lau (eds.), *Maritime Heritage of Singapore* (Singapore, 2005), 60ff.

7 R. Chakravarti, 'Seafaring, Ships and Ship Owners. India and the Indian Ocean (AD 700–1500)', in D. Parkin (ed.), *Ships and the Development of Maritime Technology in the Indian Ocean* (London, 2002), 28–61; R. Chakravarti, *The Pull towards the Coast and Other Essays: The Indian Ocean History and the Subcontinent before 1500* (New Delhi, 2020); Ptak, *Die Maritime Seidenstraße*, 326–33; S. Conermann, 'South Asia and the Indian Ocean', in W. Reinhard (ed.), *Empires and Encounters 1350–1750* (Cambridge, MA, 2015), 391–554, 983–1002 and 1078–90.

8 See A. Ibn Majid Al-Najdi and G. R. Tibbetts (eds.), *Arab Navigation in the Indian Ocean before the Coming of the Portuguese. Being a Translation of Kitab al-Fawa'id fi usul al-bahr* (London, 1971).

9 Chakravarti, 'Merchants, Merchandise and Merchantmen', 89–92.

10 G. Wolfschmidt, 'Von Kompaß und Sextant zu Radar und GPS – Geschichte der Navigation', in G. Wolfschmidt (ed.), *'Navigare necesse est.' Geschichte der Navigation* (Norderstedt, 2008), 34.

11 R. Chakravarti, 'Nakhudas and Nauvittakas. Ship-Owning-Merchants in the West Coast of India (AD 1000–1500)', *Journal of the Economic and Social History of the Orient* 43 (2000): 34–64.

12 S. D. Goitein (ed.), *Letters of Medieval Jewish Traders* (Princeton, 1973), 63.

13 Ibid., 225.

14 R. Chakravarti, *India and the Indian Ocean. Issues in Trade and Politics (up to c. 1500 CE)* (Mumbai, 2014), 15–8.

15 Alpers, *The Indian Ocean*, 51.

16 F. Reichert, *Die Erfahrung der Welt. Reisen und Kulturbegegnung im späten Mittelalter* (Stuttgart, Berlin and Cologne, 2001), 181–97.

17 North, *Expansion of Europe*, 362–3.

18 L. Blussé, *Visible Cities. Canton, Nagasaki, and Batavia and the Coming of the Americans* (Cambridge, MA and London, 2008), 9ff.

19 R. Ptak, 'Ming Maritime Trade to Southeast Asia, 1368–1567: Visions of a «System»', in C. Guillot, D. Lombard and R. Ptak (eds.), *From the Mediterranean to the China Sea. Miscellaneous Notes* (Wiesbaden, 1998), 159–65 and *Die maritime Seidenstraße*.

20 Keong, 'At the Crossroads of the Maritime Silk Route', 71; Tan and Lau (eds.), *Maritime Heritage of Singapore*.

21 K. C. Guan, D. Heng, P. Borschberg and T. T. Yong, *Seven Hundred Years. A History of Singapore* (Singapore, 2019), 19–41.

22 Ibid., 69.

23 B. Watson Andaya and L. Y. Andaya, *A History of Early Modern Southeast Asia, 1400–1830* (Cambridge, 2015), 25–6.

24 Ptak, 'Ming Maritime Trade', 159–65.

25 Watson Andaya and Andaya, *History of Early Modern Southeast Asia*, 89–90.

26 Ptak, *Die maritime Seidenstraße*, 234–47.

27 E. L. Dreyer, *Zheng He. China and the Oceans in the Early Ming Dynasty, 1405–1433* (New York, 2007), 82–91.

28 Ptak, 'Ming Maritime Trade', 248–9.

29 Ptak, *Die maritime Seidenstraße*, 244–9; Dreyer, *Zheng He*, 166–71.

30 Dreyer, *Zheng He*, 11–38.

31 Rozwadowski, *Vast Expanses*, 64–6.

32 F. Gipouloux, *The Asian Mediterranean: Port Cities and Trading Networks in China, Japan and South Asia, 13th–21st Century*, trans. J. Hall and D. Martin (Cheltenham, 2011), 59–73.

33 For a good overview, see Abulafia, *The Boundless Sea*, 212–35.

IV

Mediterranean:
The Rise of the Maritime Republics

The Mediterranean is still considered the sea par excellence. It owes this exceptional character to Fernand Braudel and his work *La Méditerranée*, the first monograph to portray a maritime region and its physiographic conditions over the centuries and to construct a single entity in which human beings were subject to these conditions. The nature of the Mediterranean had been described by various authors such as Basil of Caesarea:

> Thus, in the eyes of God, the sea is good, because it makes the under current of moisture in the depths of the earth. It is good again, because from all sides it receives the rivers without exceeding its limits. It is good, because it is the origin and source of the waters in the air. Warmed by the rays of the sun, it escapes in vapour, is attracted into the high regions of the air, and is there cooled on account of its rising high above the refraction of the rays from the ground, and, the shade of the clouds adding to this refrigeration, it is changed into rain and fattens the earth.[1]

While Braudel and those who followed him saw Mediterraneans all over the world, for example viewing the Baltic as a northern Mediterranean, nobody ever thought of regarding the Mediterranean as a southern Baltic. Before Braudel, it was ancient authors like Herodotus and Thucydides who developed the idea of a thalassocracy, or sea power. In the public mind, the Mediterranean is associated with the emergence of civilization in Greece, Rome or Renaissance Italy. More recently, scholars have criticized the exclusion of the eastern Mediterranean and with it the Ottoman Empire as well as North Africa. Currently, the focus has shifted to connections across the sea and the goods and protagonists involved as well as the sea's economic exploitation and topographical fragmentation.[2]

The above-cited quotation from Basil of Caesarea, who lived in the fourth century and was born into the elite of the city of the same name in the eastern Mediterranean, illustrates the history of the Mediterranean and its connections at a time of transition. While Basil still expressed the late antique view of a purported 'Mediterranean unity', fundamental changes were emerging at the same time. The decline of the Roman Empire and the migration of the peoples led to shifts in trade and shipping. While the Western Roman Empire dwindled away, new trading centres like Venice rose on its periphery. The Byzantine Empire claimed the eastern Mediterranean. With the Muslim victories in North Africa and the Near East, where Alexandria or Tyre took on new functions, a trade hub arose in Cairo (Fustat) with connections reaching to Damascus and Baghdad to the east, Aden and the Indian Ocean to the south and the significant ports of Kairouan and Córdoba to the west.

The conquest of the islands of Sicily and Crete added new trading posts. The Byzantine Mediterranean was subsequently limited to the eastern basin and the Black Sea, with the emperors succeeding in recapturing Cyprus and Crete.

The Muslim conquests thus did not halt trade in the Mediterranean but gave it a new structure. The north-south axis in particular, which had held great importance in Antiquity, since North Africa provided Rome with grain, was weakened, as neither Rome nor Constantinople controlled the southern coasts of the Mediterranean anymore. At the same time, the Byzantine trade network expanded from the Black Sea across the Aegean to the Adriatic, where Venice was to play an intermediary role between the Muslim and the Christian or Byzantine worlds, a role that also led to the rise of Amalfi. The situation changed again after 1000, since Latin merchants from northern Italy, Provence and the lands of the crown of Aragón increasingly dominated trade. The conquest of Sicily, the Reconquista and the Crusades set in motion a process in which cities and states in the western Mediterranean took over seafaring and soon advanced to the east. Mariners profited from new navigational techniques and aids (the compass, portolan charts) as well as changes in shipbuilding (sails, rudders, larger vessels). The new galleys in particular could spend long periods at sea, as they could be both sailed and rowed, and also carrier larger quantities of goods. They were even adapted for the Atlantic route in order to cope better with the winds and currents in the Bay of Biscay.[3]

The rise of the Maritime Republics

The protagonists of change were the maritime republics, which in the centuries that followed would put their stamp on the Mediterranean. Genoa and Pisa gained a foothold in Sicily and Sardinia at the beginning of the eleventh century. As republican entities they were ruled by oligarchies, with mercantile families such as the Doria and Spinola in Genoa or the Visconti in Pisa determining the fate of their cities. The Crusades in particular gave the maritime republics opportunities to profit from exchange with the Levant in the form of troop transport and warships. For example, during the First Crusade a Genoese fleet sailed eastwards in 1097 to support the siege of Antioch. After the city was captured, the Genoese acquired trading privileges there from the new Latin rulers, as well as in Tyre and Acre, which became their central trading post. The Pisans, who could offer similar services, settled in Acre to gain a foothold in trade with the Levant.

The most successful were the Venetians, who after modest beginnings in fishing and salt extraction developed their lagoons into a commercial centre. Their activities also included transporting crusaders and pilgrims to the Holy Land, which brought in some 40,000 silver marks on the eve of the Fourth Crusade. After the conquest and pillaging of Byzantium during this crusade in 1204, the jewel-encrusted chalices, gilded and enamelled book bindings, relics and other booty from Constantinople's imperial palace and churches ended up in the treasury of St Mark's basilica.[4] The conquest of the city and part of the Byzantine Empire, which the crusaders divided up among themselves, gave the Venetians access to the Black Sea trade, but at the same time they had to fight off threats from the East and resistance in Asia Minor and the Balkans. For a time, Genoa sought to contest Venice's possessions in the eastern Mediterranean, but then increasingly focused on the western Mediterranean.

There, the Christian kingdoms of Navarra, Aragón and Castile-Léon had increasingly gained in influence over the course of the Reconquista in the twelfth century. Barcelona in particular expanded its position in the Mediterranean trade, since the house of Aragón was interested in closing the gap left by the Muslims with foreign artisans and merchants. Pisans and Genoese came across the sea, joined in the fourteenth century by Venetians, Lombards and Florentines, who established mercantile societies there. The islands of Majorca, Menorca and Ibiza, which the house of Aragón had captured from the Muslims, offered important bases as did Valencia or the cities north of the Pyrenees (Montpellier). Catalan traders became integrated into the Mediterranean trade and expanded it to Tunis and Alexandria in the thirteenth century. The slave trade, especially in North African women, played an important role for the European market in this context. The Majorcans regularly traded with England and Flanders, allowing wool and Flemish cloth to be brought directly to the Mediterranean region, where it was finished in workshops in Florence, Barcelona and other cities. At the same time, the Catalans and Italians transported alum, which was needed for textile processing and obtained from Phocaea on the coast of Asia Minor, across the Mediterranean, Atlantic and North Sea to the Flemish textile centres of Bruges, Ghent and Ypres.[5]

The so-called commercial revolution of the twelfth and thirteenth centuries was the precondition for the expansion of trade. This term refers to the fundamental changes in business methods and commercial organization that Italian merchants employed in the thirteenth century to make their enterprises more rational and hence more effective. They thus no longer bought Flemish cloth at the fairs in Champagne, but established themselves permanently in the areas of production, notably Bruges. They were motivated by the growth of the southern European trade in luxury goods, which made a division of labour in commerce necessary and lucrative. Now, merchants engaged in long-distance trade no longer had to accompany their cargo to the fairs personally by ship but directed their firms' commercial enterprises from offices in Genoa, Florence or Pisa. Agents based in the production regions and sales markets bought and sold locally, while seafarers and waggoners transported the goods. Thus, in the fourteenth century, a company like the Florentine merchant house of Bardi maintained a network of branches stretching from Cyprus in the East to Flanders and England in the West. New forms of business partnership, bookkeeping, cashless payment and insurance followed the expansion of trade.[6]

The first evidence of maritime insurance concerns the fourteenth-century Florentine merchant Francesco del Bene's insuring of a shipment of cloth to Florence. Pisan merchants also reduced the risks of shipping cloth to Salerno with the aid of insurance policies. But pregnant slaves were also insured before embarking. This would lead to the development of a new business model in the fifteenth century.[7]

The flows of gold and silver that connected other European regions with the Mediterranean as well also offer examples of the integration of trade in the Mediterranean. Silver from the mining regions of central Europe was traded to the West and South. The Genoese and Pisans in turn used silver to make payments in Sicily and southern Italy, and the expanding Genoese and Venetian trade with the Levant brought a growing flow of silver. While in the twelfth and thirteenth centuries the Genoese and Venetians had mainly bought cotton and linen cloth, refined sugar and glass in Syria and Indian spices transported through the Levant along the caravan routes, in the late thirteenth and the fourteenth centuries Italian interest shifted to Syrian raw materials. The Italians now imported raw cotton on a grand scale and processed it in Lombardy, while in Venice raw sugar was processed and a local glass industry was established on Murano, whose products found buyers in the Near East as well as north of the Alps. For that reason, from the mid-thirteenth century increasing quantities of silver bars were transported on a new northern route to Asia Minor along the Black Sea via Constantinople, Kaffa in the Crimea and Tana on the Sea of Asov, some of which found their way to India and China.

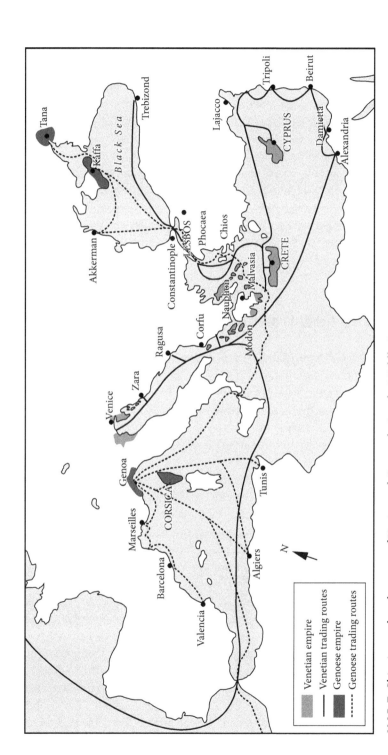

MAP 7 *Shipping and trade routes of Venice and Genoa during the Middle Ages*

While Christian Europe was mining, minting and exporting silver in growing quantities, gold was the dominant monetary metal in the Muslim world until the arrival of silver from central Europe. This gold came from the upper Senegal and Niger rivers in what was then western Sudan, from where it was transported north and east along various routes through the Sahara, to Moorish Spain, Tunis and Mahdia in present-day Tunisia as well as to Egypt. There the gold attracted Sicilians, Pisans and Genoese, who participated actively in the African trade.

Since gold coins were essential to trade with southern Italy, Sicily and Spain and also because the Genoese Mediterranean trade between the Maghreb and the Levant increasingly yielded gold, the maritime republic introduced its first gold coin, the *genovino*, in 1252. Florence, which also needed gold coins to purchase cereals in Sicily, followed that same year with the *fiorino*, which would make European monetary history as the florin or guilder.[8]

The new trading power in the Levant

With the advance of the Mamluks and Ottomans in the eastern Mediterranean, structural changes emerged in the second half of the fourteenth century that changed the western Mediterranean region. The Mamluk conquest of Acre in 1291 as well as the papal prohibition on trade with the Saracens made the Genoese, who dominated trade in the western Mediterranean and the Black Sea, consider for the first time a sea route around Africa. Although the expedition of the Vivaldi brothers in the thirteenth century probably did not get much farther than North Africa, the continent was not completely unknown to the Genoese. In the fourteenth century the Genoese, Catalans and Majorcans then advanced into the Atlantic, where they likely rediscovered the Canaries and perhaps the Madeira group and even the Azores before 1350.[9] Thus the Catalan world atlas of 1375, with a map of the Black Sea, the Mediterranean and the Atlantic coast, already shows precise distances and coastlines that could be used for orientation during navigation.[10]

The Ottoman Empire initially had no maritime ambitions. From a small emirate in north-west Anatolia, the Ottomans conquered first Bursa and the last Byzantine possessions in Anatolia. Advances on the Balkans followed in the 1350s, and the capital was soon moved from Bursa to Adrianople (Edirne). The famous 1389 battle of Kosovo, which signalled an end to Serbian rule, ensued after the capture of additional cities such as Sofia, Niš and Thessaloniki. Only the trading centre of Ragusa (Dubrovnik), Hungarian Croatia and the islands in the eastern Mediterranean, as well as the Dalmatian coastal towns belonging to Venice, were able to hold their ground. Instead, after the final conquest of the Byzantine empire in 1453, the Ottomans advanced into the Black Sea region where they occupied the port of Acre, which was frequented mainly by the Genoese. The Black Sea became the domain of Muslim merchants, but soon also of Sephardic Jews, who had been expelled from the western Mediterranean.[11]

While the Genoese suffered from this development, they made the best of the situation, for instance by shifting sugar production first to the western Mediterranean and then to the Atlantic region. Even the loss of the sources of alum in Phocaea was compensated for by the discovery of alum in Tolfa in Italy. At the same time, the merchants continued to trade with the Levant, with Aragón emerging as the main new actor alongside Venice. The conquest of Naples not only allowed the Aragonese to control trade with southern Italy, but also increased the importance of Valencia, the seat of the maritime and commercial courts. On the Iberian Peninsula, trade with the remaining Muslim territories (Granada) would come to play a significant role. There, Genoese, Florentine and Catalan merchants came together with Muslims and Jews to buy silk, dried fruit and ceramics.[12]

This trade collapsed after Granada was conquered in 1492, especially since Muslims and Jews were forced to convert or expelled. The Jews found refuge first in southern Italy and Portugal and, after being expelled from there, in North Africa and the eastern Mediterranean. Particularly in the Ottoman Empire, Sephardic Jews would make significant contributions to the economic infrastructure as merchants and artisans.

The Ottoman conquest of Syria and Egypt (1516/17) created an Ottoman Mediterranean, since three-quarters of the coastline was under the control of Istanbul.[13] The Ottomans boosted the economy and trade in the territories they occupied. Thus, Bursa became a trading centre for spices and dyes from the East, commodities that, like pilgrims, were transported to the city by camel caravans from Mecca. Although in the sixteenth century the Portuguese diverted maritime trade, especially in slaves and gold, across the Atlantic, the triumphal march of the Ottomans reopened the western Mediterranean for goods from the East. For example, cotton from Anatolia was shipped westwards via Izmir (Smyrna). At the same time, the Ottoman Empire traded via its vassal states Moldavia and Wallachia with Russia and Poland-Lithuania, on whose markets the demand for Levantine goods rose. By the late fifteenth century, a merchant from Bursa was already delivering soap and ginger from Arabia in exchange for knives from Wallachia, of which he possessed more than 11,000 at his death.[14]

Merchants from the Ottoman Empire were gaining ground in other port cities as well. The conquest of Istanbul and its expansion into a capital city led to a renewed shift in the currents of trade, away from the international trade routes maintained by the Italians and towards the provisioning of the capital. Foreign trade was accordingly dominated into the eighteenth century by trade within the Ottoman Empire. One could even say that when it came to trade, the Ottomans re-established the Byzantine Empire, with local Christian merchants, especially Greeks and Armenians, benefiting more from the withdrawal of the Italians than their Muslim counterparts.[15]

Different actors provided for Istanbul economically and culturally. Inhabitants of the Dodecanese islands took over shipping between Alexandria and Istanbul, and Ottoman merchants settled in the Egyptian port cities in the seventeenth and eighteenth centuries. Thessaloniki was an important port for goods from Egypt, chief among them coffee. Ottoman traders met Italian merchants mainly in Ancona, where they sold them textiles. The integration of Ancona into the papal states in 1532 did nothing to change this. The Black Sea was a further domain of Ottoman, especially Greek, merchants, who from there engaged in the fur trade with Russia. When the Habsburgs pushed back the Turks beginning in the late seventeenth century, trade with the Balkans flourished, where Greek merchants dealt in grain, pelts, meat, oil, wax, cotton, tobacco and wood. Independently of them French, Dutch and English merchants traded with the Ottoman Empire, receiving trading privileges, so-called capitulations, and opened consulates in Izmir (Smyrna), Thessaloniki and the Dardanelles.

The Netherlands, whose presence in the Mediterranean region Fernand Braudel has vilified as a 'northern invasion', provides an example of how the Western European maritime powers connected the Mediterranean with other trading regions of the world. In the late sixteenth century, when western and southern Europe were plagued by crop failures, the Dutch were able to capitalize on their monopoly on Baltic cereals and intensify trade with southern Europe. Dutch merchants established themselves in Venice and connected the Mediterranean with the North and Baltic Sea.[16] This gradually changed the range of goods in the Dutch Baltic trade. Salt, herring and wine were no longer the only commodities exported to this region, but also high-value goods such as spices, sugar, tropical fruits and textiles.

The Dutch trade with the Levant began around the same time. The first Dutch ship dropped anchor on the Syrian coast in 1595. On board was silver worth 100,000 ducats to purchase spices and silk in Aleppo. The Venetian, French and English merchants in the Levant were irked by the new competition, although it as yet posed no threat to Venice's old intermediate trade.

With time, Dutch ships took over transport services. They carried salt and wool from Spain to Italy and, via the Cape route, supplied the Mediterranean region with pepper and spices from the East Indies, which had previously been purchased from the Levant. They also bought cotton and Persian raw silk. After the Peace of Westphalia in 1648, the Dutch took control of the trade in Spanish wool as well as Turkish camel and goat's hair, thereby securing the raw materials for the *laken* and *camelot* manufactures in Leiden. The products were then sold in the Mediterranean region, but also the Ottoman Empire. Dutch economic dominance in this region, however, continued only until French products conquered the Ottoman markets in the late seventeenth century.[17]

Western European ships handled most passenger traffic on the Mediterranean. The travel account by the Emir Fakhr-al-Din II of Chouf (Shuf) in present-day Lebanon, for instance, describes the interruption of his journey to Italy on a Flemish ship by two galleys of Maltese pirates.[18]

A further maritime actor, Russia, arrived on the scene in the eighteenth century. While all of the Western European maritime powers were interested in trading with the Ottoman Empire, the tsarist empire also pushed for the opening of the Black Sea and free passage through the Dardanelles. To this end, Catherine the Great sent the Russian Baltic fleet around Gibraltar into the Mediterranean in 1770 with orders to blockade the Dardanelles and reach Constantinople from the west. The Ottoman monopoly on shipping through the Dardanelles and in the Black Sea crumbled and the 1774 Peace of Küçuk Kaynarca sealed free and unimpeded shipping for Russian and Ottoman trading vessels. Other European powers followed – Austria in 1784, England in 1799, France in 1802 and Prussia in 1806 – and were granted free access for their trading ships.

Goods traffic in the eastern Mediterranean and the Black Sea region continued to enjoy great importance for the European powers. This is underlined by British and Dutch trade statistics, which show that imports from the Mediterranean region were not surpassed in value by those from Asia until the late eighteenth century.[19] Although the French increasingly regarded the Mediterranean, especially in the west, as their trade and shipping domain, Greek merchants and captains from the Ottoman Empire continued to play a central role. They worked as privateers for the various European powers, especially the British, during the Seven Years' War, and Russian-Ottoman conflicts offered similar opportunities. In the 1780s, there were 400 Greek ships operating in the Mediterranean. At the same time, Greek and Armenian merchants lived in Amsterdam, Livorno, Venice, Vienna, Trieste and elsewhere, where they dominated trade and financial transactions between the Ottoman Empire and western Europe.[20]

The galley: A safe but costly mode of transport

The Arsenal of Venice, which leant its name to many armouries and ammunition dumps in early modern Europe, was the largest shipyard in mediaeval times. The name derives from the Arabic *dar al-sina'a*, which means workshop. The

Arsenal differed from a workshop by virtue of its division of labour, in which, much like a modern assembly line, prefabricated standardized components were put together. This type of manufacture, which we will encounter again in the (seventeenth century) Dutch *fluyten*, astounded contemporaries like the Castilian Pero Tafur, who visited Venice several times in the fifteenth century.

> There is an arsenal at Venice which is the finest in the world, as well for artillery as for things necessary for navigation. The sea flows into it, and the ships enter the water there after they pass the castles. They told me that, including the war galleys and merchant vessels, and others which were in the water and on the stocks, there were altogether eighty galleys, besides other ships. One day, coming from hearing Mass in St Mark's, I saw about twenty men enter the square, some carrying benches and others tables and others chairs, and others large bags of money; thereupon a trumpet was blown, and the great bell, which they call the Council Bell, was rung, and in an hour the square was full of men who received pay and went into the arsenal. And as one enters the gate there is a great street on either hand with the sea in the middle, and on one side are windows opening out of the houses of the arsenal, and the same on the other side, and out came a galley towed by a boat, and from the windows they handled out to them, from one the cordage, from another the bread, from another the arms, and from another the balistas and mortars, and so from all sides everything which was required, and when the galley had reached the end of the street all the men required were on board, together with the complement of oars, and she was equipped from end to end. In this manner there came out ten galleys, fully armed, between the hours of three and nine. I know not how to describe what I saw there, whether in the manner of its construction or in the management of the workpeople, and I do not think there is anything finer in the world.[21]

This was the final heyday of the Venetian commercial galleys. According to the doge Tommaso Mocenigo, in 1423 Venice had forty-five galleys with 11,000 sailors, along with 300 round ships[22] and 3,000 smaller vessels with crews of 25,000 men in all. By this estimate, around one-quarter of the inhabitants of the lagoon (the Venetian population) worked as mariners. The number of galleys even increased in the course of the fifteenth century, so that eventually 180 of them were in use. The largest could hold 250–300 tonnes of cargo and their deployment was precisely regulated by the Venetian senate. Because they carried arms, galleys were a safe but expensive means of transport. They were accordingly reserved for transporting valuable cargo, which was used to finance them. The galleys travelling to Alexandria, Egypt, where they took on spices from the East, were particularly profitable. The cargo the ships carried on their eastward journey, which consisted largely of silver bars, gold and silver coins worth up to 100,000 ducats[23] per galley, documents the value of this transport business. Spice transports were accordingly limited to this type of ship, while round ships were only permitted to carry spices if there was not enough room on the galleys. In order to ensure speedy transhipment, the Venetian senate also stipulated that galleys could not stay in Alexandria longer than twenty days and could not load cargo there past 20 November. This was intended to assure their arrival in Venice in time for the Christmas fair. The large ships were auctioned off by the government for specific trade routes and, if the senate accepted him, the highest bidder was granted a charter to operate the galleys on behalf of a group of investors.[24] As the master of the galley, he was simultaneously responsible for the cargo, the safe deployment of the galleys and the payment of the crew. The Venice senate also set the freight prices. While the eastward voyages were so profitable that bidding consortiums competed over them, the senate had to make attractive offers for westward journeys, for example to Flanders. The fixing of rates for freight created transparency and prevented galley masters from cheating their financiers. On board it was the ship's commander, the captain, who checked the cargo in detail.[25]

Although Venetian shipping in the Mediterranean and to Western Europe seems to have been a success story, we should not underestimate the dangers of shipwrecks. The weather and currents in the Mediterranean were quite

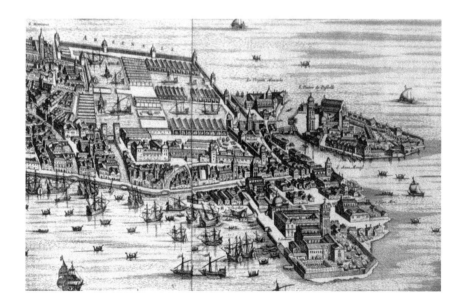

FIGURE 4 *Joan Blaeu, Arsenal in Venice, 1724.* © *Wikimedia Commons.*

different from those in the Atlantic, so that ships could easily run aground, even if they were adapted to the prevailing conditions. This is especially well documented for the disaster of the carrack *Querina*, which belonged to the Venetian Pietro Querini, who was on board at the time. The ship left the port of Crete on 25 April 1431 bound for Bruges with a cargo of wine and cypress wood. The vessel already ran aground on 2 June before Cádiz, and the repairs took quite some time. In order to avoid military conflict with Genoa, the *Querina* left the coast, reaching Lisbon in late August 1431 and Muros at the end of October. In November the ship then lost its rowlock in the Atlantic, so that it could barely navigate when a storm came up and drifted far off course. The storms in the North Atlantic battered the ship and all prayers seemed in vain. Since the ship threatened to capsize and sink, the crew took off in two life rafts. While one of them with twenty-one men was never seen again, Querini tried to keep the larger of the two on course with a crew of forty-seven rowing. After abandoning all hope at the end of December, the crew arrived near the coast in January 1432, stranding on one of the snow-covered Lofoten islands in northern Norway. In the weeks that followed, only sixteen men managed to keep themselves alive with ship's biscuits and mussels. After further deaths, the survivors finally found a fisherman's cottage where they made a fire. After noticing the smoke from the chimney, a few fishermen from the island of Røst took in the half-starved crew. By May 1433 the Venetians had recovered, after fortifying themselves for the return journey among the astonishing Christian hospitality of the fishing village. They travelled by ship to Trondheim, then on foot via Vadstena to the Swedish Baltic coast, whence some of them continued via Rostock, and others via Lödöse, London and finally on horseback to Venice. In Norway the Venetians encountered stockfish (salt cod), whose import to Italy they instigated in the years that followed.[26]

The age of the galleys came to an end around 1500 for a variety of reasons. The improvement of round ships, especially with respect to the rigging of carracks or galleons, yielded price advantages. Moreover, the Ottoman advance into the eastern Mediterranean rendered certain voyages by the galleys, for instance to the Balkans, Constantinople and the Black Sea, obsolete.

Voyages to North Africa continued, in contrast, especially since the Ottoman occupation of Constantinople and the Balkans slowed the supply of new Slavic and Tartar slaves[27] and the demand for Africans grew. Meanwhile, the Flemish galleys diminished in significance, since the Venetians were able to deliver ever fewer spices. After the Portuguese began to sell pepper from the Malabar coast in Lisbon and Antwerp, the Venetian monopoly on trade with Alexandria collapsed. In order to secure the supply of spices, in 1514 the senate allowed carracks to transport goods to Venice as well. After the carrack *Corneira* snatched the spices away from a galley in 1524, however, the senate once again granted the galleys a privilege to transport this cargo. Now, ships from other nations were taking on spices in Alexandria at all times, which led to the revocation of the privilege for the galleys in 1564. Once again, spices were brought to Venice by carrack. Alongside these partly homegrown changes in the freight system, another important factor was the reorientation of trade in the eastern Mediterranean, which increasingly focused on supplying the new centre, Istanbul.[28]

Emporia and networks

The so-called Geniza letters from Cairo, which we already encountered as important sources for shipping traffic and trade on the Arabian Sea and the Indian Ocean, offer early examples of Mediterranean trade around the year 1000. They document the life and travels of merchants from Alexandria in the western and eastern Mediterranean and hint at entire biographies.

One of these protagonists, whom Jessica Goldberg's research has brought to light, was Abu Imran Musa, known to his friends as Musa. Born in Kairouan in present-day Tunisia, he settled in Alexandria as a young man around 1045, married into a Jewish-Egyptian family and became an important merchant and member of the city's Jewish community. He is mentioned in more than sixty letters, which document a portion of his travels. Since Musa was still writing letters in 1107, he must have lived to be relatively old, since he had already built up his trading business between 1040 and 1070. He travelled a good deal to get to know people and trading centres and to cultivate and expand his personal networks. Musa visited various ports and producers not only in Egypt. He also travelled by ship to the West, visiting Tunisia or Arab Sicily, as well as present-day Palestine, then known as Al-Sham.

Many journeys were associated with specific commercial business and goods. Thus, at the beginning of his career Musa made money transfers from Mahdia and Fustat for other merchants, but also sold ammonia and pepper in Mazara, Sicily. Musa tried to complete the journey from Alexandria to Sicily via Tunisia and back during the shipping season from spring to autumn and spend the winter in Egypt. When time became short, he sold his wares in Sicily or left them for his business partners[29] with a request to sell them. In Palestine he usually bought finished textiles, especially items of clothing in Ashkelon or Tyre as well as carpets and cushions in the interior. At the same time, he brought goods from the West there if he could not sell them in his shop in Fustat or in Alexandria. His travels in Egypt took him to Fustat, Rashid or Busir and were mainly for the purpose of buying flax, one of his most important commodities, which he regularly shipped to the western Mediterranean. We should not imagine that these journeys took place all in one go; rather, ships and merchants divided their voyages into several stages, for example Fustat–Kairouan, Fustat–Palermo, Kairouan–Al-Andalus and Kairouan–Palermo. On the eastward journey traders used the Fustat–Damascus route, regularly stopping in Tyre and sometimes in Tripoli.[30]

When writing about the Geniza merchants, historians have frequently looked for famous traders who dealt in pepper, pearls, gold and spices in the Islamic-Mediterranean world. But the case of merchants like Musa demonstrates that in the eleventh century, agrarian production and the distribution of the main commodity flax took up the majority of their time and capital, showing the great influence of agricultural production on business cycles and shipping routes.[31] This changed in the following century, when trade via the Red Sea made many spices such as pepper, ginger and cinnamon cheaper and available to a less wealthy clientele. For that reason, the Geniza merchants later increasingly focused on the traffic in goods between the Red Sea and the Indian Ocean.[32]

One of the most important merchants from the standpoint of sources was Francesco di Marco Datini of Prato. Trained as a merchant in Florence and Avignon, from 1373 he had his own firm, which sold goods in the Mediterranean region and from there to Flanders, Germany, North Africa and the Levant. Aside from his trading company in Avignon, after his return to Italy he founded new firms in Pisa and Florence and participated in other trading companies, for example in Genoa. In the 1390s, the Genoese firm expanded with branches in Barcelona, Valencia and Majorca, which gave rise to Datini's Catalan trading company. A native of the cloth production centre of Prato, Datini focused on the purchase of wool from local producers, weaving and the sale of woollen cloth. He purchased some of his wool from England, but especially from the Balearic Islands, since Italian cloth manufacturers were dependent on deliveries of wool from Spain.[33] He also engaged in exchange and credit business on the model of the Tuscan merchant bankers.

The example of Datini's Catalan company illustrates the profitability and openness of trade. The company made a profit of 30,276 florins between 1396 and 1408, which corresponds to annual interest of some 24 per cent on the invested capital. The company operated in the Mediterranean region and western Europe, where sales seemed most lucrative. The most significant port was Venice, from which ships could reach both Germany and the Levant. The company sold silver, copper, paper, cotton, rhubarb and spices to Barcelona. Datini sent silk, cotton, alum and dyestuffs to Bruges, and in exchange the Florentines received Flemish woollens, stockings, linen, madder and tin destined for Spain. The merchants of the Catalan company brought silk and cotton as well as kermes insects (used to make red dye) and ostrich feathers to Montpellier and from there to other regions.

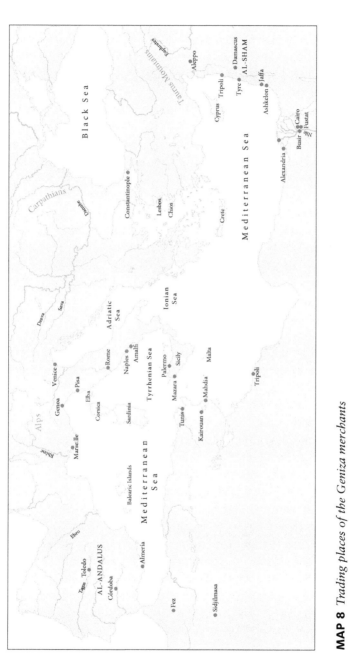

MAP 8 *Trading places of the Geniza merchants*

'It pleases me that you are sending us ostrich feathers, not too many, but fine ones', the Valencian agent of Luca del Sera's company wrote in 1397 to his colleague Cristofano Carocci on Majorca. Ostrich feathers from the Barbary Coast were luxury items that had been introduced into European markets, and they had to be treated with special care because they were quite fragile. The feathers were used to adorn hats and helmets and were also much in demand among the troops passing through. Ostrich feathers were transported by ship from Alcudia and Honaïne to Valencia and Majorca and then sent on to northwest Europe and Italy. Datini's Majorca office purchased some 36,200 feathers between 1396 and 1398 at a price of eight denarii each. Sheepskin, goatskin, calfskin and ox-skin also came from North Africa, with goatskin being the most highly prized. Kermes (lice) was also a precious commodity because the dried bodies of female kermes insects could be used to manufacture a red colour used to dye woollen and silk cloth in all shades from scarlet to violet. The insects lived on oak trees in North Africa, southern Spain and Provence and were purchased by the Valencia office from the region of Nursia and by the Majorca office from the Barbary Coast. There were certain peaks in the kermes business to which the Datinis responded, for instance in 1397 when rumours arose of growing demand for the insects in Bruges. When a maritime blockade in the eastern Mediterranean stopped shipments from the region, Datini anticipated a price rise for the dyestuff and ordered his branch offices to concentrate on buying kermes and postpone shipments of other goods. This is just one snapshot from the rich Datini correspondence and one small segment of his trading enterprise, which however shows how the activities of the Catalan offices were connected across the seas with the European commercial world of the fourteenth and fifteenth centuries.[34] In his last will, Francesco Datini, who died childless in 1410, left money to found a charitable institution for the poor, the *Ceppo*. Oversight was entrusted to four prominent personalities of the city, who are portrayed as 'honourable men' alongside the scarlet-clad donor in Filippo Lippi's painting of the Madonna in Prato.[35]

Datini is just one of many examples of the expansive trade networks of Tuscan merchants who maintained branch offices throughout the Mediterranean region. The great French merchant Jacques Coeur of Bourges falls into a similar category. As an *argentier*, purveyor to the royal court and steward of the royal expenditure under Charles VII, an office awarded to him in 1438, he also saw to the court's finances and other necessities. The son of a trader from Bourges was the most important merchant and banker produced by late mediaeval France.[36] His ships sailed from Aigues-Mortes or Marseille into the Atlantic to Bordeaux, La Rochelle and Bruges as well as eastwards to Rhodes and Alexandria. The imported Levantine goods were distributed by land in France. Close connections with the crown of Aragón, the papacy and the Florentine bankers facilitated his business undertakings. Since every ship that sailed eastwards on his behalf carried 3,000–4,000 marks of silver for the purchase of goods, he regularly faced the problem of acquiring money. And so he set about acquiring silver for the royal mints and his own Mediterranean trade by mining silver-bearing lead in the Lyon region. He also had silver coins, jewellery and silverware collected and melted down into bars. When he was accused of exporting precious metals from France, he defended himself with the same argument that Thomas Mun would use nearly 200 years later: 'He would demonstrate that for each mark of silver, he had brought one mark of gold back to the kingdom.'[37]

Despite their persecution in Spain, Jewish merchants continued to play an important role in the early modern Mediterranean region. One extended family about whom we know a good deal thanks to the research of Francesca Trivellato are the Ergases and Silveras. The founder of the family, Abraham Ergase, a Levantine Jew, took a house in Livorno in 1594 and established his business in the new centre. Some of his relatives had stayed on the Iberian Peninsula as *conversos*, while others had settled in Amsterdam or Hamburg. In the eighteenth century, Esther Ergase married David Silvera, creating a new family and business connection that extended as far as Aleppo and the Indian Ocean.

The two families specialized in the coral and diamond trade. Red corals were a Mediterranean treasure, harvested from reefs on the coasts of North Africa, Liguria, Corsica, Sardinia, Sicily, Calabria and even Tuscany. In the autumn, hundreds of coral fishers brought their 'catch' (the coral branches) to Livorno, where they were cut, polished and fashioned into chains of beads in workshops. Afterwards they were packed in paper and a company such as Ergase and Silvera sent them to Venice and Aleppo, the traditional markets for precious stones, and thence to points east. Most Mediterranean coral ended up in India and the Himalayas, where it was fashioned into traditional jewellery.

Amsterdam (as the successor to Antwerp) and London subsequently evolved into the most important markets, especially for diamonds. Sephardic Jews and *conversos* participated in the diamond business via the Portuguese trade since, unlike the spice trade, diamonds and precious stones did not fall under the monopoly of the Portuguese crown. The international connections of Sephardic Jews gave them access to information and credit across long distances, just as the discretion within family networks – similar to that among the Armenians – afforded them advantages in the diamond trade.[38] Ergase and Silvera engaged in the diamond trade through relatives in Lisbon, who in turn were in direct communication with Goa. Their contacts in Goa were connected with Indian merchants. The whole network consisted of twenty partners in Livorno, ten in Lisbon and four or five families in Goa, who had done business with one another for several generations. The Sephardi in Livorno also maintained close relations with co-religionists in London, which is why they increasingly sent their diamond shipments there. After the discovery of the Brazilian diamond mines, Lisbon became a popular replenishment location for this commodity. At the same time, a segment of the Sephardi in Livorno reoriented their trade and gave preference to the Madras–London connection over the traditional Lisbon–Goa route. The reason was that the British sailing routes around the Cape of Good Hope increasingly proved more reliable than the shipping traffic between Lisbon and Goa.[39]

In the diamond trade, Jewish merchants crossed paths with the network of Armenians, which extended from New Julfa (a quarter of Isfahan) in Persia to the coasts of the Indian Ocean in one direction and to the Mediterranean, the Atlantic and the North Sea in the other. A surviving mercantile contract demonstrates the extent of trade between the merchant Khwaja Minas in Julfa and his agent Agha di Matus of Tabriz, whom he sent with a consignment of diamonds to Izmir, Constantinople and then further west in 1673. Agha di Matus travelled on to Venice and, now a wealthy merchant, settled in Livorno in the 1680s where he enjoyed great respect among the Armenian community, as whose representative he served. New Julfa's days were numbered after the decline of the Safavid dynasty (because of the Afghan conquest of Isfahan in 1722 and the city's destruction under Nadir Shah in 1747), so that members of the local community left to seek their fortunes in the Mediterranean region or the territories on the Indian Ocean. The loss of New Julfa struck a severe blow to Armenian international trade, however, since it now lacked a centre between East and West.[40] The Sephardic diaspora, whose business focussed on the niche market in diamonds and corals, also saw their profits from international trade fall.[41]

The Greek networks, in contrast – mariners, merchants and agents, most of them subjects of the Ottoman Empire – were able to uphold their status. Since the sixteenth century, they had maintained contacts with Venice and cooperated with the English and French, for whom they worked as privateers. After the Russians conquered the Crimea, ship owners and merchants increasingly operated in the Black Sea and from there took over international shipping in the nineteenth and twentieth centuries.[42]

Pirates: Robbery and ransom

It would be hard to think of a writer who portrayed the dangers that awaited shipping in the Mediterranean more vividly than Giovanni Boccaccio did in the *Decameron*. Thus, his novellas (II, 6 and 7) recount how Madama Beritola Caracciola ran aground with her ship on the deserted island of Ponza in the northern Tyrrhenian Sea during a storm on her way from Lipari to Naples, and how the sultan's daughter Alatiel ended up on Majorca on her way from Cairo to join her husband. Pirates lurked everywhere, especially since the lines between merchant and privateer were often blurred. Boccaccio's protagonist from the fourth novella, Landolfo Rufolo, for example, turned to plundering ships after being ruined by a bad speculation on a shipload of goods bound for Cyprus.[43]

While pirates had already haunted the Mediterranean in Antiquity and the Middle Ages, the Ottoman victories of the sixteenth century unleashed forces that allowed piracy to evolve into a business model under the cover of religion. When the Medici expanded Livorno into a Tuscan Mediterranean port, they invited not just foreign merchants and ships but also French and English corsairs, who were intended above all to target Ottoman shipping. At the same time, the English also operated for a time as allies of the Muslim foe in the harbours of North Africa, where they raided Tuscan ships and enslaved their crews. English ships also offered Ottoman merchants protection for their goods when they were chased by Christian corsairs, especially from the Crusader orders on Malta. Dutch privateers also made trouble in the Mediterranean from Livorno, capturing both French and Ottoman ships. The pretext was always that these were North African ships or inhabitants with whom the privateers were at war and who thus had to be taken back to Livorno as prisoners. If necessary, they tortured the captain and crew to force the admission that they came from North Africa. For example, the Dutch captain Jacob van der Heijen captured the captain Abdurrahman 'el Borgi' with his ship and crew and his cargo of barley, wheat and honey on their way from Crete to Benghazi, and took them first to the Venetian island of Zakynthos and then to Livorno. The captain was finally freed after one year in captivity when the Dutch consul in Livorno intervened on his behalf.[44]

Frequently, piracy destroyed the fruits of many years of mercantile activity. In 1608, for example, the corsair Jacques Bierre captured a ship with which the Muslim merchant Agamaumet was sending Levantine wares to North Africa. That same year he travelled to the maritime court in Pisa and testified that he had brought 180 bales of indigo, 69 bales of turbans, 12 bales of textiles, 12 bales of other dyestuffs and 29 bales of silk from India to Mecca via Damascus in order to ship them onwards to North Africa. The English consul in Sidon had helped him to get the goods onto an English ship and transport them under his name. Agamaumet's testimony did not impress the jury, which decided that only the English goods on board the ship such as cotton, berries and rice belonged to English merchants and should be returned to them along with the ship; the Turkish goods, which belonged to the 'foe of Christendom', were recognized as Captain Jacques Bierre's legitimate booty.[45]

The endless religious war between Christianity and Islam hampered shipping in the Mediterranean even when there were no current military conflicts. This is especially evident from piracy, captivity, slavery and ransom in the western Mediterranean. Here, in the area between the Iberian and Italian peninsulas and the western coast of North Africa, some three million Muslims and Christians were captured and enslaved on land and sea between 1450 and 1850. More than one million African, Ottoman and Moroccan slaves fell into Spanish and Portuguese hands, not counting those born on the Balearic and Canary Islands. Another 500,000 were enslaved in Italy, while more than 100,000 Christians shared this fate in the Maghreb. Networks and institutions that dealt with maritime human trafficking or elevated it to a business model developed out of the practice. Apart from the act of capture, this included enslavement, smuggling and the ransom business, which involved numerous political, ecclesiastical and private actors. These networks linked the Mediterranean, the Atlantic and even the North and Baltic Sea, since the enslaved Christian mariners came from virtually every part of Europe. Wolfgang Kaiser refers to an 'economy of ransom', a rational means of regulating religious violence and rationalizing trade with Muslims.[46]

According to Kaiser, even if it is difficult, we need to distinguish between the ransoming of prisoners and the slave trade. The prisoner was living booty whose release could be purchased and brought a higher price than a slave. Accordingly, there were various options for ransom and payments. One model was the exchange of prisoners of war, which was regulated by the signing of a peace treaty or armistice. This model was practised by the diplomats of the great powers France, England and the Netherlands, who exerted political pressure on the rulers of the Maghreb. The religious orders or brotherhoods, especially on the Iberian Peninsula, which specialized in buying the freedom of prisoners, adopted a similar method, as did the *Sklavenkassen*, such as that in Hamburg, insurance funds for mariners that paid ransoms for their captive members. Some merchants organized ransoms as a sort of side-line, since they had built up long-standing relationships of trade and trust in the Mediterranean region as well as to lenders in their homelands, who advanced the funds for ransom payments.[47]

Prisoners in North Africa were partially assimilated, since conversion promised to improve their lot as slaves. For that reason, converts frequently adopted a Muslim name, underwent circumcision, visited the mosque and changed their eating habits. By dressing like their Muslim masters, the prisoners entered their world, often remaining voluntarily after they had regained their freedom. One example is the Frenchman Thomas D'Arcos, who was captured by Tunisian sailors in 1629. During his captivity he maintained a lively correspondence, especially with the scholar and antiquary Nicolas-Claude Fabri de Pereisc in Aix-en-Provence.[48] Pereisc, who created his own personal Mediterranean with the help of a far-flung network of correspondents, asked D'Arcos for information on North Africa and promised to dedicate himself to his release. Although D'Arcos attained his freedom without Pereisc's assistance, he sent him gifts and requested help for other prisoners. D'Arcos, who converted to Islam after regaining his freedom and adopted the name Osman, continued the correspondence, although he was by no means eager to return to France. On the contrary, he tried to acquire a Latin or Italian translation of the Koran. He sent Pereisc antique coins, clay lamps, dagger handles, slippers in the Christian and Moorish style and fossils. What seems remarkable is that the controversial topic of conversion to Islam barely arose in the correspondence with France. Although D'Arcos improved his status in Tunis by converting, he was still considered a Christian in France, and his correspondent Pereisc attributed his newly adopted Muslim habits to the sufferings of captivity and the influence of a woman. Captivity thus brought about a change of identity, which promoted a multi-ethnic and multi-cultural mix in the communicative space of the Mediterranean.[49]

The Venetian Beatrice Michiel, who was abducted by Ottoman pirates together with her family in 1559, met a similar but far more complex fate. While she, her mother and her sister were freed by a ransom payment, her brothers remained captives and after castration and conversion had careers as eunuchs in the Ottoman bureaucracy. Cafer died in 1582 but Gazanfer, who rose higher through the ranks, stayed in contact with his Venetian relatives as well as representatives of the Republic of Venice. In 1591 Beatrice left her second husband and her children and moved to Istanbul. Her mother had already followed her brother there. Gazanfer convinced Beatrice to convert, and she took the name Fatima Hatun and was officially divorced from her unloved Venetian husband. She remarried in 1593 but maintained contact with her children in Venice and when necessary claimed that she had been forced to convert. In the winter of 1600, Gazanfer had Fatima's son Giacomo abducted and brought to Istanbul, where he subsequently had an unremarkable career under the name of Mehmed. Although the sultan sacrificed Gazanfer to his enemies during a revolt and he was executed, Fatima remained in a harem in the Ottoman Empire until her death. Mentally, however, she alternated between the Christian and Muslim worlds and left her property in Venice and Friuli to the Franciscans as well as to a Venetian orphanage and a refuge for fallen women.[50]

Western and northern Europeans also fell victim to Muslim sailors or Barbary pirates, who often already held up and captured their ships in the Atlantic. It is estimated that 12,000 English sailors alone and some 15,000 mariners who had signed on under the Dutch flag were captured in the seventeenth century.[51] This contributed especially in England to the emergence of a new literary genre, the captivity narrative. Many accounts by English captives became popular and were reprinted many times. With time a market even emerged for this literature. The accounts were interesting because the authors reported 'first-hand' on the customs and manners of the Muslims, thus rounding out the images of stage protagonists such as Othello.[52] In the late seventeenth century, England finally succeeded in minimizing the risk of capture for English ships, on the one hand by exerting military pressure on the states of the Barbary Coast and on the other by acquiring Mediterranean passes.

The Hanseatic cities of Hamburg and Lübeck, in contrast, faced such great perils for a time that they stopped Mediterranean voyages altogether. The northern Europeans had it relatively good, however, since they were almost exclusively captured at sea and usually ransomed, whereas southern Europeans were often abducted on land and ended up in permanent slavery.

The Hanseatic cities and the northern European states established so-called *Sklavenkassen* into which captains and sailors had to pay a certain sum before embarking on a voyage. Wooden figurines were also used to raise donations in the churches by arousing the pity of the congregations. These shackled figures reminded the inhabitants of port cities of the dangers of Mediterranean and Atlantic shipping. The northern European *Sklavenkassen* had agents in Venice who handled ransom payments as a profession.

The case of a Flensburg ship travelling from Hamburg to Porto, which was raided by Algerian pirates on 9 April 1737, illustrates how this worked. The ship owner Mathias Valentiner turned to the *Sklavenkasse* in Copenhagen, with which he had insured his ship for 2,000 reichstaler and asked it to ransom his crew. Because they suspected insurance fraud and accused him of carrying uninsured cargo for Hamburg merchants, the *Sklavenkasse* at first refused to pay the ransom. Months went by before the ship owner could convince the insurer that his claim was legitimate. On 25 January 1738 the *Sklavenkasse* contacted their agent in Venice, Johannes Pommer, and instructed him to negotiate the ransom. Pommer reported a partial success on 1 August. Seven crew members were freed for the sum of 8,000 reichstaler, while only the helmsman remained a captive because he was allegedly needed in Algeria. He was not ransomed until four years later, in 1742.[53]

Not long thereafter, in 1746, Denmark was able to negotiate a favourable treaty with Algiers, followed by additional treaties with Tunis, Tripoli, Morocco and the Ottoman Empire (1756). Ships of the Danish state, including Norway and Schleswig-Holstein, were issued with Mediterranean passes. These freed ships from capture by pirates and granted them privileges as means of transport in the Mediterranean and the Atlantic on the voyage to the West and East Indies.[54]

Notes

1 Basil of Caesarea, *The Hexæmeron*, 4,7, in P. Schaff and H. Wace (eds.), *A Select Library of the Nicene and Post-Nicene Fathers of the Christian Church*, 2nd series, vol. VIII: *St. Basil. Letters and Select Works* (New York, 1895).

2 Horden and Purcell, 'Mediterranean and "the New Thalassology"', 722–40.

3 R. W. Unger, *The Ship in the Medieval Economy* (London, 1980), 176–82.

4 Abulafia, *The Great Sea*, 330.

5 Ibid., 344–7.

6 North, *Expansion of Europe*, 10.

7 B. Dini, 'Seeversicherung', in *Lexikon des Mittelalters*, vol. 7 (Stuttgart, 1995), 1691–2; F. Melis, *Origini e sviluppi delle assicurazioni in Italia (sec. XIV–XVI)* (Rome, 1975); K. Nehlsen-von Stryk, *Die venezianische Seeversicherung im 15. Jahrhundert* (Ebelsbach, 1986).

8 M. North, *Kleine Geschichte des Geldes. Vom Mittelalter bis heute* (Munich, 2009), 19–25.

9 See also below, part VI 'Indian Ocean', sub-chapter 'Conflict and cooperation' and part VII 'Atlantic', sub-chapter 'Crossing the Atlantic Ocean'.

10 E. Schmitt and C. Verlinden (eds.), *Die mittelalterlichen Ursprünge der europäischen Expansion* (Munich, 1986), 57–8.

11 North, *Expansion of Europe*, 279ff.

12 Abulafia, *The Great Sea*, 329–39.

13 G. Casale, *The Ottoman Age of Exploration* (Oxford, 2010); M. Greene, 'The Early Modern Mediterranean', in Horden and Kinoshita (eds.), *A Companion to Mediterranean History*, 92.

14 Greene, 'Early Modern Mediterranean', 93.

15 Ibid., 98.

16 M. van Gelder, *Trading Places. The Netherlandish Merchants in Early Modern Venice* (Leiden and Boston, 2009), 48–97.

17 J. I. Israel, *Dutch Primacy in World Trade, 1585–1740* (Oxford, 1989), 55, 143, 307–13.

18 Lunban Fī 'Ahd Al-Amīr Fahkr Al-Dīn Al-Ma'ni Al-Thani, reproduced in N. Matar, *Europe through Arab Eyes, 1578–1727* (New York, 2009), 163.

19 See E. B. Schumpeter, *English Overseas Trade Statistics, 1697–1808* (London, 1960), Tab.6; J. de Vries and A. van der Woude, *The First Modern Economy. Success, Failure, and Perseverance of the Dutch Economy, 1500–1815* (Cambridge New York and Melbourne, 1997), 497.

20 Greene, 'Early Modern Mediterranean', 93.

21 M. Letts (ed.), *Pero Tafur. Travels and Adventures, 1435–1439* (London, 1926), 169–70.

22 On the round ships, see Unger, *Ship in the Medieval Economy*, 182–7.

23 Thus in 1497, the galleys brought goods and precious metals worth 300,000 ducats to Alexandria and returned home with goods worth 295,000 ducats. See E. Ashtor, *Levant Trade in the Later Middle Ages* (Princeton, 1983), 477.

24 On the auction prices, see ibid., 319–20 and 475–6.

25 F. C. Lane, *Venice. A Maritime Republic* (Baltimore, 1973), 337–52.

26 G. Fouquet and G. Zeilinger, *Katastrophen im Spätmittelalter* (Darmstadt and Mainz, 2011), 48–58; L. Pezzolo, 'The Venetian Economy', in E. R. Dursteler (ed.), *A Companion to Venetian History, 1400–1797* (Leiden and Boston, 2013), 261–4.

27 S. McKee, 'Gli schiavi', in F. Franceschi, R. A. Goldthwaite and R. C. Mueller (eds.), *Commercio e cultura mercantile* (Vicenza, 2007), 339–68.

28 Lane, *Venice*, 337–52.

29 On the role played by such agents and their relationships with the Geniza merchants, see A. Greif, *Institutions and the Path to the Modern Economy. Lessons from Medieval Trade* (Cambridge, 2006), 61–90.

30 J. L. Goldberg, *Trade and Institutions in the Medieval Mediterranean. The Geniza Merchants and Their Business World* (Cambridge, 2012), 247–95.

31 Ibid., 338.

32 E. Ashtor, *A Social and Economic History of the Near East in the Middle Ages* (Berkeley, Los Angeles and London, 1976), 196–7. See also above, part III 'Red Sea, Arabian Sea, South China Sea', sub-chapter 'Ibn Battuta and Marco Polo'.

33 North, *Expansion of Europe*, 369–70.

34 A. Orlandi, 'The Catalonia Company. An Almost Unexpected Success', in G. Nigro (ed.), *Francesco di Marco Datini. The Man, the Merchant* (Florence, 2010), 347–76 and *Mercaderies i diners: la correspondència datiniana entre València i Mallorca (1395–1398)* (Valencia, 2008); P. Iradiel Murugarren, 'El comercio en el Mediterráneo catalano-aragonés. Espacios y redes', in H. Casado Alonso and A. García-Baquero (eds.), *Comercio y hombres de negocios en Castilla y Europa en tiempos de Isabel la Católica* (Madrid, 2007), 123–50.

35 M. North, 'Das Bild des Kaufmanns', in M. Schwarze (ed.), *Der neue Mensch. Perspektiven der Renaissance* (Regensburg, 2000), 233–57.

36 M. Mollat, *Jacques Coeur ou l'esprit de l'enterprise* (Paris, 1988).

37 Ibid.

38 F. Trivellato, *The Familiarity of Strangers. The Sephardic Diaspora, Livorno, and Cross-Cultural Trade in the Early Modern Period* (New Haven, 2009), 224–38.

39 Ibid., 238–50.

40 S. D. Aslanian, *From the Indian Ocean to the Mediterranean. The Global Trade Networks of Armenian Merchants from New Julfa* (Berkeley, 2011), 72–5, 215–34.

41 P. Curtin, *Cross-Cultural Trade in World History* (Cambridge, 1984).

42 M. Fusaro, 'Les Anglais et les Grecs. Un réseau de coopération commercial en Méditerranée vénitienne', *Annales. Histoire, Sciences Sociales* 58, no. 3 (2003): 605–25; G. Harlaftis, 'The "Eastern Invasion". Greeks in Mediterranean Trade and Shipping in the Eighteenth and Early Nineteenth Centuries', in M. Fusaro, C. Heywood and M.-S. Omri (eds.), *Trade and Cultural Exchange in the Early Modern Mediterranean. Braudel's Maritime Legacy* (London and New York, 2010), 223–52.

43 G. Boccaccio, *The Decameron*, trans. G. H. McWilliam, 2nd edn (London, 1995), 4th novel, 2nd day. On the female travellers in the *Decameron*, see R. Morosini, 'Penelopi in viaggio "fuori rotta" nel Decameron e altrove. "Metamorfosi" et scambi nel Mediterraneo medievale', *California Italian Studies Journal* 1 (2010): 1–32.

44 M. Greene, *Catholic Pirates and Greek Merchants. A Maritime History of the Mediterranean* (Princeton, 2010), 230.

45 Ibid., 226.

46 W. Kaiser and G. Calafat, 'The Economy of Ransoming in the Early Modern Mediterranean. A Form of Cross-Cultural Trade between Southern Europe and the Maghreb (Sixteenth to Eighteenth Centuries)', in F. Trivellato, L. Halevi and C. Antunes (eds.), *Religion and Trade. Cross-Cultural Exchanges in World History, 1000–1900* (Oxford, 2014), 108–30.

47 W. Kaiser, 'Frictions profitables. L'économie de la rançon en Mediterranée occidentale (XVIe–XVIIe siècles)', in S. Cavaciocchi (ed.), *Ricchezza del Mare, Ricchezza dal Mare Secc. XIII–XVIII* (Florence, 2006), 689–701.

48 P. N. Miller, 'The Mediterranean and the Mediterranean World in the Age of Peiresc', in P. N. Miller (ed.), *The Sea. Thalassography and Historiography* (Ann Arbor, 2013), 251–76 and *Peiresc's Mediterranean World* (Cambridge, MA:, 2015).

49 J. Tolbert, 'Ambiguity and Conversion in the Correspondence of Nicolas-Claude Fabri de Peiresc and Thomas D'Arcos, 1630–1637', *Journal of Modern History* 13 (2009): 1–24; Matar, *Europe through Arab Eyes*, 68, 186ff.

50 E. R. Dursteler, *Renegade Women: Gender, Identity and Boundaries in the Early Modern Mediterranean* (Baltimore, 2011), 1–33; S. A. Epstein, 'Hybridity', in Horden and Kinoshita (eds.), *A Companion to Mediterranean History*, 345–58.

51 M. Ressel, 'Protestant Slaves in Northern Africa during the Early Modern Age', in S. Cavaciocchi (ed.), *Serfdom and Slavery in the European Economy 11th–18th Centuries* (Florence, 2014), 532–3.

52 D. J. Vitkus, *Piracy, Slavery, and Redemption. Barbary Captivity Narratives from Early Modern England* (New York, 2001), 1–54.

53 Ressel 'Protestant Slaves,' 532–3.

54 O. Feldbæk, *Dansk Søfarts Historie*, vol. 3: *1720–1814. Storhandelens tid* (Copenhagen, 1997), 35–62.

V

Metropoles on the North and Baltic Seas

In 1420, the German merchant Hildebrand Veckinchusen wrote one of his many business letters from Bruges to his wife Margarethe in Lübeck:

Similarly, Grete my wife, please know that you will receive two crates that Claus Vrolinh is to turn over to you at Lübeck. I am sending you the key via the messenger Fyttelke. It contains 38 long strings of corals and 5 short ones […] I hoped that Hoyman would have sold them, but they are not yet sold, and so I am doing the best with them I can […]. Likewise, do your best with the corals, Hoyman has taken them to the market at Greifswald […]. Similarly, the cotton is still at Sluis; it did not arrive with Skipper Wilke van Dokkum, it is now supposed to arrive with the first ship to Hamburg, God willing […]. Similarly, Gerwin Marschede is sending you two straws of wax with Skipper Marquart Stubbe from Prussia. He intends to send you more, by the love of God, Amen […]. And with that I bid you farewell, written on the Eve of St John, Midsummer 1420 at Bruges.[1]

This prosaic business letter is evidence of the emergence of a greater maritime region on the North and Baltic Seas. In the early fifteenth century, Veckinchusen's trading company operated between Bruges, Antwerp, Cologne, Lübeck, Danzig (Gdánsk), Riga, Reval (Tallinn) and Novgorod, and also did business at the Frankfurt fairs as well as in Venice. The 'sister seas'[2] were connected by skippers like Wilke van Dokkum or Marquart Stubbe from Prussia, whom the letter mentions, and families who lived and worked in the various cities. Hildebrand Veckinchusen, for instance, who had married into a Riga mercantile family, spent most of his time outside Lübeck, while his wife Margarete ran the business there. The division of labour in this family illustrates the scope of the Hanseatic League, which linked the North and Baltic Seas more tightly than ever through trade and shipping.

The Hanseatic League: A powerful confederation of trading cities

The Hanseatic League and its cities could build on shipping and the itinerant trade of the early and high Middle Ages, but also provided the North and Baltic Sea region with a new and more solid organizational structure. From the thirteenth century, what had begun as an association of travelling merchants evolved into a powerful league of cities that would shape trade, shipping and politics in the North and Baltic Sea region for three centuries. The Old High German word *Hansa* means band or community, and in the twelfth century it referred to cooperatively organized long-distance traders who generally came from the same town. There were thus many local 'hansas' before the German Hansa first appeared on the political scene in the thirteenth century. The earliest such association was established by Cologne merchants trading in London, who acquired the special protection of the king in 1175 for their branch in the Guildhall and their goods.[3] More important for the history of the Hansa, however, were events that took place in the Baltic region in the twelfth and thirteenth centuries: the founding of Lübeck, the founding of new cities as part of German settlement in the east and the emergence of the cooperative of German merchants who traded in Gotland, known as the *Gotlandfahrer*.

With the founding of Lübeck (1143/59), German long-distance traders became settled on the Baltic coast, which enabled itinerant merchants from Lower Saxony and Westphalia to reach markets in the Baltic area and Russia without Scandinavian or Slavic middlemen. For many years, the peasant-merchants of Gotland had dominated trade with Russia, and German long-distance traders now represented serious competition. They had more capital, better mercantile training and organization and sturdier ships – in the form of the cog – than the Gotlanders. In 1161, Duke Henry the Lion gave permission for Gotlanders to trade in his Saxon territories on the condition that the privilege applied in turn to German merchants on Gotland, which stimulated German trade on that island.

A privilege issued by Countess Margarete of Flanders in 1252 made the first official mention of a German cooperative of *Gotlandfahrer* (*universi mercatores romani imperii gotlandium frequentates*). According to the document, there was a cooperative of German merchants doing business on Gotland that sailed both east- and westwards and increasingly used their base in Visby to gain a foothold on the Novgorod market. Like the Gotlanders, the German merchants established a trading post in Novgorod, which under the name Peterhof formed the future base of Hanseatic trade with Russia. Because of its hinterland, which extended all the way to the White Sea, Novgorod was the centre of the fur trade. Trade with Novgorod was overseen from Visby on

Gotland, and it was there that the remaining money was brought after the close of the trading season. From the late thirteenth century, however, Lübeck increasingly pressed to oversee trade with Russia and with the support of other cities succeeded in establishing Lübeck alongside Visby as a court of appeal in the case of legal disputes in Novgorod. This anticipated the future role of the German Baltic city as the 'patron' of trade with Russia.[4]

The founding of new cities, which were often inspired by Lübeck and its town law, contributed to this process. Thus Riga, which was founded in 1201 by a former Bremen cathedral canon at the mouth of the Daugava River, was promoted by Lübeck as a long-distance trading port. In the thirteenth century, new trading cities arose, arrayed like a string of pearls along the southern Baltic coast: Wismar, Rostock, Stralsund, Greifswald, Elbing (Elblag), Königsberg (Kaliningrad) and Reval. German merchants had also settled in the Scandinavian kingdoms. In Denmark, the main attraction was the shoals of herring on the coasts of Scania. German merchants and craftsmen migrated to the cities of southern Sweden, Lödöse, Kalmar and Stockholm, and German miners to the iron and copper mining regions. Norway was also an important commercial partner, offering dried cod in exchange for grain. Bergen, whose 'German Bridge' housed another trading post, was considered the most important trade centre. The Lübeckers held sway there, dominating trade with the Scandinavian kingdoms.

German merchants did not only trade with Russia, Scandinavia and the lands on the southern Baltic coast, however, but also with England across the North Sea, initially under leadership from Cologne. Following the privilege of 1175, Edward I's *Carta Mercatoria* of 1303 promised foreign merchants – as compensation for the rise in custom duties – freedom from all tariffs, freedom of establishment, legal protection from interference by royal officials and dispensation from future new demands. This last provision would prove to be the heart of the privilege, for at the beginning of the Hundred Years' War in the mid-fourteenth century, when Edward III raised the duty on textile exports to finance the war, the Hanseatic merchants gained exemption from it by citing the *Carta Mercatoria*. The English and other aliens had to pay it. In this way, the *Carta Mercatoria*, which had originally been granted to all foreign merchants, became a Hanseatic privilege. They used the Guildhall as their trading post and in the years that followed expanded the neighbouring Steelyard for this purpose.[5]

The last and also the most important trading region for German merchants was Flanders, where high-quality woollen cloth was produced in large quantities. The traders purchased the Flemish textiles in Bruges, whose favourable location made it the most important commodity market in western Europe. In 1252 Countess Margarete privileged the German merchants by granting them tariff concessions. One year later, they were exempted from trial by combat, liability for the debts and misdeeds of others and, especially importantly, from *jus naufragii* (right of shipwreck). According to this right, the coastal inhabitants of Flanders were no longer permitted to pillage Hanseatic ships that had run aground. These privileges gave traders greater legal security.

In 1356, in order to effectively protect the privileges in Flanders, the Bruges trading post, which had been independent up to that time, was placed under a pan-Hanseatic body, the Hanseatic diet (*Hansetag*). The 'Hansa cities', which were represented at the Hanseatic diet and mentioned for the first time in 1358, now determined trade policy in the place of the local merchants who had done so previously. It had become evident that a united Hansa was better placed to take action than groups in foreign commercial centres who were guided by local special interests. This was the end of a process that had begun in the thirteenth century in which the cities had gained increasing influence over their merchants' cooperatives abroad. They supported them in acquiring privileges, created the legal preconditions for trade and provided them with legal protection. From now on, the North and Baltic Sea cities represented in the Hanseatic League would determine shipping and trade policy in this region. Their representatives met when needed at the Hanseatic diets, which made all the important decisions. The cities were represented to the outside world by Lübeck, the head of the Hanseatic League.[6]

Fresh challenges awaited the Baltic region in the second half of the fourteenth century, and the league of cities had the opportunity to prove its newly won agency. In 1360, King Valdemar IV pursued a policy of Danish hegemony in the Baltic and captured not just Scania, which had been lost for a time to Sweden, but also Gotland. Duties and taxes were raised for Hanseatic merchants, which placed a burden on the Scania trade, which Lübeck and the eastern Hanseatic cities regarded as a *casus belli*. After the coalition's first defeat at sea, Denmark made it more difficult for the Hanseatic cities on the Zuiderzee and the Dutch cities to travel from the North Sea to the Baltic through the Sound, thus hitting their vital nerve. In 1367, all of the Hanseatic cities from Zealand to Reval then joined forces against Denmark in the so-called Confederation of Cologne. By exerting military pressure, the Hanseatic League succeeded in the 1370 Peace of Stralsund in re-establishing its privileges, especially the right of unrestricted movement in Denmark on land and water, as well as compensation for war damages. The Peace of Stralsund saw the Hansa at the height of its power, since the treaty affirmed the pre-eminence of its cities in the Baltic trade.[7] Nevertheless, it remained an interest group of merchants who used political and military means to safeguard their trade privileges.

The Hanseatic trade followed the line Novgorod – Reval – Riga – Visby – Danzig – Stralsund – Lübeck – Hamburg – Bruges – London from east to west and was based on exchange between the purveyors of foodstuffs and raw materials in northern and eastern Europe and manufacturers in north-western Europe. Merchants went beyond this function of mediators between east and west, however, by trading in Hanseatic manufactured goods and penetrating deep into the coastal hinterlands to the south. In this way they not only tapped into Bohemia and Silesia via the Elbe and Oder rivers, but also via Kraków up the Vistula to the copper-mining regions of Upper Hungary (Slovakia) and connected with the Black Sea trade via Lemberg (Lwiw, Lwów).[8]

The individual regions they visited depended on demand and production there. The range of goods was diverse and encompassed both everyday items for the mass of consumers and producers and luxury goods for a small stratum of wealthy customers. The most important commodities were wool, woollen and linen cloth, furs and pelts, herring, dried cod, salt, wax, cereals, flax, hemp, timber and forest products (ash, pitch and tar), beer and wine. Of these, pelts, wax, cereals, flax, timber and beer were sent westwards, while the west exported mainly cloth, salt and wine as well as metal goods, spices and other luxury goods to the east. Fish was sold throughout the Hanseatic region.

There were two interconnected economic areas in the east: the Russian trading area with the fur-trading centre of Novgorod and the Livonian urban region around Reval, Dorpat (Tartu) and Riga with the hinterlands of the Daugava, which produced mainly flax and hemp. There was demand throughout Europe for furs, both costly sable and cheap squirrel, and for wax for candles. In all of the Hanseatic ports, hemp was also needed for ropes and flax for linen cloth. Flemish cloth and Atlantic sea salt were the main imports to the east. To the south, the Teutonic Order and the Prussian Hanseatic cities of Danzig, Elbing and Thorn (Torún) made the produce of the Lithuanian and Polish hinterlands, notably grain, timber and forest products, available to the Hanseatic trade via the Vistula and Memel rivers. Shipbuilders needed timber for masts and planks and herring fisheries, brewers and salt works for barrels, while pitch, tar and ash were in high demand in many trades. The main export commodity of the Prussian Hanseatic cities, however, was grain, which fed part of the population in the more urbanized regions of western Europe, especially the Netherlands. And we should not forget the luxury product amber, which was gathered on the coast of the Samland (Sambia) peninsula. The Teutonic Order had a monopoly on the amber trade, and exported it to Lübeck and Bruges, where it was fashioned into precious rosaries, for example. Salt, herring and cloth were the most important goods imported into Prussia.

In the western Baltic, Sweden supplied iron, copper, butter, cattle and cowhides for the Hanseatic trade, but, except for the metals, was overshadowed in the business by Denmark. The most important 'Danish' product was Scania herring, which was so abundant in the fourteenth century that it was said one could catch the fish with one's bare hands. In the late fifteenth and sixteenth centuries, with the replacement of Baltic by North Sea herring, Dutch herring fishing became increasingly prominent. Moreover, Norway and Iceland supplied dried and salted cod, which was caught in the North Sea and dried on the Norwegian coast or the Icelandic cliffs and consumed in great quantities as ships' rations or during religious fasts.

The English trade, originally the province of Hanseatic merchants from the Rhineland and Westphalia, retained its significance in the long term. They brought Rhine wine, metals and the dyestuffs madder and woad to England and left with pewter and English wool for the Flemish and Brabant textile industry, and later with English woollen cloth. In return, the Hanseatic cities of the Baltic coast contributed typical eastern European goods such as furs, wax, cereals and timber as well as fish and metals from Scandinavia. As cloth producers and mediators with the commercial world of the Mediterranean, Flanders and later Brabant were the most important markets in western Europe. The Hanseatic merchants' main purchases in the cities of Flanders and the Brabant were woollen cloth of high and medium quality and trousers from Bruges. They also bought spices, figs and raisins from southern Europe. From France came oil and wine as well as what was known as bay salt. This Atlantic sea salt became increasingly important as a preservative. Prussian and above all Dutch ships made regular voyages to collect bay salt and brought it to the Baltic as ballast, returning west with a cargo of grain and timber and thereby undermining Lübeck's asserted monopoly on intermediate trading. Aside from the wine trade with Bordeaux, the Hanseatic presence in southern Europe remained sporadic, if we disregard the Veckinchusen family's attempts to establish fur sales in Venice.

The Hanseatic trade was organized by merchant trading companies. The dominant model was the free type, in which two partners invested capital and shared the profits according to the amount of capital they had provided, with such companies lasting up to one or two years. The large-scale international merchants were generally involved in several such companies, since this minimized the risks of trade and shipping and enlarged their range of goods. Merchants often had relatives as partners in the companies, which created the essential basis of trust for Hanseatic trade on the east-west route.

A further risk-reduction measure was the ship-owning partnership, in which ship owners acquired smaller shares of a ship for a particular journey. Apart from risk spreading, legal certainty was also a problem in shipping. There was no lack of attempts to establish uniform regulations in maritime law. On the one hand, the French Rolls of Oléron (which regulated the transport of wine from Bordeaux to the north) were translated into Flemish under the title *Vonnisse van Damme*, stipulating the responsibilities and authority of the skipper. On the other, Lübeck issued regulations establishing the rights of skippers vis-a-vis ship owners and charterers as well as penalties for violations.[9]

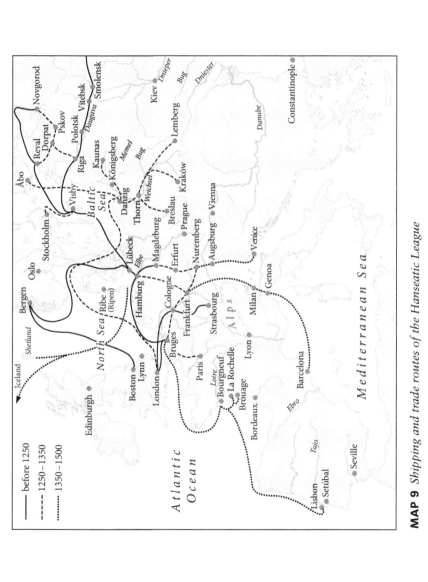

MAP 9 *Shipping and trade routes of the Hanseatic League*

Legend:
- before 1250
- 1250–1350
- 1350–1500

Iceland
Shetland
Bergen
Oslo
Åbo
Stockholm
Reval
Dorpat
Pskov
Novgorod
Polotsk
Vitebsk
Smolensk
Riga
Daugava
Kaunas
Königsberg
Memel
Visby
Baltic Sea
Danzig
Thorn
Weichsel
Bug
Kraków
Lemberg
Kiev
Dnieper
Bug
Dniester
Constantinople
Danube
Breslau
Prague
Vienna
Magdeburg
Erfurt
Nuremberg
Augsburg
Lübeck
Elbe
Hamburg
Ribe (Ripen)
North Sea
Cologne
Frankfurt
Strasbourg
Alps
Milan
Venice
Genoa
Lyon
Barcelona
Ebro
Edinburgh
Boston
Lynn
London
Bruges
Paris
Loire
Bourgneuf
La Rochelle
Brouage
Bordeaux
Atlantic Ocean
Tajo
Lisbon
Setúbal
Seville
Mediterranean Sea

The four trading posts or *Kontore* in Novgorod, Bergen, London and Bruges formed a sort of higher organizational stage of Hanseatic trade. Here, the German merchants lived in clearly demarcated areas like the *Peterhof*, the German Bridge or the walled Steelyard. It was only in Bruges that the Hanseatic merchants boarded with local hosts. Each *Kontor* had a tight structure with aldermen elected annually, fixed statutes and its own legal jurisdiction, treasury and seal. The trading posts were important for the acquisition and maintenance of trade privileges, since, with the backing of the Hanseatic cities, they represented the interests of the merchants in their dealings with the princes and cities of the host country. They also facilitated everyday trade by creating a regular system of information and messengers with their home cities and assisting with correspondence, certification, bookkeeping and raising credit. Above all, however, they sought, by enacting mandatory registration for the Hanseatic merchants active in their region, to attain a certain uniformity in the purchase and sale of goods and thus to limit competition within the Hanseatic League.

At the end of the fifteenth century, the Hanseatic trade suffered setbacks on all fronts. The old trading system based on privileges proved unenforceable in the face of growing competition and the consolidation of the European powers. The Scandinavian kings, for example, tried to limit Hanseatic trade in favour of their own merchants. At the same time, the Hanseatic merchants' Dutch competitors were often pitted against them. The Hanseatic cities accordingly participated in the power struggles in Scandinavia with maritime warfare and privateering in the hopes of holding on to their privileges. The closure of the Novgorod trading post in 1494 by Ivan III also affected the Hanseatic cities, although trade had already shifted earlier in the century to the Livonian port cities of Riga and Reval, increasing their growth and prosperity.

The situation was changing in England as well, with cloth imports and exports at the centre of conflicts. There were certainly tensions within the Hanseatic League, since in the conflicts with England Lübeck stubbornly insisted on its old privileges, while both Cologne and the Prussian trading cities were prepared to compromise. At any rate, the 1474 Peace of Utrecht produced an agreement and, after the restoration of privileges, Hanseatic trade with England experienced a final period of prosperity that lasted until the mid-sixteenth century.[10]

Competition also arose between the Dutch and the Zealanders on the one hand and the Wendish Hanseatic cities like Lübeck, Wismar, Rostock, Stralsund and Greifswald on the other, since the latter saw their position in trade and transport between the Baltic and the North Sea threatened. Lübeck, however, failed to limit Holland's access to the Baltic by either peaceful or military means. On the contrary, the Prussian Hanseatic cities of Danzig, Elbing, Thorn and Königsberg largely depended on Dutch cargo space for their trading activities.[11] From 1460, the Bruges *Kontor* was for all intents and purposes located in Antwerp, since the merchants mainly visited the Brabant fairs in Bergen op Zoom and Antwerp.

Signs of Hanseatic decline were everywhere in the sixteenth century. Historians have suggested different causes such as the growing strength of the German territorial states and the Nordic kingdoms or the superior competitiveness of South German merchant houses and the Dutch trading nation.[12] This image of decline contrasts sharply with the overall upswing in European trade in the sixteenth century, however. While the Hanseatic cities participated in this growth, it also exploded the framework of their traditional, privilege-based system. Just as innovations in shipping and trade had once given the Hansa an advantage over the peasant-merchants of Gotland, new types of ships and the expansion of the trade on commission and cashless payment now favoured the Dutch. The cities that benefited from the expansion of European trade were no longer Bruges, Bergen, Lübeck or Novgorod, but Amsterdam, Danzig and Hamburg, and the future belonged to them.

In the sixteenth century, Danzig evolved into the Baltic region's most significant port. Since the Vistula directly connected the city with the grain-producing Polish hinterland, it could use its favourable location to satisfy the growing Dutch demand for cereals and forest products. The city, which with 40,000 inhabitants was the largest on the Baltic in the second half of the sixteenth century, attracted not only merchants and mariners from western and northern Europe, but also Jews and Armenians, who attended the fairs, as well as many port workers, some of them from the coast and others, such as porters, from the hinterland.[13]

Hamburg also participated significantly in the economic upturn in the North Sea and the Atlantic by monopolizing the grain trade on the Elbe and serving as a link between the North and Baltic Seas.[14] While Lübeck's location on the Baltic and Bremen's limited river system proved to be disadvangeous, Hamburg was favoured not just by its hinterlands, which extended down the Elbe and Oder rivers. At least equally important was the continuous immigration of Dutch, Portuguese (Sephardic Jewish) and English merchants, who brought their existing trade relations with them and also elevated Hamburg's banking system to the level of western Europe. The exchange regulations of 1601 and 1603 and the founding of the Bank of Hamburg on the Amsterdam model in 1619 are evidence of this.[15] Further factors that affected seventeenth- and eighteenth-century developments were the city's permanent neutrality in European conflicts, low port charges and the fact that Hamburg emerged unscathed from the Thirty Years' War because of the European powers' financial and material interests. At first, immigration still determined trade relations, which concentrated on England, the Netherlands, Portugal and Spain. In the eighteenth century, France and England then dominated as trading partners. From London, Hamburg imported woollens and the colonial re-export goods tobacco, calicos, rice, sugar and dyestuffs, while France supplied the Hamburg and European market with products from the West Indian plantations (coffee, sugar, indigo) and French wines. On this basis, Hamburg exported coffee and sugar – which was refined in the city and processed into sugar cones (confectionary) – to central Europe. In exchange, the city mainly supplied France and England with linen, ship building materials, metals and from the 1770s increasingly grain.[16]

North Sea metropolises: Bruges, Antwerp and Amsterdam

The metropolises of Bruges and Antwerp were the trade hubs linking southern, western and eastern Europe.[17] In Bruges, cloth from Flanders and Brabant, leather from southern Europe, furs and wax from the east and spices (saffron, nutmeg, pepper, ginger, cinnamon, anise) and sugar from the Mediterranean and Asia were already being traded in the fourteenth century. Genoese, Florentine, Venetian, Lucchese, Catalan, Castilian and Portuguese merchants settled in Bruges along with traders from England and the Hanseatic cities, making the city the most important commercial centre in north-western Europe for the next century and a half. Bruges and later Antwerp profited from the flourishing of maritime overseas trade, which represented a safer and cheaper alternative to the continental trade routes from Italy to the Netherlands, which were blockaded by wars.[18]

By the early fifteenth century, the semi-annual Brabant fairs in Antwerp and Bergen op Zoom became the main hubs for English woollens. English overseas traders, the Merchant Adventurers, brought them as semi-finished goods to Brabant, where they were dyed and dressed and sold as finished products to both Hanseatic and South German merchants. The South German demand for woollen cloth as well as the Dutch need for silver attracted the expanding trade of Nuremberg and Augsburg merchants to Antwerp with silver, copper and fustian. Here they met not just English traders, but also Portuguese merchants with spices from Asia and gold and ivory from Africa, since the latter depended on South German metals as well as copper and silver for barter with Africa and India. Accordingly, English cloth, South German metal and Portuguese spices defined Antwerp's advancement in the sixteenth century to a European world marketplace.[19]

This trade waned in importance with the collapse of the Portuguese spice monopoly, at which point Antwerp shifted the focus of its trade to Spain,

Italy, France and England. The export of Dutch-manufactured goods or the re-export of English textiles also helped Antwerp to flourish again from 1540 to 1565.

When the city declined economically as a result of the Dutch Revolt, Spanish conquest (1585) and the migration of its Calvinist inhabitants to the north, several European port cities profited, with Amsterdam inheriting the largest segment of Antwerp's trade. Unlike in Antwerp, goods from the Baltic region (grain, timber, flax and hemp) and the Atlantic (fish, salt) formed the backbone of trade in Amsterdam.[20]

Holland's natural environment was an important prerequisite for its economic rise. The Dutch fight against the water was indeed legendary. Already in the high Middle Ages the 'lage landen' had to be protected against the North Sea by a number of dykes and a system of water management. The persistent danger of flooding and the creation of new land out of the sea were crucial elements of Dutch identity. Flood tides reflected the ebb and flow of prosperity, and the struggle against Spain was linked with the battle against the North Sea.[21]

The need for communal water management in a 'flood society' also helps to explain the emergence of republican structures of governance. Holland, with its many bodies of water, was especially suitable for land reclamation. Between 1590 and 1665, nearly 100,000 hectares were reclaimed with the aid of water-pumping windmills.[22] These efforts notwithstanding, disastrous floods still occurred in 1625, 1686 and 1717, when 2,500 people drowned in Christmas flooding in the Netherlands and 9,000 on the German North Sea coast.[23]

Dutch shipping, like fishing, began as a subsidiary activity alongside agriculture in the river deltas and developed into a maritime transport system.[24] Shipping and freight transport provided Holland and Zealand with access to the Baltic region, where shipping capacity was limited. The demand for Holland's and Zealand's freight capacity rose in tandem with the demand for cereal exports in the west. Thus, Dutch shippers increased their share of the shipping traffic in Danzig from one-quarter in 1475/76 to approximately one-half in 1583, and the proportion of Dutch shippers in the Baltic trade grew from 60 to 70 per cent over the course of the seventeenth century.[25]

While the Dutch Baltic trade concentrated on the transport of cheap goods for mass consumption (grain and timber), it also captured the markets in the west and south, especially on the route between the Iberian Peninsula and the Netherlands, where higher-quality products needed to be shipped. Here, by spreading risk (i.e. distributing the goods among a larger number of ships), they succeeded in lowering costs and could offer better freight rates than Spanish and Antwerp shippers, who loaded each ship with valuable cargo.[26]

The Dutch are the 'Carryers of the World'

The Netherlands astounded contemporaries and continues to fascinate historians today. How did such a small country with fewer than two million inhabitants and scant natural resources manage to become the leading seafaring nation in the seventeenth century, a period of widespread crisis?

Contemporary eyewitnesses – frequently Englishmen who resented Dutch success – cited several reasons for this. In his treatise *A Plan of the English Commerce*, for example, Daniel Defoe still wrote in 1728:

> But then the Dutch must be understood to be as they really are, the Carryers of the World, the middle Persons in Trade, the Factors and Brokers of Europe: That, as is said above, they buy to sell again, take in to send out; and the greatest Part of their vast Commerce consists in being supply'd from all Parts of the World, that they may supply all the World again.[27]

Defoe goes to the heart of Dutch success here. The combination of shipping, commerce and finance made their pre-eminence in world trade possible. Amsterdam was the emporium, the *entrepôt* where all the world's commodities were gathered and distributed. Dutch ships brought goods from the agricultural and manufacturing centres and supplied them to the markets where they were in demand.

In the late sixteenth century, the development of many new types of ships made Dutch shipwrights the leading shipbuilders in Europe for the next century and a half. One of the new and highly successful ship types was the *fluyt*, which offered several advantages: it was built in large numbers of light wood according to a uniform construction and was suited to various purposes. The standardization of this construction type lowered the cost of producing and operating ships. A vast shipbuilding industry arose in Zaanstreek north of Amsterdam, drawing its raw materials from the Baltic region and promoting mechanization and the division of labour.[28]

Dutch ships were not merely faster, but also cleaner, cheaper and safer[29] than the competition. Well-run ships with a well-fed crew increased the efficiency and speed of maritime transport and reduced the risks and thus the cost of insurance. That is why the Dutch could offer merchants and producers at home and abroad the lowest freight costs by far. Shipping increased as did the tonnage carried by the merchant fleet (*c.* 400,000 tonnes in 1670). Freight costs fell and risks and costs were further reduced by ship-owning partnerships,[30] since one ship sometimes had more than sixty owners. Thus, for example, when one Amsterdam ship owner died in 1610, he left behind shares in twenty-two ships. Of these, he owned one-sixth of thirteen ships, one twenty-third of seven ships, and one seventeenth and one twenty-eighth respectively of two ships. Risk and ownership were distributed widely, so that even the middle classes could invest in shipping.

The Dutch cost advantage in international sea transport was evident vis-à-vis not just the Hanseatic cities, but also England, Holland's strongest rival. More than half of all goods from the Baltic region were brought to England by Dutch ships. Since England lacked shipping tonnage and mariners, the Dutch conducted much of the trade between the West Indian and North American colonies and the English motherland. Dutch foreign trade was based on the well-established trading links between northern and western Europe in an area extending from the British Isles in the west and Gibraltar in the south to Bergen and the Gulf of Finland in the north and northeast. The Dutch transported herring from the North Sea (in a good year, Dutch fishermen caught more than 200 million herring), salt from the Bay of Biscay and wine from France to the Baltic region. Here they were traded for Swedish iron and copper, but primarily for cereals, timber and forest products as well as raw materials for manufacturing (flax and hemp). In the second half of the sixteenth century, the Dutch gradually pushed the Hanseatic cities out of the western trade by concentrating on the fast and cheap transport of grain, timber, herring and salt, all goods for mass consumption.[31] The Baltic trade ultimately allowed them to gain a foothold in other trade areas. In the late sixteenth century, for example, the failed harvests that plagued western and southern Europe allowed them to play up their monopoly on grain from the Baltic and intensify trade with the Mediterranean.[32]

On this basis, the Netherlands extended their trading areas to the Levant, the Azores and Madeira, and in the early seventeenth century they advanced into the West Indian, African and East Indian trade. Until then, the last two had been considered the domains of Spain and Portugal.[33]

Dutch dominance of world trade was based on their unique control of the trade in mass goods and luxury goods. The Dutch were only able to control the latter, however, because of their technically superior manufacturing. This sector profited in turn from the nearly unlimited stores of dyewoods, chemicals and rare raw materials acquired through trading. The country thus enjoyed an unassailable price advantage, which neighbouring countries could only destroy by military measures or subsidized mercantilist enterprises. But even the trade wars with England in the third quarter of the seventeenth century did not at first undermine Dutch supremacy.[34] The First Navigation Act of 1651 stipulated that imported goods had to be transported to England directly from their countries of origin, either on English ships or vessels from those countries of origin. The Act proved unenforceable, however, as long as England was not in a position to fulfil the required role of a trading power and at least properly supply their own settlers in the overseas colonies. Thus,

FIGURE 5 *Georg Braun and Frans Hogenberg, Kronborg castle and Øresund from the 1580s Civitates Orbis Terrarum, book 4, map 26. © Wikipedia Commons.*

Dutch trade returned to its previous level shortly after the Anglo-Dutch wars. What proved more deleterious in the long run were the protectionist measures adopted by the mercantilist states, which imposed import bans or high import tariffs on certain Dutch products, ruining the affected branches of trade or manufacturing.

Through continuous growth, English shipping also became competitive, leading to a demand for English transport services in the North Sea region among Dutch merchants who did business in England. To avoid sailing without cargo, English ship owners and skippers offered a triangular voyage: their ships exported coal or grain to Rotterdam, travelled on to Norway with manufactured goods and colonial goods and from there transported the Norwegian timber required for shipbuilding to England. This triangular trade, in which Hamburg and Bremen were also involved, strengthened England's position in North Sea shipping.[35]

Baltic shipping was still a Dutch domain in the eighteenth century, although the British and Scandinavians clearly participated in the boom. The proceeds from the Sound tolls (see the graph on p. 90) show that the number of ships passing through the Sound grew continuously throughout the century, with even the War of the Polish Succession, with its burdens on Danzig, and the

GRAPH *Ship Passages through the Sound (Øresund), 1503–1845*

J. Ojala and A. Räihä, 'Navigation Acts and the Integration of North Baltic Shipping in the Early Nineteenth Century', *International Journal of Maritime History* 29 (2017): 7.

Seven Years' War causing only brief declines. Overall, the Baltic trade appears to have been stable in the long term despite temporary fluctuations.

At this time, the Sound was probably the most-travelled waterway in the world. Around 1730, some 2,000 ships annually passed through the Sound into the North Sea with some 400,000 tonnes of cargo, rising to about 500,000 tonnes in 1750 or four times the volume of the Atlantic slave trade.[36]

The British and Scandinavians profited from structural change in the Baltic region, where the demand for imported textiles and colonial goods increasingly replaced that for herring and salt. British ships accordingly supplied the new Russian port of St Petersburg in particular with English cloth and colonial re-exports like sugar, coffee and tobacco. Swedish and British ships took over the transport of timber and forest products from the Baltic to Britain.[37]

Farmers, cloth-makers, entrepreneurs and artists: The Netherlandization of the Baltic region

Shipping and trade from the North Sea to the Baltic initiated a variety of cultural transfers. Altered social and economic structures created new cultural conditions. For instance, Netherlandish emigration to and culture in the Baltic region became omnipresent from the second half of the sixteenth century. One can distinguish among four main groups here: farmers, artisans, merchants and mariners and artists.[38]

The farmers who emigrated were mainly Frisian Mennonites who settled in Royal Prussia from the mid-sixteenth century. Because of their skills in reclaiming land from the sea, they were recruited by the royal domains and manorial lords along the Vistula to work their lands. The Mennonites concluded long-term tenancy agreements, enjoyed personal freedom and formed the core of a stratum of independent, self-confident and wealthy farmers, the like of which would be hard to find in other Polish regions.[39]

Another group of immigrants were the artisans. Calvinist clothmakers emigrated from the southern Netherlands not just to the north, but in large numbers also to the Baltic cities. Much as they had done in Leiden, they revolutionized textile manufacturing in Königsberg and Danzig by introducing the fabrication of light woollen cloth and cloth dyeing. Silk-weaving and *passementerie* (the manufacture of decorative braids and trim) also flourished with the arrival of Dutch migrants, with Mennonites dominant in the latter trade.[40]

Merchants, factors and bankers were of great significance. They settled temporarily or permanently in the Baltic port cities, where some of them gained citizenship rights. Most Dutch merchants initially lived in Danzig, the centre of the Baltic trade. In the mid-seventeenth century, forty to fifty Dutch factors alone managed trade and engaged in credit and exchange business on behalf of Dutch firms, a number that later grew to seventy-five. One of the Dutch immigrants even tried to establish an exchange bank on the Amsterdam model, but ran up against resistance from the Danzig town council.[41]

Sweden was another field of endeavour for Dutch entrepreneurs, the most prominent of whom was Louis de Geer. He had set his sights on the copper mines of Falun during the Thirty Years' War, when copper was needed in large quantities for weapons (cannon casting). He moved to Sweden in 1627 and built up a metal empire in Norrköping and its environs, which encompassed iron foundries and brass and weapons manufactures. He sold his products (cannon, ammunition and rifles) on the Amsterdam market and equipped the Swedish army after Sweden's entry into the Thirty Years' War.[42]

In 1643, de Geer recruited a Dutch auxiliary fleet for Sweden, which was supposed to fight against Denmark. More significant than this single action was the migration of Dutch naval officers to Sweden. In the mid-seventeenth century, they made up about one-half of Swedish captains and lieutenants. They were recruited because of their specialist knowledge, while simple sailors could hire on in Sweden and Finland.[43] Denmark and Brandenburg-Prussia also relied on Dutch experts for their ambitious Asian or African trading company projects.[44]

Apart from this human capital, Dutch atlases and nautical textbooks were much in demand. Among the most important were Claes Hendricksz. Gietermaker's *'t Vergulde licht der zeevart ofte konst der stuurlieden* (*Guilded Light of Shipping or Art of Navigation*, Amsterdam 1659) and Klaas de Vries' *Schat-kamer ofte kunst der stuurlieden* (*Treasury or Art of Navigation*, Amsterdam 1702). Gietermaker's work was used into the late eighteenth century in the nautical colleges of the North Frisian islands, where aspiring Frisian helmsmen were instructed in navigation during the long winter evenings. The works of Gietermaker and de Vries were used even longer in Copenhagen and Danzig. Navigation was also often taught in Dutch, for example on the Fischland-Darß-Zingst peninsula. The Dutch manuals showed North Germans, Danes and Swedes the way first to the Arctic waters and shortly thereafter to the Caribbean and the Indian Ocean.[45]

A final group of immigrants to the Baltic were Netherlandish architects, artists and craftsmen. They included the *fayenciers* who established ceramic production on the Delft model and cabinet makers who adorned bourgeois and noble houses along with the tapestry weavers from the southern Netherlands. It was, however, mainly architects, sculptors and painters who settled in the Baltic region.

Netherlandish culture was reflected in the reception of artists and their works. We find Netherlandish paintings in royal, aristocratic and bourgeois collections, where they arrived via the mediation of artists and later art dealers.[46] Architects and artists such as Anthonis van Obberghen (Mechelen), Willem and Abraham van den Blocke (Mechelen), the painters Jan Vredeman de Vries (Leeuwarden) and Isaak van den Blocke and the copper engravers Clas Jansz. Visscher (called Piscator) and Willem Hondius (The Hague), among others, worked for various patrons in both Copenhagen and Danzig.

One example is Hans van Steenwinckel the Elder, who was born in Antwerp and whose family fled during the Dutch Revolt to Emden, where his father built the town hall. In 1578, Anthonis van Obberghen hired van Steenwinckel as an assistant for the construction of Kronborg Castle on the Sound. As royal architect to Christian IV, he worked on Danish and Norwegian coastal fortifications and also erected the new fortified town of Christianopel (1599) while his sons redesigned Copenhagen.[47]

Jan Diricksz. van Campen's 1611 view of Copenhagen shows many new gabled houses in the Dutch style, few of which survive. Public buildings like the orphanage, the stock exchange and housing for sailors and textile workers followed this 'progressive' style. Dutch architects also worked in Sweden, where they participated in the fortification of Gothenburg (1603–7) and Kalmar (1613), and above all in Danzig.[48]

Notes

1   W. Stieda, *Hildebrand Veckinchusen. Briefe eines deutschen Kaufmanns im 15. Jahrhundert* (Leipzig, 1921), no. 248, letter of 23 June 1420 from Veckinchusen in Bruges to his wife Margarethe in Lübeck.

2   Mörke, *Geschwistermeere*.

3   V. Henn, 'Was war die Hanse?' in J. Bracker, V. Henn and R. Postel (eds.), *Die Hanse. Lebenswirklichkeit und Mythos*, 2nd edn (Lübeck, 1998), 14–23. See the overview in R. Hammel-Kiesow, *Die Hanse*, 5th edn (Munich, 2014).

4   E. Hoffmann, 'Lübeck im Hoch- und Spätmittelalter. Die große Zeit Lübecks', in A. Graßmann (ed.), *Lübeckische Geschichte* (Lübeck, 1988), 134–50; E. Groth, *Das Verhältnis der livländischen Städte zum Novgoroder Hansekontor im 14. Jahrhundert* (Hamburg, 1999).

5   T. H. Lloyd, *England and the German Hanse, 1157–1611. A Study of Their Trade and Commercial Diplomacy* (Cambridge, 1991); S. Jenks, 'Die "Carta mercatoria". Ein "Hansisches" Privileg', *Hansische Geschichtsblätter* 108 (1990): 45–86.

6   H. Wernicke, *Die Städtehanse 1280–1418. Genesis–Strukturen–Funktionen* (Weimar, 1983).

7   N. Jörn, R.-G. Werlich and H. Wernicke (eds.), *Der Stralsunder Frieden von 1370. Prosopographische Studien* (Cologne, 1998); K. Fritze, *Am Wendepunkt der Hanse. Untersuchungen zur Wirtschafts- und Sozialgeschichte wendischer Hansestädte in der ersten Hälfte des 15. Jahrhunderts* (Berlin, 1967).

8   P. Dollinger, *Die Hanse*, 4th edn (Stuttgart, 1989), 275–340; Bracker, Henn and Postel (eds.), *Die Hanse*, 700–57; H. Samsonowicz, 'Die Handelsstraße Ostsee-Schwarzes Meer im 13. und 14. Jahrhundert', in S. Jenks and M. North (eds.), *Der hansische Sonderweg? Beiträge zur Sozial- und Wirtschaftsgeschichte der Hanse* (Cologne, Weimar and Vienna, 1993), 23–30.

9   G. Landwehr, 'Das Seerecht im Ostseeraum vom Mittelalter bis zum Ausgang des 18.Jahrhunderts', in J. Eckert and K. Å. Modéer (eds.), *Geschichte und Perspektiven des Rechts im Ostseeraum* (Frankfurt/M., 2002), 275–304, and 'Seerecht (Seehandelsrecht)', in A. Erler and E. Kaufmann (eds.), *Handwörterbuch zur Deutschen Rechtsgeschichte*, vol. 4: *Protonotarius Apostolicus – Strafprozeßordnung* (Berlin, 1990), 1596–614.

10 S. Jenks, *England, die Hanse und Preußen. Handel und Diplomatie, 1377–1474* (Cologne and Vienna, 1992); J. D. Fudge, *Cargoes, Embargoes, and Emissaries. The Commercial and Political Interaction of England and the German Hanse, 1450–1510* (Toronto, 1995).

11 D. Seifert, *Kompagnons und Konkurrenten. Holland und die Hanse im späten Mittelalter* (Cologne, 1997); J. Schildhauer, 'Zur Verlagerung des See- und Handelsverkehrs im nordeuropäischen Raum während des 15. und 16. Jahrhunderts. Eine Untersuchung auf der Grundlage der Danziger Pfalkammerbücher', *Jahrbuch für Wirtschaftsgeschichte* 9, no. 4 (1968): 187–211.

12 Bracker, Henn and Postel, *Die Hanse*, 110–95.

13 E. Ciéslak, *Historia Gdańska*, vol. 2: *1454–1655* (Gdańsk, 1982).

14 Y. Kikuchi, *Hamburgs Ostsee- und Mitteleuropahandel 1600–1800*: *Warenaustausch und Hinterlandnetzwerke* (Cologne, Weimar and Vienna 2018).

15 M. A. Denzel, 'Die Errichtung der Hamburger Bank 1619. Ausbreitung einer stabilen Währung und Ausdehnung des bargeldlosen Zahlungsverkehrs', in D. Lindenlaub, C. Burhop and J. Scholtyseck (eds.), *Schlüsselereignisse der deutschen Bankengeschichte* (Stuttgart, 2013), 38–50.

16 M. North, *Kommunikation, Handel, Geld und Banken in der Frühen Neuzeit*, 2nd edn (Munich, 2014), 19–20.

17 W. Blockmans, *Metropolen aan de Noordzee. De Geschiedenis van Nederland 1000–1560* (Amsterdam, 2010), 532–87.

18 H. van der Wee, 'Structural Changes in European Long-Distance Trade, and Particularly in the Re-Export Trade from South to North, 1350–1750', in J. D. Tracy (ed.), *The Rise of Merchant Empires. Long Distance Trade in the Early Modern World 1350–1750* (Cambridge, 1990), 13–33.

19 H. van der Wee, *The Growth of the Antwerp Market and the European Economy (Fourteenth – Sixteenth Centuries)* (Louvain, 1963).

20 C. Lesger, 'De wereld als horizon. De economie tussen 1578 en 1650', in W. Frijhoff and M. Prak (eds.), *Geschiedenis van Amsterdam*, II/1: *Centrum van de wereld, 1578–1650* (Amsterdam, 2004), 107–15.

21 S. Schama, *The Embarrassment of Riches. An Interpretation of Dutch Culture in the Golden Age* (New York, 1987), 34–8.

22 G. P. van de Ven, *Man-Made Lowlands: History of Water Management and Land Reclamation in the Netherlands*, 4th edn (Utrecht, 2004), 143–91.

23 M. Jakubowski-Tiessen, *Sturmflut 1717. Die Bewältigung einer Naturkatastrophe in der Frühen Neuzeit* (Munich, 1992), 57–62.

24 W. P. Blockmans, 'Der holländische Durchbruch in die Ostsee', in Jenks and North (eds.), *Der hansische Sonderweg?*, 49–58; W. Scheltjens, *Dutch Deltas. Emergence, Function and Structure of the Low Countries' Maritime Transport System ca. 1300–1850* (Leiden and Boston, 2015).

25 Schildhauer, 'Zur Verlagerung des See- und Handelsverkehrs im nordeuropäischen Raum', 187–211, 205–7; J. T. Lindblad, 'Foreign Trade of the Dutch Republic in the Seventeenth Century', in K. Davids and L. Noordegraaf (eds.), *The Dutch Economy in the Golden Age* (Amsterdam, 1993), 232.

26 L. Sicking, 'A Wider Spread of Risk. A Key to Understanding Holland's Domination of Eastward and Westward Seafaring from the Low Countries in the Sixteenth Century', in H. Brand and L. Müller (eds.), *The Dynamics of Economic Culture in the North Sea and Baltic Region in the Late Middle Ages and Early Modern Period* (Hilversum, 2007), 122–35.

27 D. Defoe, *A Plan of the English Commerce* (London, 1728), 192.

28 R. W. Unger, *Dutch Shipbuilding before 1800* (Assen, 1978), 4–9, 24–40.

29 C. Wilson, *Profit and Power. A Study of England and the Dutch Wars* (London, 1957), 111.

30 Israel, *Dutch Primacy*, 21–2.

31 M. van Tielhof, *The 'Mother of all Trades'. The Baltic Grain Trade in Amsterdam from the Late Sixteenth to the Nineteenth Century* (Leiden and Boston, 2002); Wilson, *Profit and Power*, 40–7; Vries and Woude, *First Modern Economy*, 372–9.

32 See also above, part IV 'Mediterranean', sub-chapter 'The new trading power in the Levant'.

33 See below, part VI 'Indian Ocean', sub-chapter 'Conflict and cooperation' and chapter 'Atlantic', sub-chapter 'Sugar, slaves and furs'.

34 For a thorough account, see Wilson, *Profit and Power*.

35 D. Ormrod, *The Rise of Commercial Empires. England and the Netherlands in the Age of Mercantilism, 1650–1770* (Cambridge, 2003), 276, 287–306.

36 Y. Kaukiainen, 'Overseas Migration and the Development of Ocean Navigation. A Europe-Outward Perspective', in D. R. Gabaccia and D. Hoerder (eds.), *Connecting Seas and Connected Ocean Rims. Indian, Atlantic, and Pacific Oceans and China Seas Migrations from the 1830s to the 1930s* (Leiden and Boston, 2011), 371–86.

37 Ormrod, *The Rise of Commercial Empires*, 276, 284–7.

38 North, *The Baltic*, 110–6, 135–44.

39 E. Kizik, *Mennonici w Gdańsku, Elblągu i na Żuławach wiślanych w drugiej połowie XVII i w XVIII wieku* (Gdańsk, 1994).

40 M. Bogucka, *Gdańskie rzemiosło tekstylne od XVI do połowy XVII wieku* (Wrocław, 1956); F. Gause, *Geschichte der Stadt Königsberg*, vol. 1 (Cologne and Graz, 1965), 310ff.

41 M. Bogucka, 'The Baltic and Amsterdam in the First Half of the Seventeenth Century', in W. J. Wieringa (ed.), *The Interactions of Amsterdam and Antwerp with the Baltic Region, 1400–1800* (Leiden, 1983), 55–6 and 'Dutch Merchants' Activities in Gdansk in the First Half of the Seventeenth Century', in J. P. Lemmink and J. S. A. M. van Koningsbrugge (eds.), *Baltic Affairs. Relations between the Netherlands and North-Eastern Europe 1500–1800* (Nijmegen, 1990), 22ff.

42 J. T. Lindblad, 'Louis de Geer (1587–1652). Dutch Entrepreneur and the Father of Swedish Industry', in C. Lesger and L. Noordegraaf (eds.), *Entrepreneurs and Entrepreneurship in Early Modern Times. Merchants and Industrialists within the Orbit of the Dutch Staple Market* (The Hague, 1995), 77–84.

43 H. v. Nieuwenhuize, *Niederländische Seefahrer in schwedischen Diensten. Seeschifffahrt und Technologietransfer im 17. Jahrhundert* (Cologne, Weimar and Vienna, 2021).

44 M. Krieger, *Kaufleute, Seeräuber und Diplomaten. Der dänische Handel auf dem Indischen Ozean (1620–1868)* (Cologne, 1998).

45 M. North, 'Modell Niederlande. Wissenstransfer und Strukturanpassung in Zeiten der Globalisierung', in Deutsch-Niederländische Gesellschaft e.V.

(ed.), *Deutsch-Niederländische Beziehungen in Vergangenheit, Gegenwart und Zukunft, 4th symposium, 27–28 November 1998 in Berlin* (Berlin, 1999), 165–76.

46 M. North, 'The Hamburg Art Market and Influences on Northern and Central Europe', *Scandinavian Journal of History* 28 (2003): 253–61, and 'The Long Way of Professionalisation in the Early Modern German Art Trade', in S. Caviciocchi (ed.), *Economia e arte, secc. xiii–xviii* (Prato, 2002), 459–71.

47 J. Roding, 'The Myth of the Dutch Renaissance in Denmark. Dutch Influence on Danish Architecture in the Seventeenth Century', in Lemmink and Koningsbrugge (eds.), *Baltic Affairs*, 343–53, and 'The North Sea Coasts, an Architectural Unity?' in J. Roding and L. Heerma van Voss (eds.), *The North Sea and Culture (1550–1800), Proceedings of the International Conference held at Leiden, 21–22 April 1995* (Hilversum, 1996), 95–106.

48 M. Wardzyński, 'Zwischen den Niederlanden und Polen-Litauen. Danzig als Mittler niederländischer Kunst und Musterbücher', in M. Krieger and M. North (eds.), *Land und Meer. Kultureller Austausch zwischen Westeuropa und dem Ostseeraum in der Frühen Neuzeit* (Cologne, 2004), 23–50.

VI

Indian Ocean:
Europe meets Asia

In Vasco da Gama's logbook, its anonymous author described the spice trade in the Indian Ocean region. He also indicates the profits that the Mamluk Sultan of Egypt made thanks to demand from the Venetians and Genoese, who loaded the spices onto their galleys in Alexandria:

> From this country of Calecut, or Alta India, come the spices which are consumed in the East and the West, in Portugal, as in all other countries of the world, as also precious stones of every description. The following spices are to be found in this city of Calecut, being its own produce: much ginger and pepper and cinnamon, although the last is not of so fine a quality as that brought from an island called Çillan [Ceylon], which is eight days journey from Calecut. Calecut is the staple for all this cinnamon. Cloves are brought to this city from an island called Melequa [Malacca]. The Mecca vessels carry these spices from there to a city in Mecca called Judeâ [Jeddah], and from the said island to Judeâ is a voyage of fifty days sailing before the wind, for the vessels of this country cannot tack. At Judea they discharge their cargoes, paying customs duties to the Grand Sultan. The merchandise is then transshipped to smaller vessels, which carry it through the Red Sea to a place close to Santa Catarina of Mount Sinai, called Tuuz, where customs dues are paid once more. From that place the merchants carry the spices on the back of camels, which they hire at the rate of 4 cruzados each, to Quayro [Cairo], a journey occupying ten days. At Quayro duties are paid again.[1]

The author already addresses an explanation for why the Portuguese, Dutch and other Europeans expanded their maritime activities to the Indian Ocean: to participate in the spice trade.

Conflict and cooperation

Portuguese efforts to find a sea route to India began in the fifteenth century and were long impossible to separate from Atlantic shipping. The Atlantic islands of Madeira and Porto Santo were important stages on both routes. The ancient knowledge of these islands had been lost, and voyages by Majorcans into the Atlantic had left no traces. The Portuguese Prince Henry (later known as The Navigator) undertook the colonization of the islands and appointed the Italian-born Bartolomeu Perestrelo, the future father-in-law of Christopher Columbus, as governor. The settlement of colonists began on the islands, where sugar cane and grapevines were cultivated. In 1427, the Portuguese arrived at the Azores, and beginning in 1439 Henry opened some of them to economic exploitation. The islands would be of great importance for future voyages to the South Atlantic and to India.[2] In 1433, Gil Eanes took a further step in this direction and circumnavigated Cape Bojador. All of the sailors' fears of encountering monsters and antipodes (a race of people who occupied the opposite end of the world) near the equator and being unable to bear the high temperatures there proved unfounded. More than fifty ships must have sailed beyond the Cape by 1448; on their return journeys, they brought enslaved Africans and African gold home with them. A maritime trading triangle stretching from the African coast near the Cape Verde Islands across the Azores and Madeira to the Algarve began to take shape. A trading post was established on the island of Arguin (off the coast of present-day Mauritania).

Advances along the African coast continued in the years that followed. Following the death of Henry the Navigator in 1460, the occupation of new territories was entrusted in 1468 to Fernão Gomes, who in exchange for a trade concession was charged with exploring 100 miles of coastline each year. João de Santarém and Pedro Escobar accordingly reached what is now Ghana, and shortly thereafter Fernão do Póo arrived in the territories of present-day Nigeria and Cameroon. At the same time, ships sailed into the islands in the Gulf of Guinea – São Tomé, Príncipe and Annobón. The mariners named the new coastal areas after the main goods traded there: Costa da Malagueta or do Grão (Pepper or Grain Coast, now Liberia), Costa da Marfim (Ivory Coast), Costa do Ouro (Gold Coast, present-day Ghana) and Costa dos Escravos (Slave Coast, now Togo and Benin).[3]

In 1482, Diogo Cão explored the Congo River estuary and during a later voyage (1485–6) present-day Namibia. From there it was not far to the Cape of Good Hope, which Bartolomeu Dias circumnavigated in 1488. He realized that he had reached the southern tip of Africa and thus found a sea route to India. Aside from these advances, which were crowned just ten years later by Vasco da Gama's success, the explorations within Africa continued. Europeans searched there for gold and spices as well as for Christians, especially the legendary king Prester John at the Horn of Africa.

To this end, John II of Portugal sent a mission under the leadership of Pero de Covilhã and Afonso de Paiva in 1487. Two priests had already been dispatched the year before, but although they reached Jerusalem, their lack of linguistic skills forced them to return soon afterwards. Covilhã, in contrast, was well qualified, having learnt Arabic during several diplomatic missions in North Africa. Dressed as Muslim merchants, he and Paiva travelled via Alexandria and Cairo to Aden, which they reached in 1488. Paiva then continued on to Ethiopia, where he died. Covilhã for his part first took a boat to Cannanore (Kannur) and then visited Calicut and Goa. On his return journey, he travelled via Hormuz and Aden to Cairo, where he met two Jewish envoys who were searching for him and Paiva on behalf of the king. Covilhã presented them with his account of the details of the spice trade and the sea route from Guinea to Madagascar. It is impossible to say for certain whether John II ever received the report, but around the same time (1488) an Ethiopian priest travelled via Rome to Portugal and was received at court there. After the meeting in Cairo, Covilhã himself continued his journey via Jeddah, Mecca and Medina to Ethiopia, where he reached the court of the putative Prester John and died in 1526.[4]

Unlike Christopher Columbus, after leaving Belem on 8 July 1497 Vasco da Gama could sail towards India using known routes for much of the way. He spent Christmas in a bay (now Durban Bay) beyond the Cape of Good Hope, which he therefore gave the name Natal, and with the help of an Arab pilot reached Calicut on the Malabar Coast in May 1498 after a voyage across the Arabian Sea.

The locals did not welcome Vasco da Gama with open arms, however.[5] The Portuguese had not yet realized that Calicut was one of the most important economic centres, where merchants met to trade treasures from the Far and Middle East. The presents that Vasco da Gama hastily assembled ('twelve pieces of *lambel* [striped cloth], four scarlet hoods, six hats, four strings of coral [...] six wash-hand basins, a case of sugar, two casks of oil and two of honey')[6] did little to impress the Zamorin of Calicut, who lived in a splendid palace and was accustomed to gifts of gold and ivory.[7] Since the Arab traders who dominated the spice trade sensed a new competitor, Vasco da Gama had difficulty collecting a spice cargo and turned instead to Goa farther north, which later became the most important Portuguese trading post. But even the small quantities of pepper that da Gama brought back to Lisbon caused the European pepper market to collapse. A second voyage in 1502 served mainly to establish trading posts in Asia and push back the Arab competition. In the process, the Portuguese deployed their superior artillery at sea with deliberate terror – ships were plundered and set aflame along with their passengers and crews – towards Arab merchants and pilgrims to Mecca. The yields of pepper were now so great that they led to a run on Portugal by South German and western European merchants and at the same time motivated the Portuguese king to establish a permanent presence in India. In 1505, the *Estado da Índia* was founded to manage trade in India, and Francisco de Almeida was appointed viceroy with the task of expanding and fortifying trading posts on the eastern coast of Africa and in Goa. Moreover, Almeida was supposed to close off the traditional pepper route by blockading the Red Sea. Although the latter operation did not succeed, Almeida expanded Portugal's position in India up until 1508, when he was beaten to death by local tribe members in the Cape amidst attempts by his crew to steal some of their cattle. In 1511, his successor Afonso de Albuquerque captured Malacca, whose position on the straits of the same name represented an important point of access to the Indian Ocean in the Indonesian archipelago and South China Sea.[8] The Portuguese reached Canton (Guanghzou) in 1516, but it was only in 1554 that they established a permanent trading post in China in Macao. The route heading south towards Java, Celebes (Sulawesi), the Bandas and Moluccas (the so-called the Spice Islands), and Timor was of similar importance. The short-lived colony in Nagasaki on Kyushu in Japan and the founding of a trading post on the cinnamon island of Ceylon formed the centre of a network of fortified and unfortified trading posts.[9]

Portuguese trade was based on exclusive licences granted by the Portuguese Crown to organize concession voyages (*viagens)* between two specific ports for a limited period, generally between one and three years. Concessions were sold or granted by royal favour.[10] In the mid-sixteenth century, a carrack was then regularly dispatched to connect all the regions of the Indian Ocean and the South China Sea, something that had last occurred under the Chinese Admiral Zheng He. The voyage was undertaken in several stages (Goa–Malacca, Malacca–Moluccas, Malacca–Macao and Macao–Hirado) and rendered especially lucrative in the latter segments by the import of Chinese goods to Japan.[11]

Portugal also possessed a few territories, which supplied the Portuguese colonial system with consumer goods and people. Albuquerque had already recognized that the population of Portugal was insufficient to send new men out to Asia every year. They also remained without legitimate issue there, since Portuguese women rarely ventured into these regions. The promotion of marriages between Portuguese men and the baptized women of the local upper class proved more effective than sending orphan girls from the motherland.[12]

The number of men remained small, however (12,000–14,000), so that in everyday life the colonizers relied on enslaved people, who were brought from

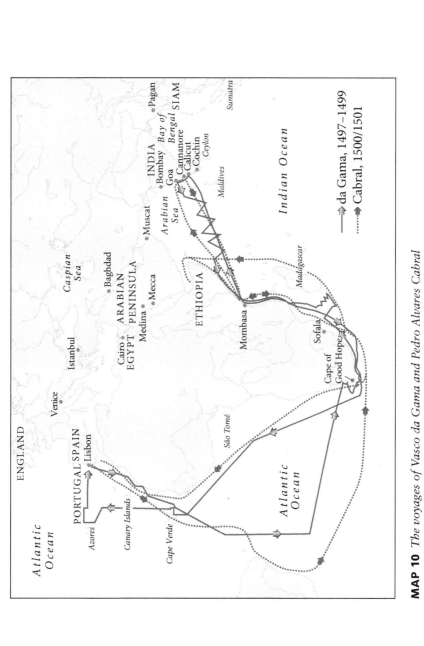

MAP 10 *The voyages of Vasco da Gama and Pedro Alvares Cabral*

all regions of the Indian Ocean. The support of local princes was needed in order to maintain trade and a military presence. The extension of the Portuguese trading post system accordingly proved highly vulnerable to hostile influences, when alliances collapsed or were challenged by rivals.[13]

When purchasing Asian products, the Portuguese depended on services provided by the local people or overseas Chinese who controlled trade. Neither the Portuguese nor the Dutch nor the English succeeded in monopolizing trade with respect to other European or Asian merchants. Instead, they opened trade up to a variety of actors and groups from all parts of the known world of their day.

The Dutch trade with India and Southeast Asia seems to have been the most successful. Adventurers awakened an interest in Asia. One of them was Jan Huyghen van Linschoten, who trained as a merchant in Portugal and Spain and became secretary to the archbishop of Goa in 1581. There he became interested in the trade in Asian goods and gained insights into the nascent Portuguese maritime empire and nautical charts, which were treated as secret. He left India after the archbishop's death and was shipwrecked on his home journey, returning to the Netherlands via Lisbon after an involuntary stay of two years on the Azores. Linschoten settled in Enkhuizen, the port town on the Zuiderzee, where he met another trader returned from Asia, Dirck Gerritsz. Pomp, also known as Dirck China.

Pomp had also trained as a merchant in Lisbon and worked as a trader in Goa, undertaking journeys to Japan and China from there. Linschoten's main work, the *Itinerario* (1596), incorporates the accounts by Pomp as well as his own, and also insights gained from nautical charts. The book, with many illustrations purporting to depict life in Goa, the Malabar Coast and China, attracted the Dutch to Asia.[14]

Cornelis de Houtman was carrying a copy of the *Itinerario* when he arrived in Java in 1595 with the first fleet. Thereafter, the Dutch and Zealand *voorcompagnieën* involved in the East Indian trade combined to form a monopolist association, the *Vereenigde Oost-Indische Compagnie* (VOC) or Dutch East India Company.[15]

The VOC was a joint-stock company with a charter from the Estates General, which was granted sovereign rights and permitted to establish forts, recruit soldiers or make contracts with foreign rulers. The Company was divided into six chambers (Amsterdam, Zealand, Rotterdam, Delft, Hoorn and Enkhuizen), which independently built and outfitted ships and sold the imported goods.[16] Soon people were speculating with their shares, stocks that over the course of the century were traded well above their original value. The chambers were headed by the so-called *bewindhebbers*, directors with lifetime tenure, who elected the governing body, a central board of directors comprising seventeen members known as the *Heeren XVII*. In 1609, operations in Asia were turned over to a governor general, who was supposed to secure Dutch access to spices on the ground by peaceful or military means.

Given the fact that pepper grew on Java and Sumatra and fine spices like cloves and nutmeg on the Moluccas, the VOC needed a headquarters in the region from which they could coordinate the pepper and spice trade. This was the idea of Admiral Cornelis Matelieff de Jonge, who had unsuccessfully besieged Malacca in 1606 and was championed by Governor-General Jan Pietersz. Coen. He founded the fortress of Batavia (the present-day Indonesian capital Jakarta) close to the pepper port of Bantam on Java, on the site of the ruins of Jacatra. Unlike Malacca, Batavia was easy to reach year-round thanks to its location on the Sunda Strait.[17]

Coen had to continue to tolerate competition from the English, who however had less capital and a smaller volume of trade. The actual aim of the VOC was the lucrative intra-Asian trade, in which the Portuguese, Spanish and English participated. Exclusive supply contracts were supposed to ensure a Dutch monopoly on cloves and nutmeg. If their partners did not honour the contracts, the VOC enforced them by violence. To keep prices on the European market high, they not only killed or enslaved the producers but also destroyed a portion of the production resources.

The VOC made great efforts to break into the Portuguese system of trading posts in India. The main commodities were cinnamon from Ceylon, which was conquered by 1658, and textiles from the Coromandel Coast and Bengal. Although textiles were used from the outset to barter for Asian products, in the late seventeenth century cotton cloth and silk replaced pepper as the dominant product in the VOC's intercontinental trade.[18] Especially lucrative was trade with Japan, where in 1641 the Dutch moved from Hirado to Deshima near Nagasaki, two years after the Portuguese were finally forbidden to trade there. Thus, the Dutch acquired an exclusive trading position under the so-called *sakoku* policy. The VOC imported silks, textiles, timber and sugar to Japan, while exporting mainly precious metals – silver, copper and golden kobang coins – which the VOC needed for purchases in India and the Indonesian archipelago.[19] The 1668 ban on silver exports and the decline of Japanese trade overall drastically reduced the VOC's Asian silver supplies, which is why they increasingly had to resort to importing silver from Europe. Since the European-Asiatic trade grew apace and the textiles in demand in Europe as well as the new stimulants coffee and tea could only be had for silver in Asia, this trade devoured ever more bullion.

We know more about the profits in the Dutch trade in Asia than any other area of trade, since the VOC kept precise records of the purchase and sale of goods. The proceeds from commodity auctions in Holland were on average around three times the purchase price in Asia. The situation changed in the eighteenth century, when the profit margins became narrower but the

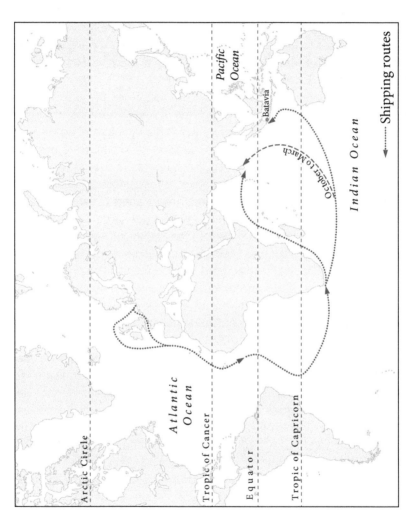

MAP 11 *Shipping routes from the Netherlands to Asia*

investment costs higher and the VOC – above all as a result of high dividend payments of up to 36 per cent – ended up in the red.[20] Those who profited from the Asiatic trade were stockholders, on the one hand, who received high dividends, and Dutch traders on the other, who re-exported Asian goods to the European or American market. It is thus no surprise that leading Amsterdam merchants like Gerrit Bicker or Gerrit Reynst were involved in trade in both the West and East Indies. Trading in the East Indies also allowed many employees of the VOC to rise socially in the Netherlands, provided they survived the long sea voyages and life in the tropics.

In the new centre of Batavia, Dutch East Indiamen met Chinese junks, and European and local merchants from southeast Asia lived together with soldiers and slaves, who outnumbered the Dutch. The Dutch colony was composed of Company personnel and the so-called free citizens, many of whom had served the Company as merchants or soldiers. The men generally lived with native partners and with time married Eurasian women or women from other parts of Asia. Chinese had already been living in Jacatra before the Dutch arrived, while others came as artisans; a further group were Chinese landowners involved in sugar production. The Mardijkers were baptized former slaves who

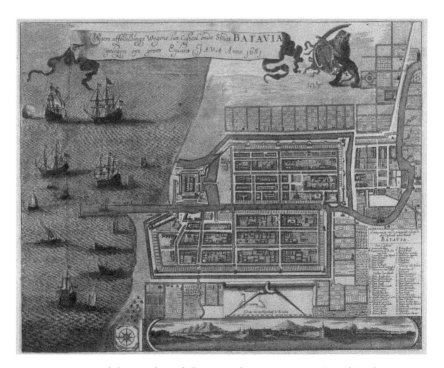

FIGURE 6 *Map of the Castle and the City of Batavia, 1682.* © *Wikipedia Commons.*

had already been freed by the Portuguese, bore Portuguese names and spoke Portuguese. Some of them had been given Dutch names when they were christened. During their military campaigns, the Dutch used the Balinese as auxiliary troops. They were joined by Malays and Bugis, groups of Muslim sailors and traders. Dutch, Chinese and Mardijkers, but also Malays and Balinese were rivals in the slave trade. They acquired slaves in many places around the Indian Ocean and the Indonesian archipelago and took them by ship to the slave markets, especially in Batavia.[21] In other VOC trading posts, though, for example on the Cape of Good Hope, names such as Rosetta of Bengal or Pieter of Macassar point to the origins of the enslaved people.

The role of Malacca changed once again with the founding and successful expansion of Batavia and the VOC network on the Indian Ocean. The arrival of the Portuguese had already caused shifts in trade. The Muslim merchants reorientated themselves towards the ports of Sumatra and Java, while a segment of Chinese traders moved to Patani and Siam. In the medium term, Manila evolved into an important Chinese hub, since this was where they received silver from America coming across the Pacific. Malacca itself also changed under the Portuguese, becoming a Catholic, Portuguese-speaking Eurasian city. Despite its shifting economic significance, the Dutch still regarded Malacca as a rival, which they conquered in 1641 after several unsuccessful earlier attempts. Although the Dutch tolerated both the Portuguese language and Catholicism in order to promote economic recovery after the long siege, it would be several years before Malacca was appreciated as a Dutch depot for

TABLE 1 *Ethnic composition of Batavia, 1679*

Ethnicity	Number	Per cent
Dutch	2,227	7
Eurasian	760	2.4
Chinese	3,220	10
Mardijkers	5,348	17
Javanese	1,391	4.3
Malay	1,049	3.3
Balinese	1,364	4.2
Slaves	16,695	51.8
Total	32,054	100

H. E. Niemeijer, *Calvinisme en koloniale stadscultuur, Batavia 1619–1725* (Amsterdam, 1996), 26.

the Indian markets and a strategic fortress.[22] It continues to play a role today in collective memory, thanks to the town hall and the many depictions, of which the English were already aware, at least visually, when they took over Malacca along with the other VOC possessions in 1795, while concentrating their power and trade in Penang and later Singapore.

After its founding in 1600, the English East India Company (EIC) began equipping ships and acquiring land for trading posts. The first one was established in Bantam on Java, where the Sultan offered the English the possibility of settlement. Others were in the Mogul kingdom in Surat and in southern India on the Coromandel Coast in Masulipatam. The EIC succeeded in acquiring, from a Nayak of the disintegrating Vijayanagara Empire, the right to establish a fortress in the region of Madras (Chennai), which evolved into a safe port and a base for trade with southern India. In alliance with the Safavid Empire, the English also managed in 1622 to expel the Portuguese from Hormuz at the entrance to the Persian Gulf and establish a trading post there as well as to draw revenues from the local customs duties.

Although the English were violently expelled from Java and Ambon, they were able to acquire new trading posts. Fort Cormantin on the Gold Coast of Africa and the island of St Helena in the Atlantic, which the English permanently occupied in 1673, provided them, as the Cape did the Dutch from 1651, with supply and provisioning stations for shipping with Asia and the Americas. Bombay (Mumbai) became a further station, which the Portuguese Infanta Catherine of Braganza brought as a dowry into her marriage to Charles II. Although contemporaries did not yet appreciate this 'poor little Island' as Samuel Pepys called it, it provided the Company with a permanent base with opportunities for expansion. Administrative and judicial structures were set up in both Bombay and Madras, which were intended to solidify the Company's authority within the settlements. In future, governors, soldiers, clerics, settlers, merchants, prisoners and enslaved people could be transferred from one place to another and encounter the same legal system everywhere.[23]

Aside from the official branch offices of the EIC, however, a large portion of English trade in the Indian Ocean region was conducted by private traders or merchants of the Company engaging in private business. Thus, within a very brief period, the governor of Madras Elihu Yale amassed a fortune of £200,000 on his own account, a small amount of which he donated in 1716 to the college in Connecticut that later bore his name. The English trade with Bengal initially began on a private basis with the ports of Hugli (Hooghly) and Balasore (Baleshwar) and gradually shifted to Calcutta (Kolkata), which was founded in 1690 and became the contact point for the English.

English merchant ships transported cargoes of textiles from Indian traders from Bengal to Surat, the Persian Gulf and the Red Sea. English trade was not limited to the Indian Subcontinent, however, but extended across the Bay of Bengal to Pegu (Burma), Junk Ceylon (Phuket), Aceh and Ayutthaya. English ships also landed in Manila in the Philippines and Canton, although the great boom in the China trade began only after 1760.

At this time the EIC became the ruler of Bengal and its connections with the locals as well as private English traders substantially increased its profit margins. Bengali opium and cotton from Bombay provided the basis for trade expansion to China, which influenced English shipping in the Indian Ocean and the South China Sea. The importance of Madras waned, while ships from Calcutta and Bombay monopolized much of trade. At the same time, they increasingly undermined the monopoly on the Southeast Asian trade claimed by the Dutch East India Company. In both Aceh and Ayutthaya, they encountered Chinese traders whom they sold opium, textiles, rice and slaves from the Indian Ocean region. The main Chinese commodity was tea, which was purchased either from junks or increasingly directly in Canton, where there was a market for both cotton cloth from Bombay and opium from Bengal.[24]

Other nations were also attracted by the prospect of profit. Thus, individual French merchants were already active in the region before France founded a company specializing in trade with the West and East Indies in 1719, the *Compagnie des Indes*. Although the Compagnie was part of the conglomerate of institutions founded by John Law to provide debt relief for the state, and a speculative bubble already burst in 1720, it was able to resume its activities in the 1720s and organize voyages to Pondicherry. The greatest profits, however, were accrued by company employees acting on their own accounts. Pondicherry nevertheless evolved into a permanent French settlement lasting until 1954.

One of the driving forces behind French trade in India was Joseph François Dupleix, who established a trading post in Chandernagore in Bengal in 1731, in collaboration with Dutchmen, former employees of the Austrian East India Company (Ostend Company) and local merchants. Together they invested in trade and shipping enterprises, with the greatest demand for freight services coming from Armenian and Muslim traders. Dupleix's ships sailed to Surat, Basra, the Maldives, East Africa and the Arabian Peninsula as well as Aceh, Manila and Canton.

French activities around the Indian Ocean suffered, however, from global conflicts with England, which played out not just in Europe and North America, but from the 1740s on the Indian Subcontinent. The only trade connection remaining at the end of the century was that between Pondicherry and Mauritius.[25]

Silver for cotton fabrics

Two main types of commodities connected the Indian Ocean with the other seas: precious metals and textiles. Silver from central Europe and later the Americas made the expansion of European trade in and with Asia possible in the first place, because European-manufactured goods (with the exception of copper and brass objects or weapons) found few buyers in Asia. Thus between 1660 and 1720, some 80 per cent of English exports consisted of precious metals in the form of bullion or coins; the figure for the Dutch East India Company was often up to 90 per cent.

Precious metals reached the Indian Ocean along three routes: first, via the Mediterranean, the Levant, the Arabian Peninsula and the Red Sea or Persian Gulf; second, via the Atlantic around the Cape of Good Hope; and third from Mexico and Peru via the so-called Manila galleons. Indian merchants played an important role in transfers through the Near and Middle East.

Thanks to Dutch and English trade statistics, we are well informed about the transfer of precious metals on the Cape route and possess possibly reliable estimates of trade across the Pacific, while individual transfers across the Red Sea and Persian Gulf are virtually impossible to quantify.

The expansion of the exchange of goods with China helped to further swell the stream of silver in the late eighteenth century. India played the central role in the trade in textiles between the Atlantic, the Indian Ocean, the South China Sea and the Pacific, with the wealth of cotton products from the Coromandel Coast, Bengal and Gujarat providing the largest portion. Demand for these fabrics in the Indonesian archipelago, the Malay Peninsula, Siam, Burma, the Red Sea, the Persian Gulf and East Africa ensured a high level of production and employment in Indian textile manufacturing.

A number of steps and trades were required to turn raw cotton into saleable products. Hundreds of thousands of yarn spinners supplied the weavers, whose product, unbleached cloth, was purchased by wholesalers and sent to other artisans to dye, print and embroider. As to these finishing processes, Indian artisans were technologically superior to Europeans until well into the eighteenth century. The Europeans, but also Indian exporters, exerted no direct influence over production. This was the province of local middlemen, who bought products from the weavers or dyers and also sought to direct production towards the needs of exporters. To increase production, the number of workers had to be increased, for example. The European trading companies vied for these middlemen, while trying at the same time to keep the international markets in mind. Merchants of the companies cooperated on the ground with the same local merchants, since the arrival of the Europeans had not changed the demand for various types of cloth. Japan, Southeast

Asia, East Africa, and the Safavid and Ottoman Empires preferred high-quality printed, painted and embroidered fabrics, while with time the Europeans came to favour cheaper and less elaborately finished cotton cloth, and in the eighteenth century exported white calicos, which were printed in European cotton printing workshops. In West Africa, which produced its own cloth, demand was greatest for blue textiles dyed with indigo as well as stripes and chequerboard patterns in red and blue.[26]

Overall, a variety of local, regional and international forces influenced production. Thus, merchants from Gujarat orientated the production of 'their' weavers towards the Arabian Peninsula and the Persian Gulf as well as Bantam and Aceh, for in order to trade in spices, sandalwood and tin from the Indonesian islands, it made sense to send textiles as well as silver. Bengal, in contrast, exported foodstuffs, raw silk and fine muslin to Surat and brought back tobacco and raw cotton. With the arrival of the Europeans, Bengal's previous inland trade was reorientated towards the sea. The Europeans became their main trading partners and boosted Bengali textile production, which had previously been overshadowed by the manufactures of Gujarat and the Coromandel Coast.[27]

In the eighteenth century, the British then promoted an increase in opium production in Bengal, which was closely connected to the tea trade. Tea altered the trade and production structures in the Indian Ocean yet again and made Canton the most important port for Europeans and soon Americans as well. The almost insatiable demand for tea – in 1800, per capita consumption of tea in England was 2.5 pounds, sweetened with 17 pounds of sugar – could only be met by payment in silver, weapons or opium. For that reason, the European trading companies directed a large proportion of their cargo capacity to tea. Since the VOC, which had long procured the cheaper sorts of tea via Batavia, could no longer satisfy growing demand in this way, its directors now organized the voyage to China directly from Amsterdam to Canton. This left them a market share of some 20 per cent, while the EIC met one-third of the demand for tea. Meanwhile, the ships of other nations, all of which had trading centres in Canton, transported tea to England on a smaller scale.[28]

Merchant dynasties

The Indian Ocean experienced growing mobility in the early modern period. Maritime traffic on the routes from the Middle East to India and China, which had been known since the Middle Ages, was fundamentally intensified. Merchants, seamen, soldiers, envoys, pilgrims and enslaved people travelled the world's seas. In the Indian Ocean, the expansion of maritime trade revived old ports while stimulating the establishment of new trading centres. Coastal dwellers and migrants from the inland areas alike, hoping to participate in the economic boom, profited.[29]

The Europeans arriving in Asia operated within a trade network dominated by local dynasties. The merchants of Surat, for example, worked not just as importers, exporters and shipowners, but also as brokers and agents for the Europeans. One such merchant family were the Parekhs, who for generations acted on behalf of the EIC in Surat. In the mid-eighteenth century, Jagannath Laldas Parekh bought English imported goods and procured Indian goods, such as textiles, for the company to export. He also had contracts with countless weavers and sub-contractors, and his sons followed in his footsteps. As one of the wealthiest merchants, he promoted English predominance in the 1750s as well as his sons' role as mediators between the EIC and local traders and producers.[30]

The networks of Gujarati merchants extended to Persia as well as Aceh in the Indonesian Archipelago. In the chapter on the Mediterranean, we already encountered another network, that of the Armenians of New Julfa,[31] which also extended to India, the Indian Ocean and Southeast Asia.

Particularly in India, the Armenians were appreciated and envied by the Europeans for their success in buying Indian textiles at a far lower price than that paid by the English, for example, through their middlemen. For that reason, the EIC entered into a number of contracts with Armenian merchants, which ensured a steady supply for the Company in Bengal. Thus, the European presence offered new opportunities for the Armenians and their trading centres in Bengal, which they grasped in Hugli, Calcutta or Kasimbazar. One of these merchants was Khoja Wajid, who played a leading role in Bengali economic life in the first half of the eighteenth century. He not only made his money from the inland trade in saltpeter, salt and opium, but also engaged in overseas trade extending from Bengal to Surat, the Persian Gulf and the Red Sea.

At the same time, Wajid maintained close contacts with the French, Dutch and English, controlling a large portion of French trade with India. He had a monopoly on the trade in salt and saltpeter, which he supplied to European companies. Wajid also built up a merchant fleet whose ships sailed from Hugli to Surat carrying rice, sugar, textiles and silk and returned with a cargo of raw cotton, rosewater, corals, almonds and porcelain. He maintained a branch office in Surat for his business with Gujarat. His close contacts with the French were a thorn in the side of the British, however. In 1757 they captured Hugli, burnt down his warehouses and seized another one of his ships under the pretext that it was sailing under the French flag. As a consequence, his business did not survive the year. He lost his salt monopoly as well as his role as a supplier to the European trading companies.[32]

The networks that merchants and sea captains controlled from the western Indian Ocean and the Arabian Gulf were of great importance. Merchants, dhow captains (*nakhudas*) and seamen sailed frequently between Kuwait, Bahrain, Oman, Yemen and East Africa. Although this trade had been going on for centuries, the nineteenth century saw an expansion fostered by the British presence in the Gulf and the pearl and date booms. The demand for pearls among *nouveau riche* Europeans and North Americans stimulated pearl diving and trading on the banks between Bahrain and Kuwait. Furthermore, merchants and *nakhudas* established communities in the western Indian ports in order to supply rice, sugar, tea and spices as well as timber for the dhow-building industry. Travelling west, Zanzibar-bound dhows carried and sold salt in African ports and purchased mangrove poles to be sold as building materials in the Gulf ports.[33]

Another of these networks were the Hadhramis, who migrated from Yemen to Southeast Asia, India and East Africa. Although they often married local women, the Hadhramis maintained economic, social and religious ties with their homeland.[34] They were traders, shipowners and Muslim scholars who carried Sufism with them across the Indian Ocean. Their command of Arabic fostered the rise of local Muslim societies. Some of them founded small sultanates, while others were entrepreneurs and landowners in British Singapore and Dutch Indonesia. In the western Indian Ocean, Zanzibar, with its markets for slaves and African products, and the Comoro islands were attractive destinations for Hadhrami dhow masters and traders.[35]

The rise of one trading dynasty was often closely linked to the fall of another. Frequently, it was merchant bankruptcies that left their mark in the archives, and this offers insights into mercantile life. The Armenian traders in Batavia, too, found that success and failure often went hand in hand.

Thus, the record of an auction held in 1798 reports on the business activities of the bankrupt late Armenian merchant Cosorop Petrus. Apart from a large stock of Madeira wine, Petrus had possessed lavish household furnishings, which the Dutch, Chinese and Muslim inhabitants of Batavia bought up. A Chinese man named Sim Tjimko appears to have been attracted by the decorative objects. He bought not only a large – presumably Netherlandish – painting, but also costly copper lamps, copper spittoons, beds, chairs and side and gaming tables. Another person purchased the valuable table clock in a glass case, thereby demonstrating the role of the material culture of the merchant diaspora, which crossed ethnic and social boundaries.

Particularly in Southeast Asia, traders of diverse origins worked together closely. The largest group were the Chinese, who were present everywhere. From the port cities they built up contacts across the rivers to producers in the hinterland and procured the goods that were in demand overseas. They supplied the Dutch, for example, with porcelain, silk and later tea.

Much of shipping also occurred on Chinese junks. There were large Chinese communities not just in Batavia, but also in Ayutthaya, Malacca or Hội An, and they established contacts to the Pacific[36] and Spanish America via Manila. The Japanese merchants who were also active there brokered Chinese goods to Japan, the shipping of which overseas was also limited or regulated by ship's passports.[37]

The Hokkien Chinese from Fujian in particular dominated trade in the South China Sea for centuries. Although the Ming and later Qing dynasties sought to limit seafaring and trade, tens of thousands of families lived from illegal goods traffic, which they engaged in under the pretext of visits to foreign relatives. The Hokkien Chinese settled mainly in Java among the local Javanese and Muslim traders. In the course of the sixteenth century, Hokkien junks received concessions to trade with Southeast Asia, but also with Manila. The junks set sail around the Chinese New Year (January/February) and reached their destinations in Southeast Asia three or four weeks later. They returned in early June. Unlike the Indian Ocean, where many ports were inaccessible for months depending on the direction of the monsoon winds, shipping in the South China Sea was possible all year round, thanks to the many coastlines and islands that offered shelter. The threat here came from the typhoons, so that seafarers but also those responsible for the VOC's merchant vessels did their best to reach their home ports before typhoon season. American silver was attractive for Chinese traders. After settling in Manila, the Chinese took over petty trade and with it the provisioning of the local population as well as the Spanish with food.

On Java, trade was at first concentrated in Bantam, which was visited by travelling traders from China and where a Chinese mercantile community that supplied the Indonesian archipelago gradually arose. Before the Europeans arrived, the Chinese provided Bantam with the basic necessities, and it was only after the Europeans came that they began to trade Chinese luxury goods such as silk and porcelain for South American silver. Like the Gujaratis, they also exported pepper grown on Java and Sumatra.

After the VOC had put down roots in Batavia, the Dutch forcibly rerouted trade, and junks began to travel regularly from Fujian to Batavia. The Chinese mainly supplied silk, porcelain and sugar, screens and paper, while in Batavia they loaded their boats with precious metals, pepper and other spices as well as sandalwood, buffalo horn, birds' nests, ivory and later tin and cloth.[38]

Merchants from China also mediated between the global trade networks and the local producers in Southeast Asia. One example is the developing market for lacquer from Southeast Asia. This natural lacquer was produced when female lac bugs settled onto branches, especially of banyan trees, and secreted a scarlet-red resin. The resin was dried and ground and shipped to China and Japan. There artisans used it as lacquer to protect and embellish wooden cupboards, boxes, screens and other furniture. Chinese and Japanese lacquerware was prized around the Indian Ocean and above all in Europe, leading to rising demand and a veritable boom in production.[39]

Taiwan and Nagasaki accordingly became destinations for Chinese junks, with two or three ships travelling regularly from Batavia to Japan. The Hokkien Chinese traded with their local compatriots in both Taiwan and Japan. An interest in Chinese tea, which had long evaded the Dutch, grew in the late seventeenth and early eighteenth centuries.

Although maritime traffic was interrupted several times during the eighteenth century, the Hokkien networks, which extended from Nagasaki in the east to Malacca in the west, remained intact. Clans played an especially important role here.[40]

The main partners of the Chinese and Europeans in the Indonesian archipelago were the Malays, the Bugis of Sulawesi and the Muslims of the Coromandel Coast, who appear in the sources as Chulia. After the Portuguese conquest of Malacca, they moved to Aceh and Johor, among other places. At the same time, relations with the Coromandel Coast remained intact, where they provided textile producers with money and credit. They focused on the trade in goods about which Europeans were ignorant or that did not interest them. These included betel (areca) nuts, which were widely enjoyed in India and Southeast Asia. The Chulia could distinguish between the different varieties of betel nuts and the preferences of various regions (red betel nuts for Pegu, white ones for China and the Malabar Coast). They correspondingly ensured that their ships were ready to land on the northeast coast of Sumatra in time for the harvest, for example of the precious red betel nuts. The Chulia merchants also proved themselves to be experts in the trade in elephants from the Malay Peninsula. The Dutch and English tried to break into this business but lacked the requisite knowledge of how to treat the animals and were forced to acknowledge the superiority of Indian merchants in this area and in negotiations with the local producers.[41]

Another Tamil trading community were the Hindu Chettiars, who had begun as itinerant salt traders before expanding into the pearl fisheries in the Straits between India and Ceylon and later trading with the Malay Peninsula. Their business was based on moneylending, since they financed indigenous rice production as well as the opium trade. Establishing operations as far away as Vietnam, they consolidated their position in Southeast Asia by investing in temples and religious practices as well, retaining close connections to their ancestral home on the Coromandel Coast.[42]

Shipping was in the hands of many native seafaring families, who operated from Malacca and the islands of the Indonesian archipelago. Every year several junks sailed from Amoy (Xiamen) to Malacca. Malay and Javanese captains engaged in small-scale shipping with the ports of Sumatra or Java. While at the beginning of the eighteenth century ten to twenty ships a year came from India, fifty to one hundred ships each embarked from Sumatra or the Malay Peninsula and some forty from Java. Malays captained the largest number of ships, before the Chinese, Javanese and Bugis. In the late eighteenth and early nineteenth centuries, the Malay captains reorientated their activities and increasingly sailed to the growing English trading centre of Penang. Nevertheless, the Malays were soon overshadowed by the Chinese, who because of the immigration or growth of the local Chinese population and their clan and family networks were better placed to exploit the new opportunities offered by tin mining and commercialized agriculture on the Malay Peninsula.[43]

The population of the islands played an important role in trade and shipping. The Orang Laut (literally sea peoples), for example, lived on boats along the coastlines of the western Indonesian Archipelago and were well acquainted with the dangers of the Straits of Malacca and Singapore. They worked as pilots, fished and harvested resources from the sea, including sea grass, corals, pearls, shark's fins and sea turtles for their shells, which were in demand mainly by Chinese merchants. While the Orang Laut served native rulers as advisors, merchants and mercenaries, the Europeans feared them as pirates. Their contacts extended into the Pacific, with whose island societies they shared a number of features.[44]

Life at sea

When it comes to source materials and breadth of activities, Dutch traders and seafarers stand out. From the early seventeenth century to the second half of the eighteenth century, they ran more ships and transported more people from Europe to South Africa and Asia than all other European nations combined. Overall, around one million individuals travelled to Asia on Dutch ships between 1600 and 1795, approximately 5,000 per year. One third of them returned to the Netherlands by ship. Exact figures for certain chambers of the VOC, such as the Delft chamber, show that 60 per cent of sailors recruited by the VOC returned, but only 30 per cent of soldiers. This would seem to indicate a higher mortality rate for soldiers, who were confined to barracks for long periods in Asia and exposed to diseases.[45]

The ships sailed first along the African coast, then set their course for South America with the trade winds and finally used the west winds off the coast of Brazil to reach the Cape of Good Hope. After that, the Dutch felt their way along the East African coast and past Madagascar, finally crossing the Indian Ocean towards Java. This journey took 258 days on average in the 1620s, but mariners soon noticed that it was quicker if they did not sail along the

African coast but instead followed the west winds directly from the Cape to the western Australian coast and then took off in a northerly direction towards Java. In this way, they needed only around 200 days for the passage, which also became safer as nautical charts improved.

In Batavia, the fleet had to wait until the ships returned from other outposts in Asia with their goods. This happened in September and October, so they could reload the ships and begin the journey in December. If the wind was blowing from the southeast, it was possible to sail directly to the Cape, but in an emergency, they made for Mauritius. The ships then sailed from the Cape of Good Hope across the Atlantic and past St Helena via the Azores to Europe, either through the English Channel or around Scotland and through the North Sea. The return journey took 218–230 days.[46]

The many tasks on board required specialized personnel. On VOC ships, along with the captain or skipper the supercargo (head merchant) was responsible for voyages and goods. Next in the hierarchy were the first mate, the second officers like the boatswain, boatswain's mate, steward, quartermaster, cook and their respective deputies (mates) as well as the constable or *provoost*. The craftsmen on board included the ship's carpenters, sailmakers, barbers and surgeons. Ordinary seamen, cabin boys and private servants to officers and the VOC personnel occupied the lowest rungs on the ladder. There were always clerics on board and often travellers with their families on their way to Batavia. Also present were a number of soldiers who had entered the service of the VOC for a time, since military service offered members of other European nationalities the opportunity to work for the Dutch.

Most seamen came from the Netherlands, with northern European coastal areas becoming increasingly important for recruitment. Notable among them were the duchies of Schleswig and Holstein, Denmark, Norway and Sweden, but also Poland and the eastern Baltic coast.

A significant proportion of foreign sailors and skippers married in Amsterdam and settled in the Netherlands, while others, if they survived the voyages, returned to their homelands after a few decades. These returnees were highly prized among the officers of warships in the Baltic region because of their nautical experience.

Despite the at times arduous climate in Southeast Asia, the VOC gradually succeeded in making the long voyages in the Indian Ocean safer. The relatively nutritious provisions on board helped. In the late seventeenth century, Dutch sailors consumed 4,700–5,000 calories a day on VOC ships and warships and thus were at the top of the nutrition hierarchy. This is underlined by the fact that textile workers in Leiden received at most 3,500 calories per day.

There were clear regulations about provisions for the crews of Dutch warships and the VOC followed them. Breakfast consisted of porridge with prunes and raisins. Around 12 o'clock the crew was served a hot soup of dried peas or beans. Butter, mustard or vinegar were added as flavourings. On meat days the cook added some meat. At 6 in the evening, the remains of the midday soup were reheated. Four times a week they ate salt cod along with the soup and three times meat or bacon. Each crew member also had a weekly ration of bread, butter, cheese and vinegar. They drank water and beer as well as rations of wine and brandy. Officers and cabin passengers of course ate more lavishly, which meant that along with the standard dishes of peas and beans they were also served honey, sugar, spices, various kinds of meat and beer and wine.[47]

Despite abundant food, sailors often suffered from a lack of vitamin C, which led to scurvy among many seamen. Although the relatively high mortality rate fell over the course of the seventeenth century, it was still 9 per cent in the 1670s and 1680s, although there were decades with up to 15 per cent mortality. On land, in contrast, only 2 per cent of men aged twenty-five to thirty-five died. Apart from diseases of deficiency such as scurvy, work accidents, battle injuries including wound infections and shipwreck were the most frequent causes of death. Infectious diseases in the tropics also played a role.[48] The health risks remained great, since poor nutrition had weakened the crew members' immune systems. Between 1725 and 1786, some 95,000 employees of the VOC died in hospital in Batavia, more than 1,500 per year, with yearly arrivals of 6,000 Europeans.[49] Mortality on the return journey was at least lower at 6 per cent, and if no epidemic diseases broke out, the rate could drop still further.[50]

Apart from being well-fed, the crews were also comparatively well paid. The captain or skipper was near the top of the pay hierarchy with 60–80 guilders monthly (720–960 per year), but the first mate was also very well paid with 40–50 guilders a month. The predicant or pastor was in the highest pay category at 80–100 guilders. The ship's carpenter was well remunerated at 30–36 guilders and the carpenter's mate at 24–28 guilders. Ordinary sailors, in contrast, received just 7–11 guilders per month, or 84–132 per year. Ordinary soldiers fell into the same category. If we consider, however, that sailors were housed and fed, they could save a good deal by the end of the voyage, especially because they had little opportunity to spend money on board the ship.[51]

Apart from their wages, illegal private trade promised varying degrees of profit. The eighteenth-century inventories that inform us about the contents of sailors' sea chests mention a rich assortment of goods. Sailors also smuggled silver ducatons, whose export was officially forbidden by the Netherlands, to Batavia. For example, Daniël van Staden (1738) and Dirck Pomp (1740) carried 231 and 195 of these coins with them. The skipper Reinier Jan Elsevier even had an entire storehouse on board – not just 19 different types of wine and beer, but also black trousers, embroidered camisoles, 300 spectacle cases,

56 pairs of snaphances and 30 pistols, 24 men's hats, 12 crystal fruit bowls, 400 glass lampshades, 66 wine cups and 320 pieces of window glass. He also carried cheese, butter, herring, ham, smoked meat, ox tongues and salmon. Others specialized in metal objects, so-called *Neurenburger cramerij*, such as spectacles, scissors, knives, mirrors, shearing blades, skewers and buttons.[52]

Career prospects were another incentive to enter the services of the VOC. Those who did were given a three-year contract and anyone who died was immediately replaced by a new sailor, soldier or employee. This meant that a man who left the Netherlands as an ordinary seaman had good chances of returning with a higher rank. There were admirals who had begun as cabin boys. The personnel recruited from Europe did not, however, suffice to satisfy the VOC's needs in their Asian outposts. For that reason, large numbers of sailors, soldiers, craftsmen and shipbuilding and port workers were recruited from the local population. Europeans and Eurasians made up just one-sixth of VOC personnel in Asia. In Ceylon, for instance, two-thirds of VOC staff and half of all soldiers came from the region. The Company's ban on taking Asian wives or partners back to the Netherlands meant that many Dutchmen chose to remain in the tropics.

As we have seen, there was lively Chinese, Javanese and Malay maritime traffic. At the same time, the VOC recruited local and Chinese sailors in large numbers for voyages within Asia, and in the ports from which the Company's ships embarked directly for Europe the crews were completed with native sailors. Thus, the VOC took on board Christian Tamils on the Coromandel Coast, Muslims in Bengal and Ceylon, Portuguese Chinese in Macao, and Javanese and Chinese in Batavia. Accordingly, around 1790 some 1,000 Asian seamen travelled from Asia to the Netherlands and back every year.[53]

Bengal and Surat sailors were also recruited by the English East India Company and by private traders. These so-called *lascars* (after *lascarin*, a term used for native soldiers) served on East Indiamen and privately owned country ships, but also on Pacific whalers.[54] With the help of lascars, European captains were able to operate their country ships in the Indian Ocean, calling at ports that European ships were unable to visit.[55] The role of lascars in (Indian Ocean) seafaring is reflected in their maritime vocabulary, which originated in the South Asian ports and entered into the nautical slang of the Malay maritime world.[56] Despite their importance, they were paid far less than the Muslim sailors on VOC ships, where the latter earned about the same wages as European sailors.[57]

While those captains and high VOC officials who managed to survive their deployment in the tropics usually returned home, a significant proportion of ordinary sailors and soldiers remained in the 'colonies' for longer periods because of the good career prospects there.

The Company's great need for personnel also gave former employees the opportunity to re-enter their service when required. One fascinating example was Hubert Hugo, who after fourteen years of service in the VOC and attaining the status of a merchant in Surat tried his hand at piracy for a while. Together with his friend Laurens Davidsz., who had worked for the admiralty of the Maas as a seaman and privateer, and six others, he founded a pirate company (*Reederij*) with the aim of capturing Muslim ships in the Red Sea. Each partner invested 8,000 guilders to build a ship and recruit a crew. After leaving Dutch waters, the pirates changed the ship's name from *de Seven Provintien* to *den Swarten Arent* and at the port of Le Havre received a French letter of marque authorizing them to take pirates, corsairs and infidels as well as 'savages' and enemies of France captive, seize their goods and bring them to Le Havre.

In 1661 they set sail for the Red Sea, where, as in the Indian Ocean, they plundered and burnt a number of ships. The booty consisted of money, gold bullion, jewels, cowry shells, rice, textiles, spices and domestic animals. They captured sailors and stole VOC and EIC ship's passports. The local rulers of Mocha who resisted the pirates were met with violence. The 'biggest catch' was the ship belonging to the queen mother of Bijapur (Vijayapura), which was supposed to bring a valuable cargo of gold, muslin, carpets, money and rosewater to Mecca and Medina. After scouring the Indian Ocean, the pirates sailed via St Helena to the Caribbean, where they continued their raids off the islands of Martinique and St Kitts.

When Davidsz. tried to share his profits with his 'investors' in Amsterdam, he was discovered, arrested as a pirate and sentenced to death and the confiscation of his goods. Shortly before the execution of the sentence, he was transferred to his home city of Dordrecht and tried anew. There he was sentenced to thirty years in prison and banishment from Holland and West Frisia. Since Dordrecht had no secure prison, he was sent to the penitentiary in Amsterdam, but he managed to escape through a chimney two months after his arrival in November 1663. He may have travelled to Le Havre, where his friend Hugo was in hiding. Two years later he appears to have been in the employ of the admiralty of the Maas once more, where he commanded the warship *Gorinchem* as captain during the Second Anglo-Dutch War (1665–7). In the years that followed he rose to commander of one of the largest warships, the *Gelderland* with a crew of 280 men and thirty-six cannons – a position he held until his death in 1672.

Herbert Hugo, in contrast, who had not only stolen VOC ship's passports and wreaked havoc in the Company's waters, re-entered the service of the VOC in 1671, after which his career truly took off: he rose to head of the VOC outpost on Mauritius and although he had to promise not to visit the coasts of the East Indies, he died a well-respected man in Batavia in 1678.[58]

The Dresden native Zacharias Wagener (1614–68), who after leaving school in Saxony underwent further training as a draughtsman with the cartographer Willem Blaeu in Amsterdam and travelled to Brazil in 1634 with the Dutch West India Company, is an example of an international career in the Dutch service. Hired by the governor, Prince John Maurice of Nassau-Siegen, who extended the Dutch holdings in Brazil, he worked as a clerk and draughtsman. The surviving *Thier-Buch* (Book of Animals) with depictions of animals, plants and people is evidence of these activities. After returning to Europe and trying to establish himself in Dresden, Wagner signed on again in the 1640s, this time with the VOC, and after his arrival in Batavia rose to the position of assistant to Governor General Anton van Diemen. He quickly advanced and in 1651 was sent to Tonkin and Formosa (Taiwan) as legation secretary and in 1653 as envoy to Canton. In 1656 he was supposed to represent the VOC in Japan. There he was a member of the mission to Edo and witnessed the great fire in the city. In 1660 he concluded a peace and friendship pact with the sultan of Macassar. For his services, he was appointed governor of the Cape Colony in 1662, succeeding Jan van Riebeeck. Although he returned to Amsterdam after five years on the Cape, he was not able to enjoy retirement in Europe and died without ever seeing Saxony again. He did leave behind his personal recollections in the 'Brief Description of 35 Years of Travels and Activities, which Mr Zacharias Wagner Gloriously Performed and Completed in Europe, Asia, Africa and America, Mostly in the Service of the Dutch East and West India Companies, From the Late Man's Own Handwritten Journal'.[59]

Jan Brandes also had a remarkable career. He was born in 1743 into a Thuringian family that had resettled in the Netherlands, and after school and initial studies in Leiden, he moved to Greifswald to study theology. After some time as a Lutheran pastor in Doetinchem (Geldern), he hired on as a pastor to the VOC. On 6 May 1778, he and his wife Truy and their fifteen-year-old ward Maria Margaretha Wiese embarked for Batavia on the East Indiaman *Holland*. After a brief stay on the Cape, they sailed on to Batavia, arriving on 23 January 1779. He worked there until 1785. On 22 June 1779, their son Jantje was born and just one year later his wife died. Brandes's correspondence, diary and the many drawings he left behind make him probably the best chronicler of the lives of the many ethnic groups in Batavia and Ceylon, which he and his son visited on their return journey to Europe in 1785/1786.

Before Brandes returned to Europe, the church council in Batavia issued a negative assessment claiming that he had not fulfilled his duties properly. He was accused among other things of spending most of his time drawing, painting, taxidermying birds and working on his land. During the return voyage Brandes stopped for a while on the Cape to get to know the region and make drawings. Since the assessment meant that his chances of gaining a new position were low, he looked for other opportunities.

He found Sweden, which was familiar to him from his studies in Swedish Pomerania, increasingly attractive. In Batavia he had also made the acquaintance of Sven Johan Wimmercrantz, who performed an important task within the VOC as overseer of the locks, canals and waterworks there. Wimmercrantz collected rare birds, minerals and plants and discussed them with Brandes. Wimmercrantz left Batavia in 1783 and moved first to Stralsund on the Baltic, and later bought a farm in Småland. He persuaded Brandes to follow his example, and the latter travelled to Gothenburg in November 1787 and bought land near Wimmercrantz in Skälsebo. Not long thereafter he married into the local elite and had two daughters. Unfortunately, his son Jantje, who had survived the tropics, died in Sweden of smallpox in January 1792, aged twelve. Jan Brandes, who continued to keep a journal and draw (his journals are preserved in Linköping), died in 1808.[60]

The examples of Wagener and Brandes illustrate the international networks that were established through the Dutch trading posts. It was quite common to remain in contact through letters, sometimes over many years, albeit with interruptions. Pastor Carl Ludwig Scheitz of Steinberg in the parish of Flensburg, for instance, corresponded with his brother, who worked as a bookkeeper for the Dutch East India Company in Cochin (Kochi), and not only sent him silhouettes of his family – much as we send now photos – but also explained how to transfer money:

Dearest Brother! You inform me that you are prepared to transfer money to me […] Following your wishes, I have sought to find two safe companies in Amsterdam to which you may send money or remittances. They are Mr Frans de Wilde Boekhouder bij het Oostindishe Compagnie tot Amsterdam, who has agreed to take care of the letters to you, and the other is called Mr Erdwin Borgtede. You should regard Mr Frans de Wilde as the main person and mention him as the recipient and collector of the money in your procuration. The abovementioned men will see to it that the money is sent to me safely. I commend you, dearest Brother, along with your dear wife and children, whom I and our dear mother and my wife and children send tender greetings and embraces, to God's grace and blessings. Farewell, very well indeed, and think frequently of your Brother, who loves you dearly.[61]

Unfortunately, the letter never arrived, as the ship carrying it was captured by an English vessel, and it is now housed in the so-called *Prize Papers* in the National Archives in London.

Europe meets Asia

The Dutch presence significantly stimulated cultural exchange in the Indian Ocean region. A number of actors were involved in this communication system, which linked not just the maritime regions from the Arabian Sea to the East China Sea but also the oceans, since Dutch merchants were also active in the North and South Atlantic. Dutch success depended at the same time on a great willingness to adapt. The Dutch quickly learned the customs of the various Asian societies around them and performed the ceremonies demanded of them in a manner that benefited their business. They corresponded in Malay, Farsi, Portuguese and Chinese, kowtowed in keeping with Japanese custom (unlike the English or Russians) and also submitted to the complicated manners of the Moghul courts or the rulers of Kandy and Mataram in Ceylon or the court of Siam. At the same time, they made controlled use of their European hegemonic knowledge towards the locals, so that they were frequently the only source of knowledge about the world.[62] The colonial societies differed from place to place with respect to both the goods traded and cooperation with native merchants. While the Dutch lived alongside many other ethnic groups in Batavia or Cape Town, they were quite isolated in Deshima and could only occasionally receive visitors.

Every year the director, a medical doctor and the trading post scribe had to undertake an official journey to Edo to pay their respects to the shogun. With time, the delegations expanded to 100–150 persons, including Japanese interpreters and attendants. The journey took some three months and involved large expenditures for gifts for the shogun and other dignitaries. As a rule, the Dutch were sent a list of the expected gifts in advance. The *Dagregisters* from Deshima, for example, give precise details about this reciprocal process and thus represent an important source of information about cultural exchange between Japan, the Netherlands and Europe. The delegations not only gave the Dutch the opportunity to leave Deshima once a year, but in turn allowed the Japanese to meet people from the West. Especially when the Dutch stopped in Kyoto, Japanese officials came to acquaint themselves with Western customs and habits. Scholars specialized in Western studies (*rangaku* or Dutch studies), while European mediators such as Engelbert Kämpfer or Carl Peter Thunberg brought scholarly knowledge from Japan to the Netherlands and the rest of Europe.[63]

In Batavia and elsewhere, the Dutch tried to adapt practices and cultural goods to local customs and needs. This applied not only to house building, which had to take account of the monsoon rains, but also ways of life, which represented a symbiosis between European and local customs. Thus, the material culture of the Dutch and the Chinese or Armenians in Batavia exhibited both European and Asian elements. Homes were adorned with Dutch and Chinese paintings, drawings and prints as well as Chinese porcelain, lanterns and birdcages. People equally prized seating furniture in the European Rococo style and 'Chinese' chairs, as well as Japanese lacquer furniture and clocks, with the Chinese much preferring Frisian clocks.[64]

The scholarly preoccupation with languages, customs and habits is remarkable. One of the earliest instances is Frederik de Houtman's *Spraeck ende woord-boeck, Inde Maleysche ende Madagaskarsche Talen met vele Arabische ende Turcsche woorden (Grammar and Dictionary of the Malay and Malagasy Languages with Many Arab and Turkish Words)*. Houtman participated in the first journeys to Asia and was captured in 1599 in Aceh, where he spent twenty-six months as a prisoner. In this period he learnt the Malay language so well that after his return home in 1603 he could publish his dictionary, which not only gave the Malay equivalents for Dutch words but also provided dialogues that one could use when arriving by ship or during an audience with a king. The appendix also included a number of his astronomical observations.[65]

This began a long tradition of knowledge exchange that would see a veritable explosion in the eighteenth century. It included Georg Everhard Rumphius' *D'Amboinsche Rariteitkamer*[66], a cabinet of curiosities in book form, as well as François Valentyn's *Oud en Nieuw Oost-Indiën (Old and New East India)*.[67] This influential work reported not just on geography, natural history and the various ethnic groups in East Indies but also on the religions. As a Protestant proponent of the Enlightenment who believed in progress, Valentyn, a cleric, grappled with 'superstition' in the region while also propagating projects to translate the Bible into Malay. In this way, the Dutch created an image of the world around the Indian Ocean at the same time as they communicated their own worldviews to the local societies.

Encounters with the inhabitants of the Indian Ocean and their ways of life were not the only matters communicated to Europe, however; these also included the conflicts between the European powers in this region, which for example had a lasting impact on the development of international law or notions of dominion over the seas. Thus, the Portuguese claimed sovereignty over maritime traffic and tried to enforce it by issuing passes[68] known as *cartazes*. Any ship found without one of these passes was seized and the crew either killed or enslaved.

The Dutch naturally refused to recognize the Portuguese shipping monopoly. An incident in the Singapore Strait unleashed a protracted debate over international law. On 25 February 1603, the Dutch Admiral Jacob van Heemskerk seized the Portuguese carrack *Santa Catarina*, which was carrying a valuable cargo of Chinese silks and porcelain. What began as an action by privateers culminated in a political strategy to weaken Portugal's position in

Asia. In 1604, the VOC asked the humanist and jurist Hugo Grotius, who had already given legal support to the plundering of Spanish ships by the Dutch vessel *Zwemmende Leeuw* off Havana in the 1590s, to write a defence of the seizure. This was the background to his treatise *De Jure Praedae*, from which the chapter *Mare Liberum* was published in 1609. In this text, Grotius laid out the legal basis for free shipping on the world's seas, unleashing a debate: in his pamphlet *De Iusto Imperio Lusitanorum Asiatico*, the Portuguese priest Seraphim de Freitas defended Portugal's control of shipping in the waters that bordered on its territories, without however declaring the open sea to be a Portuguese possession. The Englishman John Selden opposed the *Mare Liberum* in his *Mare Clausum*, in which he asserted English sovereignty over the North Sea against the Dutch herring fisheries.[69] Legal implementation followed in the Navigation Acts, which stipulated that import goods had to be brought to England directly from their country of origin and transported only by ships from their country of origin or England.[70] Naturally, this could not be enforced in the Indian Ocean because of the initially limited English cargo capacities. Only in the nineteenth century, after the British had taken over the former Dutch possessions in South Africa, Malacca and Ceylon, could these regulations be tightened. Thereafter, merchants who wished to trade with British overseas possessions had to use ships whose crews were at least three-quarters British, and they could dock only at ports under British control. The customs duty that had to be paid in an Indian harbour was accordingly twice as high if the cargo was transported on a non-British ship, regardless of where it had originated.[71]

Meanwhile, the Anglo-Dutch rivalry continued, as the two colonial powers sought to intervene in native conflicts and in this way secure allies. In the Anglo-Dutch Treaty of 1824, the two powers lastingly defined their spheres of interest in Southeast Asia by drawing a line through the middle of the Straits of Malacca and Singapore to the South China Sea. Henceforth, the islands, countries and waters north of the line would belong to Britain and those south of the line to the Netherlands. The Dutch accepted the expansion of the British port of Singapore, while the British agreed not to set up trading posts on Sumatra or the islands south of Singapore.[72]

Notes

1   E. G. Ravenstein (ed.), *A Journal of the First Voyage of Vasco da Gama 1497–1499* (London, 1898), 77–8.

2   P. E. Russell, 'Prince Henry the Navigator', in P. E. Russell (ed.), *Portugal, Spain and the African Atlantic. 1343–1490. Chivalry and Crusade from John of Gaunt to Henry the Navigator* (Aldershot, 1995), xi, 3–30.

3   B. W. Diffie and G. D. Winius, *Foundations of the Portuguese Empire, 1415–1580* (Minneapolis, MI, 1977), 57–106.

4   C. R. Boxer, *The Portuguese Seaborne Empire 1415–1825* (Harmondsworth, 1973), 15–38; Diffie and Winius, *Foundations of the Portuguese Empire*, 144–65.

5   On the misunderstandings and disappointments that the Portuguese encountered in Calicut, see J. Sarnowsky, *Die Erkundung der Welt. Die großen Entdeckungsreisen von Marco Polo bis Humboldt* (Munich, 2015), 72–7.

6   Ravenstein, *Journal of the First Voyage of Vasco da Gama*, 60.

7   Alpers, *The Indian Ocean*, 70–1.

8   See above, part III 'Red Sea, Arabian Sea, South China Sea', sub-chapter 'The maritime Silk Road'.

9   W. Reinhard, *Geschichte der europäischen Expansion*, vol. I: *Die Alte Welt bis 1818* (Stuttgart, 1983), 50–67; Boxer, *The Portuguese Seaborne Empire*, 39.

10 P. Borschberg (ed.), *Jacques de Coutre's Singapore and Johor 1594–c.1625* (Singapore, 2015), 347–8.

11 C. R. Boxer, *The Great Ship of Amacon. Annals of Macao and the Old Japan Trade, 1555–1640* (Lisbon, 1959), 15–6.

12 Reinhard, *Geschichte der europäischen Expansion*, vol. I, 50–67; Boxer, *The Portuguese Seaborne Empire*, 39–64.

13 S. Subrahmanyam, *The Portuguese Empire in Asia 1500–1700. A Political and Economic History*, 2nd edn (Chichester, 2012).

14 K. Zandvliet, *De Nederlandse ontmoeting met Azië 1600–1950* (Zwolle, 2002), 13–16; Arun Saldanha, 'The Itineraries of Geography: Jan Huygen van Linschoten's Itinerario and Dutch Expedition to the Indian Ocean, 1594–1602', *Annals of the Association of American Geographers* 101 (2011): 149–77.

15 F. S. Gaastra, *The Dutch East India Company: Expansion and Decline* (Zutphen, 2003), 17–23.

16 Ibid., 23–6; Reinhard, *Geschichte der europäischen Expansion*, vol. I, 114.

17 P. Borschberg (ed.), *Journal, Memorials and Letters of Cornelis Matelieff de Jonge. Security, Diplomacy and Commerce in 17th-century Southeast Asia* (Singapore, 2015), 133–8; P. Emmer and J. Gommans, *The Dutch Overseas Empire, 1600–1800* (Cambridge and New York, 2021).

18 K. Glamann, *Dutch-Asiatic Trade 1620–1740* (Copenhagen and The Hague, 1958), 12–21, esp. 14 (Tab. 2); Emmer and Gommans, *The Dutch Overseas Empire*, 254–388.

19 I. Schöffer and F. S. Gaastra, 'The Import of Bullion and Coin into Asia by the Dutch East India Company in the Seventeenth and Eighteenth Centuries', in M. Aymard (ed.), *Dutch Capitalism and World Capitalism* (Cambridge, 1982), 215–33.

20 Gaastra, *The Dutch East India Company*, 127–38.

21 J. G. Taylor, *The Social World of Batavia. European and Eurasian in Dutch Asia*, 2nd edn (Madison, 2009), 3–20; H. E. Niemeijer, *Batavia. Een koloniale samenleving in de zeventiende eeuw* (Amsterdam, 2005).

22 P. Borschberg, 'Ethnicity, Language and Culture in Melaka after the Transition from Portuguese to Dutch Rule', *Journal of the Malaysian Branch of the Royal Asiatic Society* 83, no. 2 (2010): 93–117.

23 P. J. Stern, *The Company-State. Corporate Sovereignty and the Early Modern Foundations of the British Empire in India* (Oxford, 2001), 19–40.

24 O. Prakash, 'The Trading World of the Indian Ocean. Some Defining Features', in Prakash (ed.), *The Trading World of the Indian Ocean*, 24–8; P. A. Van Dyke, *The Canton Trade. Life and Enterprise on the China Coast 1700–1845* (Hong Kong, 2005).

25 Prakash, 'Trading World', 28–30.

26 Ibid., 36–8.

27 K. N. Chaudhuri, *The Trading World of Asia and the English East India Company 1660–1760* (Cambridge, 2006), 237–312; P. Parthasarathi, 'Cotton Textiles in the Indian Subcontinent, 1200–1800', in G. Riello and P. Parthasarathi (eds.), *The Spinning World. A Global History of Cotton Textiles, 1200–1850* (New York, 2009), 17–42.

28 Blussé, *Visible Cities*, 53–5; Chris Nierstrasz, *Rivalry for Trade in Tea and Textiles: The English and Dutch East India Companies (1700–1800)* (Houndmills, 2015).

29 Watson Andaya and Andaya, *Early Modern Southeast Asia*, 338–6.

30 G. A. Nadri, 'Sailing in Hazardous Waters. Maritime Merchants of Gujarat in the Second Half of the Eighteenth Century', in Prakash (ed.), *The Trading World of the Indian Ocean*, 267.

31 See above, part IV 'Mediterranean' and part III 'Red Sea, Arabian Sea, South China Sea', sub-chapter 'The maritime Silk Road'.

32 S. Chaudhury, 'Trading Networks in a Traditional Diaspora. Armenians in India, *c.* 1600–1800', in I. Baghdiantz McCabe et al. (eds.), *Diaspora Entrepreneurial Networks. Four Centuries of History* (Oxford and New York, 2005), 51–72.

33 F. A. Bishara, 'Mapping the Indian Ocean World of Gulf Merchants, *c.* 1870–1960', in A. Sheriff and E. Ho (eds.), *The Indian Ocean. Connections and the Creation of New Societies* (London, 2014), 69–93.

34 A. Sheriff, 'Globalisation with Difference: An Overview', in Sheriff and Ho, *The Indian Ocean*, 27–8.

35 E. A. Alpers, *The Indian Ocean in World History* (Oxford, 2014), 121–4; U. Freitag and W. C. Smith (eds.), *Hadhrami Traders, Scholars and Statesmen in the Indian Ocean, 1750s to 1960s* (Leiden, 1997).

36 See below, chapter VIII 'Pacific', sub-chapter 'Between Canton and California'.

37 J. K. Chin, 'The Hokkien Merchants in the South China Sea, 1500–1800', in Prakash (ed.), *The Trading World of the Indian Ocean*, 433–61; Blussé, *Visible Cities*, 20–3.

38 Chin, 'The Hokkien Merchants', 433–61.

39 Watson Andaya and Andaya, *Early Modern Southeast Asia*, 149.

40 Chin, 'The Hokkien Merchants', 433–61; N. C. Keong, *Trade and Society. The Amoy Network on the China Coast, 1683–1735*, 2nd edn (Singapore, 2015).

41 B. Watson Andaya, '"A People That Range into All the Kingdoms of Asia". The Chulia Trading Network in the Malay World in the Seventeenth and Eighteenth Centuries', in Prakash (ed.), *The Trading World of the Indian Ocean*, 353–86.

42 L. Subramanian, 'Commerce, Circulation and Consumption. Indian Ocean Communities in Historical Perspective', in S. Moorthy and A. Jamal (eds.), *Indian Ocean Studies. Cultural, Social, and Political Perspectives* (New York, 2010), 148–54.

43 M. R. Fernando, 'Commerce in the Malay Archipelago, 1400–1800', in Prakash (ed.), *The Trading World of the Indian Ocean*, 387–431.

44 Watson Andaya and Andaya, *Early Modern Southeast Asia*, 149; P. Borschberg, *The Singapore and Melaka Straits. Violence, Security and Diplomacy in the Seventeenth Century* (Singapore, 2010), 14, 53, 63.

45 J. Lucassen, 'A Multinational and Its Labor Force. The Dutch East India Company, 1595–1795', *ILWCH* 66 (2004): 12–39, 12–17.

46 H. Ketting, *Leven, werk en rebellie aan boord van Oost-Indiëvaarders (1595–1650)* (Amsterdam, 2002), 29–37.

47 Ibid., 88–9.

48 J. R. Bruijn, 'De personeelsbehoefte van de VOC overzee en aan boord, bezien in Aziatisch en Nederlands perspectief', *BMGN* 91 (1976): 218–48, 223; J. Lucassen, 'Zeevarenden', in L. M. Akveld, S. Hart and W. J. van Hoboken (eds.), *Maritieme geschiedenis der Nederlanden,* vol. 2: *Zeventiende eeuw, van 1585 tot ca 1680* (Bussum, 1977), 126–58, 145–50.

49 Lucassen, 'A Multinational and Its Labor Force', 16.

50 Bruijn, 'Personeelsbehoefte van de VOC', 223; Lucassen, 'Zeevarenden', 145–50.

51 Lucassen, 'Zeevarenden', 126–58.

52 J. R. Bruijn, *Schippers van de VOC in de achttiende eeuw aan de wal en op zee*, 2nd edn (Amsterdam, 2008), 163–5.

53 Lucassen, 'A Multinational and Its Labor Force', 19–24; M. van Rossum, *Werkers van de wereld. Globalisering, arbeid en interculturele ontmoetingen tussen Aziatische en Europese zeelieden in dienst van de VOC, 1600–1800* (Hilversum, 2014).

54 D. A. Chappell, 'Ahab's Boat: Non-European Seamen in Western Ships of Exploration and Commerce', in Klein and Mackenthun (eds.), *Sea Changes*, 77.

55 A. Jaffer, *Lascars and Indian Ocean Seafaring, 1780–1960. Shipboard Life, Unrest and Mutiny* (Woodbridge and Rochester, 2015).

56 T. Hoogervorst, 'Sailors, Tailors, Cooks and Crooks. On Loanwords and Neglected Lives in Indian Ocean Ports', *Itinerario* 42, no. 3 (December 2018): 516–48, 519–21.

57 M. van Rossum, 'A "Moorish World" within the Company. The VOC, Maritime Logistics and Subaltern Networks of Asian Sailors', *Itinerario* 36, no. 3 (2012): 39–60, 55.

58 V. W. Lunsford, *Piracy and Privateering in the Golden Age Netherlands* (New York, 2005), 170–5.

59 Wagener, *Kurtze Beschreibung der 35-jährigen Reisen und Verrichtungen, welche Weyland Herr Zacharias Wagner in Europa, Asia, Africa und America, meistentheils zu Dienst der Ost-und West-Indianischen Compagnie in Holland, rühmlichst gethan und abgeleget, aus des Seeligen gehaltenen eigenhändigen Journal.* See C. Ferrão and J. P. Monteiro Soares (eds.), *The 'Thierbuch' and 'Autobiography' of Zacharias Wagener* (Rio de Janeiro, 1997).

60 M. de Bruijn and R. Raben (eds.), *The World of Jan Brandes, 1743–1808. Drawings of a Dutch Traveller in Batavia, Ceylon and Southern Africa* (Zwolle, 2004).

61 'Brief van C. L. Scheitz vanuit Steinberg aan zijn broer, 23 maart 1780', in E. van der Doe, P. Moree and D. J. Tang (eds.), *De Dominee met het stenen hart en andere overzeese briefgeheimen* (Zutphen, 2008), 75–6.

62 Blussé, *Visible Cities*, 35, 49.

63 Zandvliet, *De Nederlandse Ontmoeting*, 24–6.

64 M. North, 'Art and Material Culture in the Cape Colony and Batavia in the Seventeenth and Eighteenth Centuries', in T. DaCosta Kaufmann and M. North (eds.), *Mediating Netherlandish Art and Material Culture in Asia* (Amsterdam, 2014), 111–28.

65 Zandvliet, *De Nederlandse Ontmoeting*, 24–6.

66 G. E. Rumphius, *D'Amboinsche Rariteitkamer* (Amsterdam, 1705).

67 F. Valentyn, *Oud en Nieuw Oost-Indiën* (Dordrecht, 1724–6).

68 Borschberg, *Journal, Memorials and Letters of Cornelis Matelieff de Jonge*, 467f.; J. Villiers, 'The Estado da India in South East Asia', in P. Kratoska and P. Borschberg (eds.), *South East Asia. Colonial History*, vol. 1: *Imperialism before 1800* (London, 2001), 151–78.

69 P. Borschberg, *Hugo Grotius, the Portuguese and Free Trade in the East Indies* (Singapore, 2011), 78–105, and *Singapore and Melaka Straits*, 68–77; T. Brook, *Mr. Selden's Map of China. Decoding Secrets of a Vanished Cartographer* (New York, 2013), 19–44; C. H. Alexandrowicz, *An Introduction to the History of the Law of the Nations in the East Indies (16th, 17th and 18th Centuries)* (Oxford, 1967), 61–82; Steinberg, *Social Construction*, 68–110.

70 See above, part V 'Metropoles on the North and Baltic Sea', sub-chapter 'The Dutch are the "Carryers of the World"'.

71 Steinberg, *Social Construction*, 98.

72 Watson Andaya and Andaya, *Early Modern Southeast Asia*, 301; P. Borschberg, 'Dutch Objections to British Singapore, 1819–1824: Law, Politics, Commerce and a Diplomatic Misstep', *Journal of Southeast Asian Studies* 50, no. 4 (2019): 540–61.

VII

Atlantic:

Expanding horizons and exchanges

In a letter of 1553 the Seville merchant Francisco de Escobar to his business partner in Lima reflects the uncertainties of trade and shipping in the Atlantic, where people on both sides of the ocean eagerly awaited the fleet:

> With the changing times we here [in Seville] may have an excess of merchandise, though you will not there [in Lima]. When you come to Tierra Firme you should in no way or manner sell the house in the city of Lima, because we want to make a new company and have you go back to reside there. Don't take it into your head to come to Castile now, because all Spain is so expensive and high priced that people need great means to be able to support themselves here. I would like you to be there another five or six years, whichever you think best, for the time that the company we are organizing should last [...]. At the moment we are all in necessity because the fleet of which Carreño was general and which left on the 4th of November of last year has not been heard from to this day, nor has any ship come from New Spain or Santo Domingo.[1]

Despite the many imponderables, the Atlantic had been tamed by the mid-sixteenth century and exchange was taking place regularly. This conquest had taken place in several stages, in which perceptions of this ocean as a space changed. When the Vikings crossed the North Atlantic from Iceland to Greenland, it is not clear whether they realized that they were sailing across an ocean or through a number of seas. For the majority of Europeans, the 'Pillars of Hercules' were a barrier, and it was only Christopher Columbus who thought that it was possible to manage the Atlantic. Thereafter, Europeans understood the Atlantic Ocean as a space that could be physically overcome and connected through various hubs. Later seafarers, explorers and merchants recognized that they could also use the Atlantic to reach other oceans such as the Pacific.[2]

Crossing the Atlantic Ocean

In the first half of the fourteenth century, the Genoese Lanzarotto Malocello and Niccoloso da Recco visited the Canary Islands, about which people had vaguely known since antiquity. Portugal at first laid claim to the archipelago, but Castile set out to conquer the islands in 1477 based on a bill of sale between the Catholic kings, Ferdinand and Isabella, and the king and queen of the Canary Islands. It would be some time, however, before the aboriginal population, the Guanches, was subjugated in 1496 and the Canary Islands integrated into the Castilian kingdom. The Canaries served as a sort of launch pad for later expansion to the Americas. Since the islands could be reached by ship in one week from southern Spain, assimilation proceeded quickly. Imported diseases also decimated the native population.[3]

As everywhere in the Americas, the motives of the conquerors were economic, political and religious. The settlers were granted large estates as well as smaller plantations where they grew grain and above all sugar cane. Genoese and Flemish merchants played a large role in the port towns, for it was their capital that built the sugar industry. The islands had about 25,000 inhabitants in 1516. One quarter of them were indigenous and the rest were composed of Spanish and Portuguese settlers and enslaved Africans and Muslims brought to the Canaries to work the sugar plantations.

The islands were an important intermediate stop for ships to stock up on provisions on their way to the Americas. This was also true of the first voyage of the Genoese Christopher Columbus. After his plan to sail westwards and find a sea route to India found no support in Portugal, Columbus was supported for a time by Andalusian magnates. In the autumn of 1491, he was finally able to interest the Catholic Monarchs in his enterprise. The united Spanish Crown was supposed to facilitate loans for the expedition costs and to provide two caravels (the *Pinta* and the *Niña*), while Columbus himself equipped the *Santa Maria*. The agreement, which was quite favourable to him, was surely a result of the Crown's great eagerness to conquer new lands fact in the light of Portuguese advances in India.

On 3 August 1492, Columbus embarked on his voyage from Palos. His first stop was the Canary Islands, which he already departed on 6 September, sailing westwards. He arrived in the Caribbean on 12 October, landing on the island of Guanahani, which he named San Salvador (now Watling Island in the Bahamas). After passing other islands with his ships, he sailed along the coast of Cuba and on 6 December dropped anchor off an island he called La

Española (Hispaniola). The return journey, which began on 16 January 1493, had to be interrupted because of storms both in the Azores and in Lisbon. After an audience with the Portuguese king, who laid claim to the Caribbean islands, Columbus reached Spain on 15 March 1493. There the king and queen received him and the natives he had brought back with him in Barcelona. A few months later, on 25 September 1493, he was able to embark on a second voyage with a larger fleet. It lasted until 1496 and once again sailed to the Antilles. This time, he explored Puerto Rico and the southern coasts of Cuba, Haiti and Jamaica and founded the colony of La Isabela on Hispaniola. In the course of his third voyage Columbus sailed as far as South America and the mouth of the Orinoco River before returning to Hispaniola. In the meantime, however, settlers had complained to the Spanish court about Columbus and his brother who for a time served as commander in La Isabela, so that a new governor was sent there. He had the brothers returned to Spain in chains. The court rehabilitated the explorer and approved a fourth expedition, during which Columbus hoped to find a passage between Cuba and South America. He sailed along the Central American coast from Honduras to Panama, but accidents, hunger, illness and mutinies forced him to turn back. He died in Valladolid in 1506, a disappointed man, who firmly believed that he had been to Asia.[4]

The exploration of the Atlantic world continued without Columbus, however. Amerigo Vespucci reported on the coasts of northern South America, which was named after him although he probably never saw the continent with his own eyes. Giovanni Caboto (John Cabot), an Italian in the service of the English, landed in North America in 1497. Pedro Álvares Cabral reached Brazil and Vasco Núñez de Balboa crossed the Isthmus of Panama in 1513 and saw the Pacific Ocean for the first time, which he named *Mar del Sur*. Juan Ponce de León began exploring the coast of present-day Florida, while Juan Díaz de Solís reached the Rio de la Plata in 1516. The division between the Portuguese and Spanish spheres of interest was significant for the further course of European expansion. For that reason, Isabella of Castile and Ferdinand of Aragón ordered bulls from Pope Alexander VI that were intended to ensure them a monopoly, including a missionary mandate for recently discovered and as yet undiscovered territories. John II of Portugal, in contrast, entered into direct negotiations with Spain. On 7 June 1494, in the Treaty of Tordesillas, the two powers agreed to a demarcation line at 46°30' W of Greenwich. The line ran some 1,200 nautical miles west of the Cape Verde Islands, making part of Brazil (the northeast) Portuguese. Overall, the two nations had divided their spheres of influence in such a way that the Portuguese secured for themselves the African Atlantic coast south of Cape Bojador and thus the route to Asia, while the Spanish could sail the Atlantic north of Cape Bojador unimpeded. The Spanish could travel south-west of the demarcation line, which is how the estuary of the Rio de la Plata, later Argentina, became Spanish.

It was the circumnavigation of the globe by Ferdinand Magellan (1515–22), a Portuguese working for the Spanish, that led to a collision of interests in Southeast Asia. In 1527, the Spanish gained a foothold in the Philippines. They pawned the Spice Islands (Moluccas) to Portugal. With the signing of the Treaty of Saragossa in 1529, the dividing line between the Portuguese and Spanish spheres of influence was defined as 297.5 miles east of the Moluccas.

Columbus was the first to transform the Atlantic from a barrier into a space, although he did not realize he had done so. Since he had wrongly calculated the distance between Europe and Asia, he had as little idea of the size of the Atlantic as Magellan did of the Pacific. It was only with time that people realized that crossing the Atlantic Ocean led not to Asia but to a new continent. Logically enough, the act of passing the 'Pillars of Hercules' came to justify the motto of Spanish world domination (*plus ultra* – further beyond).

The Spanish prepared nautical charts, assisted in their efforts to understand the world by globes produced in Nuremberg. Martín Fernández de Enciso's *Suma de geographia* (1519) already contained sailing instructions for large segments of the world, including the Caribbean. The book was soon translated into English and went through many editions, much like the navigation manual of another Spaniard, Martín Cortés' *Breve compendio de la sphera y del arte de navegar* (1551, 1554).[5]

Those who wished to cross the Atlantic had to be familiar not just with the winds but also with the specific currents. The Canary or Caribbean Current, which ran from Portugal past the Canaries and into the Atlantic, for example, made it easier to reach Barbados or the South American mainland, while the Gulf Stream led from the Caribbean past Bermuda and the Azores or the North Atlantic to the North Sea. It was correspondingly easy for ships to sail to western Europe, while progress in the opposite direction was slower.[6] To determine the ship's position, mariners used navigational instruments like the astrolabe, the Jacob's staff or the quadrant as well as tables of the sun's declination, with the aid of which they sought to discover the height of the stars and thus the latitude.

Ports of departure and routes influenced how people viewed the Atlantic. Thus, from their perspective, the English referred to the North Atlantic as the 'Western Ocean' or North Sea, while viewing the South Atlantic as the 'Ethiopian Sea' and later the 'Spanish Sea'.[7]

There was therefore not just one Atlantic Ocean, but at least three, which differed according to their climate, environment, wind and currents: the North Atlantic initially linked the societies of northern Europe with the fishing grounds of Newfoundland and later the settlements on the East Coast of North American and some Caribbean islands. The Spanish Atlantic connected Seville to the Caribbean and the Spanish possessions in Central and South America. Then there was the Luso-Atlantic (Portuguese Atlantic), which

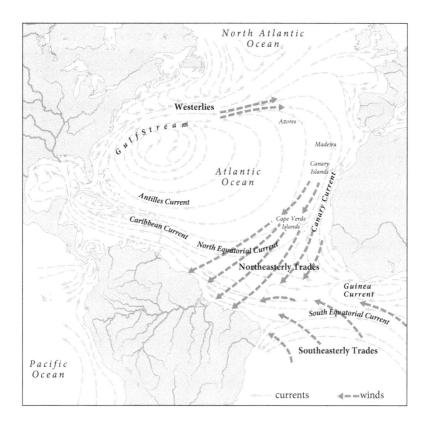

MAP 12 *Winds and currents in the Atlantic Ocean*

extended from Lisbon to Brazil, but also to Africa and to Asia. In the course of the seventeenth and eighteenth centuries the systems grew together, with enslaved Africans serving as an involuntary medium of this cohesion. In this way, with many overlaps, a Black and a White Atlantic arose alongside the American-indigenous one.[8]

The rivalry between the Spanish and the Portuguese

Setting off from the Canaries and the Azores, the Spanish and Portuguese put their stamp on the Middle and South Atlantic. The thirst for gold kept alive the idea of expansion. Since panning for gold in the Caribbean soon proved unproductive and the riches there rarely met explorers' expectations, the conquistadors moved on to Mexico, Central America and Peru. The conquests of Hernán Cortés in Mexico and Francisco Pizarro in Peru profited from the support of indigenous allies who were rebelling against the Aztec and Inca states. The conquistadors strengthened their position by forming strategic alliances with indigenous kingdoms or local elites and laid the foundations of the Spanish Atlantic system.

The indigenous population was decimated by the introduction of European diseases, dropping from 5–10 million in 1519 to 1.5 million in Mexico a century later. At the same time, the discovery of new silver mines and the founding of colonial cities encouraged immigrants to undertake the perilous journey across the Atlantic. Up to 1600, some 50,000[9] Spaniards emigrated to the Caribbean, but above all to New Spain and Peru. The Crown, which issued migration permits,[10] gave preference to officials and clerics, especially members of the religious orders, for the purposes of administering the new territories and converting the native population to Christianity. Viceroys were installed for New Spain (the Caribbean, Mexico and Central America) and Peru (from Panama to the southern tip of South America). Trade as well as travel across the Atlantic was organized by the *Casa de la Contratación* in Seville, while in Seville, Mexico City and Lima merchant guilds known as *consulados* regulated commercial affairs on the ground.[11]

The most significant factor in this connection was the *carrera de Indias*, which was largely conducted using a newly developed type of ship, the galleon. Beginning around 1564 the fleet was divided into two convoys, which set sail from Seville and later from Sanlúcar de Barrameda or Cádiz. The Tierra Firme fleet, known as *galeones*, sailed in August to the ports of Cartagena and later to Nombre de Dios (subsequently replaced by Portobelo) on the Isthmus of Panama. The famous trade fairs took place after their arrival, with merchants purchasing the goods brought by the fleet and transporting them southwards with the help of pack animals, trains of porters and ships. Peruvian silver was transported in the opposite direction from Callao on the Pacific across the Isthmus of Panama to the returning fleet and taken on board. The second fleet, the *flota de Nueva España* (Fleet of New Spain), sailed in April with the help of the trade winds to the Caribbean and further through the Straits of Yucatan (between the Yucatan peninsula and western Cuba) and the Gulf of Mexico to Veracruz, the port of Nueva España (New Spain). For their return journey, the two fleets met in the roads of La Habana, Cuba, where they repaired and provisioned their ships before sailing – with the aid of the westerlies and the Gulf Stream – home to Seville or to Cádiz and Sanlúcar (depending on the size of the ships). The outbound journey of the New Spain fleet took an average of seventy-five days from Cádiz and ninety-one days from Sanlúcar, the same number of days as the return voyage from the Isthmus of Panama to the ports of origin. The mainland fleet (*flota de Tierra-Firme*) took about the same time. The average should be understood solely as orientation, since most voyages were longer or shorter. Apart from bullion, the ships mainly transported cochineal, indigo, skins, sugar, pearls, dyewood and in later centuries also tobacco and cocoa to Spain.[12]

The discovery of silver mines in Potosí (in present-day Bolivia) and the smelting of silver using the amalgamation process led to an expansion of silver exports. The silver was transported across the Andes from Potosí to Lima by lama caravan and then by ship to the Isthmus of Panama and onwards to Europe. From Seville, or in the course of Spain's military engagement in Europe, the silver circulated through the European trade networks. American silver also represented an important component of trade with Asia, which could scarcely have functioned without it. Regular maritime traffic across the Pacific between Acapulco und Manila ensured the circulation of this silver.[13]

In the late sixteenth century, merchants from Mexico facilitated the exchange of commodities between Peru and Asia. Silk and porcelain as well as highly prized lacquer work from China were traded for silver, so that in the seventeenth century, the trade with Manila sometimes surpassed the Spanish Atlantic trade. At the urging of merchants from Seville, the Crown then limited the size and number of ships sailing from Acapulco to Manila. The Atlantic trade declined in the seventeenth century, since Spain, faced with Dutch and English competition, was at times unable to guarantee or safeguard the shipping routes. While official trade declined, smuggling flourished, which meant that American silver continued to flow into Europe in large amounts in the late seventeenth century.[14]

Silver production in Mexico developed more slowly than in Peru and only surpassed it in the 1650s. Cochineal accordingly represented Mexico's most important export commodity. The natives extracted this red dyestuff from insects that lived on cacti. The Crown and its officials demanded that indigenous communities provide tribute in the form of cochineal. Because of silver production and manufactures, a division of labour evolved according to which the rural *haciendas* both produced wheat for the Spanish and maize for the rest of the population and provided beasts of burden (mules, oxen, horses) for the urban and artisanal economy. Apart from local ceramic production, luxury trades for the elites also emerged (gold- and silversmiths, luxury clothing, coaches, furniture). In this way, Mexico became the centre of an intercolonial network, in which wheat from Puebla was traded for tobacco from Cuba, and cocoa and chocolate, which the pre-Columbian elites had consumed, rose to the status of key products in the regional trade system.[15] While a large proportion of the cocoa came from present-day Guatemala, in the seventeenth century 'Venezuela' became the most important producer of cocoa, which was exported in growing quantities to Spain.

At the same time, Cuba's volume of trade and population were rising. The Havana Company took over the monopoly on the tobacco trade in

1740, sending three million pounds of Cuban tobacco annually to the royal tobacco factory in Seville. The growing commodities traffic mirrors not just the successful activities of the trading companies, but also the emergence of a Spanish Atlantic trade system, in which previously peripheral regions such as the Río de la Plata, Chile, Venezuela and Central America were connected by the Atlantic and Pacific Oceans.[16]

The fleets were financed as public–private partnerships, with private individuals providing the funds for equipment and reaping the profits. The Crown or royal legislation guaranteed legal certainty, so that business contracts made in the motherland were equally binding and enforceable in Mexico, Lima or Manila. Local elites ruled the colonies in the king's name and pledged loyalty in return for privileges. Bureaucrats sailed across the Atlantic to take up temporary posts overseas before returning to the metropolises of Madrid and Seville. Family relationships also remained intact, as is evident from wills. Even sailors who were at home throughout the world maintained close relationships to their families in the coastal cities.[17]

Portuguese shipping established the South Atlantic region en route to India. Thus, the exploration of islands like Madeira, the Azores, Cape Verde or São Tomé played an important role in voyages to the Cape of Good Hope. They were not merely the first ports of call for trade and migration, but also intermediate stops for navigation and communication in the Portuguese-speaking Atlantic – a function they continue to fulfil to this day, alongside the booming tourism sector. Islands were important for access to the new mainland. In order to provide for the inhabitants of the islands, agrarian crops were planted that could also be sold in the motherland. Apart from European crops, the Portuguese also cultivated plants native to America and Africa. In the fifteenth century Portuguese farmers and traders settled on Madeira and the Azores along with Flemish farmers recruited by entrepreneurs from the southern Low Countries.

In addition to resins and dyestuffs, the islands provided grain, grapes, wine, salt and beef. Later, sugar production was conducted with slave labour, along with whaling and fishing. Less attractive for Europeans but essential as a resupply station on the voyage to India or Brazil were the volcanic Cape Verde islands some 500 kilometres off the coast of Senegal. The islands were mainly populated by Africans and the Luso-African descendants of interracial relationships, which led to the development of a creole variant of the Portuguese language. Here, too, sugar cane was cultivated alongside cattle, which supplied the needs of ships. Also significant was the archipelago of São Tomé and Príncipe in the Gulf of Guinea, where Portugal settled both marginalized social groups and Jewish children who had been taken away from their parents. The tropical climate with two rainy seasons, water and forests made São Tomé appear ideal for sugar production, in which thousands of enslaved Africans would work. São Tomé evolved into an important hub for enslaved people from the Gulf of Guinea or Angola, who were transported onwards to America.[18]

In the course of the sixteenth century, Portuguese interests extended to Brazil and Angola. In the Kongo, there had initially been a positive exchange between the ruling dynasty, which hoped for military and technical support, and Portugal, which sought to promote Christianization. Soon, however, the interests of slave traders gained the upper hand so that the region served henceforth solely as a source of slaves and ivory. The Portuguese focused on the region of Ndongo (Kongo) in the south of the kingdom and called it Angola after the word for ruler, *ngola*. In Ndongo, as everywhere in Africa, the colonizers encountered established political and social structures as well as traditional trade networks. Accordingly, they could only profit from or participate in the existing structures by cooperating with indigenous networks or by force. In Ndongo they chose force and established the colony of Angola in 1571 with a governor and fortified trading posts. But they could hold their positions only by military aggression, punitive expeditions and temporary alliances with local rulers.

The slave trade continued and attained new dimensions after Pedro Álvares Cabral claimed Brazil for Portugal in 1500. Cabral had landed on the Brazilian coast on his way to India. He abandoned a sailor, who had actually been sentenced to death, among the aboriginal people there, thus inadvertently laying the groundwork for further colonization. It was above all France's interest in the journey to Brazil and the pirate war between the two powers that moved Portugal to recruit European settlers in the 1530s. In those places where the cultivation of sugar cane by enslaved Africans was introduced for economic reasons, there was an impetus for Portuguese settlement. It gained a further boost in 1559 with the appointment of a governor-general and the establishment of a central financial, judicial and military administration as well as the creation of ecclesiastical structures and the activities of Jesuit missionaries.[19]

At this time the coasts were settled from the northeast to Santa Catarina in the south, while the important ports of Salvador, Recife and Rio de Janeiro were laid out on estuaries. Sugar was the largest export commodity. The shared Atlantic world of the Portuguese in Africa and Brazil was shaped by Brazilian sugar and enslaved Africans. Although it was challenged by the Dutch Brazilian adventure between 1630 and 1654,[20] contacts remained, since the Brazilian planters and gold prospectors alike needed labour that only Angola provided. Brazil accordingly became the focal point of the African slave trade. This led to the development of a triangular trade managed mainly by Portuguese in Rio de Janeiro or Lisbon, in which they supplied African trading partners with sugar, tobacco and rum as well as smuggled American silver.[21]

Sugar flowed across the seas from Brazil to Portugal and further to the Netherlands, England and other European countries where it was traded for textiles and other finished goods. Colonial products like rum and tobacco were used to pay for slaves. Portuguese ships also supplied Asian spices, again in exchange for sugar.[22]

The Brazilian gold boom had a substantial impact on the European world. Extensive gold deposits were discovered in the years 1693–5 in the Brazilian territories that now make up the state of Minas Gerais. The news unleashed a gold rush and attracted prospectors from the Brazilian coastal areas as well as Portugal to the gold mining town of Vila Rica de Ouro Preto. As part of the royal right of mineral extraction, the Portuguese Crown taxed each gram of gold found in Minas Gerais and the other mines of Goiás and Mato Grosso. In this way, and through trade, 10–15 tonnes of gold annually came from Brazil to Portugal and Europe in the eighteenth century. The main beneficiary of the gold was England, which supplied both textiles and enslaved people to Portugal or rather Brazil.[23]

Sugar, slaves and furs: The Dutch, English and French

Connections between the South and North Atlantic, but also between the Atlantic and the North and Baltic Seas and the South Atlantic and the Indian Ocean, were maintained by the Dutch, who devoted themselves to the Atlantic trade from the late sixteenth century. Dutch voyages to the West Indies and Africa are inextricably linked with the West India Company (WIC), which was founded in 1621, after the Twelve Years' Truce between the Netherlands and Spain in the Eighty Years' War. Like the earlier VOC, the WIC's aim was to concentrate Dutch trade with these parts of the world and above all to put an end to the competition between the existing Dutch trading companies. The WIC was organized as a joint-stock company. Only a few merchants long involved in trade with the Caribbean, Brazil and Guinea invested larger sums, and they also became directors of the company. The initial capital of some seven million guilders could only be raised, however, because the inhabitants of cities not directly associated with shipping also invested substantial sums.

At first, the WIC enjoyed only modest success. The conquest of Spanish and Portuguese possessions soon exhausted the capital. Had Piet Heyn not seized the silver fleet coming from Mexico off the coast of Cuba and brought more than eleven million guilders into the WIC's coffers in 1628, the Company would soon have been forgotten. In order to expand, it needed not just gold imports from Africa but also a solid economic base across the Atlantic. An opportunity opened up in Brazil, where the sugar centre of Olinda was captured and the Dutch entered into alliances with the indigenous population.[24]

The Dutch now dominated the international sugar trade for the first time and, as a consequence, the slave trade as well. Their exploitation of sugar production came to an abrupt end in 1644, however, when a rebellion broke out among Brazilian sugar planters and the Dutch failed to bring it under control. In 1661, north-eastern Brazil was returned to Portugal in exchange for a payment of eight million guilders. Heavily in debt, in the second half of the century the WIC concentrated on supplying the other European powers' West Indian colonies as well as on the slave trade and gold imports from Dutch possessions in Africa. Sugar production had spread in the Caribbean with Dutch know-how and capital, and the Dutch supplied Portuguese, Spanish and English planters with the necessary labour and equipment. The Black population of the islands grew rapidly – from 5,680 individuals in 1645 to 82,023 in 1667 on Barbados – and ever more planters amassed debts with the Dutch traders.

The trade with Spanish America proceeded directly as well as indirectly through the motherland, for it was there that the Dutch earned the silver they needed for purchases in the Baltic but above all in Southeast Asia. The WIC's monopoly on the slave trade with the Spanish colonies ended in 1679, when the Spanish themselves purchased their labour force at the slave markets of English Jamaica. Because of its convenient location off the American coast, Dutch Curaçao continued as the centre of the transit trade with Spanish America and other islands in the Caribbean, which were supplied from there with linen, spices, wax candles, silk and paper.[25]

The Dutch initially settled the North American continent by accident. In 1609, the VOC commissioned the Englishman Captain Henry Hudson to find a northeast passage to Asia. Hudson was actually supposed to sail past Scandinavia and Russia, but when he found himself blocked by Arctic ice he turned around and tried sailing northwest instead. Hoping to find a passage to the Pacific, he encountered the river delta that would later bear his name. After sailing up the river he landed near present-day Albany, where Fort Orange would later become the centre of New Netherland. His account of the voyage, which was published in 1611, attracted seafarers and merchants (the admiralty in Amsterdam sent expeditions in 1611–12) and led to the mapping of the east coast of North America. In 1614, a small Dutch trading company was granted a patent for four years, and traders established Fort Nassau on the upper Hudson that same year. From 1621, New Netherland came under the rule of the WIC. The attraction for the Dutch was furs, especially the beaver pelts offered them by the Algonquin on the Hudson delta and the Mohawk on the upper Hudson.

With time, Dutch settlers also arrived in the Hudson region. In 1624, the *Nieu Nederlandt* docked near Manhattan, with a cargo including seeds, seedlings, cattle and agricultural implements to set up a colony. In 1626 the WIC governor-general Peter Minuit, together with a few settler families from the Netherlands, founded Fort Amsterdam, which would evolve into New Amsterdam and later New York. A vibrant colony arose with 8,000–10,000 inhabitants.[26]

The Dutch Atlantic economy was not based solely on the WIC monopoly over the gold and slave trades and agricultural production in New Netherland, however. It also encompassed merchants who financed sugar production on the Spanish, French and British Caribbean islands. These planters also depended on the Dutch ships that transported Caribbean sugar to the Netherlands, more precisely to the sugar refineries in Amsterdam. In 1660, these refineries processed more than half of all the sugar consumed in Europe.[27]

Dutch supremacy in the Atlantic, however, was diminished by the mercantilist policies of France and England. The first threat came from England, which provoked the First Anglo-Dutch War (1652–4) with the proclamation of the Navigation Act of 1651. The prelude to the Second Anglo-Dutch War (1665–7) played out in the colonies, where the English Royal African Company had succeeded in breaking the Dutch monopoly over the slave trade with the West Indies. England declared war in 1665, but the Dutch fleet bested the financially strapped English fleet. The 1667 Treaty of Breda was a compromise, since the Dutch held back on any excessive claims out of deference to France, which was growing stronger in the south. They sought to remove the most dangerous bones of contention and therefore relinquished New Netherland to the English. In the Caribbean they retained Curaçao and a few smaller islands, and in the North of South America Guyana, which had been conquered in 1667, became Dutch and provided the base for the establishment of the colony of Suriname.[28]

From there Sephardic Jewish merchants in particular built up new trade networks, which extended both across the Caribbean and to the North and South American mainland. One example of this type of trader was David Cohen Nassy. During the uprising of Brazilian planters against Dutch rule and the subsequent persecution of the Jewish population he initially sought refuge in Curaçao. In 1659 he travelled to Cayenne, and from there moved in 1667 to the colony of Guyana, which was English before it was captured by the Dutch. A small group of Jewish settlers were already living there. Nassy was still in contact with Amsterdam and expanded his trading business. It made no difference that New Netherland had become New England. His trading partners were co-religionists in New York, Newport, Rhode Island and above all Boston. Ships from Boston, New York and Connecticut regularly delivered horses, fish and kosher meat, products for which there was strong demand in Suriname. On the return journey from Suriname the ships were loaded with sugar, which they often transported on to Amsterdam via Boston and New York.[29]

Although after its final defeat in the Third Anglo-Dutch War (1672–4) the Netherland could no longer defend its military position in the Atlantic, the WIC continued to trade with the Spanish Caribbean and the mainland from Curaçao until 1713, when the Company had to give up the contract (*asiento*) for the importation of slaves in favour of the English. Nevertheless, a Dutch Atlantic economy developed in the new-won territory of Suriname, with the expansion of a plantation economy based on sugar, coffee and indigo. The launch of a special plantation bond by the banking house of Deutz sparked an economic boom in the Dutch Caribbean. Between 1765 and 1772, some six million guilders a year were invested in bonds, which financed plantations in the Caribbean and Suriname as well as Sumatra.[30]

The Dutch thus continued to shape the Atlantic economy, which however represented but one segment of their global maritime network.[31] Their presence in the Atlantic differed accordingly, both quantitatively and qualitatively, from that of other Europeans. The Dutch colonies were multi-ethnic, multi-lingual and multi-religious. Dutch, Germans, Huguenots, Jewish settlers and people of other European origins lived there together with enslaved Blacks and mestizos as well as the indigenous population.[32] Specific creole languages, such as the Papiamentu spoken on Curaçao and other islands, are evidence of this multicultural interaction. Papiamentu began on the West Coast of Africa as an Afro-Portuguese creole and came to the Dutch Caribbean with enslaved people from the region. Unlike Jamaican Patois or Haitian Kreyòl, it did not derive from the language of the colonizers but was probably also fostered by the immigration of Sephardic Jews from Brazil.[33]

England sent mainly indentured servants and convicts to North America in the seventeenth century. The lofty words Richard Hakluyt used in the programme for Atlantic expansion that he presented to Elizabeth I in 1584, which aimed to make England economically self-sufficient by settling America, soon gave way to disenchantment.[34]

While propaganda by Hakluyt and others led to a number of settlement endeavours such as those in Roanoke Island (1580s), Jamestown, Virginia (1607) and Bermuda (1609) or New England in the 1620s with the arrival of the so-called Pilgrims,[35] despite enthusiasm most English colonies in North America remained inhospitable places whose settlers had to struggle for sheer survival. Britain was overpopulated in the sixteenth and seventeenth centuries, but the resulting migration went mainly to the large towns and then above all to Ireland, which English, Welsh and Scottish settlers made increasingly British over the centuries. While Scots migrated to Ireland – but in the seventeenth century to the Baltic region as well – the English left for North America, especially the Chesapeake Bay, and the Caribbean.[36] Frequently, the settlers' masters treated them like chattel and traded them for goods or land. John Stotter, who arrived in Barbados from London on the *Falcon* in 1635, was still an indentured servant five years later, and was sold along with a hog and some farm implements.

In this early period, ship's passages were still uncertain and irregular. It was up to every captain, ship owner or merchant to give priority to the needs of trade or of passengers.[37] Companies and plantation owners used promotional flyers to recruit a labour force. Two-thirds of the 300,000 English migrants ended up in the Caribbean, where many succumbed to the murderous climate. They represented but a fraction of overall migration, with the forced migration of enslaved Africans making up the majority of arrivals. The European immigrants were largely male, while one-third of enslaved people were female. This explains the divergent demographic development, since white indentured servants could not reproduce, and slaves could do so only under difficult conditions. This means that the colonies could not have survived without further migration. It was only in the late seventeenth century, with the founding of Pennsylvania, that England possessed a number of viable colonies whose inhabitants however no longer came solely from the British Isles. The mobility of migrants, who moved from the American mainland to the Caribbean and other regions, proved important for future developments.

Sailors built networks between the emerging central ports and the territories on the periphery. At the same time, ties were retained with London, so that a fabric of relationships arose between the motherland, the North American mainland and the West Indies. Trade and migration across the Atlantic and to the Caribbean linked the various regions and cemented contacts between England and its colonies as well as those of the other European states. These connections were also maintained by a steady stream of letters and personal encounters on both sides of the ocean.[38]

At first, fishing and fur-trapping provided the only economic benefits for those English settlers who crossed the Atlantic. It was not until they began cultivating agricultural products that could be sold for such high prices on the European market that transporting them across the Atlantic was worth the expense that settlers gained a more solid economic footing. This was what supplied 'the Americans' with the money and credit to buy the European goods and tools they needed. Until then, they tried their luck with Caribbean products. The seizure of Jamaica from Spain in 1655 also allowed the English to participate in the wealth of Spanish America through trade, smuggling and plunder. Ships from New England smuggled sugar or tobacco, covered with a thin layer of fish or flour. The export regulations of the Navigation Act hindered trade, however.

The tobacco that was grown in Virginia from the second decade of the seventeenth century accordingly put settlers on the American mainland on a new economic basis. Tobacco was easy to cultivate and required no large investments. The high price commanded by tobacco in Europe made it extremely profitable. This led to the expansion of cultivation in the Chesapeake colonies and other regions as well as to further emigration to America. The tobacco import figures (10 million pounds in 1660; 50 million in 1730; 100 million in 1770 with a growing proportion of re-exports) point to the commodity's central significance as well as shifting consumer demand in the eighteenth century. Tobacco had also played a role in the Caribbean, but it was displaced by sugar. In the late seventeenth century, these crops were joined by a further agricultural product grown mainly in the Carolinas: rice. Indigo cultivation also began on a grand scale. All three commodities – sugar, rice and indigo – depended on slave labour and brought with them a further stream of enslaved people into the Caribbean and the American mainland. The plantation colonies in the South became an important market for the colonies in the North, which offered no products – apart from furs – for which there was a market in England. Apart from cereals and fish, the North supplied salted meat and timber as a raw material for barrels and building as well as firewood to the South and the Caribbean, where clearing for sugar plantations had largely destroyed the forests.[39]

The 'wealth gap' between the Northern and Southern colonies was very apparent. Merchants who operated super-regionally, such as Philip English in Salem, who sent his ships to Barbados, Honduras, Suriname, Bilbao, Madeira, the Azores and along the coast of Nova Scotia as well as to Virginia, profited from this gap.[40] In the course of the eighteenth century, new Atlantic shipping connections were also established to Vigo, Bilbao, Campeche, Cayenne, Ceuta, Cowes, Providence Island and more.

The Indian Ocean with its range of goods was also integrated into the Atlantic trade via Europe. Asian silk, porcelain and, in the eighteenth century, Chinese tea were shipped to the North American colonies via England. Ships also regularly sailed to the Indian Ocean from New York, Boston or Rhode Island. The lines between trade and privateering were not always clear, since any private commercial enterprise outside the monopoly claimed by the East India Company was deemed piracy and could become deadly if the ship encountered an English warship. Nevertheless, American merchants like the New Yorkers Frederick and Adolph Philips ordered porcelain and lacquer work. They equipped the *Margarete* and commissioned its Captain Samuel Burges to trade for these commodities in Madagascar and elsewhere.[41]

French migration across the Atlantic began with fishermen from St Malo on the Atlantic coast, whose economy was closely associated with colonial expansion. The main attraction was the furs offered by the native peoples, which were prized as especially fashionable in Europe. Even before the establishment of permanent settlements, the French engaged in close economic exchange with native tribes.

Jacques Cartier arrived at the St Lawrence River while searching for the fishing grounds of Newfoundland in the 1530s, but returned to France, and it was only Samuel de Champlain's discoveries in the early seventeenth century that provided the impetus to found a trading company, the Compagnie de la Nouvelle France, in 1627.[42]

Apart from a small number of French settlers who emigrated to Canada at this period and from there to French Louisiana in the eighteenth century, most of the French, like the English, settled in the Caribbean. In the French Caribbean, too, African slaves made up the majority of new arrivals. Some 800,000 Africans were brought to Saint-Domingue (Haiti) and 200,000 to Martinique. The slave population was smaller on Guadeloupe and the North American mainland. Since the French Crown forbade non-Catholics from emigrating to their colonies, French Huguenots settled in the Dutch or English territories, in New York or the Cape Colony.

Unlike mainland North America, France's Caribbean colonies became centres of large-scale sugar, coffee and indigo production. Especially in Saint-Domingue, planters, often free Blacks, founded coffee plantations in the mountains. The colonial plantation economy would give a new impetus to French commerce in Europe. For example, thanks to the boom in the plantation economy, French merchants came to dominate markets like Hamburg in the mid-eighteenth century. Settlement projects such as Kourou in French Guyana failed, since the majority of settlers fell victim to endemic yellow fever. This settlement was accordingly recalled in France primarily as a deadly prison camp. Like most Caribbean islands, Saint-Domingue, Martinique and Guadeloupe depended on food and timber from New England, and the ships returned north with legal or illegal cargoes of molasses.[43]

The plantation boom on the French islands in the Atlantic had far-reaching political consequences. The French national assembly banned slavery throughout France in 1794 as a result of the slave uprising in Saint-Domingue. The attempt to reverse emancipation in the early nineteenth century led to renewed revolution in Haiti and independence in 1804. In Guadeloupe and Guyana, in contrast, Blacks were enslaved again, and in Martinique, which was under British occupation, slavery had never been abolished. The outcomes of Haitian independence included the rise of Cuba as a significant sugar producer and the sale of Louisiana to the United States in 1803.

As a consequence of the defeat by Britain, France withdrew from the North American continent in 1763 and ceded Louisiana to Spain. In 1800, Napoleon took Louisiana back to re-establish a French colonial empire in North America and the Caribbean. The continual resistance in Haiti, however, motivated Napoleon to accept President Jefferson's offer, and 530 million acres changed hands for 15 million dollars. The native peoples who lived on the land transferred from France to the United States were not asked, although they controlled most of it.[44]

Refugees from Haiti, white and free Black planters, at first sought refuge in Cuba, but the Spanish governor drove them out after receiving news of the French invasion of Spain. In 1809 these Haitians moved on to Louisiana, where they settled in New Orleans and gradually disseminated French Revolutionary ideas about slavery and emancipation.[45]

Black Atlantic

While the role of Africans and thus of the Black Atlantic[46] are now at the centre of historical interest, 'Atlantic' historians have paid comparatively less attention to the earlier periods. Before the arrival of the Europeans, the seas played only a minor role in the lives of Africans. There were a few ports, especially on the Indian Ocean, but connections to the Arab world and the Mediterranean were maintained via the Trans-Saharan trade route and organized by Muslim slave traders. Naturally, people fished in the sea and traded salt on the coasts, but the great rivers and lagoons of West Africa rendered journeys into the Atlantic superfluous. This would change fundamentally in the sixteenth century, since some twelve million enslaved Africans would be transported across the Atlantic over the following three centuries. Around 1.5 million of them never arrived in the Americas because they died along the way. In the course of the slave trade, an infrastructure[47] developed with thousands of interpreters, soldiers, skippers and guards who facilitated the operation of the slavery system. Accordingly, many Africans gathered maritime knowledge by supplying the European ships, which anchored a few miles off the coast, from shuttle boats. Former fishing villages, salt production sites like Luanda, Cabinda and Benguela in present-day Angola or James Fort and Saint Louis in the Senegambia became ports. This was in addition to the numerous settlements of the European powers, such as Elmina, which was Portuguese and after 1637 Dutch. Although historians long viewed gold and slaves as the most important commodities in trade with Western Africa and claimed that the Europeans were dominant, more recent scholarship reveals a more varied range of goods as well as the central role of Africans[48] in this exchange. In order to concentrate trade on the coast or small islands, local rulers long restricted European trading posts to the coastal regions. Only in Angola were the Portuguese able to conquer and permanently occupy land. The so-called European forts and trading posts were also in reality African-European joint ventures and served primarily as protection from other European powers.[49]

The slave trade accelerated commercialization in West Africa. The merchants gained in significance along with new dynasties in the hinterlands. Relationships of credit and trust developed between Europeans, especially representatives of the trading companies, and Africans; this also applied to ship's captains, who regularly returned to the same towns and their familiar trading partners. Above all, African rulers and merchants were well informed about the available European goods and compared them with their own manufactured products. Colleen Kriger has made a detailed study of African textile production and the textile trade. Africans were producing cotton fabrics before the arrival of the Europeans, such as the so-called Benin Cloth, which Europeans transported to the Gold Coast, to Angola, São Tomé, the West Indies and Brazil. Alongside local fabrics, imported textiles such as dyed and printed cottons from India were also in demand.[50]

West African traders familiar with the variety of goods were highly selective, which increased the cost of trading with the Africans. Thus, for example, the king of the Ashanti kingdom on the Gold Coast ordered a brass bed with cotton curtains from the merchants of the Royal African Company in 1706, leading the English to wonder about the origin of his concrete wishes.[51]

As to payment, there were marked regional preferences, for instance for cowries from the Indian Ocean on the Bight of Benin and tobacco from Brazil on the Slave Coast. In exchange, the Europeans acquired leather, pepper, beeswax, gum arabic, dyewoods and palm oil as well as gold, ivory and enslaved Africans.

Enslavement was widespread and considered perfectly legitimate. The trans-Saharan slave trade, as well as that with the Indian Ocean, which dated back to antiquity, was similar in scope to the transatlantic slave trade. The Europeans therefore merely had to integrate into and expand existing networks. The slave trade also had structural effects within Africa. Since the slave trade promised profits, more Africans were captured and enslaved than sold across the Atlantic, that is, the number of enslaved people in Africa increased as well. Historians have argued that Africans were willing participants in and beneficiaries of the slave trade, often even dictating the terms of trade.[52] Although African leaders were involved, many Africans opposed participation.[53] Especially in the second half of the eighteenth century, there were revolts, rebellions and the famous revolution of Senegambia. This movement was led by African Muslim clerics and their peasant disciples, who overthrew hereditary slaving kings in 1776 and abolished the Atlantic slave trade in the Senegal River Valley.[54]

One result of the trans-Atlantic slave trade was the emergence of an African diaspora in the Americas, which led among other things to the spread of African religious beliefs and practices. Maintaining their religious beliefs was also a form of resistance to enslavement. A continuity of religious practice is very apparent in places such as Brazil and Cuba where Africans lived in large numbers. There, Africans merged their existing beliefs with Christianity. In both Brazil and Cuba, enslaved people linked the *orisas (orichas)*, the deities of their Yoruba religion, with Catholic saints. For example, in the Afro-Cuban syncretic religion of *Santería* (way of the saints), the *oricha* Babalú Ayé, originally associated with disease and healing, is identified with St Lazarus. Like Brazilian *Candomblé* (dance in honour of the gods), *Santería* rituals incorporate song, dance, drumming (*toque de santo*) and animal sacrifice. Similar practices are discernible in Haitian *voudou*, which had its origins in a mixture of indigenous Kongolese traditions and Portuguese Catholicism in the sixteenth and seventeenth centuries but was later overlaid with West African elements in the Caribbean.[55]

These religious practices are examples of a syncretic cultural continuity from Africa to the Americas, also reflected in the Black African-Iberian brotherhoods that already existed in Africa before Africans were shipped to the Americas as slaves. The brotherhoods served as strategies of cooperative resistance aimed at negotiating life in bondage, not just in Latin America, but possibly also in North America.[56] Another form of resistance by enslaved people was to escape and join forces in *maroon* communities to protect their independence from plantation owners. In some places, runaway slaves allied with indigenous peoples. One such instance was the Black Seminoles, African Americans who escaped from the rice plantations in Carolina and established their own free settlements in the Florida wilderness, adopting elements of Native American and Spanish cultures.

How Africans became (African-)Americans differed from place to place. However, a variety of African identities emerged that remain visible today in festivities such as carnival.

Africans were more important for the Atlantic world than the Atlantic world was for Africans.[57] This becomes clear when we examine the introduction of African plants and ways of life into the Americas. After their arrival, for example, Africans cultivated plants they had brought with them by ship. They also consumed the fruits of Asian plants that had arrived in Africa long before the transatlantic slave trade. These included taro and yam roots, ginger and bananas. In West African ports, slave ship captains bought not just South American imports such as maize, manioc, peanuts and sweet potatoes, but also African foods such as millet, rice, yams and black-eyed peas. The kola nut, which was known for its stimulant properties, was also used to improve the quality of the drinking water stored on ships. With the help of this nut, which was placed inside the water barrels, water that had grown brackish during the long transatlantic voyage could be purified and made potable again. After arriving in the Americas, enslaved people tried to cultivate familiar plants. Plantation owners discovered new plants in their slaves' gardens and cooking pots and to this day some dishes, like the famous gumbo from New Orleans, bear African names.[58]

Africans crossed the Atlantic on the Middle Passage not just as slaves, but also as sailors. One of the most interesting protagonists was Olaudah Equiano, who published an autobiography in 1789. In this book he recounts his birth in West Africa, his capture, enslavement and transportation to the Caribbean on a slave ship. According to other sources, Equiano was born in South Carolina and, after buying his freedom, was given the name Gustavus Vassa after the Swedish king.[59] He spent only a brief time on a plantation, however, and was sold in 1754 to Lieutenant Michael Henry Pascall of the Royal Navy. As the lieutenant's servant he participated in several naval battles during the Seven Years' War and eventually arrived in London. Contrary to his hopes, he was again sold as a slave in the West Indies, but his new master Robert King, a Quaker on the island of Montserrat, recognized Equiano's abilities and sent him on slaving voyages to South Carolina and Georgia as a skipper. His private trading activities allowed Equiano to buy his freedom for 70 pounds in 1766 and return to London. From there he not only sailed back to North America and the Caribbean but also to Smyrna (Izmir) in the eastern Mediterranean. In 1773 he even took part as a volunteer in the Royal Navy's expedition to the North Pole.[60] After a further interlude as a slave overseer on the Mosquito Coast,[61] he was entrusted after the American Revolutionary War with the task of settling impoverished Black loyalists in Sierra Leone. He was dismissed before he could do so, however, and thereafter devoted himself to the cause of abolishing slavery.[62] He travelled through Britain on a reading tour and married one of the female admirers he met along the way.[63]

Indigenous Atlantic

Although the indigenous Americas made up much of the western hemisphere into the late nineteenth century, they are often mentioned only in connection with the so-called Columbian Exchange, which the historian Alfred W. Crosby defines as the transfer of American plants and animals such as maize, potatoes, peanuts, tobacco, coffee, cocoa and also turkeys to Europe and vice versa.[64] When the indigenous side is discussed, it is frequently primarily in reference to the introduction of diseases from Europe such as smallpox, which decimated a significant proportion of the native population of Central and South America. This discussion overlooks the fact that the indigenous peoples played different roles in different places, not just because Europeans dictated the conditions, but also because the indigenous communities were characterized by a variety of environments and ways of life both before and after the arrival of the Europeans.

Only in Spanish America was the native population integrated administratively and religiously into a colonial empire. In other cases, the indigenous population existed on the margins and frontiers of a colonial empire or colonial settlements, where the *modus vivendi* was always being renegotiated. Native peoples interacted and communicated with traders, missionaries and soldiers, with negotiation processes ranging from peaceful exchange to military conflict. A large number of them also lived outside the empires, and they have accordingly been ignored by colonial history.

Europeans first encountered the indigenous population in the Caribbean. Inhabitants of the region had crossed from the mainland some 6,000 years before by boat. They lived from the sea and soon also found animals and plants in the interior of the islands. Later generations engaged in agriculture and trades.[65] The colonial sources describe indigenous Caribbean society as hierarchically structured, with elected chieftains referred to as 'captains' at the top. Especially in conflicts with the English or French, these captains commanded a large number of warriors. One example was 'Captain' Warner, son of the English governor of St Christopher (St Kitts) and a Caribbean native woman, who, as leader of Dominica, came to the aid of the English with 600 men in 17 canoes during the 1663 assault on St Lucia. The captain's position included the possession of a canoe, known as a *piragua*, with a crew of forty to fifty men, which could transport larger cargoes and operated in fleets or convoys. The Caribs turned plundering Spanish ships into a lucrative sideline, which inspired the English on Jamaica to engage them to attack Spanish towns, ships and mule trains.[66]

Another group were the Taínos, whom the Europeans distinguished from the warlike Caribs, describing them as 'peaceful farmers' and adopting their hammocks. The Taínos had settled the Bahamas, the Greater Antilles and the northern Lesser Antilles by canoe, probably navigating northwards from the Orinoco valley. Columbus encountered them on Hispaniola and soon demanded tribute in the form of gold dust. Since the Taínos could not produce as much as gold as expected, men, women and children were forced to work in the gold fields. Mortality among the Taínos rose tremendously, and the Spaniards began to import enslaved people from West Africa and the Canary Islands to replace the dwindling population.[67]

In the past decade, historians have turned their attention to relations between indigenous peoples and Europeans on the northern Atlantic coast. In these cold and temperate climate zones, the initial encounter between Europeans and Native Americans proved less deadly and even economically advantageous for both sides. The fur trade in North America developed via the Algonquin, who as fishermen learnt to appreciate the usefulness of metal (for instance for kettles, fishhooks, knives or axes). In exchange, the Algonquin offered beaver pelts from which modern beaver hats were fashioned in Europe.[68]

The Native Americans were experts in shipbuilding and their longest canoes could transport more people than the smaller European ships. Many native peoples regarded the Europeans, most of whom could not swim, as unseaworthy. For peoples such as the Wabanaki of northern New England and the Canadian Maritimes, the sea was imbued with spiritual power, and it was the sea with its rich population of mammals, fish and shellfish that had caused the Wabanaki to move from the hinterlands to the coast some 3,000 years before.[69] The animating power of water was reflected not just in Wabanaki folklore, but in practices such as bathing infants in seal oil and acquainting two-year-old toddlers with the sea.[70] The divergent maritime cultures nevertheless began to interact with one another. The Native Americans learnt fishing and sailing techniques from the Europeans, while the colonists imitated the native canoes, which were better suited to navigating in shallow waters.

The Wabanaki traded with the Europeans, but also raided their fishing camps, settlements, ships and sailors. With the decline of the beaver population around 1700, plundering ships and taking sailors captive opened up new economic perspectives.[71] Through cooperation and competition, the Wabanaki succeeded in playing the French and the English against each other, and partially integrated the European settlers into their dominion. This changed with France's withdrawal from the North American continent in 1763.

Further south, we witness the interactions between various Algonquin-speaking tribes and a small number of Europeans on the so-called saltwater frontier.[72] Trade with foreigners empowered chiefs to overcome their native rivals. Wampum, strings of polished beads made of shells originally used by the north-eastern native peoples as sacred objects in rituals of diplomacy and storytelling, became the means of exchange not only between the native peoples and the Europeans, but also in New Netherland and New Amsterdam.[73] With the arrival of new colonists and English expansion at the end of the seventeenth century, exchanges between the various maritime cultures took new forms, as conflicts over coastal resources rose. Whale oil replaced wampum as a key commodity that linked communities and fostered whaling by the coastal natives, and whaling shaped their economic activities. A few of them, such as Paul Cuffe, rose to prominence as whalers and shipowners. Born on a farm as the son of a freed slave and a native Wampanoag mother (and later also married to a native girl), Cuffe went on several whaling voyages in the 1770s. After the Revolutionary War, he opened a shipyard and a shipping business for whaling expeditions and trading voyages. He became an active abolitionist, and in the early nineteenth century personally participated in the resettlement of free Blacks in the British colony of Sierra Leone, sailing there several times.[74]

European fur traders were integrated into indigenous societies and networks early on, aided by their alliances with native women. European goods were already circulating in Huron and Iroquois society before they ever saw settlers in larger communities. Apart from fur traders, who were in close contact with their Indian suppliers, Jesuit missionaries were the only Europeans interested in exchange and contact with native societies, and who succeeded in establishing 'Christian' communities among the Iroquois.[75] The French did little to consolidate their state power in North America, and the competition between France and Britain in the eighteenth century gave the indigenous tribes ample opportunity to renegotiate their autonomy.[76]

The native tribes were primarily interested in acquiring firearms. The French delivered them to the Hurons and Innu of the St Lawrence River in Québec and the Dutch to the Iroquois on the Hudson. The Iroquois in turn monopolized the trade in arms, tools and textiles by supplying these goods to other tribes in the hinterlands in exchange for furs.[77]

In southern North America, in the Carolinas, furs and skins, especially deerskin, were also much sought-after commodities. Trade convoys were sent several thousand miles into the interior from Charleston, where the Creeks had long been exchanging goods and gifts with the Spanish in Florida, the French in Louisiana and the English in Carolina.[78]

The horse offered the Native Americans new mobility and new economic opportunities. The Comanches are a good example, since they managed to build their own empire based on horse breeding and trading. Their trade network encompassed not just Spanish and French territories but also the Indian societies of the Great Plains and tribes in the East and West. Horses, weapons, furs and agricultural products flowed through these commercial channels and the Comanche empire expanded with the aid of trade, war, treaties and clientele systems.[79]

The emerging European colonial structures offered incredible new possibilities for Native Americans in particular. The colonial powers were able to operate and pursue their own agenda within the often-overlapping frontier territories of the various nations. Accordingly, intercultural spaces of interaction arose that were characterized – independent of European-native relations – by both violence and peaceful exchange. Clientele relationships were at the heart of determining affiliation and proximity to or distance from the chief and tribal elders.[80] This complexity would not change fundamentally up to the second half of the nineteenth century, although the European sources sometimes suggest otherwise.

Seamen, buccaneers and pastors

Transatlantic connections were created through commercial, administrative, religious and familial networks. They would have been impossible, however, without the hardships and perils faced by seafarers. What Edward Barlow, for example, wrote in his journal around 1700 offers eloquent testimony about life as a sailor:

> At night when we went to take our rest, we were not to lie still above four hours; and many times when it blew hard were not sure to lie one hour, yea, often [we] were called upon before we had slept half an hour and forced to go up into the maintop or foretop to take in our topsails, half awake and half asleep, with one shoe on and the other off, not having time to put it on: always sleeping in our clothes for readiness; and in stormy weather, when the ship rolled and tumbled as though some great millstone were rolling up one hill and down another, we had much ado to hold ourselves fast by the small ropes from falling by the board.[81]

After finding apprenticeships to a bleacher and a publican not to his liking, Edward Barlow signed on as a ship's boy. When he ended his seafaring days in 1703 at the age of sixty-one, he had spent nearly fifty years on some thirty different ships and seen most of the known world. He sailed not just the Baltic and the Mediterranean but also the Atlantic and the Caribbean on his way to Brazil, Barbados and Jamaica. He had not only been to India and China several times on the ships of the East India Company, but had experienced a good deal more besides: a near-shipwreck off Mauritius, imprisonment by the Dutch in the East Indies, the brothels of Calicut and the regular bloody conflicts on board among the ragtag crews. British seamen served with sailors from the Netherlands, France and Spain, but also Africa, North America and the Caribbean as well as parts of Asia. For Black sailors from the Caribbean, in particular, seafaring represented a freedom unavailable to them as plantation slaves, although they often encountered discrimination on board and worked in lower status positions as cooks, servants or musicians.[82]

The complaints of Barlow and other sailors revolved around the same topics: strict discipline, uncertain pay, poor food and frequent injustice. The 'tyranny' of ship's captains and officers in particular, which often led to mutinies that were violently put down, shows the seas in a different light than we are accustomed to from mercantile correspondence or private letters. Aside from the dangers to life and limb from corporal punishment, shipwrecks, capture and imprisonment, sailors found wage cuts especially painful, a method resorted to by merchants when they held the crew responsible for the loss of or damage to their goods.

This was particularly important because sailors' more meagre wages meant that they could not afford sufficient food in port either. In the light of this circumstance, it is truly surprising that Barlow held out for so many decades and did not look for alternative employment.[83]

Alongside those pirates who operated on their own account, and who were feared and pursued as marauders on the high seas, freebooters operated on public commission and were referred to as buccaneers or privateers. The governors of Jamaica issued letters of marque or licences to the buccaneers who were to terrorize Spanish settlers and ship's captains. Their activities included the capture of Porto Bello in 1668 and Panama in 1670 by Henry Morgan. The freebooters fought on all sides, but also resisted control by their masters. A successful buccaneer like Morgan was able to rise to the position of governor of Jamaica but, once fallen into disfavour, he found himself imprisoned in the Tower of London. The line between pirates and freebooters was unclear, although the private business of freebooters, who frequently acted on commission from the state, was often in the foreground.

One of the most famous of these was William Dampier, who also undertook voyages of exploration on a grand scale. He was especially notable for linking the world of the Atlantic with that of the Pacific and the Indian Ocean. Over the course of his life (1651–1715), Dampier circumnavigated the globe three times, primarily in pursuit of Spanish silver. But he was also interested in exotic flora, fauna and people, and wrote about them in his famous journal.

The son of a Somerset farmer, Dampier crossed the Atlantic to Newfoundland on a merchantman in order to participate in the Third Anglo-Dutch War in the Caribbean. He then joined a group of buccaneers who attempted to plunder Porto Bello and Panama following the example of Captain Morgan. The failure of this enterprise took him to the Pacific, where he and his cronies reached Guam while in pursuit of a Manila galleon. Since they only managed to capture smaller ships, however, Dampier spent his time describing the native plants and people. Finally, they sailed to Australia via the Philippines and from there further into the Indian Ocean. His 1697 book *A New Voyage Round the World*[84] became a bestseller and attracted the attention of the English admiralty.

Several freebooter missions during the War of the Spanish Succession (1700–13/14) eventually led to the capture of a Spanish galleon off the coast of Mexico. After retiring to London, Dampier wanted to do something for his reputation and secure his legacy as a naturalist. This was understandable at a time when the European states were trying to draw a line between privateering and war, that is, between piracy on the one hand and the legal exercise of violence on the other.[85]

Although piracy continues to be mythologized in films and books, it represents a continuous chapter of violence on the seas.[86] The years 1716–27 are considered the golden age of piracy, in which the only recently established 'Atlantic' economic cycle was lastingly disrupted and destabilized.

Pirates followed the pattern of buccaneers and freebooters and chose to base themselves in the Caribbean, but also in the Indian Ocean. The Bahamas, in particular, which the English Crown neither defended nor governed, attracted

FIGURE 7 *Thomas Murray, Portrait of William Dampier (1651–1715).*
© *National Portrait Gallery, London (NPG 538).*

pirates in large numbers. The African coasts were also not free of piracy, and Madagascar, for example, was used to store booty and also served for a time as a pirate base.

The pirates mainly came from the merchant vessels. Given the working conditions on these ships, it could be quite attractive to hire on with pirates. The food was more abundant, the pay better and the working hours shorter. The spoils were shared according to abilities and functions on the ship, with the profit differentials less than on merchant or naval ships. While the pirate flag, the Jolly Roger, conveyed a group identity, the sailors on merchantmen identified far less with their captains, shipowners or charterers.

Pirates were, however, considered a threat to commercial networks and pursued as such. At the end of the seventeenth century, the British tried to convince the pirates to give up by offering them amnesty, which was unacceptable to the majority of pirates, though, since it would have meant a return to their previous miserable conditions on board the merchant ships. For that reason, the British intensified the war against pirates and enjoyed some success. As a deterrent, between 500 and 600 pirates were publicly hanged in the Caribbean ports in the years 1716–21. Similarly, all those who aided pirates were threatened with execution.

The mass hangings, for example of the crew of Black Bart Roberts (1722), together with a publicity campaign by clerics and officials, finally led to success. Piracy as an occupation became less attractive and the number of pirates fell, also because the Royal Navy was looking for sailors again. Unlike their opponents, the merchants and the government, the pirates, at least in the Caribbean, did not manage to build stable social and economic networks, which would have helped them to secure their position and ensure permanent recruitment.[87] Only the Barbary pirates of North Africa, who operated in the Mediterranean and the eastern Atlantic, succeeded in doing so.[88]

Sailors, privateers and pirates were not the only ones to influence or connect the Atlantic or other seas. The many soldiers who served in the Dutch East and West India Companies sailed the oceans of the world and wrote accounts from time to time and were also part of this world, as were missionaries, pastors and merchants with their extensive family networks.

A good example is that of Margrieta van Varick, who arrived in New York in 1686 with her second husband, a Dutch Reformed pastor, and spent many years living in Flatbush in what is now Brooklyn. Since her parents had died when she was young, Margrieta, who was born in the Netherlands in 1649, travelled to Malacca with her sister and uncle. There in 1673 she married Egbert van Duins, a merchant active in the trade between Malacca and Bengal. After Duins' early death, she met Roelof (Rudolphus) van Varick, pastor of the Reformed Church in Malacca. The couple returned to the Netherlands, where they married, but Roelof van Varick was soon offered a position in Flatbush, whereupon the family, including their children, made their way to North America. Margrieta, however, brought not just her Dutch household belongings across the Atlantic, but also goods purchased in Asia. These included furniture, porcelain, clothing, fabrics, lacquer work, Chinese figurines and a betel box. She also brought a collection of Dutch paintings, representations of the East Indies, and silver vessels. Although this extensive inventory of Eastern and Western goods appears unique, it is merely the best documented one we have for such a seventeenth-century globetrotter.[89]

The many Englishmen and -women who sailed to America often also had experience of other worlds, including not just crossing the Irish Sea but frequently also sojourns in the Mediterranean. John Winthrop the Younger, the future governor of Connecticut, for instance, not only participated in the campaign to relieve the Huguenots besieged by the French in La Rochelle (1628), but also – like many of his compatriots – had travelled in the Mediterranean and the Levant.

John Smith, the founder of Jamestown, had different experiences as a mercenary in Wallachia, where he fought against the Ottomans and was taken prisoner by the Turks. He compared his trading contacts with the indigenous communities in North America with the commercial activities of the Muscovy Company in Russia. Smith also had success with the tried-and-true trade strategy of cultural assimilation, when the chief's daughter Pocahontas fell in love with him, by his own account, and saved his life. Assimilation went still further in the case of the tobacco planter John Rolfe, one of the founders of Jamestown, who married Pocahontas.

Colonial experiences from other maritime regions were applied with profit to new enterprises. Thus, Admiral William Monson planned an English colony on Madagascar, whose advantages he compared to those of the American and Caribbean settlements.[90]

Perceptions of the Atlantic

As we have seen, the Atlantic was long associated primarily with crossings and passages to other continents and seas. It would be several centuries before the name Atlantic, which goes back to classical mythology and means 'sea of Atlas' (Ἀτλαντὶς θάλασσα), would appear on maps. In 1570, Abraham Ortelius, who as court cosmographer to Philip II in Seville had an opportunity to study Spanish maps, would divide the Atlantic into the *Mar del Nort* and the *Oceanus Aethiopicus*.[91] Lucas Jansz. Waghenaer called the Atlantic *Maris Oceani* or *De Groote Zee Oceanus*, accompanied on the map's legend with two whales. Waghenaer also offered mariners information on navigation and cosmography as well as tide tables and sailing instructions as a sort of manual.[92]

Over time, the focus then shifted mainly to coastal and marine areas, as we see in Dampier's description of his circumnavigation of the globe. His 1699 account *A Discourse of Winds, Breezes, Storms, Tides, and Currents* describes the problems that could arise during an ocean passage and also maps the winds over the Atlantic, the Indian Ocean and the Pacific. Dampier was one of the first – perhaps following some English seafarers – to use the word Atlantic to refer to the north and south of this ocean.

The Royal Society also promoted hydrographic knowledge and research. English efforts to navigate the Atlantic then led to Parliament setting the famous Longitude Prize in 1714, following the shipwreck of Sir Cloudsley Shovell.

After much back and forth, the clockmaker John Harrison ultimately won the prize for his chronometer, beating out all his competitors and the experts who sought to determine longitude using old navigational techniques.[93]

Under Jean-Baptiste Colbert, a hydrographic office was set up at the Académie Royale des Sciences in France and a set of maps commissioned under the title *Le Neptune françois*, which was intended both to serve scientific purposes and to increase royal and national prestige. In the old colonial powers Spain and Portugal, navigation routes and technologies, especially with regard to the South Atlantic, were elaborated at the *Casa de la Contratación* in Seville and the *Casa da Índia* in Lisbon. Into the eighteenth century, however, the Dutch were ahead in both mapmaking and writing about navigation, and unlike most of their competitors, their knowledge was published on the free market. By the late sixteenth and early seventeenth centuries, Wagenaar's atlases already offered precise descriptions for navigation on the North and Baltic Seas, the Atlantic coast and the Mediterranean. In the years that followed, with the expansion to Brazil and above all the East Indies, extensive maps, descriptions and travel accounts were published, opening up the world for Europeans. One milestone was the appointment of John Maurice, Prince of Nassau-Siegen, as governor of the Dutch West India Company in Brazil in 1636. His staff of learned men included the painters Frans Post and Albert Eckhout, who were to describe the country through the arts and sciences. The two artists painted nearly everything they saw – Post mainly landscapes, Eckhout largely people – thereby making a major contribution to knowledge of Brazil in seventeenth-century Europe. Although Dutch rule in Brazil remained a brief episode and John Maurice returned to Europe in 1644, the more than one hundred pictures by Post and Eckhout strongly influenced the image of Brazil.[94] Together with Jacob Steendam's poem *'t Lof van Nieuw-Nederland* (1661), Johan Nieuhof's *Gedenkweerdige Brasiliaense Zee- en Lantreize* (1682) and the decorative maps by Johannes Janssonius and Willem Blaeu in the *Nova Belgica* collection (1635), they can be regarded as a multi-media show about the Dutch Atlantic world.[95]

In addition to the luxury volumes by Olfert Dapper on Africa (1668) and Arnoldus Montanus on America (1671), Johan Nieuhof's 1703 *Voyages and Travels, into Brasil, and the East Indies* offered an overview that took readers and sailors alike from the West Indies and Brazil to the Indian Ocean and the Pacific, thereby preparing the way for a new genre of Dutch global travel accounts.

People in North America had been busy as well, though. In 1768, while serving as deputy postmaster general of the American colonies, Benjamin Franklin commissioned a map of the Gulf Stream. The Board of Trade had inquired into why the post took longer to travel from England to Boston than it did in the opposite direction. Franklin posed the question to a cousin on Nantucket Island, a centre of whaling and shipping. Timothy Folger, who had himself captained ships between England and New England and who was personally acquainted with numerous whalers, was able to explain the matter to Franklin. The Gulf Stream slowed ships sailing in a westerly direction, but accelerated ships travelling eastwards towards England. Franklin asked his cousin to sketch the currents and suggested that charts indicating them be engraved and published for the benefit of the captains of ships carrying the mail.[96]

Other factors that heightened awareness of the Atlantic were the conflicts between France and Britain during the Seven Years' War (1756–63 [1754–63]) and the War of the American Independence. Now the word Atlantic increasingly appeared in the newspapers to refer to the ocean between Britain and North America. At the same time, the Admiralty commissioned a new atlas (*Atlantic Neptune*) as well as a study of the coastlines. The search for a northwest passage in particular gained new momentum. In 1745, Parliament had already set a prize of £20,000 for anyone who could sail from Hudson Bay to the South Sea, as the Pacific was known in those days. Although only the icebreakers of the twentieth century and the global warming of our own time have made the northwest passage passable, knowledge about the North Atlantic and interest in the Pacific were growing.[97]

Notes

1　Francisco de Escobar, Letter from Escobar in Sevilla to his junior partner Diego de Ribera in Lima, 1553. Quoted in http://faculty.smu.edu/bakewell/bake well/texts/sevillemerchant.html. J. Lockhart and E. Otte (eds.), *Letters and Peoples of the Indies* (Westport, 1976), 86–113.

2　J. E. Chaplin, 'The Atlantic Ocean and Its Contemporary Meanings, 1492–1808', in Greene and Morgan (eds.), *Atlantic History*, 35–51.

3　F. Fernández-Armesto, *Before Columbus. Exploration and Colonisation from the Mediterranean to the Atlantic, 1229–1492* (London, 1987); D. Abulafia, 'Neolithic Meets Medieval. First Encounters in the Canary Islands', in D. Abulafia and F. Berend (eds.), *Medieval Frontiers: Concepts and Practices* (Aldershot, 2002), 255–78.

4　F. Mauro, *Die europäische Expansion* (Wiesbaden, 1984), 33–41.

5　L. Martín-Merás, 'Fabricando la imagen del mundo. Los trabajos cartográficos de la Casa de la Contratación', in G. de Carlos Boutet (ed.), *España y América. Un océano de negocios: quinto centenario de la Casa de la Contratación, 1503–2003* (Madrid, 2003), 89–102; Chaplin, 'The Atlantic Ocean', 38–9.

6　J. K. Thornton, *A Cultural History of the Atlantic World 1250–1820* (Cambridge, 2012), 9–11.

7 I. K. Steele, *The English Atlantic, 1675–1740. An Exploration of Communication and Community* (New York, 1986), 14–5.

8 J. H. Elliott, 'Atlantic History: A Circumnavigation', in Armitage and Braddick (eds.), *The British Atlantic World*, 254–5.

9 N. Sánchez-Albornoz, *La población de América latina. Desde los tiempos precolombinos al año 2025* (Madrid, 1994), 80.

10 W. Stangl, *Zwischen Authentizität und Fiktion. Die private Korrespondenz spanischer Emigranten aus Amerika, 1492–1824* (Cologne, 2012), 99–107.

11 R. M. Serrera, 'La Casa de la Contratación en Sevilla (1503–1717)', in G. de Carlos Boutet (ed.), *España y América. Un océano de negocios: quinto centenario de la Casa de la Contratación, 1503–2003* (Madrid, 2003), 47–64; H. Pohl, 'Die Consulados im spanischen Amerika', *Jahrbuch für Geschichte von Staat, Wirtschaft und Gesellschaft Lateinamerikas* 3 (1966): 402–15.

12 E. Schmitt et al. (ed.), *Dokumente zur Geschichte der europäischen Expansion*, vol. 4: *Wirtschaft und Handel der Kolonialreiche* (Munich, 1955), 48–51, based on P. Chaunu, *Sevilla y América siglos XVI y XVII* (Seville, 1983), 204–5.

13 See chapter VIII 'Pacific'. For a time there was also a South America run between Manila and Peru.

14 M. A. Burkholder and L. A. Johnson, *Colonial Latin America*, 8th edn (Oxford and New York, 2012), 162–3.

15 C. S. Assadourian, *El sistema de la economía colonial. El mercado interior, regiones y espacio económico* (Mexico City, 1983).

16 Burkholder and Johnson, *Latin America*, 182–5, 303.

17 C. Rahn Phillips, 'The Organization of Oceanic Empires. The Iberian World in the Habsburg Period', in Bentley, Bridenthal and Wigen (eds.), *Seascapes*, 71–86.

18 A. J. R. Russell-Wood, 'The Portuguese Atlantic, 1415–1808', in Greene and Morgan (eds.), *Atlantic History*, 81–109.

19 North, *The Expansion of Europe*, 117.

20 See below, chapter 'Atlantic', sub-chapter 'Sugar, slaves and furs'.

21 Russell-Wood, 'The Portuguese Atlantic', 89–96.

22 Burkholder and Johnson, *Latin America*, 185–6.

23 North, *Kleine Geschichte des Geldes*, 2nd edn, 121–3.

24 H. den Heijer, *De geschiedenis van de WIC*, 2nd edn (Zutphen, 2002), 13–54; C. R. Boxer, *The Dutch in Brazil, 1624–1654* (Oxford, 1957); W. Klooster, *The Dutch Moment. War, Trade, and Settlement in the Seventeenth-Century Atlantic World* (Ithaca and London, 2016).

25 L. M. Rupert, *Creolization and Contraband. Curaçao in the Early Modern Atlantic World* (Athens, GA, 2021); Heijer, *Geschiedenis van de WIC*, 151–62.

26 O. A. Rink, 'Seafarers and Businessmen. The Growth of Dutch Commerce in the Lower Hudson River Valley', in R. Panetta (ed.), *Dutch New York. The Roots of Hudson Valley Culture* (New York, 2009), 7–34.

27 J. de Vries, 'The Dutch Atlantic Economies', in P. A. Coclanis (ed.), *The Atlantic Economy during the Seventeenth and Eighteenth Centuries. Organization, Operation, Practice, and Personnel* (Columbia, SC, 2005), 8.

28 M. North, *Geschichte der Niederlande*, 4th edn (Munich, 2013), 40–2.

29 C. Schnurmann, *Atlantische Welten. Engländer und Niederländer im amerikanisch-atlantischen Raum 1648–1713* (Cologne, 1998), 231–4, 293–301.

30 de Vries, 'Dutch Atlantic Economies', 12.

31 B. Schmidt, 'The Dutch Atlantic. From Provincialism to Globalism', in Greene and Morgan (eds.), *Atlantic History*, 181–2.

32 K. Fatah-Black, *White Lies and Black Markets. Evading Metropolitan Authority in Colonial Suriname, 1650–1800* (Leiden and Boston, 2015); J. B. Hochstrasser, 'The Butterfly Effect. Embodied Cognition and Perceptual Knowledge in Maria Sibylla Merian's *Metamorphosis Insectorum Surinamensium*', in S. Huigen, J. L. de Jong and E. Kolfin (eds.), *The Dutch Trading Companies as Knowledge Networks* (Leiden and Boston, 2010), 59–101.

33 J. Dewulf, 'From Papiamentu to Afro-Catholic Brotherhoods. An Interdisciplinary Analysis of Iberian Elements in Curaçao and Popular Culture', *Studies in Latin American Popular Culture* 36 (2018): 69–94.

34 R. Hakluyt, *Divers Voyages Touching the Discovery of America and the Islands Adjacent*, ed. J. W. Jones (London, 1850), 8–9.

35 See P. Mancall, *Hakluyt's Promise. An Elizabethan's Obsession for an English America* (New Haven, 2007); K. O. Kupperman, *The Jamestown Project* (Cambridge, MA and London, 2007).

36 A. Games, *Migration and the Origins of the English Atlantic World* (Cambridge, MA and London, 1999), 39–40.

37 A. Games, 'Migration', in Armitage and Braddick (eds.), *The British Atlantic World*, 39–40.

38 Ibid., 32–4. See also A. Games, 'Beyond the Atlantic. English Globetrotters and Transoceanic Connections', *The William and Mary Quarterly*, Third Series 63, no. 4 (2006): 675–92; S. M. S. Pearsall, *Atlantic Families. Lives and Letters in the Later Eighteenth Century* (Oxford and New York, 2010).

39 N. Zahedieh, 'Economy', in Armitage and Braddick (eds.), *The British Atlantic World*, 53.

40 P. W. Hunter, *Purchasing Identity in the Atlantic World. Massachusetts Merchants, 1670–1780* (Ithaca, 2001), 48–9, 66, 78, 83–5.

41 C. Frank, *Objectifying China. Imagining America. Chinese Commodities in Early America* (Chicago and London, 2011), 30–4, 43–6.

42 G. Havard and C. Vidal, *Histoire de L'Amérique Française*, 2nd edn (Paris, 2008), 61–6.

43 L. Dubois, 'The French Atlantic', in Greene and Morgan (eds.), *Atlantic History*, 140–4. See also C. C. Bell, *Revolution, Romanticism, and the Afro-Creole Protest Tradition in Louisiana, 1718–1868* (Baton Rouge, 1997).

44 P. Hämäläinen, *Lakota America: A New History of Indigenous Power* (New Haven and London, 2019), 118–20.

45 Dubois, 'French Atlantic', 144–6.

46 P. Gilroy, *The Black Atlantic: Modernity and Double Consciousness* (Cambridge, MA and London, 1993).

47 M. Zeuske, *Sklavenhändler, Negreros und Atlantikkreolen. Eine Weltgeschichte des Sklavenhandels im atlantischen Raum* (Berlin, 2015), 21–5.

48 P. D. Morgan, 'Africa and the Atlantic, *c.* 1450 to *c.* 1820', in Greene and Morgan (eds.), *Atlantic History*, 223–48.

49 D. Northrup, *Africa's Discovery of Europe, 1450–1850* (Oxford and New York, 2002), 50–69.

50 C. Kriger, 'Mapping the History of Cotton Textile Production in Precolonial West Africa', *African Economic History* 33 (2005): 87–116.

51 C. Kriger, 'The Importance of Mande Textiles in the African Side of the Atlantic Trade, ca. 1680–1710', *Mande Studies* 11 (2011): 1–21, 16.

52 J. K. Thornton, *Africa and Africans in the Making of the Atlantic World, 1400–1800*, 2nd edn (Cambridge, 2016).

53 S. A. Diouf (ed.), *Fighting the Slave Trade. West African Strategies* (Athens, OH, 2003).

54 R. T. Ware, *The Walking Qu'ran. Islamic Education, Embodied Knowledge, and History in West Africa* (Chapel Hill, 2014), 110–62.

55 J. Dewulf, *The Pinkster King and the King of Kongo. The Forgotten History of America's Dutch-Owned Slaves* (Jackson, 2017), 128.

56 Dewulf, *Pinkster King*, 11.

57 Morgan, 'Africa and the Atlantic', 223–4, 232, 235–40; D. Eltis, 'Precolonial Western Africa, and the Atlantic Economy', in B. L. Solow (ed.), *Slavery and the Rise of the Atlantic System* (New York, 1991), 97–119.

58 J. A. Carney, 'African Plant and Animal Species in 18th-Century Tropical America', in V. Hyden-Hanscho, R. Pieper and W. Stangl (eds.), *Cultural Exchange and Consumption Patterns in the Age of Enlightenment. Europe and the Atlantic World* (Bochum, 2013), 97–116; H. S. Klein, *The Atlantic Slave Trade* (Cambridge, 2010), 182–7.

59 V. Carretta, *Equiano the African. Biography of a Self-Made Man* (Athens, GA, 2005), 1–16.

60 Ibid., 135–61.

61 Ibid., 176–201.

62 Ibid., 236–70.

63 M. Ogborn, *Global Lives. Britain and the World 1550–1800* (Cambridge, 2008), 276–80; Carretta, *Equiano*, 330–9.

64 A. W. Crosby, *The Columbian Exchange. Biological and Cultural Consequences of 1492* (Westport, 2003).

65 J. E. Chamberlin, *Island. How Islands Transform the World* (Katonah, NY, 2013), 8–13.

66 Thornton, *Cultural History*, 104–7.

67 J.-P. Rubiés, 'The Worlds of Europeans, Africans, and Americans, c. 1490', in N. Canny and P. Morgan (eds.), *The Oxford Handbook of the Atlantic World c. 1450–c.1850* (Oxford, 2011), 32–6.

68 A. Turner Bushnell, 'Indigenous America and the Limits of the Atlantic World, 1493–1825', in Greene and Morgan (eds.), *Atlantic History*, 191–204.

69 M. R. Bahar, *Storm of the Sea. Indians and Empires in the Atlantic's Age of Sail* (Oxford and New York, 2019), 30–1.

70 Bahar, *Storm of the Sea*, 34.

71 Ibid., 133.

72 A. Lipman, *The Saltwater Frontier. Indians and the Contest for the American Coast* (New Haven and London, 2015), 1–54.

73 Lipman, *The Saltwater Frontier*, 105–11.

74 Ibid., 249–51.

75 Havard and Vidal, *Histoire de L'Amérique Française*, 172–6, 318–29.

76 Dubois, 'French Atlantic', 140–4.

77 See chapter VIII 'Pacific'.

78 J. M. Hall, *Zamumo's Gifts. Indian-European Exchange in the Colonial Southeast* (Philadelphia, 2009), 1–11, 117–67.

79 P. Hämäläinen, *The Comanche Empire* (New Haven, 2008), 3.

80 Fundamental studies include R. White, *The Middle Ground. Indians, Empires, and Republics in the Great Lakes Region, 1650–1815* (Cambridge, 1991); C. F. Smith, 'Native Borderlands. Colonialism and the Development of Native Power', in J. W. I. Lee and M. North (eds.), *Globalizing Borderlands Studies in Europe and North America* (Lincoln, 2016), 179–92; Hämäläinen, *Lakota America*.

81 B. Lubbock (ed.), *Barlow's Journal of His Life at Sea in King's Ships, East and West Indiamen* and *Other Ships from 1659 to 1703* (London, 1934), 162.

82 Ogborn, *Global Lives*, 148–52.

83 P. Earle, *Sailors. English Merchant Seamen 1650–1775* (London, 2007), 145–63.

84 W. Dampier, *A New Voyage Round the World* (London, 1697).

85 Ogborn, *Global Lives*, 171–7.

86 M. Rediker, 'The Pirate and the Gallows. An Atlantic Theater of Terror and Resistance', in Bentley, Bridenthal and Wigen (eds.), *Seascapes*, 242.

87 Rediker, *Outlaws of the Atlantic*, 63–88.

88 See part IV 'Mediterranean', sub-capter 'Pirates: Robbery and ransom'.

89 M. North, 'Towards a Global Material Culture. Domestic Interiors in the Atlantic and Other Worlds', in Hyden-Hanscho, Pieper and Stangl (eds.), *Cultural Exchange*, 92; D. L. Krohn, M. De Filippis and P. Miller (eds.), *Dutch New York between East and West. The World of Margrieta van Varick* (New Haven, 2009), 356.

90 W. Monson, 'Advice How to Plant the Island of Madagascar, or St. Lawrence, the Greatest Island in the World, and a Part of Africa', in M. Oppenheim (ed.), *The Naval Tracts of Sir William Monson in Six Books Edited with a Commentary Drawn from the State Papers and Other Original Sources by M. Oppenheim* (London, 1913), 437–8; Games, 'Beyond the Atlantic', 675–92.

91 See A. Ortelius, *Theatrum Orbis Terrarum* (Nuremberg, 1572; Darmstadt, 2006).

92 L. J. Waghenaer, *T'eerste deel vande Spieghel der zeevaerdt, van de navigatie der Westersche zee […] in diversche zee caerten begrepen* (Leiden, 1584; Amsterdam, 1964).

93 Sobel, *Longitude*.

94 M. de Campos Françozo, *De Olinda a Holanda. O gabinete de curiosidades de Nassau* (Campinas, 2014); M. North, 'Koloniale Kunstwelten in Ostindien. Kulturelle Kommunikation im Umkreis der Handelskompanien', *Jahrbuch für Europäische Geschichte*, 5 (2005): 55–72, 55.

95 Schmidt, 'Dutch Atlantic', 178. See also K. Zandvliet, *Mapping for Money. Maps, Plans and Topographic Paintings and Their Role in Dutch Overseas Expansion During the Sixteenth and Seventeenth Centuries* (Amsterdam, 1998).

96 Chaplin, 'The Atlantic Ocean', 35–51, 45 and *The First Scientific American. Benjamin Franklin and the Pursuit of Genius* (New York, 2006), 195–200.

97 Chaplin, 'The Atlantic Ocean', 45–8.

VIII

Pacific:

Exploration and Encounter

The exploration of the South Sea, as the Pacific was long known, awakened many European longings. Apart from exotic flora and fauna, people believed they had found the 'noble savage' there. Fanny Burney, for example, sang the praises of the Polynesian Omai, whom Cook had taken on board during his second voyage and brought home to England, where he was introduced to the king and polite society:

> Omai […], with no Tutor but Nature, changes after he is grown up, his Dress, his way of Life, his Diet and Country and his Friends; […] and appears in a new world like a man who had all his life studied the Graces, and attended with unremitting application and diligence to form his manners, to render his appearance and behaviour politely easy, and thoroughly well bred: I think this shews how much more Nature can do without art, than art with all her refinement, unassisted by Nature.[1]

Adelbert von Chamisso, who sailed around the world on the *Rurik* from 1815 to 1817, also believed that the Polynesians retained a naturalness that he had sought in vain in Europe.[2]

The encounters between Europeans and South Sea islanders were not always as amicable as people in Europe imagined, or as they glorified them in retrospect. On the contrary, they could prove disillusioning (at best) for both sides, if not dangerous or even deadly. Like Francisco de Almeida on the Cape of Good Hope, Fernando Magellan on the Philippines and James Cook on Haiti lost their lives in conflicts with indigenous peoples, while the latter died in huge numbers of diseases introduced by Europeans.

Before the Europeans, trapped in their own nautical worlds, encountered the Pacific Islanders, however, the latter had been settled in the Pacific region for many thousands of years. Ever since the voyage of the French explorer Jules-Sébastien-César Dumont d'Urville, this region, which extends over

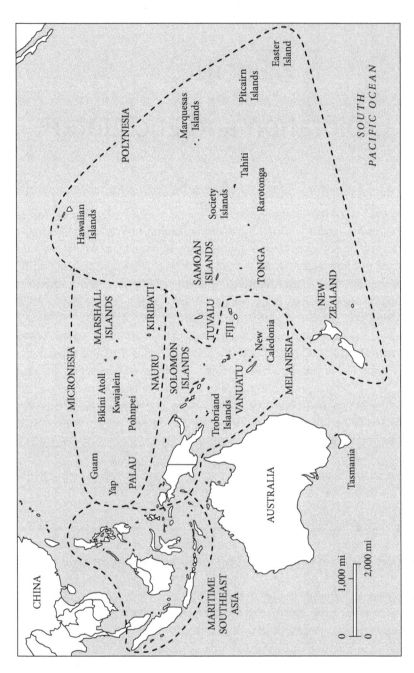

MAP 13 *The Pacific Ocean*

12,000 km^2 and where more than 1,000 languages are spoken, has been divided into Micronesia, Melanesia and Polynesia.

Alongside the 'small' islands (Micronesia) north of New Guinea and east of the Philippines, the 'black' islands (Melanesia), which were named for the dark skin of their inhabitants, extend from New Guinea to Fiji. The 'many islands' (Polynesia) stretch from Hawaii in the north to Easter Island in the east and New Caledonia in the south.[3]

Some 60,000 to 40,000 years ago, when because of low sea levels New Guinea and Australia formed one land mass, settlers from Southeast Asia reached Australia via New Guinea, and still live there today as Aboriginal Australians. Other peoples travelled by sea around 4000 BCE from Taiwan to Melanesia, Micronesia, Polynesia, Hawaii and Easter Island.

The Austronesian navigators used outrigger canoes and navigated by the stars or orientated themselves by water, air, clouds or birds to recognize nearby land. They distinguished between the waters inside and outside the reefs and venerated the spirits and gods who lived in the depths of the ocean.[4] Nautical knowledge passed down over generations allowed the Austronesians to maintain and build cultural, economic and social contacts over wide expanses of the Pacific Ocean. To populate the Eastern Pacific, the islanders brought their food crops, domestic birds, animals and tools with them and combined their usual diet with fish and plants from their new homes. These seafarers and their contacts are evident in the so-called Lapita culture, which left behind a particular style of ceramic pottery, which has been found in more than 100 sites in the Pacific region from the Bismarck Archipelago to the Solomon Islands and Fiji, Tonga and Samoa. Other objects such as obsidian, seashells, hearth stones, jewellery and axes circulated far from the places where they were produced and document the extended and narrower exchange networks, which are also reflected in the navigators' oral traditions.[5] After the first encounter in 1521, it would be more than four centuries before most Pacific Islanders would set eyes upon a European.

Encounter

As was mentioned above, the first European to lay eyes upon the Pacific was Vasco Núñez de Balboa, who did so after passing through the Isthmus of Panama in 1513. One year before, the Portuguese had approached the Pacific from the other side in the course of seizing the Moluccas. Since the Spanish Crown also laid claim to this territory according to the 1494 Treaty of Tordesillas, they sent a fleet of five ships in 1519 under the command of the Portuguese native Ferdinand Magellan with a commission to reach the islands from the Atlantic in a westerly direction. It took months and several unsuccessful attempts before Magellan managed to find a passage to the Pacific Ocean, which was later named the Strait of Magellan after him. The course he chose unwittingly took him to the high seas, past all the islands he (like later mariners) could have used as way stations to gather supplies. His crews starved, many died of scurvy and other diseases and mutinies erupted as described in the gripping travelogue by Antonio Pigafetta.[6] In March 1521 the survivors reached Guam, where they immediately clashed with the indigenous Chamorros. Magellan ordered that they sail on, only to lose his life in another fight on the Philippines. Just one ship under the command of Sebastian Elcano, with the chronicler Antonio Pigafetta on board, reached Spain in 1522 via the Indian Ocean and the South Atlantic, thus completing the first circumnavigation of the globe.

Further attempts followed in the years 1525–1527 under the commander García Jofre de Loaísa. The ships of this fleet were blown off course after passing through the Straits of Magellan, so that only two of them reached the island of Mindanao. The few survivors who made it to the Spice Islands had to be taken to Portugal on Portuguese ships. One of the survivors was the Basque Andrés de Urdaneta, who returned to New Spain (Mexico) and joined the order of Augustinian Hermits. In 1564 Fray Andrés, as he was now known, participated in another expedition, which left Mexico to strengthen the Spanish presence in the Philippines. For the return journey, which began on 1 June 1565, Urdaneta chose a route on the 32nd parallel north and laid his ship's spiritual fate in the hands of its patron saint, Peter. Without an opportunity to take on water and food, the San Pedro crossed the expanses of the North Pacific until the California Current finally drove it south. Urdaneta reached Acapulco on 8 October. He had travelled more than 12,000 nautical miles in 130 days, and sixteen of the original forty-four crew members had died, mostly of scurvy. Urdaneta's route became the standard one for galleons sailing between Mexico and the Philippines, after the founding of Manila in 1571.[7] His maps of winds and currents were still being used into the eighteenth century, for example by James Cook. California, in contrast, whose name was derived from a legendary island, was long of little interest to the Spanish. During his voyages along the coast in 1540, however, Juan Cabrillo explored what are now San Diego, the Santa Barbara Islands and the Bay Area.[8]

American silver and the Spanish silver fleets soon attracted the English and Dutch to the Pacific as well. Whilst sailing around the world from 1577 to 1580, Francis Drake plundered any Spanish possessions he could lay hands on. The Nassau fleet, the first larger Dutch nautical undertaking in the Pacific, was also tasked with capturing the Spanish silver fleet on its way from Peru to the Isthmus of Panama, thereby cutting off the Spanish foe from their source of silver. The route was known, since Olivier van Noort had already sailed across the Atlantic and Pacific to Java in 1598–1601 and Joris van Spilbergen in 1614–16. After returning to Holland in 1617, Spilbergen had published a corresponding travel account. As to the Nassau fleet (1623/24), anything that could go wrong did. It was held up by a leak in the North Sea and by a murderous barber who poisoned part of the crew off the coast of Africa. As a result, after an arduous voyage around Cape Horn the Dutch missed the Spanish fleet by five days. The Dutch made up for this by blockading Callao harbour in Peru and destroying a number of ships, but they were forced to return to Europe via the East Indies without the hoped-for treasure. It therefore made more sense to capture the Spanish silver fleet in the Caribbean, as Piet Heyn successfully did off Cuba in 1628.[9] Dutch interest in the Pacific nonetheless remained intense. In the 1640s, a smaller fleet was sent to the Pacific to construct an alliance against Spain with native chiefs in Chile.[10]

Independent of its activities in the eastern Pacific, the VOC made several attempts from Batavia to explore the Pacific Ocean, which according to the founding charter of 1602 was also part of its field of operations. To this end, Governor General van Diemen sent his colleague Abel Tasman on a voyage to find Australia in 1642. Tasman sailed past Australia to the south, arrived at Van Diemen's Land, the island of Tasmania, which was later named after him, New Zealand (after the Dutch province) and continued his journey to Tonga, Fiji and New Guinea before returning to Batavia. On the voyage from Europe to Southeast Asia VOC ships also regularly sailed along the north-western coast of Australia, where the *Batavia* ran aground spectacularly on a reef in 1629. The inhospitable coast offered no economic perspectives, so that no further efforts were made to exploit the land.

It was not until the eighteenth century that the European maritime powers would again pay greater attention to the Pacific. The reason was the rivalry between France and Britain, which affected conflicts not just on land in Europe, the Americas and India, but also on the seas. In the Pacific, they operated in an ocean that the Spanish claimed as their own, since it bordered on the Spanish colonies.[11] Nevertheless, a race began to take possession of islands. Thus in 1765 the British government instructed John Byron not just to claim the Falkland Islands in the South Atlantic, but also to search for the southern continent (Australia) as well as the Northwest Passage. Louis Antoine de Bougainville received almost the identical commission from the French king. Since Byron only secured the Falklands for Britain, further captains were dispatched. In 1767 Samuel Wallis took possession of Tahiti for the king of England, and Bougainville did the same for the French Crown one year later. Bougainville's travel account spread the myth of Tahiti as a 'Garden of Eden' and also inspired James Cook, who arrived in Tahiti in 1769, this time on behalf of the British.

Cook's first circumnavigation of the globe was inspired by scientific interests. The year 1769 witnessed a transit of Venus, in which the planet's passage across the sun could be observed from Earth. This phenomenon was noted and measured from various locations on Earth, which people hoped would provide important navigational information for the determination of longitudes. Tahiti seemed to be a suitable location. James Cook, who had made a name for himself as a Royal Navy navigator und cartographer in the North Atlantic off the coast of Canada, set sail on the refurbished former collier HMS *Endeavour* on 26 August 1768 and reached Tahiti on 13 April 1769. After taking measurements, Cook followed orders from the Admiralty and went off in search of Australia. He reached and mapped New Zealand first, and in April 1770 he landed at the southeast coast of Australia, disembarking at the site of present-day Sydney and meeting the indigenous peoples for the first time. He laid claim to this part of Australia, known until then as New Holland, for Britain under the name New South Wales. The *Endeavour* later ran aground on the Great Barrier Reef but managed, by jettisoning some of the cargo, to make the ship seaworthy again and continue towards New Zealand.[12]

The encounter with the indigenous population was remarkable in every respect and over the course of the voyage ranged from participant observation to friendly contacts, but also to rejection and military conflict. In the process, Cook tolerated the killing and eating of crew members by Maoris in New Zealand, but mercilessly punished anyone who stole from his ship.

His most impressive encounter was probably on Tahiti, when he met the priest and navigator Tupaia. Tupaia not only piloted Cook around the Pacific, but also, together with Cook, applied his rich store of knowledge about the Pacific islands to create a map.[13] This map portrays 70 islands out of an original list of 130 in concentric circles, with Tupaia's home island of Ra'iātea (Ulietea) at the centre. Cook, who drew the surviving map – Tupaia's draught has been lost – thereby translated traditional local knowledge into a European medium, which was remedialized in Johann Reinhold Forster's publication. Tupaia also depicted the encounter between Pacific Islanders and Europeans later in the journey in watercolour. The journey did not, however, take him into the Indian Ocean or to Europe as he had hoped, for he died of malaria in Batavia.

Before the *Endeavour* arrived in Britain on 10 July 1771, many more crew members would die on the way to the Cape of Good Hope and the further journey. The voyage was nevertheless considered a success, which left its mark in published works as well as collections. There was never any question that Britain would equip another expedition by Cook, this time on the *Resolution*. Between 1772 and 1775 it twice crossed the Atlantic and the southern Indian Ocean – with forays to the southern polar circle – to New Zealand and from there to the South Pacific. The voyage was documented not just by the printed and illustrated journal, but also and above all by the paintings of William Hodges, who accompanied Cook. He portrayed and conveyed the South Sea landscape to the English public, including the sea and icebergs.[14]

This media success led the Royal Navy to begin planning an additional expedition. This time, the aim was finally to find the long-sought Northwest Passage, the existence of which had been speculated upon for many years. In 1776, Cook sailed the usual route across the Atlantic and the Indian Ocean to New Zealand and from there to Tonga and Tahiti, before heading north past Hawaii to the west coast of North America, which he intended to map. He followed the coast through the Bering Strait until the ice of the Bering Sea forced him to turn back. Wishing to spend the winter in warmer climes, he again sailed to Hawaii, where he was killed on 14 February 1779 in a clash with the locals. His navigator William Bligh, against whom the crew of the *Bounty* would later mutiny, sailed the *Resolution* back to England. Cook's successes attracted interest in France, where Louis XVI commissioned a Pacific expedition in 1785 under the nobleman Jean-François Galup de La Pérouse, also with the intention of finding the Northwest Passage. After this undertaking proved fruitless once again, La Pérouse sailed south past Japan and on to Tonga and Samoa. In Australia he encountered the first British convicts who had been left there in 1788. Shortly thereafter, the ships ran aground off the Solomon Islands and there were no survivors. People in France waited in vain for news, and the ships sent out to discover what had happened found no traces.[15] Further unsuccessful attempts to discover the Northwest Passage were undertaken in 1791–5 by the Briton George Vancouver and in 1789–94 by the Italian Alessandro Malaspina, who was sent by the Spanish. Malaspina, who also surveyed the northwest coast of America including the mountains of Alaska, demonstrated that the consumption of citrus fruits prevented scurvy, and thus suffered fewer cases of the illness among his crew.[16]

Spanish interest also focused on the California coast, where, arrayed like beads on a string, a number of so-called missions were founded over the course of the eighteenth century. This was the work of Father Miguel José Serra, a priest from Majorca, who despite a promising ecclesiastical career on the Balearics felt called to be a missionary to the native peoples. In the middle of the century, he travelled to Spanish America and, as legend has it, was forced along the way to contend not just with an English 'heretic' as a captain but also with storms and dwindling supplies of food and water. Having arrived in Mexico, he was stung by a scorpion or tarantula on his way to the capital and arrived limping in Mexico City. Serra set out for the wilderness of the Sierra Madre, where for eight years he preached, baptized natives and awaited a new assignment. In 1765 he joined an expedition under the leadership of Gaspar de Portola, governor of Baja California, whose aim was to colonize California and convert the indigenous population. They set out in five groups, three by ship and two by land on horseback with pack mules and finally reached the Bay Area.

Serra founded missions he named after San Gabriel, San Buenaventura, San Luis Obispo and San Antonio de Padua; more followed in San Juan Capistrano, Santa Clara and Santa Barbara. The army founded *presidios* in San Diego, Santa Barbara, Monterey and San Francisco, and the first settlers arrived with the support of the Spanish Crown. The missions proselytized the local tribes like the Chumash, but also exploited them as agricultural labour and in the trades and exported the agricultural products they grew along with cowhides and tallow.[17] In the early nineteenth century, ships with merchants from Boston and elsewhere regularly landed at the anchorages near the California missions, where they traded finished goods for cowhides, which were then processed into leather on the East Coast.[18]

During their voyages, the ships also visited Russian trading posts in the North Pacific. Russian traders were active there, and from 1799 the Russian-American Company, which established a branch at Fort Ross north of San Francisco in 1812. Russian expansion in the North Pacific and especially in North America occurred in several stages. At first, two expeditions explored Kamchatka and the Russian Pacific coast from the Russian Pacific trading post of Okhotsk under the command of the Danish captain Vitus Bering and discovered the Aleutian Islands and Alaska. Russian merchants soon sent fur hunters to capture seals and sea otters along the coast. Trading posts in Kodiak and Sitka followed, but it proved difficult to provision them from Russia, so that it made sense to turn to the Spanish in northern California or to cultivate their own supplies in the Russian River Area, where they founded the trading post of Fort Ross.

Russian economic interests in the region encouraged further expeditions, the most significant of which were undertaken by Krusenstern and Kotzebue. Interestingly, they were led by Baltic German officers who had previously been active on other seas. Thus, Adam Johann von Krusenstern had served not just in the Swedish-Russian War (1788–90) but also in the Royal Navy in the Atlantic and the Indian Ocean. On his journeys, he had also visited Canton (Guanghzou) and witnessed the riches of the Asian trade.

The circumnavigation of the globe commissioned and financed by Tsar Alexander I was intended above all to initiate trade with Japan. Krusenstern's ship, the *Nadežda*, went to sea on 7 August 1803, sailed around Cape Horn on 3 March 1804 and after stations on the Marquesas and Hawaii landed on the Kamchatka Peninsula. Its east coast was explored and mapped along with Sakhalin and the Aleutian and Kuril Islands. The ship followed the Japanese coastline to Nagasaki, where the Dutch however still held a monopoly on trade with Japan. The *Nadežda* landed in Kronstadt on 19 August 1806, after a return voyage through the Indian Ocean and the Atlantic. Krusenstern published the research findings in the *Reise um die Welt* (*Voyage Round the World*) as well as an atlas of the Pacific Ocean.[19] Also on board the *Nadežda* was the young Otto von Kotzebue, son of the era's most popular playwright August von Kotzebue, who was able to gather maritime experience. Krusenstern accordingly recommended him to the Russian foreign minister Count Rumjancev to captain another expedition to the Far East.

This research expedition (1815–18) was remarkable not just for its scientific results, which included mapping more than 400 islands. Also on board were the author Adelbert von Chamisso and the painter Louis Choris, who processed their impressions for a broader public. The French-born had already made a name for himself with the Romantic novel *Peter Schlemihl* and used his connections to accompany the voyage as a 'naturalist'. His contribution to Kotzebue's account of the expedition[20] and his subsequent publications, especially his *Reise um die Welt (Voyage Round the World)*, thus have a different quality from the previously published journals of world travellers and explorers.

This begins with his extensive description of his arrival – he joined the crew of the *Rurik*, which had begun its journey in Kronstadt – in Copenhagen. Here, he compares the three-day torture of the regular post coach with the speedy crossing of the Baltic from Kiel to Copenhagen:

> On the trip from Kiel to Copenhagen one does not even get into the middle of it [the Baltic Sea], as one never loses sight of land. But it became quite apparent how the seas are really the roofs of the land in the face of all the sails one could see round about, and of which we never counted fewer than fifty between the green plain of Sjælland and the low coasts of Sweden.[21]

Chamisso had a similar association in the Atlantic, which the *Rurik* sailed through from Plymouth to Tenerife and from there to Santa Catarina in Brazil:

> The Atlantic Ocean never seemed wide to me. I always felt as if I were on a well- traveled stretch whose shores I did not have to see in order to feel them. On the contrary, the seas we had sailed on hitherto, the coastal fires of which, like the lanterns in a city, we seldom lost sight of, and where you have to fear that you will run another ship down or be run down yourself, seemed to me to be too narrow.[22]

This changed when, after rounding Cape Horn and spending several weeks in Concepción in Chile, the *Rurik* set course across the Pacific for Kamchatka via Easter Island, the Marquesas and the Marshall Islands:

> The routes that cross this wide ocean basin are traveled much more sparsely than those of the Atlantic, and no shore borders them against

which the seafarer could lean in imagination, but the flight of sea birds and other signs often let him suspect land, islands he doesn't see and doesn't seek, and still he is not lost in this unlimited space. Ships as a rule only encounter each other in the vicinity of harbours, which serve them as gathering places: the Sandwich Islands, etc.[23]

Chamisso's accounts and the body of pictorial representations of the encounter with the inhabitants of the Aleutians, the native peoples on the San Francisco coast and the island societies of Micronesia and Polynesia in particular can be understood as 'thick description' as described by Clifford Geertz,[24] and both met with interest in various branches of science. Above all the meeting with the Polynesian Kadu, who spent several months on board the *Rurik* and was extensively questioned by Chamisso, is among the best contemporary observations:

The present was not without charm for me. The result of Kadu's statements about his known world, from the Pelew [Palau] Islands to Radak, can be perused by the reader in my 'Notes and Opinions'. But to get what was written down there into words, to determine these facts, that was the task, that was the pleasurable torture of this first period. First the medium of understanding had to be expanded, developed, and practiced. The language was composed of the dialects of Polynesia that Kadu spoke and a few European words and expressions. Kadu had to become accustomed to understanding, and, which was harder, to making himself understood. Concrete and historical things could soon be negotiated, and the narration was without difficulty. But what else did the curtain conceal? His answer never went beyond the question. Natural history books with illustrations settled many doubts about questionable objects. Further inquiries were made on the basis of the letter of Pater Cantova about the Carolines in the Lettres édifiantes. Then Kadu's joyous astonishment was great when he heard so much about his native islands from our mouths. He confirmed, corrected; many a new connecting point presented itself, and every new path was diligently followed.[25]

It turned out that Kadu had learnt how to count in Spanish, and that he also knew songs from other islands. Foreign and indigenous (maritime) travellers, merchants, missionaries and beachcombers linked the Pacific islands with each other and with other seas and continents. A body of knowledge emerged that offered the basis for communication and was continually being expanded.[26] The admiration was certainly mutual. Thus, Kadu followed with interest the naturalist observations and collecting activities of the scientists on the *Rurik*, while Chamisso stressed 'the beauty in the simple, unadulterated nature'[27] of

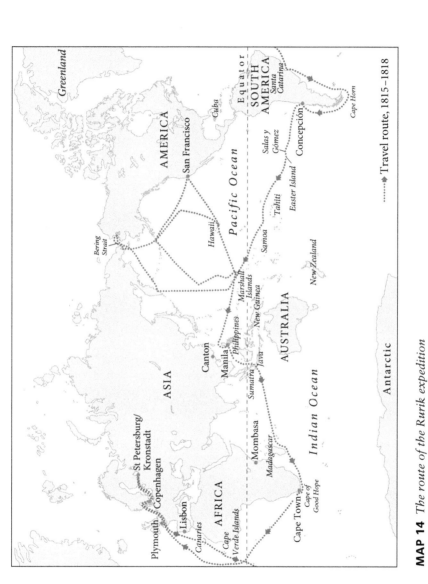

MAP 14 *The route of the Rurik expedition*

Greenland

AMERICA

San Francisco

Cuba

Equator

SOUTH
AMERICA

Santa
Catarina

Cape Horn

Pacific Ocean

Concepción

Salas y
Gómez

Easter Island

Tahiti

Samoa

Bering
Strait

Hawaii

New Zealand

Marshall
Islands

New Guinea

AUSTRALIA

ASIA

Canton

Manila

Philippines

Java

Sumatra

Indian Ocean

Mombasa

Madagascar

St Petersburg/
Kronstadt

Copenhagen

Plymouth

Lisbon

Canaries

AFRICA

Cape
Verde Islands

Cape Town

Cape of
Good Hope

Antarctic

········→ Travel route, 1815–1818

FIGURE 8 *Portrait of Kadu by Louis Choris, 1822. From Adelbert von Chamisso, Reise um die Welt (Berlin, 1978), 280.*

the Polynesians, including their tattoos as an 'artistic whole'.[28] Unfortunately, Chamisso's ambition to acquire a tattoo as a memento went unfulfilled.

At almost the same time as reports of the *Rurik* expedition were being published in Europe, the first Pacific Islander, Harry Maitey, reached Germany. In 1823, this young Hawaiian had asked the crew of the Bremen-based *Mentor* for permission to come on board when it was anchored off Honolulu. The *Mentor* was supposed to explore opportunities for trade in the Pacific region on behalf of the *Preußische Seehandlung* (Prussian Maritime Trading Company).

Maitey managed to persuade Captain Harmssen and the supercargo Willem Oswald and arrived at the Prussian Baltic port of Swinemünde (now Świnoujście) in 1824 after sojourns in Canton and St Helena. From there he travelled by coach to Berlin, where he lived first in the house of the Prussian Maritime Trading Company's director Christian Rother and later at the recently founded school for boys at Hallesches Tor, where Maitey had to work hard to learn German and prepare for baptism and confirmation. At the same time, he was expected to pose at the trading company's headquarters among the treasures brought back from the South Seas and Canton. Zoological and mineralogical objects intended for museums were on display alongside tea, cinnamon, bales of silk cloth, ivory and mother-of-pearl objets d'art, porcelain and paintings on rice paper. From Hawaii came tapa cloth, drinking gourds, feather fans, weapons, fishhooks and household items. In this way, the Prussian Maritime Trading Company helped to create a romantic image of the South Seas alongside the travelogues by Kotzebue and Chamisso.

After his baptism in 1830, Maitey worked as an assistant to the engine master on Peacock Island in the Havel River, which served as a landscape garden and menagerie (with exotic animals and plants) for the recreation and entertainment of the court. He married the daughter of the animal keeper Becker, with whom he had three children, and died of smallpox at the age of sixty-four.[29]

Sandalwood, sea cucumbers and sea otters

The explorers were followed by traders, although exploration was also economically motivated. The captain-explorers repeatedly called at trade centres such as Batavia, Manila, Valparaiso or Kamchatka. Thus, Europeans could participate through local barter in the centuries-old exchange networks that already existed in the Pacific, while new regional and global relationships emerged in the region through the exploitation of indigenous resources. Moreover, many Islanders joined the expedition, merchant and whaling ships. William Dampier had already taken natives from the Caribbean to the Pacific, where their skill in catching turtles and manatees ensured the crew's survival on the long journey. He also bought the freedom of Joely, a native of the Miangas Atoll who had travelled to Madras as a slave on a spice ship, from his English master and brought him to London.[30]

Apart from prominent passengers such as Tupaia, Omai or Kadu, most Pacific Islander crew members worked on deck and sailed to harbours such as Sydney/Botany Bay, Canton, Macao and Manila, but on British ships they also sailed to the Indian Ocean and the Atlantic. One of the first Hawaiian women to travel the various regions of the Pacific in this way was probably 'Winee' (*wahine* is Hawaiian for woman), who in May 1787 boarded the British *Imperial Eagle*, which sailed under the Austrian flag and had stopped in Hawaii on its way to the sea otter grounds on the northwest coast of North America. Frances Barkley, the captain's sixteen-year-old fiancée, brought Winee onto the ship – which took on furs in Nootka Sound and sold them in Macao – as her personal maid. Suffering from homesickness, Winee left the ship and, while waiting to return home, met Tianna (or Kaiana), a Hawaiian man who had travelled to Canton and Macao on another ship. Together they embarked for

Hawaii, but Winee died on the voyage. Shortly before her death she presented Tianna with a mirror and a bowl made of fine porcelain as well as a dress, a petticoat and a cap given to her by Frances Barkley. Tianna finally reached home in 1788 via the Philippines and Nootka.[31]

Trade and shipping also brought Pacific Islanders to other islands, where they settled in the short or longer term: Hawaiians to Tahiti and the Marquesas, Tahitians to Tonga and New Zealand. In this way, they met not just Europeans, but also the inhabitants of other islands. Their chiefs were eager to learn about the unfamiliar regions of Polynesia.[32]

Encounter and exchange with the societies of the Pacific region led to a variety of economic relationships. Initially, the Europeans received water, firewood, food and sexual services in exchange for nails, needles, knives, axes, jewellery and textiles. Iron objects were much in demand, given that most of the existing tools were made of stone or shells. As time went on, however, objects from other islands, which natives like Tupaia, Omai or Kadu had seen on board European ships, also became desirable. For example, red feathers from Samoa or Tonga became popular among Tahitians, alongside European goods. In Tahiti, the Islanders sought guns, gunpowder and boats in order to dominate rivals on other islands. Alcohol was also in demand. Furthermore, the Europeans imported citrus fruits, grapevines, pineapple and papaya and even potatoes and grain to feed the ships' crews.

On the islands, the Europeans discovered previously unfamiliar goods that were in demand on the Asian markets. Thus, for example, members of Cook's crews sold furs when they docked in Macao on their home journeys and expanded to the entire ocean the trade in which the Russians already engaged in the North Pacific. A beachcomber, Oliver Slater, who had lived in Canton, recognized the value in Asia of the sandalwood that could be found on various Pacific islands. The first stocks to be exploited were in Fiji and later the Marquesas. The Hawaiians even undertook long voyages to tap the resources of other islands. At the same time, sea cucumbers (Indonesian, *trepang*) came to the attention of traders. Sea cucumbers were harvested in Southeast Asia and considered a delicacy in China. Since they were found in the lagoons of various Pacific islands, agreements were reached with the local chiefs to set up sea cucumber breeding stations on their islands.[33]

Hunting and trapping, especially of sea otters, was orientated from the beginning towards the Chinese market, where the new Manchu dynasty had popularized the wearing of fur. In the early nineteenth century, for example, the imperial minister Ho-K'un owned some 67,000 furs.[34] Hunting sea otters began in the North Pacific in the eighteenth century and would expand to the East Pacific in the nineteenth century. The point of departure was the old Russian Pacific settlement of Okhotsk. This is where Vitus Bering embarked for the Aleutian Islands, bringing furs back with him which the Russians sold to Chinese traders in Kyakhta on the Russian-Chinese border. This led to a thriving trade in which tens of thousands of otter pelts changed hands every year. To hunt these animals and process their pelts, the Russians relied on the skills of the Aleut and Kodiak peoples, which explains the Russian presence in the region. The Russian-American Trading Company in particular established a system of contract workers, monopolized the fur trade and expanded it after rich sea otter grounds were discovered in California as well. In cooperation with American sea captains and businessmen, Aleutian hunters and their families were sent to California on ships from Boston, for example to Bodega Bay and the region around San Francisco. While the men went out hunting the women skinned the animals. Most of the pelts were brought back to Alaska with the hunters and from there sold on the market in Canton.[35]

Hawaiians like the Native chief Naukane (nicknamed John Coxe) also worked in the fur trade. After his ship was destroyed by local people on the Columbia River, he set off on foot for the interior to buy furs. There he met the British traders of the Northwest Company, who took him with them overland to Fort William on Lake Superior and finally by ship to London. He enjoyed English pub life until travelling to the Pacific Northwest in 1813 as a pilot on the warship *Racoon*. After a sojourn in Hawaii, he worked for several years in Fort Vancouver, before spending his final years as a swineherd on the Columbia River.[36]

Following the dramatic decline of the sea otter population, the hunt was expanded to seals, which were to be found throughout the Pacific. The Juan Fernández Islands off the Chilean coast became a centre where British, French and Spanish ships vied in the hunt. Boston seal hunters soon gained the upper hand and in 1793 ships like the *Jefferson* and the *Eliza* supplied 13,000 and 38,000 furs to Canton, respectively.[37]

Between Canton and California

The Pacific networks were recast by trade and later, naturally, by whaling as well – new trading centres arose, and the significance of older ones changed. Manila was long the *entrepôt* of the Pacific region. Several hundred Spaniards and Japanese lived there alongside the largely indigenous population and a large Chinese community. Trade focused on the exchange of American silver for Asian goods. The merchants of New Spain were astonished by the low cost of Chinese goods in Manila, while silver attracted traders from Asia. Apart from silver, the Spanish sent wine, vinegar, oil, almonds, books and medicines from Acapulco to their outposts. Ships sailed regularly from Manila, or rather its harbour, Cavite, to Siam, Cambodia, Macassar, Cochinchina and even Dutch Batavia. Ships also docked at Chinese harbours like Macao, where Portuguese and Chinese traders vied for Philippine custom. The main commodities to reach Acapulco were porcelain, silk and other textiles as well as lacquer work and the corresponding furniture. Even the clerics from the Manila cathedral chapter exported silk to Mexico. Imported porcelain has come to light in the excavations on the Zócalo in Mexico City, but also in the salvaged wreck of the *San Diego*, which sank during a battle with the Dutch in 1600. Local ceramic production in Puebla and Cuzco was inspired by imported Chinese porcelain. The most important sources of information about Asian objects in the households of the colonial elites of Mexico and Peru, aside from estate inventories, were objects such as Japanese-inspired folding screens (*biombos*), which spread first through the Spanish-American world and later to Europe.[38]

In Chamisso's eyes, early nineteenth-century Manila was still a significant commercial city where Americans, English and French docked, and where the *Rurik* was thoroughly overhauled during the northeast monsoon for the return voyage to Europe.[39] One of the new centres was the Chinese treaty port of Canton, where foreign merchants could trade with locals and each other and where the strands of world commerce now converged. Here Europeans and traders from around the Indian Ocean encountered the Chinese merchant houses known as hongs. Along with textiles from India and Britain and opium from Bengal, traders here offered silver from Mexico, furs from Siberia and the Pacific, and sandalwood from Hawaii and Tahiti, with tea, porcelain and silk being the most important Chinese export goods. Although the English East India Company tried to monopolize trade with Canton, Europeans, especially Danes and Swedes, as well as Americans, increasingly worked their way in.[40]

In the wake of the booming Chinese market, California and Hawaii were integrated into this exchange network. California evolved into a trade hub between North and South America, China and Siberia/Alaska. Hawaii, where King Kamehameha granted privileges to foreign traders and lured them to Honolulu, became another hub of exchange between the west coast of North America and the east coast of Asia.

One example of the new quality of shipping routes and ports is the voyages of the British schooner *Columbia*, which between June 1814 and Christmas 1817 travelled constantly between the west coast of North America, Hawaii and Canton selling North American furs and Hawaiian sandalwood in Canton, trading food for furs in Sitka (the capital of Russian Alaska), taking on furs and other goods on the Columbia River and grain on the California coast. Four times the *Columbia* dropped anchor in Hawaii where repairs were made, goods and provisions brought on board and new crew members recruited. In other ports, too, local workers boarded ships, for example in Macao, where the English ship *Isaac Todd* had 'forgotten' sixteen Hawaiians. At the end of the journeys, Captain Peter Corner sold the already rather dilapidated *Columbia* to King Kamehameha for two shiploads of sandalwood, which he transported to Canton on another vessel.

In the 1820s and 1830s, British and American merchant houses opened branches in Hawaii, importing or negotiating onward trade on a large range of European and American goods, as is evident from their correspondence with business partners in Canton, California, Callao, Boston and London.[41]

Whaling gave a new significance to Hawaii as well as to the exploitation of the Pacific more generally. This phenomenon was anchored in cultural memory by Herman Melville's *Moby Dick*: Queequeg, the indigenous harpooner on Captain Ahab's ship, represents the large number of so-called Kanakas (the word for person in Hawaiian) who worked on American whaling vessels.

Whaling had a long tradition in New England. By the late seventeenth century, whalers from Nantucket and New Bedford were already setting sail for the North Atlantic to hunt sperm whales, whose blubber was processed into lamp oil. Whalebone was also used to make corset stays. In the eighteenth century, the whalers sailed further into the Davis Strait, but also to the Azores and the South Atlantic. From there it was just a short hop to the South Pacific, where the British whaler *Emilia* caught the first whale off the Chilean coast in 1789. This attracted a veritable stream of whalers from New England, first to the west coast of South America and then further into the Pacific. In 1828, 200 American whalers were active in the Pacific, a number that would rise to 571 in 1844, while the British and French were active with just a few dozen ships.[42] On the other side of the Pacific, hunters from Port Jackson in New South Wales established whaling stations on the coasts of Australia, Tasmania and New Zealand.

A whaling expedition lasted three years on average. This meant that whalers needed stations along the way to take on supplies, repair their ships, process the catch and provision and entertain the crew. One of these stations was Honolulu, where whaling vessels from New England docked with a skeleton crew which they then supplemented with Hawaiians. Tahitians and Maoris were also sought-after crew members, especially by the British and French, which naturally changed their way of life as well as that of the islanders the crews encountered elsewhere.[43] This was especially true when native and foreign whalers left the ships and settled in the Pacific region as beachcombers, innkeepers or brothel keepers.

The discovery of rich oil deposits diminished the economic importance of whale oil, so that the American whaling fleet dwindled from the 1860s. The Norwegians, Japanese and Russians, however, continue to hunt whales even today.

Missionaries and scientists

Apart from seafarers and merchants, it was missionaries who linked the Pacific region with the Indian Ocean, the Atlantic world and the Mediterranean and North Sea. Portuguese expansion to the Spice Islands, Macao and Japan went hand in hand with missionary activities, which led to numerous conversions but not to the permanent establishment of ecclesiastical structures, except at Macao. In the early seventeenth century, the Jesuits were expelled from the Moluccas by their Muslim rulers and the Dutch, while in Japan there were several waves of persecution against (Portuguese) Christians. The Jesuits accordingly concentrated their activities on the Philippines, where an archdiocese was established, and the Inquisition soon oversaw the purity of the faith from Mexico. Into the eighteenth century, the (Jesuit) missionaries succeeded in gaining a foothold only in Guam, where the indigenous population, the Chamorros, were killed or resettled by the Spanish, or were decimated by the diseases introduced by Europeans. Missionary attempts to convert the Caroline Islands from the Philippines failed, but the maps that emerged familiarized the Europeans with the islands of Micronesia.[44]

Cook's discoveries in the late eighteenth century brought about a turning point in missionary activities. Protestant missionaries wanted to save the souls of the 'savages' described by Cook and others, and in 1796 the London Missionary Society chartered the *Duff*, which was supposed to bring thirty missionaries to the Pacific, the first destination being Tahiti. Only four of them were ordained ministers, the rest pious tradesmen inspired by their faith who wished to save the 'savages' by a combination of mission and labour. The first missionaries arrived in Matavai Bay on Tahiti with their families in March 1797, another nine volunteers docked on Tongaptapu and a further missionary, William Pascoe Crook, landed on the Marquesas in June. The missionaries separated and tried to settle in small groups under the protection of local chiefs. Three missionaries were killed in Tonga, while others escaped on an English ship. Only George Vason, a bricklayer from Nottingham, stayed, since he had fallen in love with a local woman. Instead of converting the locals, he 'went native', married, adopted Tongan dress and had himself tattooed. Thanks to his relationship with the local chief Mulikiha'amea he was provided with land, rose in Tongan society and associated with other chiefs through marriage contracts. When his patron was murdered, he took the opportunity in August 1801 to embark on the missionary ship *Royal Admiral*, which was bound for China. There he joined the crew of an American vessel which brought him to the Caribbean and New York, and after a few voyages he returned to England. He remarried, joined the Baptist Church and ended his career as governor of Nottingham Gaol. He wrote a travel account, the *Authentic Narrative of Four*

Years' Residence at Tongataboo in which he reflected upon his reception by the Tongans.[45]

This example shows that although missionaries are generally regarded as bigoted white European men, the reality on the ground could be more diverse and more colourful. Missionaries' activities and how they were received varied from place to place.[46] Thus while they sought to protect their newly won congregations from the predations of merchants and sea captains, they also punished and exploited the people they styled their 'children'. For this, however, they preferred to use the inhabitants of other islands. Thus, in the 1870s, missionaries transported 250 inhabitants of Easter Island to Tahiti to work as forced labourers on the church-owned farms.[47] While the churchmen were relentless in their efforts to eradicate paganism, they initially depended on local interpreters to spread the gospel and had to find rituals that could be reconciled with Christian beliefs and practices. In the process, the missionaries became linguists and ethnographers.

Whether or not they met with success depended on a variety of local factors as well as the character of the missionaries themselves, and their social origins and theological training also played a role. Indigenous teachers, catechists and pastors, whose cultural competence was essential for spreading the Christian faith locally, were a key factor. We should also not underestimate the role of female family members in community work.

Let us return to Tahiti, where the London Missionary Society's 'godly mechanics' laboured more or less unsuccessfully for fifteen years until, after his victory over his rivals, King Pomare I presented them with his family gods, which they sent to London as trophies. The result was a mass conversion quite reminiscent of early and high medieval conversions in Europe.[48]

The activities of the London Missionary Society on Tahiti and other islands inspired American ministers trained in the theological seminaries of New England to undertake a mission in Hawaii, and to establish the American Board of Commissioners for Foreign Missions. One innovation was the training of Pacific Islanders in the United States. The first student was the Hawaiian Obookiah, who had arrived in New Haven with a sea captain and studied at the theological seminary in Andover. Although Obookiah died of typhus in 1818 before he could work as a missionary, his fellow students Hiram Bingham and Asa Thurston led a group of missionaries with strict Calvinist convictions of sin and morality to Hawaii, where they met with favourable conditions. King Kamehameha had opened the islands to Europeans and Americans and their goods, and the belief in the old gods and ways of life was waning. Soon Christian devotional works and catechisms were being printed in the Hawaiian language and in the mid-1820s, the most distinguished chieftains had themselves publicly baptized. Hawaii became a Christian island.[49]

The missionaries' success was not without controversy, especially because at the same time thousands of islanders fell victim to diseases introduced from across the seas. Critics like Otto von Kotzebue also lamented the destruction of the Pacific Islanders' traditional ways of life by British and American missionaries. He openly asked whether the prohibitions on traditional dress and customs such as dance and tattoos helped the natives. The Tahitians had forgotten how to build their boats or produce their traditional tapa cloth, their flutes had gone silent and they no longer engaged in dancing, mock battles or games. The Baltic nobleman was especially horrified that the former sailor Charles Wilson and a few freshly christened Tahitians had set out to convert the region: 'The London Missionary Society is less demanding. They consider a half-savage, confused by a sailor with a few dogmas, to be wholly suitable.'[50]

Naturally, the missionaries did not let this criticism stand. In their attitudes towards the 'heathens', the missionaries found themselves in agreement with a new generation of explorers. One of them was the young Charles Darwin, who in 1831 set off to circumnavigate the globe with Captain Robert FitzRoy on the board the *Beagle*. One of their first destinations was Tierra del Fuego, where they were supposed to take geographical measurements. The encounter with the 'savages' of Tierra del Fuego helped to form his image of human development as later formulated in *The Descent of Man*. In the *Voyage of the Beagle* Darwin wrote, 'The perfect equality among the individuals composing these tribes (the Fuegians), must for a long time retard their civilization.'[51] For, as in the animal kingdom, those ruled by a chief were best placed to improve their situation. Later, in *The Descent of Man*, he speculated that changing living conditions had a negative effect on peoples who had long enjoyed conditions of equality.[52] Unlike preceding generations of travellers such as Forster or Chamisso, Darwin was no participant observer, but gazed down upon the natives from the lofty heights of Britain's looming world dominance, apparently no longer dependent upon their hospitality and help.

Nevertheless, when looking back at the voyage of the *Beagle*, during which he collected more than 1,000 objects, and which would take him across all the oceans and back to England in 1836, Darwin regarded it as the most important event in his life as a scientist. He was fascinated by the unhindered development of species, for example on the Galapagos Islands, as well as the geological composition of other volcanic islands from Hawaii and Tahiti to St Helena and the Azores.[53] Apart from the travel account, Darwin soon published his theory on the formation of coral reefs. He corresponded on the subject with the American geologist James Dana, who took part in the first American scientific expedition to the Pacific in 1838–42, which produced important findings on the mountains of California, the volcanoes of Hawaii and the coral reefs, among other topics. These would later culminate in his theses on the origins and structure of oceans and continents.[54]

Dana's research on the California mountains, especially his publication on the geology of Mount Shasta, was well publicized after the discovery of gold in California. The gold rush changed the Pacific region once again, since it unleashed new waves of migration across the ocean. This process was accompanied by the establishment of a plantation economy in both California and Hawaii, which in turn attracted workers from Japan, China and Latin America. The cultural interactions between these groups in particular and the Pacific Island dwellers shaped the Pacific in a different way than the seafarers from Oceania did. The latter knew that the sea represented a road map, not a barrier, and that shipping routes connected the world. They met foreign sailors in a contact zone. Like the white seafarers who explored the islands, Pacific seafarers also combed the foreign coasts. Although they only ever saw segments of the countries where they docked, they played an important role in cultural exchange within the maritime networks of the eighteenth and nineteenth centuries. The global shipping routes gave the inhabitants of Oceania previously unknown mobility and knowledge, which they used when they returned to their home islands.[55]

Notes

1   F. Burney, *Journals and Letters*, ed. P. Sabor and L. E. Troide (London, 2001), 33 (letter 24). Quoted in E. H. McCormick, *Omai. Pacific Envoy* (Auckland, 1977), 128.

2   A. von Chamisso, *Reise um die Welt* (Berlin, 1978), 345.

3   R. Wendt, 'Einleitung. Der Pazifische Ozean und die Europäer. Ambitionen, Erfahrungen und Transfers', *Saeculum* 64 (2014): 1–7, 1.

4   Matsuda, *Pacific Worlds*, 21.

5   D. Salesa, 'The Pacific in Indigenous Times', in Armitage and Bashford (eds.), *Pacific Histories*, 31–52, 34–6; B. Fagan, *Beyond the Blue Horizon. How the Earliest Mariners Unlocked the Secrets of the Oceans* (London and New York, 2012), 37–41.

6   A. Pigafetta, *Magellan's Voyage around the World*, trans. J. A. Robertson (Cleveland, 1906).

7   A. Giráldez, *The Age of Trade* (Lanham, 2015), 119–44.

8   W. A. McDougall, *Let the Sea Make a Noise. A History of the North Pacific from Magellan to MacArthur* (New York, 1993), 25–7.

9   See part VII 'Atlantic', sub-chapter 'Sugar, slaves and furs'.

10   On the two fleet projects, see B. Schmidt, *Innocence Abroad. The Dutch Imagination and the New World, 1570–1670* (Cambridge, 2001).

11   R. F. Buschmann, *Iberian Visions of the Pacific Ocean, 1507–1899* (Basingstoke and New York, 2014), 55–68.

12 J. Cook, J. Banks and J. Hawkesworth, 'The Unfortunate Compiler', in J. Lamb, V. Smith and N. Thomas (eds.), *Exploration and Exchange. A South Sea Anthology 1680–1900* (Chicago and London, 2000), 84–8.

13 J. R. Forster, *Observations Made during a Voyage Round the World on Physical Geography, Natural History, and Ethic Philosophy* (London, 1778), 513.

14 H. Guest, *Empire, Barbarism, and Civilization. James Cook, William Hodges, and the Return to the Pacific* (Cambridge, 2007).

15 P. Bérard, *Le voyage de La Pérouse. Itinéraires et aspects singuliers* (Albi, 2010), 133–42; S. R. Fischer, *History of the Pacific Islands* (Basingstoke and New York, 2002), 92–3.

16 Buschmann, *Iberian Visions*, 164–9.

17 McDougall, *Let the Sea*, 62–71.

18 For details, see R. H. Dana, *Two Years before the Mast. A Personal Narrative* (New York, 1840; London, 1969).

19 A. J. Krusenstern, *Reise um die Welt 1803–06*, 3 vols (Petersburg, 1810–1812); English: I. F. Krusenstern, *Voyage Round the World in the Years 1803, 1804, 1805, & 1806*, trans. R. B. Hoppner (London, 1813); A. J. von Krusenstern, *Atlas de l'Océan Pacifique*, 2 vols (Petersburg, 1824–1827).

20 O. v. Kotzebue, *Entdeckungsreise in die Südsee und nach der Berings-Straße zur Erforschung einer nordöstlichen Durchfahrt. Unternommen in den Jahren 1815, 1816, 1817 und 1818, auf Kosten Sr. Erlaucht des Herrn Reichs-Kanzlers Grafen Rumanzoff auf dem Schiffe Rurick unter dem Befehle des Lieutenants der Russisch Kaiserlichen Marine Otto von Kotzebue*, 3 vols (Weimar, 1821).

21 A. von Chamisso, *A Voyage around the World with the Romanzov Expedition in the Years 1815–1818 in the Brig Rurik, Captain Otto von Kotzebue*, trans. and ed. H. Kratz (Honolulu, 1986), 16–7.

22 Ibid., 32.

23 Ibid., 63.

24 C. Geertz, *The Interpretation of Cultures. Selected Essays* (New York, 1973), 310–23.

25 Chamisso, *Voyage*, 159.

26 H. Liebersohn, *The Travellers' World. Europe to the Pacific* (Cambridge, MA and London, 2006), 161–2.

27 Chamisso, *Reise*, 352.

28 Ibid., 355.

29 A. Moore, 'Harry Maitey. From Polynesia to Prussia', *Hawaiian Journal of History* 2 (1977): 125–61.

30 D. Chappell, *Double Ghosts. Oceanian Voyagers on Euroamerican Ships* (Armonk, NY, 1997), 27, 118.

31 J. Barman, *Leaving Paradise. Indigenous Hawaiians in the Pacific Northwest, 1787–1898* (Honolulu, 2006), 18–22.

32 Ibid.

33 N. Thomas, 'The Age of Empire in the Pacific', in Armitage and Bashford (eds.), *Pacific Histories*, 82.

34 J. M. Beurdeley, *The Chinese Collector through the Centuries. From the Han to the 20th Century* (Fribourg, 1966), 181–5.

35 D. Igler, *The Great Ocean. Pacific Worlds from Captain Cook to the Gold Rush* (Oxford, 2013), 99–111.

36 Chappell, *Double Ghosts*, 103–4.

37 Igler, *Great Ocean*, 111–15.

38 See D. Leibsohn, 'Made in China, Made in Mexico', in D. Pierce and R. Y. Otsuka (eds.), *At the Crossroads. The Arts of Spanish America & Early Global Trade, 1492–1850, Papers from the 2010 Mayer Center Symposium at the Denver Art Museum* (Denver, 2012), 11–40; D. Pierce (ed.), *Asia & Spanish America. Trans-Pacific Artistic & Cultural Exchange, 1500–1800* (Denver, 2009); R. Pieper, 'From Cultural Exchange to Cultural Memory. Spanish American Objects in Spanish and Austrian Households of the Early 18th Century', in Hyden-Hanscho, Pieper and Stangl (eds.), *Cultural Exchange and Consumption Patterns*, 213–34.

39 Chamisso, *Reise*, 380–4.

40 Blussé, *Visible Cities*, 50–5, 60–6; Matsuda, *Pacific Worlds*, 175–96.

41 Igler, *Great Ocean*, 29–30.

42 Fischer, *History of the Pacific Islands*, 100–1.

43 Ibid., 101; Chappell, *Double Ghosts*, 94–5.

44 U. Strasser, 'Die Kartierung der Palaosinseln. Geographische Imagination und Wissenstransfer zwischen europäischen Jesuiten und mikronesischen Insulanern um 1700', *Geschichte und Gesellschaft* 36, no. 2 (2010): 197–230.

45 Matsuda, *Pacific Worlds*, 144–6; Thomas, *Islanders*, 40–3; V. Smith, 'Falling from Grace. George Vason', in J. Lamb, V. Smith and N. Thomas (eds.), *Exploration and Exchange. A South Sea Anthology 1680–1900* (Chicago and London, 2000), 156–69.

46 Thomas, *Islanders*.

47 Chappell, *Double Ghosts*, 95.

48 D. Bronwen, 'Religion', in Armitage and Bashford (eds.), *Pacific Histories*, 201–5.

49 Liebersohn, *Travelers' World*, 245–62.

50 O. von Kotzebue, *Neue Reise um die Welt in den Jahren 1823, 24, 25 und 26. Mit 2 Kupferstichen und 3 Charten*, ed. W. Hoffmann (Weimar, 1830), 88 and *A New Voyage round the World in the Years 1823–1826* (London 1830, Reprint Amsterdam, 1967).

51 Quoted in Liebersohn, *Travelers' World*, 283.

52 Ibid., 287.

53 Chamberlin, *Island*, 125–62.

54 Igler, *Great Ocean*, 155–85.

55 Chappell, *Double Ghosts*, 173–4.

IX

Global Seas:

From Sail to Steam and the Communication Revolution

In his *Inquiry into the Nature and Causes of the Wealth of Nations,* Adam Smith points to the superiority of water over land transport:

> A broad-wheeled waggon, attended by two men, and drawn by eight horses, in about six weeks' time carries and brings back between London and Edinburgh near four ton weight of goods. In about the same time a ship navigated by six or eight men, and sailing between the ports of London and Leith, frequently carries and brings back two hundred ton weight of goods […]. Since such, therefore, are the advantages of water-carriage, it is natural that the first improvements of art and industry should be made where this conveniency opens the whole world for a market to the produce of every sort of labour, and that they should always be much later in extending themselves into the inland parts of the country.[1]

Had he not died in 1790, Adam Smith would have experienced the success of the railways. Nevertheless, the flourishing of river, canal, coastal and ocean shipping fundamentally changed the transport of goods and people. Adam Smith observed this phenomenon in the case of coastal shipping: one ship could transport fifty times as much freight as a waggon pulled by eight horses.

From sailing ship to steamship

Adam Smith prophesied the nineteenth-century transport revolution, in which the costs for international transport dropped and the seas were connected even more closely and regularly. Historians long regarded the introduction of the steamship as responsible for this development, but in recent years they have come to realize that the introduction of steam technology was a drawn-out process, accompanied for quite some time by sailing ships and improvements in shipbuilding.

In 1807, the American Robert Fulton presented the paddle steamer *Clermont* to an enthusiastic national audience, who used the new ship on the Hudson River between Albany and New York City. Fulton's invention unleashed a boom on US rivers, especially the Mississippi, which however was only gradually emulated on the narrower rivers of Europe.

The paddle steamers were less suitable for ocean travel. The SS *Savannah*, for example, the first hybrid steamship, which crossed the Atlantic in 1819, was converted back to a pure sailing vessel for reasons of profitability. The paddle technology was unsuited to the sea and the ships had to carry massive amounts of coal to run the steam engine, which took up nearly all their freight capacity. Saltwater also damaged the steam engine's boilers. Only the introduction of the ship's screw or propeller starting in 1840 made the steamships ocean-worthy. Improvements in engineering like Alexander Kirk's compound or triple expansion engine used steam more effectively and slowly reduced the amount of coal needed. It would nevertheless take at least until the end of the century nearly everywhere for steamships to gradually replace sailing ships. The displacement process began in the 1870s.

The *Parliamentary Papers*, which recorded the arrival of international ships in British ports, offer insight into the proportion of steamships. While around 1880 steamships dominated among vessels arriving from the Mediterranean and western Europe, sailing ships were still in use on many other routes. It was not until 1910 that up to 90 per cent of ships arriving in British ports in Europe ran on steam. The adoption of steam technology depended on a variety of factors. Apart from the efficiency of steam engines, these included the type of cargo and the distance and duration of journeys. Since steamers had to carry their own fuel, they became increasingly expensive the longer the distance to be travelled. Starting at a distance of 500 nautical miles, sailing ships could compete with steamships, and they could even perform better over longer journeys. This also applied to northern Europe and the Baltic region, where mainly timber and grain were transported on wooden sailing ships.[2]

Norway and Finland in particular participated in the international economic boom of the nineteenth century less as producers of raw materials than as service providers. Although Norwegian timber and tar were important for English shipping and industrialization, the role of the Scandinavian merchant fleets was changing. They would come to transport a significant portion of freight worldwide. Although they originally focused on exporting timber to England, Norwegian ships increasingly shifted to the so-called tramp trade in the Atlantic; that is, they travelled without fixed routes or scheduled ports of call to harbours where they unloaded their cargo or awaited new cargo. Although in the Baltic sailing ships had lost their cost advantage by around

1860, on the Atlantic routes they long remained profitable over the competition. Above all, they could be bought cheaply on the second-hand ship market or built inexpensively of local timber, such as northern pine, by local carpenters at small shipyards. Whether or not one made the capital-intensive transition from sailing to steamships depended on local conditions. Large ports – like Copenhagen or Stockholm – shifted to steamships early on. Bergen soon also preferred steamers in order to guarantee rapid and regular fish sales on the European markets. Provincial ports, which had specialized in different routes, initially saw no reason to switch.

In Finland, steamships did not supersede sailing ships until the twentieth century. Finnish sailing ships first specialized in the transport of timber and tar across the Danish Sound to western Europe, but they increasingly offered corresponding services in the Black Sea and the Mediterranean as well. In the 1870s they participated in the transport revolution in the Atlantic trade and brought not only grain from New York, Philadelphia and Baltimore to Ireland and the British North Sea ports but also petroleum to western Europe and even to the Baltic region. Other freight included timber exports (e.g. pine wood) from the American South and Canada.

Canadian shipowners also still used sailing ships to transport timber across the Atlantic, while the Anglo-American trade was largely conducted via steamship. Sailing ships dominated in trade with the Indian Ocean. It was only with the opening of the Suez Canal in 1869 that the travel time became short enough to use steamships, which depended on a dense network of coaling stations that allowed for more pit stops to take on coal, water and food. In coastal and tramp shipping in the Indian Ocean as well as the South and East China Sea, the sailing ship long remained the dominant mode of transport. Since the American and European sailing ships could sail against the monsoon winds, they had an advantage over local junks, which depended on the monsoons. Accordingly, ships from Hamburg took over the transport of rice from Akyab (Sittwe) in Burma to the Chinese coast via Singapore and Hong Kong. Steamers were used for the first time to transport rice in the 1870s.[3]

Sailing ships remained competitive in the grain and ore trade with the North American west coast and above all on voyages to South America until the early twentieth century, as documented by the Hamburg shipping company Laeisz's Flying P-Liners, which were used to transport saltpeter.

Overall, the international merchant fleet was continually expanding throughout the nineteenth century with ever more and larger ships. This can be measured by the tonnage, which exploded between 1850 and 1911 from 9 to 34.6 million net register tonnage. Atlantic shipping in particular, which represented 75–80 per cent of world registered tonnage, was able to increase its capacities substantially.

The British fleet dominated the world's seas around 1900, with 9.3 million tonnes, followed by Germany (1.9 million), Norway (1.5 million) and France (1.04 million), while the United States had allowed its merchant fleet (0.8 million) to decay during the Civil War.[4]

With rising freight capacities, freight rates fell by more than one third worldwide between 1870 and 1900. Thus in 1885, the cost of shipping grain from New York and cotton from New Orleans was just half what it had been in 1873.[5] Consumer prices fell accordingly, and cheap maritime transport brought together producers and consumers across the globe. This changed production landscapes throughout the world. Falling transport costs fostered specialized agricultural production and settlement in distant regions like North and South America, Australia, parts of South and Southeast Asia but also southern Europe, while in the more densely populated areas on the US East Coast or in Europe agriculture declined with the rise of industry.[6] Atlantic wheat prices converged, as did rice prices in the Indian Ocean region and the Chinese seas and stimulated the worldwide integration of the wheat and rice markets.[7]

As in the seventeenth-century Netherlands, which could feed the population with cheap grain imports from the Baltic, the nineteenth-century maritime transport revolution enabled the industrial centres of Europe and North America to become independent of local agricultural production, which shifted to the fruitful plains of North and South America, south-eastern Europe, Asia and Australia.

At the same time, countries less suited to agriculture, such as Norway, Finland or Greece, profited from the new opportunities offered by the international shipping industry. Greece, too, grasped the possibilities of its maritime location and the long tradition of shipping in the eastern Mediterranean to build a competitive shipping sector. After the opening of the Black Sea to merchant shipping as a consequence of Russian-Ottoman conflicts in the 1770s, Greek merchants and shipowners took over grain transports to the European market from South Russia and south-eastern Europe and dominated seafaring in the Mediterranean. In the mid-nineteenth century, this sector contributed up to one third of national income. Greek shipowners were integrated into the world economy as service providers and competed with the most important maritime nations, which gave them a leading role in international tanker shipping in the twentieth century. Only Britain succeeded in combining and dominating all aspects of shipping and trade because it had access to both the largest supply of capital and relatively cheap iron or coal as well as the technological innovations of the Industrial Revolution. While British shipping had lost ground to Americans in the Atlantic and Scandinavians in the Baltic around the middle of the century, British innovation paid off once again with the rise of iron-hulled vessels and steamships.[8]

Along with freight traffic on the world's oceans, passenger transport also underwent fundamental transformations in the nineteenth century, without which mass emigration across the Atlantic would have been impossible. By 1846/47, 300,000 emigrants were crossing the Atlantic every year, and the figure would double to 600,000 between 1876 and 1896. In the early twentieth century, some one million people left Europe annually to cross the Atlantic.

A look at the ships highlights the fundamental transformation of ocean voyages: in the late eighteenth century, a Falmouth packet ship brought passengers and post to New York via Halifax, a journey lasting approximately fifty days. The luxury ocean liners of the late nineteenth century, in contrast, which carried up to 2,500 passengers, took just five or six days. The efficiency of ocean transport, especially the speed on the route from the West of England to New York, had risen rapidly from 2.5 knots (4.5 km/h) to 20–25 knots per hour. Moreover, the steamers could choose the shortest route across the Atlantic, while sailing ships took the route with the most favourable winds via the Azores and the Caribbean and thus had to travel up to 12,000 nautical routes more than the steamers. This went hand-in-hand with a rediscovery of the open sea and the use of hydrological and oceanographic knowledge about winds and currents to plan shipping routes.

The packet boats of the eighteenth century could not transport more than about 100 passengers on their three or four journeys a year, while at the beginning of the twentieth century an ocean liner could take 20,000–30,000 emigrants a year across the Atlantic. Until that time, emigrants took sailing ships, mainly embarking for overseas from Antwerp, Rotterdam or Bremen as well as London and Le Havre. Two hundred-tonne ships were often packed with up to 300 emigrants, so that hygiene and mortality on board were scarcely better than they had been on the slave ships. British convicts were also transported to Australia on sailing ships along with those emigrating there or to South Africa. The duration of the passage to Australia had been reduced to 100–120 days in the first half of the nineteenth century through the use of larger and better ships and shorter stops along the way. This was about half the time needed a century before.

The introduction of steamship lines to North America not only made for speedier crossings; they also enabled ships to more easily combine passenger and freight traffic. Thus, on the return journey, the steerage decks used by passengers were filled with grain. Cotton and frozen meat (ships with cold storage were an innovation of the 1880s) became increasingly important as return cargo for emigrant ships.

The steamers changed the skills required of sailors as well as the maritime infrastructure. Ships no longer needed men with sailing skills, but rather stokers to keep the furnaces filled. These men were no longer recruited from the coasts, but for example from inland Germany, and often worked only for a short period between the ages of twenty and thirty.[9] Large lighthouses were erected from which the ship's position could be more readily determined even in the dark. This expedited shipping, as did the construction of passenger terminals in the ports, which made the embarkation and landing of passengers more convenient and effective.[10]

The communication revolution

The maritime transport revolution was accompanied by a communication revolution that also took place on the seas, albeit underwater on the ocean floor. The new medium of the telegraph played a key role here.[11] Along with innovations in electrical engineering, the discovery of gutta-percha – a flexible natural latex derived from trees that does not corrode in saltwater and possesses a high level of viscosity to prevent the cable coating from cracking – was a precondition for the worldwide use of this medium. Furthermore, iron ships large enough to transport the vast length of cables and stable enough to allow them to be laid successfully were also needed.[12]

The first submarine telegraph cable was laid in the English Channel between Calais and Dover in November 1851 and proved both technologically and economically successful. Further Channel cables between Britain, Belgium and the Netherlands followed; Copenhagen and Flensburg were linked telegraphically in 1854, and one year later Denmark and Sweden were connected via the Sound. In 1859, this connection was extended to Haparanda on the Swedish-Finnish or rather Russian border.

That same year, the cable reached Alexandria and with it the Mediterranean. In 1870, starting from Alexandria, Bombay, Madras and Singapore were connected via the Red Sea, Suez and the Indian Ocean. Cables were then laid from there to Shanghai and one year later to Australia, Hong Kong and Yokohama.

The North Atlantic cable went into operation in 1866 and connected London with New York via Ireland and Newfoundland. In 1874, England was finally connected with Brazil and Argentina via Lisbon, Madeira and the Cape Verde Islands. Within twenty years, the submarine cables had linked three quarters of the world telegraphically, and most of these cables belonged to British companies. In the decades that followed, however, French companies would operate additional submarine cables in the Mediterranean and along the West African coast, just as Americans operated submarine cables in the Atlantic, the Caribbean and South America as well as between San Francisco and the Philippines.

Laying cables in the world's oceans radically reduced the time it took information to travel. While a letter took thirty to forty days from India to

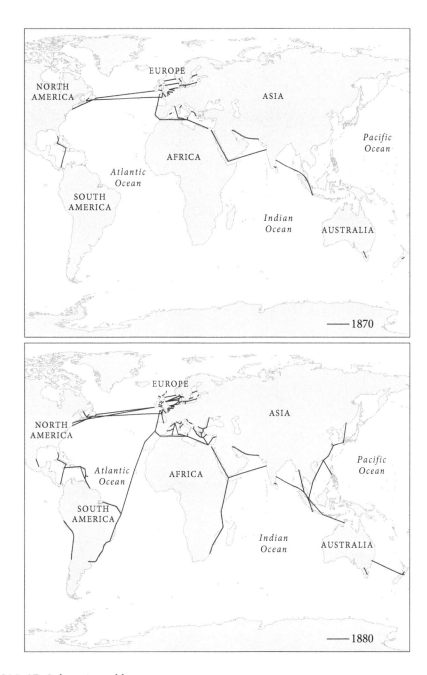

MAP 15 *Submarine cables*

London and fourteen to seventeen days from North America to London in the years 1866–9, after 1870 the time between sending a message by telegraph and publishing it in the press was just two to three days, whether

TABLE 2 *Comparison of the Time, in Days, Needed to Transmit Information from London to Overseas Destinations*

From London to	Postal shipping 1866–9	Transmission by Gulf telegraph 1866–9	Transmission by telegraph 1870	Year connected to the inter-continental telegraph system
	Days			
Australia				
Sydney	60	-	4	1876
New Zealand	65	-	4	1876
Asia				
Bombay	29	9	3	1870
Calcutta	35	12	3	1872
Hong Kong	51	29	3	1871
Madras	40	15	3	1870
Shanghai	56	30	4	1870
Yokohama	70	30	5	1871
Africa				
Alexandria	11	5	2	1868
Cape Town	30	-	4	1868
Lagos	12	-	3	1886
Madeira	8	-	2	1874
North America				
Galveston	17	-	3	1866
Montreal	14	-	2	1866
New Orleans	17	-	3	1866
New York	14	-	2	1866
Central America				
Barbados	26	-	4	1868
Havana	24	-	4	1868
Jamaica	25	-	4	1868
South America				
Bahia	15	-	3	1873
Buenos Aires	32	-	3	1875

From London to	Postal shipping 1866–9	Transmission by Gulf telegraph 1866–9	Transmission by telegraph 1870	Year connected to the inter-continental telegraph system
Days				
Colombo	33	-	3	1875
Natal	36	-	4	1875
Rio de Janeiro	30	-	3	1875
Valparaíso	46	-	4	1875

J. Ahvenainen, 'The Role of Telegraphs in the 19th-Century Revolution of Communications', in M. North (ed.), *Kommunikationsrevolutionen*, 75–6.

the communication came from India or North America. Because of the high cost – ten French francs to transmit one word from the West Indies to Europe in 1875 – the main users of this medium were news agencies and periodicals that published currency exchange rates and commodity prices, thus creating market transparency. Accordingly, the main beneficiaries of the telegraph, apart from governments, were bankers and merchants and thus commercial and financial centres such as London and New York. But shipowners could also use the medium to guide their tramp ships from harbour to harbour in Southeast Asia or South America.

For the majority of people, communication with the new medium was prohibitively expensive.[13] The old medium of the letter thus remained competitive, even after the telephone came into use not long thereafter for brief verbal communications. Letters profited from the massive fall in postage prices brought about by the founding of the General Postal Union (1874) and the Universal Postal Union (1878) on the one hand and the reduction of travel time for letters internationally and intercontinentally because of the railway postal and mail steamer networks on the other. At the end of the nineteenth century, overseas mail was carried by the international post steamer lines, which had regular timetables and whose numbers were continually growing. The German post steamer lines of Hamburg American Line (HAPAG), North German Lloyd (Bremen) and the German-American Sea Post Service, which in 1895/96 made 98 journeys from New York to Germany and 102 to New York, carrying some 15 million letters. It was a safe and secure means of transport and operated in both directions. And it was profitable for the shipping companies to take on mail, since both the American and German postal authorities paid substantial sums to transport the transatlantic mails. Matters were different on the less travelled routes to Africa, the Pacific and China, where the letter post had to be subsidized. These state subsidies for the establishment and acceleration of mail transport to far-off colonies contributed to the world-wide concentration of shipping lines, with postal administrations helping to determine the timetables, routes and speed of the mail steamers, which also carried freight and passengers.[14]

Emigration and exploitation

The reduction of crossing times linked the seas to a degree not seen before and set off worldwide movements of population. Everywhere in the world, people now left their homes willingly or unwillingly by ship to seek new living and working conditions. From 1850, some 55 million Europeans crossed the Atlantic, the majority of whom migrated to the United States, but around 13 million left for Latin America.[15] Between 1880 and 1930, nearly four million Europeans emigrated to Argentina and the same number to Brazil. For several hundred thousand of them, the destination was Cuba, Uruguay or Chile.[16] The majority came from southern Europe. But Germans, too, for instance from Hunsrück and Pomerania, also settled in southern Brazil. They were joined by Jewish immigrants fleeing persecution and discrimination in Europe, as well as former inhabitants of the Ottoman Empire, who were known as *turcos* in South America. A number of Chinese and Italians went to Argentina as seasonal labour. Although some Europeans returned home, their mobility contributed to the growth of South American cities, which remained closely tied to the immigrants' homelands, for instance Portugal, Spain, Sicily or Naples. The value of remittances from Argentina to Europe corresponded to about one-half that of Argentine meat exports. Apart from European re-migrants, former Black slaves were also returned to Africa in connection with settlement enterprises, for example in Monrovia, in which people placed great hopes. After the Bahia revolt of 1835, the Brazilian authorities also expelled enslaved people to Africa, where they soon formed so-called Brazilian communities.[17]

Britain's abolition of the slave trade in the *Slave Trade Act* of 1807, however, set wholly new population flows in motion. In order to meet the emerging need for labour on sugar, coffee, tea and cotton plantations as well as in the mines and railway construction, contract workers (so-called coolies) were recruited from India and China and transported great distances over the world's oceans, particularly the Pacific, where the mortality rate, at 25 per cent, was similar to that of the Atlantic slave trade. Although the coolies – a name presumably derived from the Hindi *kūlī* (porter) – theoretically enjoyed personal freedom and received a fixed wage, they were treated so poorly that their individual situation scarcely differed from that of slaves. While some coolies returned to their home countries, others successfully settled in the countries where they worked and were followed by additional labour migrants.

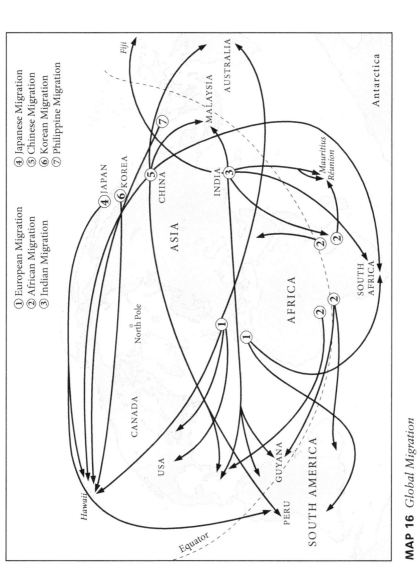

① European Migration   ④ Japanese Migration
② African Migration   ⑤ Chinese Migration
③ Indian Migration   ⑥ Korean Migration
                          ⑦ Philippine Migration

MAP 16 *Global Migration*

In all periods of history, the societies around the Indian Ocean had witnessed various forms of slavery and bonded labour. In South Asia, individuals sold either themselves or family members into slavery during times of famine. In Southeast Asia, debt bondage was more common and served as a strategy for securing credit.[18] Slave raids were also conducted, for example by pirates of the Sulu Zone near Mindanao. Unlike the Atlantic system, the demand for slaves around the Indian Ocean was limited to a few cash-crop plantations, for example in Mauritius and Zanzibar, and captains therefore did not specialize in the slave trade.[19] Instead, the British tried to control the supply of and demand for labour in their Indian Ocean empire by establishing a system of indentured servitude.

It all began in 1815, when Indian convicts were sent to Mauritius to work on the sugar plantations. Then, forced labourers were 'recruited' from Bengal and the Coromandel Coast and transported to Mauritius, South Africa, Ceylon, Burma and the Malay Peninsula (known until 1963 as Malaya). After France abolished slavery in 1848, coolies were sent to Réunion; later, workers were hired to build the Ugandan railway. The contracts generally ran for three to five years, but the inclusion of women meant that former coolies began to settle permanently. Of the approximately 450,000 Indians who went to Mauritius to work as coolies between 1834 and 1910, only about one third returned to India. This changed the population structure in Mauritius, in which Indians became quantitatively dominant in the 1870s. Alongside those with long-term labour contracts, millions of Indian workers took up seasonal work on the coffee and tea plantations of Ceylon, during the rice harvest in Burma or on the sugar plantations of Natal. Better educated Indians like the young lawyer Mohandas Gandhi, however, also went out to South Africa, for the sake of their careers.[20]

The other large group of labour migrants were the Chinese, who toiled in Southeast Asia and the Caribbean as well as North and South America. There had long been a Chinese merchant diaspora in Southeast Asia and in some regions like the Dutch East Indies Chinese entrepreneurs ran sugar plantations with slave labour. At the same time, Chinese labourers worked in the tin mines of Malaysia (Malaya) and the opium plantations of Java, for example.

In the British Empire, the ports of Singapore and Hong Kong would become the main transition points for coolies and labour migrants. Singapore, which under British rule evolved from a small port into a metropolis of nearly 100,000 in 1870, attracted Chinese traders, European merchants and shipowners and itinerant labourers. The latter hailed mainly from Fujian, Guangdong, Taiwan, Hainan and Canton and signed contracts that required them to work off the money advanced to them for the passage to their new workplaces. This was

FIGURE 9 *Coolies and Orang Laut (sea people) in Singapore harbour, drawing by Charles Dyce, 1842–3. Courtesy of NUS Museum Collection. Singapore (S1970-0052-039-0).*

known as the credit-ticket system. For the middlemen, the 'coolie trade' was a business that also benefited Hong Kong, which around 1870 replaced Singapore as the most important 'emigration port' especially for those bound for Australia, New Zealand and North America.

The global migration of Chinese workers was promoted by the British, who had already sent 200 Chinese to Trinidad in the Caribbean in 1806. Ships were sent from Cuba, which experienced a boom in its sugar and coffee plantations in the nineteenth century, to Amoy (Xiamen) in China to recruit workers. On 3 June 1847, after 131 days at sea, the ships returned with 206 Chinese workers on board. Six of them had lost their lives at sea, and seven died shortly after arriving in Cuba. Thereafter, the import of Chinese labourers, mainly from Macao, increased and included some 125,000 persons up to 1874. Other Chinese labourers (c. 95,000) were transported to Peru, where they largely performed the degrading work of guano mining on the Chincha Islands. Because of the unbearable conditions – more than two-thirds of the coolies in Peru died before completing their work contracts – small revolts against the Chinese and foreign agents frequently broke out in the ports, ships and workplaces.[21]

Chinese migrants were initially transported to Australia, Canada and the United States on sailing ships, but by the 1860s regular steamship routes had been established and were served by the New Zealand and Australia Royal Mail steamers as well as the Pacific Mail Steamship Company, which sent vessels from San Francisco to Japan and China every week. Chinese made up the majority of the passengers as well as crew members.[22] Emigration was more or less voluntary and proceeded on the basis of the abovementioned credit-ticket system. The first Chinese labourers in North America worked in the California gold fields. They were employed to build the Central Pacific Railroad from 1863 and the dams in the Sacramento-San Joaquin River Delta in the 1870s.[23]

Since most of the labourers were men, a regular trade in women developed between China and California. One such woman was Yip Mun Chun, who had been sold by her parents in Canton at the age of fourteen. After arriving in Hong Kong, she was sold on to San Francisco, where she worked as a prostitute. She later found a Chinese partner, but he left her after running through her savings. In desperate straits, she returned to Hong Kong and worked her way up through various brothels and eventually owned one.[24]

The cruel treatment of coolies on American ships led to a ban on unrestricted human trafficking in 1862. Thus, an American consul in Hong Kong had to certify that the coolies had left the country of their own free will. Since the consuls issued certificates without much scrutiny, the more or less uncontrolled migration, including the trafficking of women, continued. Soon, however, some Americans began to complain of being overrun by foreigners, leading to nativist unrest and attracting the attention of politicians. At first, the government tried to make it unattractive to hire Chinese labour in California by taxing the workers. In 1882, the Chinese Exclusion Act then suspended labour immigration from China for a period of ten years. This was extended for another ten years in 1892, and in 1902 Chinese immigration was outlawed permanently. The Exclusion was repealed on 17 December 1943 by the Magnuson Act, which allowed 105 Chinese per year to enter the country. President Theodore Roosevelt had initially succeeded in forestalling an extension of this discrimination to the Japanese population by urging the Japanese government to limit emigration. The Immigration Act of 1924 prohibited all migration to the United States from Asia and set a quota for European immigrants, which limited their numbers to 2 per cent of each nationality already living in the United States.

Fear of immigrants was also rife in Australia and New Zealand, so that migration from Asia was also restricted there in 1899 and 1901.[25] In the preceding decades, Australians had not objected to the recruitment of forced labourers from Melanesia to work in the cotton, sugar and pineapple plantations, however. Aside from three-year coolie contracts, so-called blackbirding also played a role – recruitment by trickery or kidnapping with the participation of native chiefs who attacked neighbouring islands as well as British sea captains. Although the British parliament passed the Pacific Islanders Protection Act in 1872 to regulate the recruitment of labour, workers from the Pacific islands continued to be exploited on the plantations of Queensland. The plantation economy even travelled further into the Pacific Ocean, where the rulers of Fiji (King Cakobau) and Hawaii (King Kamehameha III) attracted foreign capital to establish new plantations.[26]

This process was associated with continuous labour migration. While thousands of Hawaiians followed the lure of California gold, 46,000 Chinese, 20,000 Portuguese, 180,000 Japanese, 8,000 Koreans, 5,600 Puerto Ricans and 126,000 Filipinos came to Hawaii between 1870 and 1930, most of them to work on the plantations. When one ethnic group such as the Japanese went on strike, the plantation owners tried to replace them with workers of another nationality, for example Filipinos. Some of them returned home, while others moved on to their ultimate destination, the United States.[27]

Schooners and trawlers

On 23 March 1870, the *Gloucester Telegraph* reported from Portsmouth, New Hampshire, that local fishermen had caught or rather brought to Portsmouth harbour more than one million pounds of cod with ten ships in the previous winter. The reporter also noted that 63 miles of nets had been cast with more than 96,000 hooks. The apparent success in Portsmouth masks the decline of cod fishing in other regions such as the Gulf of Maine or the waters off Nova Scotia, where local fishermen as well as New Englanders and Frenchmen fished. The especially efficient French factory ships with their trawl nets were blamed for declining catch numbers there.[28] There were thus two opposing trends, with increasingly elaborate new technologies being used in the same or other places to compensate for falling catch numbers. This led to overfishing, which was recognized as both an economic and an ecological problem, but which was exacerbated by the new technologies. The term 'fisheries revolution' was coined for this phenomenon.

This revolution was not, as one might expect, associated with the introduction of steam technology, since Atlantic fishing continued to be conducted largely by sailing ship, and from there by rowboat. Nevertheless, the new types of ships such as schooners and sharpshooters were larger and faster than their predecessors and could sail higher to the wind because of their sharper hull form.

Nets were now also increasingly machine-made and were so tight that few fish could escape them. These bottom trawl nets facilitated deep-sea fishing but likewise threatened the spawning grounds. Apart from traditional fish like cod and mackerel, fishermen now hunted new species such as halibut, swordfish and above all sardines. Lobstering also reached new dimensions, which in turn created a great demand for bait such as clams, herring or flounder.

The fisheries revolution was accompanied by new forms of distribution. The ships took ice on board and refrigerated fish was brought to market by railway from the harbours. Fish that could not be preserved with salt and that had previously only been sold fresh in the port towns now reached American cities and wholesale fish merchants specialized in marketing them.[29] The demand in New York City, for example, grew continuously so that in years with poor catches, such as 1885/86 for mackerel, prices exploded. Mackerel was accordingly imported on a grand scale for the first time from Ireland, where this fish was still available at a low price. Mackerel, which was also purchased from South Africa, became the most important imported fish in the United States.[30]

Moreover, British steam trawlers expanded their radius of operations ever further into the North Sea and the Atlantic to supply the growing European population with fish. In the early twentieth century, fish was also available everywhere in America because of support for native fishing fleets. At the same time, the state promoted fisheries in Alaska and the establishment of new species in the Pacific, for instance by transporting adult lobsters by rail from the Atlantic coast to Seattle and releasing them in the waters there. After the overfishing of halibut in the Atlantic, halibut fishing also moved to Puget Sound on the West Coast.[31] Unlike in Europe and North America, fish was the mainstay of the East and Southeast Asian diet, alongside rice. Particularly in Southeast Asia the population used nearly every kind of seafood in their everyday lives. They consumed fish in various ways: coastal dwellers ate fresh fish, while the rest of the population enjoyed fish in preserved form, since it spoiled quickly in the hot, humid climate. Fish was usually dried in the sun and was often salted. Various pastes and sauces were also made from fish and other seafood. Fish roe was considered a delicacy and swim bladders – especially barramundi swim bladders – were in demand for medicine in China and Europe. In China shark fin soup was popular and fish oil was processed to light lamps. The sea cucumbers we already encountered in the Pacific were deemed a delicacy, and the Chinese prized crocodile penises as an aphrodisiac, while in the Moluccas seahorses were purchased as talismans. Ambergris, a substance excreted by sperm whales, was used in Europe to manufacture expensive perfumes, and in Asia as medicine. Sea turtles also had many uses; they were captured for their meat, their eggs and above all their shells, which were used to make precious decorative objects. Corals and pearl oysters were the most valuable products of the sea.[32]

The exploitation of the Indian Ocean and the South and East China Seas had scarcely changed over the centuries. In the mid-nineteenth century only a small part of the ocean was affected, mainly the waters along whose coasts most people lived and in regions where the most valuable sea creatures could be found. Fish was abundant and there was no need to transport it across long distances. The ecosystem was not yet under threat. Marketing only began on a large scale around 1900, when fish was transported on ice by railway from Selangor or Malacca to Kuala Lumpur. Steamers could bring salt for preservation to locations where the supply of fish was plentiful. The Chinese trade network exported dried fish and dried shrimp paste (belacan) from Singapore to all of Southeast Asia. The industrialization of Japan, which led to a higher demand for fish to feed the growing urban population of industrial workers, proved more influential. The Japanese government offered high subsidies to boost fisheries on its own coasts as well as in Southeast Asia and the South Pacific. This support included expedition ships charged with collecting oceanographic, ichthyological information from the lesser-known regions as well as the establishment of schools of fisheries. Japanese fishermen accordingly operated not just in Manila and Singapore, but also in Malaysia, the Dutch East Indies and Siam. European pearl companies also entered into contracts mainly with Japanese divers.

Fish consumption in Southeast Asia appears to have remained constant into the 1930s. While fishing shifted to the Gulf of Thailand or the Strait of Malacca and Japanese fishermen increased their haul in Philippine waters, demand and prices remained stable. We do not find the beginnings of the industrial fishing and overfishing we encountered in the Atlantic here until after the Second World War and the advent of trawling.[33]

Whaling reached new dimensions in the nineteenth century and drew whalers out into the depths of the open sea. The peoples of the Arctic had been hunting whales for food and oil for centuries, and in the early modern period Dutch and North German whaling crews had regularly gone whaling off the Spitsbergen archipelago. When whales became scarce near shore, hunters such as the Basque whalers pursued these large mammals into the open sea. In the nineteenth century, American whaling crews extended their activities into the North and South Atlantic as well as the Pacific. Tryworks made it possible to boil the blubber on board. During this period, sperm whales became the new objects of desire. Their blubber provided a better quality of oil, which could be used as a lubricant in industrial machinery. Furthermore, so-called spermaceti, a waxy substance in their heads, was in high demand for making high-quality, smokeless candles. As a result, by the 1870s American whalers had killed over 200,000 sperm whales and some 190,000 right whales. The

American whaling fleet provided jobs to Native Americans, African Americans, white Americans, Europeans and Pacific Islanders, who occupied a prominent position on board the ships, while most of the profits ended up in the pockets of shipowners and captains from New England. Around 1900, the Norwegian, Russian and Japanese whaling fleets took over an important part of previously American activities, not only in the Arctic and Antarctic regions, but also in the Pacific, which became a whaling ground for Japan and later the Soviet Union.[34]

The battle for maritime supremacy

The Battle of Trafalgar, at which Britain defeated Napoleon and his allies, became a symbolic expression of the British maritime supremacy that would persist for a century. The takeover of Dutch possessions (South Africa, Ceylon, Malacca) on the Indian Ocean turned it into a 'British lake'.

Britain now had access to a series of ports and trading posts that were continually expanding and would be manned by Indian sepoys.[35] The old centres such as Calcutta, Bombay and Madras were joined first by Cape Town, Mauritius, Colombo and later Durban, Aden, Karachi, Penang, Singapore, Hong Kong and Fremantle in Australia. Modern port facilities with rail connections opened up the hinterland, and the Suez Canal connected the motherland more closely with the colonies. In order to safeguard this route, British bases in the Mediterranean – Gibraltar, Malta and later Cyprus – acquired a new strategic significance. This development also led to a militarization of the seas, in which steam-powered warships facilitated the enforcement of British hegemony.[36]

In the Opium Wars that Britain conducted against China with the aim of opening the Chinese market to drugs, steamships like the HMS *Nemesis* offered the decisive advantage of being able to navigate rivers and canals. In 1840, it destroyed the Chinese war junks and threatened the capital of Beijing. The Qing emperor then saw himself compelled to sign an unequal treaty and open up Canton, Xiamen, Fuzhou, Shanghai and Ningbo to the Europeans as treaty ports as well as to cede Hong Kong to the British.

About a decade later, the American Commodore Matthew C. Perry arrived in Tokyo with a fleet of warships to open Japan to American trade. This was followed by the so-called Meiji Restoration, in which the shoguns lost their power and the imperial authorities tackled a programme of reform. Japan adapted Western technologies and transformed the feudal state into an industrial one. This included establishing a navy, which defeated China in 1894/95 in the war over Korea. In Europe, Japan's rise as a sea power was regarded with suspicion. Conflicts with Russia led to the Russo-Japanese war of 1904/05. After the Russian naval base of Port Arthur surrendered to the Japanese at the beginning of 1905, the Russian Baltic fleet, which had departed for the Pacific from the port of Libau via Africa, was also decimated in May of that year by the Japanese navy at the Battle of Tsushima. This defeat was the main trigger for the Russian Revolution of 1905.

Although Britain's Royal Navy had the largest fleet of warships in the world, the Pacific was increasingly the domain of the Americans, who in keeping with the Monroe Doctrine regarded the Caribbean and the South Atlantic as their exclusive sphere of influence. Apart from the Philippines they also occupied Guam, Hawaii and Puerto Rico.

The Panama Canal was an expression of American ambitions to play a leading role in the Atlantic as well as the Pacific. After an initial effort by Ferdinand de Lesseps, the developer of the Suez Canal, in the 1880s, which was thwarted by malaria and yellow fever, the United States undertook a successful second attempt under Theodore Roosevelt, which led to the opening of the Canal in 1914 and to US control of the Canal Zone until 1979.[37]

Theodore Roosevelt was an apt pupil of Alfred Thayer Mahan. In his book *The Influence of Sea Power upon History* (1890), Mahan wrote a theoretical treatise rooted in his experience on Union blockade ships during the American Civil War and his admiration for British sea power. For Mahan, sea power was based on maritime trade and communications networks, which had to be protected by the navy, with colonies and trading posts supplying the necessary infrastructure.[38]

Mahan was read avidly not just in Britain, where people found affirmation in his work, but also at the Japanese naval academy and in Alfred Tirpitz's circles in Wilhelmine Germany. Tirpitz aimed to build a fleet of warships to assist Germany, a latecomer to empire, in gaining an 'equal position in the world'.[39] The construction of a fleet of sixty large battleships was intended to put Germany's navy in a position to defeat Britain at sea.

This launched a naval arms race in which England gained an unassailable advantage with the introduction of the dreadnought class of battleships, named after the prototype HMS *Dreadnought*. Intended to dissuade Germany and other powers from engaging in an arms race because of the especially high cost of the dreadnought programme, the effect was the opposite. Germany reacted by building four ships of the so-called Nassau class. At the same time, Imperial Chancellor Bernhard von Bülow sought to reach a political agreement with the British.[40] When these attempts failed and England continued to expand its fleet programme, Tirpitz was still convinced that he could win the arms race. This proved illusory, as became evident at the beginning of the First World War: The Royal Navy launched a successful blockade that prevented the German fleet from leaving its bases, and the undecided Battle of Jutland brought no tangible success. The deployment of submarines was intended to bring about a breakthrough. However, after the ocean liner RMS *Lusitania* was torpedoed, causing nearly 1,200 deaths, outraged public opinion in the United States brought an end to the use of unlimited submarine warfare against enemies and neutral nations. The desperate resumption of submarine warfare against American merchant ships, among others, in 1917 led to the US entry into the war and ultimately to the defeat of Imperial Germany and the revolution, which the Kiel sailors sparked with their November 1918 mutiny.[41]

The maritime dimension of the First World War extended well beyond the German perspective, however. British and French colonial troops were transported to Europe by ship from Africa and Asia. The best-known example is probably the British Admiralty's attempt to attack the Ottoman Empire at what was believed to be its weakest point. To that end, a large contingent of soldiers from Australia and New Zealand were transferred to the Dardanelles to open up access to the Black Sea. The attempt ended in the retreat of the British, Australian and New Zealand troops. With more than 200,000 dead and wounded on both sides, the Battle of Gallipoli went down in history as one of the bloodiest military confrontations ever. It has, however, also become a site of memory for Australian military identity and is commemorated in Australia and New Zealand every year on Anzac Day.[42]

Oceanography and a new understanding of the sea

The nineteenth-century globalization of the sea went hand-in-hand with oceanographic research and the emotional appropriation of the sea. The first step in marine research was to measure the depth of the seas. Sailing in shallow waters, and confronted with frequent fogs, sailors were always concerned with the depth of the water through which they sailed. Depth was measured by sounding, which involved using a sounding line, a rope with a lead plummet on the end. In order to determine the depth of the sea and ascertain the composition of the seabed, a 'leadsman' on the ship threw the plummet into the water. When the plummet was smeared with tallow, it picked up grains of the bottom sediment and enabled navigators to fix their position, due to their knowledge of the composition of the seabed off various coasts. Furthermore, the marked sounding line gave an idea of the actual depth, measured in so-called fathoms (1.8 m or 6 ft), the arm span of a man.

Sounding practices enabled navigators to establish ocean routes as well as to explore unfamiliar waters. Studying the seabed also helped to find new fishing grounds. Information about sea depths, the seabed, shipping routes, adverse winds and currents was recorded by captains in their logbooks and on maps, but most of the data did not survive the individual captain or his ship. That is why Matthew Fontaine Maury, a former US Navy midshipman and later superintendent of the United States Naval Observatory, decided to systematize this forgotten sailors' knowledge and make it available to all sea captains. Maury's *Explanations and Sailing Directions to Accompany the Wind and Current Charts* (eight editions, 1851–9) showed sailors the fastest way over the Atlantic, and his charts provided a line of soundings along the new steamship routes and the later submarine telegraph cable between Newfoundland and Ireland.[43] What is more, Maury initiated international cooperation in meteorology, inviting colleagues and scientists to a first international conference in Brussels in 1853. As a result of the conference, many seafaring nations agreed to provide Maury with their oceanographic observations. Maury processed the land and sea weather data and shared them worldwide.

It was, however, the Scottish naturalist Charles Wyville Thomson who put deep sea research on the British agenda. After two deep sea dredging expeditions with Royal Navy HMS *Lightning* and HMS *Porcupine* in 1868 and 1869, which showed that animal life existed in the deep sea, Thomson convinced the Navy to provide him with another ship, HMS *Challenger*, for a global expedition. This oceanographic expedition lasted from 1872 until 1876 and carried out 363 station measurements during its 69,000 nautical mile voyage in all the oceans. The expedition took 494 deep sea soundings, 263 temperature measurements at various depths, 151 trawl catches and conducted 133 dredges to obtain seabed samples and deep-sea organisms. Some 4,700 new species of marine life were discovered as a result. The expedition conducted meteorological, hydrographic, geological and biological investigations. Before this voyage, the ocean depths were largely unknown, with the exception of the North Atlantic. The *Challenger* expedition produced the first depth maps of the oceans with the deepest sounding at 8,184 metres in the southwest Pacific Ocean between Guam and Palau. The processing and evaluation of the samples were carried out in institutes in many countries. In 1880 and 1895, the results were published in fifty large-format volumes, which were made available to the most important oceanographic institutes in the world.

German, Norwegian and French deep-sea expeditions followed, and European nations founded the International Council for the Exploration of the Seas (ICES) in 1902. Inspired by the Kiel scholar Victor Hensen's pathbreaking discovery of the importance of phytoplankton for the marine food chain, the use of science to preserve and restore fisheries became a common European aim, which was tied to the notion of European scientific dominion over the oceans.[44]

Public interest in the oceans and the deep sea had grown since the 1850s. The aquarium at the London World Exhibition of 1851 attracted many visitors, and public aquariums sprung up in European and American cities, while readers devoured novels such as Jules Verne's *20 000 Leagues under the Sea*.

At the same time, the sea became a place of longing. The Romantic rediscovery of the sea in the nineteenth century coincided with doctors' recommendations to spend time at the seaside, since they were convinced that gazing upon the water and breathing salt air were beneficial for the health and recreation of city dwellers.

While journeys to inland spas had enjoyed some popularity since the sixteenth century and became fashionable in the eighteenth century, seaside resorts arose in large numbers only in the second half of the eighteenth century. The pioneer in this regard was England, where the physician Richard Russell's oft-reprinted *A Dissertation Concerning the Use of Sea Water in Diseases of the Glands* recommended using sea water internally and externally to treat numerous ailments such as rheumatism, scurvy, gonorrhoea, herpes and tumours.[45] The first English towns to introduce public bathing around 1720 were Whitby und Scarborough, but the business of seaside resorts soon moved to the south coast. Brighton, Harwich, Margate, Southampton, Weymouth and Plymouth in particular established a new bathing culture. This quickly spread to the Continent, across the Channel to Scheveningen, Boulogne, Dieppe and to the French and Italian Riviera. Dieppe and Brighton were the watering places of the European aristocracy, who stayed for long periods, often in the entourage of a member of the royal family, which became a popular topic of interest for the local press.[46]

In the United States as well as Australia and South Africa, too, the seaside offered swimming experiences that were no longer limited to bathing machines, but included a new beach culture, such as surf bathing (swimming in the sea) in Australia, that anticipated twentieth-century developments.

After returning from a journey to England in 1793, the German scientist and author Georg Christoph Lichtenberg asked, 'Why does Germany not have a large public seaside resort yet?' This inspired a debate on the relative advantages and disadvantages of the North and Baltic Sea as locations for such a resort. While proponents of the North Sea stressed the higher salt content of the water, supporters of the Baltic praised the lack of tides and consistent water temperature. It was Samuel Gottlieb Vogel, personal physician to Grand Duke Friedrich Franz I of Mecklenburg-Schwerin, who took the initiative, however, and convinced the ruler to establish a seaside resort. When Friedrich Franz, accompanied by his retinue and his officials, took his first sea bath at Heiligendamm near Doberan on 22 July 1793, it sealed the symbolic founding of Heiligendamm as a resort.[47] The years that followed saw the construction of residential as well as sociable and cultural buildings like the Salon building (1802), the Grand Palais (1806–9) or the pavilions, all designed by Carl Theodor Severing, a pupil of the famous Prussian architect Carl Gotthard Langhans.

Bathing facilities and lodgings for the growing number of Baltic tourists were also built. In the first half of the nineteenth century, an average of 1,200 guests visited the seaside resort every year, although not all of them came to bathe, since the presence of the grand duke's family and other members of the European high nobility was a tourist attraction in its own right. At the same time, Heiligendamm now had competition, since seaside resorts had sprung up all along the North Sea and Baltic coasts, including Norderney (1797), Travemünde (1802), Warnemünde (1805), Spiekeroog (1809), Putbus (1816), Binz (1825) and Jüst (1840).

Seaside tourism in the eastern Baltic enjoyed a veritable boom in the 1820s and 1830s because of Russian visitors.[48] After foreign travel became more difficult for inhabitants of Tsarist Russia, they shifted their focus to the coastal towns of Finland and the Baltic provinces. Petersburgers spent their summers in Helsinki or at the seaside further south. A tourist infrastructure emerged with typical wooden hotels, for example in Pernau (Pärnu), Hapsal (Haapsalu), Arensburg on the island of Ösel (Kuressaare on Saaremaa island), Hanko in southern Finland, and Öregrund on the eastern coast of Sweden. With time, some of them were replaced by stone structures, while splendid luxury hotels were constructed in Saltsjöbaden (near Stockholm), Kulosaari (near Helsinki), Skodsborg at the Sound Binz on Rügen, Heringsdorf on Usedom and Zoppot (Sopot, near Gdánsk).

Summer leisure time also led to the advent of sailing as a sport. Yacht clubs were founded everywhere, and regattas organized. Yacht club pavilions dotted the Baltic coast and lent maritime glamour to Riga's beach (known since 1920 as Jūrmala). Sport sailing came from England, and was closely associated with the expansion of the fleets and the increasing prestige of the navy before the First World War. A prime example is the port city of Kiel, which evolved into an imperial military harbour for the naval fleet that grew rapidly especially under Emperor Wilhelm II, and into a maritime armoury. Regattas were regularly staged here on the inlet known as the Förde beginning in 1882. In 1887, naval officers and officials founded the Marine-Regatta-Verein (Naval Regatta Association), which Emperor Wilhelm II granted the title 'Imperial Yacht Club' in 1893 in his capacity as honorary chairman (commodore). The emperor and his brother Heinrich visited the so-called Kiel Week regularly from 1894 and promoted the sport of sailing, which in Germany followed the lead of the Kiel Yacht Club.

In Russia the tsar's family also lent the sport prestige by becoming patrons of the imperial 'St Petersburg River Sailing Society'. Finally, before the First World War, it became the fashion for ruling monarchs to meet at sea. Nicholas II and Wilhelm II, who were cousins, did so at Björkö in 1905 and in Swinemünde two years later. Edward VII also travelled by yacht to Reval in 1908 to pay his respects to his cousin Nicholas II.[49]

Moreover, the summer recreations of Europe's crowned heads also inspired a new form of pleasure trip for an upper middle-class public. The travels of Wilhelm II to Norway on his yacht, the *Hohenzollern*, popularized trips to Scandinavia, which were organized by North German Lloyd and HAPAG from the 1890s. Around the same time, British, Dutch and French shipping companies offered cruises lasting several weeks that targeted the new group of leisure travellers.

To this end, ships that had previously transported emigrants were remodelled and refitted by interior designers experienced in furnishing hotels. The main clientele were Americans travelling from New York to Britain and from there to Paris, along the Rhine or to the Alps or Italy.[50] Artists and writers also made use of these services. Italian opera companies travelled the Pacific and the Indian Ocean on steamers and performed in the most important port cities such as Manila, Macao, Hong Kong, Singapore and Batavia.[51] The Bengali poet Rabindranath Tagore had also taken a leisure voyage across the Indian Ocean to England and the United States even before receiving the Nobel Prize for Literature in 1913. In 1916, during the First World War, he left India for Burma and then continued by steamer to Southeast Asia, Japan and North America. In 1924/25, Tagore travelled to Buenos Aires via the Indian Ocean, the Suez Canal, the Mediterranean and Marseille. He used his return journey for a longer sojourn in Italy before returning home to India.[52]

Those who did not go on sea voyages enjoyed the beach and the sea air in their summer houses, whether in *bastides* on the French Mediterranean coast or skerry landscapes on the Baltic. Those who could not afford their own holiday home spent the summer boarding with fishermen or sea captains who offered rooms to guests.

The idyllic skerry became an important motif in Baltic art. Anders Zorn painted summer life near Stockholm and Albert Edelfelt captured the mood of the skerries of Uusimaa. In this way, the experiences of nature and art mutually influenced one another.

Artists like the Impressionists Camille Pissarro and Eugène Delacroix repeatedly visited the new beach resorts; others settled by the sea, seeking inspiration from it and the life of fishermen. The Danish painters in Skagen – a fishing village where the North and Baltic Seas meet – devoted themselves to depicting light and water as well as the working population of the coast. In this way, Michael and Anna Ancher, Viggo Johansen, P. S. Krøyer, Marie Krøyer, Christian Krohg, Carl Locher, Karl Madsen and Lauritz Tuxen paved the way for Danish Impressionism.

The most important marine painter of the nineteenth century, William Turner, regularly took lodgings in Margate and went to sea to gather a variety of impressions. One of his most significant paintings – *Steam Boat off a Harbour's Mouth Making Signals in Shallow Waters, and Going by the Lead*,

The Author was in this Storm on the Night the Ariel left Harwich – depicts a steamer, and the artist had been on board to capture the moment. We see the ship grappling with the forces of nature and attempting to master it with new technology.

Caspar David Friedrich, too, who grew up on the Baltic coast and went on to become the pioneer of Nordic Romanticism, portrayed the yearning gaze upon the sea as well as the view from water to land. While studying at the art academy in Copenhagen he became familiar with Joseph Vernet's paintings of ships on the Mediterranean and was inspired by the marine landscapes of his teacher Jens Juel. In paintings like *On the Sailing Boat* Friedrich thus depicted not just the distant city on shore, but also the subjects of the gaze on board the ship. In *Monk by the Sea*, the water becomes an object of projection for the viewing subject. His painting *The Sea of Ice* would be virtually inconceivable without contemporary accounts of Arctic expeditions.

Paul Gauguin went a good deal further. His longing took him from Brittany and Provence across the Caribbean to the South Pacific, and his colourful 'exotic' paintings set the stage for Expressionism.

At the Pacific itself, the Japanese printmaker Katsushika Hokusai, inspired by Dutch engravings, captured the power of the sea. His dramatic 'Great Wave off Kanagawa' became important to European painters and is regarded as an iconic piece of marine art. Furthermore, in his series 'One Thousand Pictures of the Ocean' he depicts the various forms of fishing, especially fishing boats in the waves of the wild sea (see cover illustration).[53]

Notes

1 A. Smith, *An Inquiry into the Nature and Causes of the Wealth of Nations.* Books I, II, III, IV and VI (1776; Amsterdam, 2007), 19 (Book I, ch. 4).

2 J. Armstrong and D. Williams, 'An Appraisal of the Progress of the Steamship in the Nineteenth Century', in G. Harlaftis, S. Tenold and J. M. Valdaliso (eds.), *The World's Key Industry. History and Economics of International Shipping* (Basingstoke and New York, 2012), 43–63.

3 W. Kresse, *Die Fahrtgebiete der Hamburger Handelsflotte 1824–1888* (Hamburg, 1972), 184–9.

4 S. Palmer, 'The British Shipping Industry 1850–1914', in L. R. Fischer and G. E. Painting (eds.), *Change and Adaptation in Maritime History. The North Atlantic Fleets in the Nineteenth Century* (St John's, 1984), 87–115; L. R. Fischer and H. W. Nordvik, 'Maritime Transport and the Integration of the North Atlantic Economy, 1850–1914', in W. Fischer (ed.), *The Emergence of a World Economy 1500–1914. Papers of the IXth International Congress of Economic History* (Stuttgart, 1986), 519–46.

5   Fischer and Nordvik, 'Maritime Transport', 539.

6   C. Knick Harley, 'Late Nineteenth-Century Transportation, Trade and Settlement', in Fischer (ed.), *Emergence of a World Economy*, 593–618.

7   A. J. H. Latham, 'The International Trade in Rice and Wheat since 1868. A Study in Market Integration', in Fischer (ed.), *Emergence of a World Economy*, 645–64; A. J. H. Latham and L. Neal, 'The International Market in Rice and Wheat, 1868–1914', *Economic History Review* 36, no. 2 (1983): 260–80.

8   C. Knick Harley, 'Shipping and Stable Economies in the Periphery', in Harlaftis, Tenold and Valdaliso (eds.), *World's Key Industry*, 29–42.

9   M. North, 'German Sailors, 1650–1900', in J. R. Bruijn, J. Lucassen and P. C. van Royen (eds.), *'Those Emblems of Hell'? European Sailors and the Maritime Labour Market, 1570–1870* (St John's, 1997), 258. See also J. Ojala, J. Pehkonen and J. Eloranta, 'Deskilling and Decline in Skill Premiums during the Age of Sail: Swedish and Finnish Seamen, 1751–1913', *Explorations in Economic History* 61 (2016): 85–94.

10 Y. Kaukiainen, 'Overseas Migration and the Development of Ocean Navigation. A Europe-Outward Perspective', in Gabaccia and Hoerder (eds.), *Connecting Seas and Connected Ocean Rims*, 371–87.

11 R. Wenzlhuemer, *Connecting the Nineteenth-Century World: The Telegraph and Globalization* (Cambridge, 2013).

12 R. Boyce, 'Submarine Cables as a Factor in Britain's Ascendancy', in M. North (ed.), *Kommunikationsrevolutionen. Die neuen Medien des 16. und 19. Jahrhunderts*, 2nd edn (Cologne, 2001), 81–99.

13 Ahvenainen, 'The Role of Telegraphs', 73–80; M. North, 'Einleitung', in North (ed.), *Kommunikationsrevolutionen*, ix–xix.

14 C. Neutsch, 'Briefverkehr als Medium Internationaler Kommunikation im ausgehenden 19. und beginnenden 20. Jahrhundert', in North (ed.), *Kommunikationsrevolutionen*, 129–55.

15 S. Hensel, 'Latin American Perspectives on Migration in the Atlantic World', in Gabaccia and Hoerder (eds.), *Connecting Seas*, 289.

16 Sánchez-Albornoz, *La población de América latina*, 129–42.

17 Hensel, 'Latin American Perspectives', 281–301.

18 G. Campbell and A. Stanziani (eds.), *Bonded Labour and Debt in the Indian Ocean World* (Oxford and London, 2013).

19 G. Campbell, *Slavery and the Trans-Indian Ocean World Slave Trade*, in H. P. Ray and E. A. Alpers (eds.), *Cross Currents and Community Networks: The History of the Indian Ocean World* (New Delhi, 2007), 291–4.

20 Alpers, *The Indian Ocean*, 116–18.

21 E. Hu-Dehart, 'Chinese Coolie Labor in Cuba in the Nineteenth Century. Free Labor of Neoslavery', *Contributions in Black Studies* 12 (1994): 38–54.

22 R. J. Chandler and S. J. Potash, *Gold, Silk, Pioneers & Mail. The Story of the Pacific Mail Steamship Company* (San Francisco, 2007); E. M. Tate, *Trans-Pacific Steam: The Story of Steam Navigation from the Pacific Coast*

of North America to the Far East and the Antipodes, 1867–1941 (New York, 1986).

23 A. McKeown, 'Movement', in Armitage and Bashford (eds.), *Pacific Histories*, 152–3.

24 E. Sinn, *Pacific Crossing. California Gold, Chinese Migration, and the Making of Hong Kong* (Hong Kong, 2013), 231–40.

25 McKeown, 'Movement', 152–3.

26 Matsuda, *Pacific Worlds*, 216–32.

27 C. Skwiot, 'Migration and the Politics of Sovereignty, Settlement, and Belonging in Hawai'i', in Gabaccia and Hoerder (eds.), *Connecting Seas*, 440–63.

28 W. J. Bolster, *The Mortal Sea. Fishing the Atlantic in the Age of Sail* (Cambridge, MA and London, 2012), 158–63.

29 Ibid., 133–68.

30 Ibid., 191–7.

31 Ibid., 223–7.

32 J. G. Butcher, *The Closing of the Frontier. A History of the Marine Fisheries of Southeast Asia c. 1850–2000* (Singapore, 2004), 27–59; P. Borschberg, 'O comércio da âmbar cinzento asiático na época moderna', *Revista Oriente* 8 (2004): 3–25 and 'Der asiatische Ambra-Handel während der frühen Neuzeit', in J. Alves, C. Guillot and R. Ptak (eds.), *Mirabilia Asiatica II. Seltene Waren im Seehandel* (Wiesbaden and Lisbon, 2004), 167–201.

33 Butcher, *Closing of the Frontier*, 60–74. See chapter X 'Dangerous Seas', sub-chapter 'Overfishing'.

34 Rozwadowski, *Vast Expanses*, 106–7; M. Johnson, 'Whales and Whaling', in R. F. Buschmann and L. Nolde (eds.), *The World's Oceans. Geography, History, and Environment* (Santa Barbara, 2018), 309–422; D. H. Cushing, *The Provident Sea* (Cambridge, 1988), 109–14. See chapter VIII, 'Pacific', sub-chapter 'Between Canton and California'.

35 S. S. Amrith, *Crossing the Bay of Bengal. The Furies of Nature and the Fortunes of Migrants* (Cambridge, MA and London, 2013), 74–5.

36 Alpers, *The Indian Ocean*, 98–112.

37 R. F. Buschmann, *Oceans in World History* (Boston, 2007), 104–7.

38 A. T. Mahan, *The Influence of Sea Power upon History 1660–1783* (1889; 2nd edn, Bremen, 2010).

39 Quoted in M. Epkenhans, *Die wilhelminische Flottenrüstung 1908–1914* (Munich, 1991), 409.

40 Ibid., 31–51.

41 M. Epkenhans, 'Flotten und Flottenrüstung im 20. Jahrhundert', in J. Elvert, S. Hess and H. Walle (eds.), *Maritime Wirtschaft in Deutschland. Schifffahrt – Werften – Handel – Seemacht im 19. und 20. Jahrhundert* (Stuttgart, 2012), 176–89.

42 P. Hart, *Gallipoli* (London, 2011).

43 Rozwadowski, *Vast Expanses*, 111.

44 H. M. Rozwadowski, *The Sea Knows No Boundaries. A Century of Marine Science under ICES* (Copenhagen, 2002), 475–80.

45 D. Richter, *Das Meer. Geschichte der ältesten Landschaft* (Berlin, 2014), 147–9.

46 A. Corbin, *The Lure of the Sea. Discovery of the Seaside in the Western World 1750–1840*, trans. J. Phelps (Berkeley and Los Angeles, 1994), 269–77.

47 W. Karge, *Heiligendamm. Erstes deutsches Seebad. Gegründet 1793* (Schwerin, 1993). For a good overview of the origins of Bad Doberan and other German seaside resorts, see A. Brenner's thesis '"Wenn jemand eine Reise tut, so kann er was erzählen … ". Die Anfänge des Bädertourismus am Beispiel des ersten deutschen Seebades Doberan-Heiligendamm', State Examination thesis, University of Greifswald, 2010.

48 O. Kurilo (ed.), *Seebäder an der Ostsee im 19. und 20. Jahrhundert* (Munich, 2009).

49 For this and what follows, see Klinge, *Die Ostseewelt*, 130–3 and *The Baltic World*. Revised, expanded edn. (Helsinki, 2010).

50 D. Bellmann, *Von Höllengefährten zu schwimmenden Palästen. Die Passagierschifffahrt auf dem Atlantik (1840–1930)* (Frankfurt and New York, 2015), 37–46.

51 A. Sugiyama, 'The Transmission and Circulation of Western Opera in the Netherlands East Indies, 1835–1869: Preliminary Observations', *SEJARAH: Journal of the Department of History* 26, no. 2 (2017): 98–105 and 'Maritime Journeys of European Opera in the Indonesian Archipelago, 1835–1869', *International Journal of Maritime History* 31, no. 2 (2019): 248–62.

52 S. Bose, *A Hundred Horizons. The Indian Ocean in the Age of Global Empire* (Cambridge, MA and London, 2006), 233–71.

53 M. Forrer, *Hokusai. Prints and Drawings* (Munich, 2010), 9–26, illustration 10, 11, 47–9.

X

Dangerous Seas:

Exploitation, Pollution and the Refugee Crisis

This account by the fisherman Mahyuddin recalls the most recent disaster on the Indian Ocean, when on 26 December 2004, a 9.1 magnitude earthquake off the coast of Sumatra unleashed a tsunami that destroyed countless settlements:

On Saturday I went fishing around Pulau Weh, an island off Aceh, and we spent the night there. We were on the way back to the mainland on Sunday morning when our boats started rocking. After that we could see a huge wave in the distance. It was extraordinary, about 20 meters high. Another boat crew heading to land started yelling at us, telling us to return to the middle of the ocean. Three waves passed and at noon we got a radio call asking for us to help rescue the victims. On the way back we saw bodies floating in the water. It was unbelievable. We picked up many survivors. When we got to land we saw that it was flat, debris was everywhere and there was a clear view of the mountain. We helped rescue people all day and before it got dark I returned to my home in Kampoeng Jawa village. Sadly, my house had been swept away. I had lost my wife and my son and I didn't know what to do. I went to the great mosque and slept there on the terrace and the tremors continued into the night.[1]

Tsunamis – the word means 'harbour wave' in Japanese – though not unknown on the Indian Ocean, are relatively rare there. The 2004 tsunami, however, exceeded anything ever seen. The wave wreaked havoc in Indonesia, Malaysia, Thailand, Myanmar, Bangladesh, India, Sri Lanka (Ceylon), the Maldives, Kenya, Tanzania and Somalia. More than 200,000 people died and some two million lost their homes. The effects were also felt on the Pacific. The tsunami was widely reported in the press, especially because around 2,000 mainly European tourists on their Christmas holidays lost their lives at various beach resorts.[2]

In recent years, only the people who have drowned trying to flee across the Mediterranean to Europe have received comparable media attention. While the sea has always presented dangers to humankind, people now present far more and varied dangers to the sea. These include the rising volume of shipping worldwide as well as industrial exploitation, CO_2 emissions, war and nuclear testing.

Pearl Harbor and the Bikini Atoll

The maritime military conflicts that had begun in the First World War assumed new dimensions in the Second World War. To be sure, Nazi Germany was initially in a position to endanger Allied supply convoys with its submarines. In November 1942, the Germans sank 725,000 tonnes of Allied ships and threatened supplies to Britain, but over the course of 1943 the Allies largely succeeded in containing the German submarine fleet through air dominance in the North Atlantic, new radar systems and breaking German naval codes (Enigma).

The fundamental changes occurred in the Pacific, where Japan occupied the Philippines, British Malaysia and the Dutch East Indies from December 1941. The attempt to decimate the US naval fleet anchored in Pearl Harbor in Hawaii by a surprise attack was only partially successful. While Japanese planes destroyed and damaged twenty-one ships and killed some 2,500 sailors and civilians, the American aircraft carriers were out at sea during the assault and fuel and replenishment supplies remained intact. Aircraft carriers would accordingly prove to be an important new weapon during the war in the Pacific. The Americans emerged victorious from the Battle of the Coral Sea (7 and 8 May 1942) and the Battle of Midway (4 to 7 June 1942). Operating from aircraft carriers, American pilots were able to halt a further Japanese invasion and limit the Japanese Navy's radius of action by destroying several aircraft carriers and some 300 planes. Thereafter, the way was clear for the Americans to reconquer the Pacific, which ended with the dropping of the first atomic bomb, *Little Boy*, on Hiroshima on 6 August 1945 and *Fat Man* on Nagasaki on 9 August.

The militarization of the Pacific region continued, however, even after the American victory. The US Navy discovered the 'uninhabited' Bikini Atoll as an ideal site for future nuclear testing. The United States detonated sixty-seven nuclear bombs on the Bikini and Enewetak Atolls between 1946 and 1958, since they were far away from shipping routes. The islanders were asked to leave their homes and gradually resettled on various atolls, without providing them with a new means of livelihood. The inhabitants of the Bikini Atoll now lacked a lagoon for their traditional fishing and the stormy seas often prevented supply ships from landing on the islands. The population therefore demanded to return to their home atoll, but the deadly effects of nuclear testing soon became apparent: since the inhabitants consumed the radioactively contaminated fish, shrimp and coconuts, the rate of miscarriages and birth defects rose.

The islanders were then resettled again, especially to Kili, which belonged to the Marshall Islands. The surviving inhabitants of the Bikini Atoll and their descendants have now fallen victim to climate change, since the low-lying island of Kili regularly floods and saltwater contaminates the groundwater, making it unsuitable for human consumption and agriculture.

While the United States stopped its tests in the Pacific in 1963, France began nuclear testing there in 1966 and did not even stop at sinking the Greenpeace ship *Rainbow Warrior* in Oakland in 1985. New Zealand and Australia had protested the French nuclear tests in the 1970s, and the anti-nuclear movement quickly spread. The sinking of the *Rainbow Warrior* gained the movement international attention, and in 1996 French President Jacques Chirac had to abandon his plan to resume French testing, which had ended in 1974.

The movement for a Pacific free of nuclear weapons brought together a variety of political groups who were both opposed to nuclear testing and supportive of the independence movements of small nations in the Pacific region. The United States nevertheless maintained dominance in the region by linking their naval and air force bases in California, Hawaii, the Philippines and Japan. When Subic Bay Naval Base in the Philippines had to be closed in 1992 because of political pressure, the troops stationed there were transferred to Guam.[3]

When the end of the Cold War reduced the confrontations between the great powers at sea, piracy offered new challenges to international shipping. While in the Strait of Malacca cooperation among the littoral states reduced threats to maritime traffic, the western Indian Ocean, especially the coast of Somalia, experienced a veritable boom in piracy starting in 2005. In order to protect free shipping and UN aid deliveries for Somalia, the EU decided to carry out a naval operation aimed at repelling pirate attacks and destroying their infrastructure. Apart from a military presence, only regional agreements could combat piracy in the long term.[4]

Further conflicts at sea arise from claims to alleged mineral resources. One example is the Spratly Island archipelago, which extends across 1,000 km in the South China Sea. The islands are claimed in whole or in part by Vietnam and the People's Republic of China, but also by Malaysia, the Philippines and Brunei. The key factors here are their strategic location as well as putative oil and gas deposits. All of the abovementioned states, with the exception of Brunei, have occupied parts of the islands, and the expansion of the Chinese presence through the creation of artificial islands has attracted the involvement of neighbouring countries and the United States. China has refused to participate in arbitration proceedings initiated by the Philippines before the International Court of Justice in The Hague.

Beijing sought to create precedents in the region in order to attain sovereignty over the South China Sea, based on the regulations of the 1982 UN Convention of the Law of the Sea. In the course of exploiting marine natural resources, this convention established a twelve-nautical-mile (c. 22 km) territorial limit as well as a 200-mile zone for coastal states for their exclusive economic use, whether for fishing or the exploitation of the mineral deposits of the continental shelf. Although freedom of navigation still exists in these areas, this means that around one third of the world's seas are now under territorial control.

Flight and migration

Flight and migration across seas are closely associated with war. Television reports on Africans desperately trying to reach the Canary Islands on flimsy boats while tourists from all over Europe sun themselves on the beaches drew public attention to this problem in the summer of 2006. The arrival in Lampedusa of thousands of refugees on boats and their precarious situation in 2015, however, did not move European politicians to take action. It was only in September when the photo of the drowned three-year-old Alan Kurdi was seen around the world that some countries opened their borders for refugees fleeing the Syrian civil war. Nevertheless, more than 1,000 people continue to drown in the Mediterranean every year.[5]

Although the dimensions or public perception of people fleeing across the sea may seem extraordinary, the phenomenon is not new and represents just one part of overall migration internationally. In the twentieth century, the murderous policies of Nazi Germany in particular drove millions of people from their homelands, hundreds of thousands of whom travelled by sea. It is not only today that fleeing by sea is organized by people smugglers; in the past, too, refugees were forced to use their services, since as is the case today, many countries refuse to take them in. This primarily affected Jewish refugees from Nazi Germany. Although the United States was the most coveted destination, the fixed immigration quotas, closure of consulates, the ban on immigration (1941) and negative public opinion led to the rejection of most Jewish refugees. Thus, for example, the 930 Jewish refugees on board the St Louis in 1939 were turned away by the United States, Cuba and Canada and sent back to Europe. As a result, half of the passengers were killed in the Holocaust. South America took in approximately 35,000 Jews between 1939

FIGURE 10 *Tourists and refugees on a Mediterranean beach.* © *Picture alliance/ REUTERS/Yannis Behrakis.*

and 1945, some of whom later moved to the United States or Palestine or to Israel after the war.

Britain took strong measures to prevent migration to Palestine. At the time most refugees were already forced to travel illegally with false papers on unseaworthy ships, often first crossing the Danube and the Black Sea to arrive in Palestine. Illegal migration continued after Germany's defeat in the Second World War, since Jewish organizations tried to bring ships with Holocaust survivors to Palestine but were often thwarted by British policy. One example is the *Exodus*, which was supposed to transport 4,515 people from Marseille to Palestine in July 1947. British ships captured the *Exodus* shortly before it could land in Tel Aviv, transferred the passengers to British troop carriers and took them back to France. Since the refugees refused to disembark there, they were simply transported to Hamburg and stuck in internment camps near Lübeck. After international pressure led to their release many of them succeeded in making their way to Palestine via France. Only the founding of the state of Israel cleared the way for permanent immigration.[6]

The decolonialization process in Africa and the Caribbean in particular brought waves of emigration to Europe. For France, this so-called repatriation meant that 1.8 million persons, about 800,000 of them former colonial settlers known as *Pieds-Noirs*, departed from Algeria between 1954 and 1964 to settle mainly on the other side of the Mediterranean.[7] Around the same time, West

Indians from the former British, French and Dutch colonies in the Caribbean moved to the motherlands where they had an unlimited right to settle until the colonies gained their independence.[8]

Cold War military and political conflicts also regularly set waves of refugees in motion. After the Vietnam War there was a mass exodus from South Vietnam. Some 1.6 million Vietnamese tried to flee by boat across the South China Sea. Nearly 250,000 of these so-called boat people died at sea or fell prey to pirates in the Gulf of Thailand. Malaysia, Thailand, Indonesia and the Philippines turned them away or forced them back to sea, leaving thousands of boats adrift on the South China Sea. Ultimately the problem was resolved, if not permanently, and many lives saved, because the United States exerted political pressure on countries to accept the refugees temporarily and offer guarantees for future asylum.

In other parts of the world, too, flight from Communist regimes also forced people onto the seas. Thus 5,500 East German citizens tried to escape across the Baltic, but only one in ten reached Denmark or Schleswig-Holstein. Many of them drowned or were picked up by the East German Navy and sent to prison.

Flight across the sea from Cuba, especially to Florida, assumed larger dimensions, as did the later wave of refugees from Haiti to the United States, which the American government tried to prevent. Australia was also keen to halt growing migration from Bangladesh, Afghanistan or Indonesia and to this end introduced the so-called Pacific Solution: refugee ships were either turned away and sent back to Indonesia or the people on board were interned in detention camps on the island nation of Nauru or the island of Manus, which belongs to Papua-New Guinea until they either left voluntarily or received asylum. In the latter case, however, they were granted a residence permit only for Papua-New Guinea, not Australia.[9]

All these factors notwithstanding, people continue to flee across the Indian Ocean, especially from Bangladesh and Myanmar, hoping to reach Thailand, Malaysia or Indonesia. The crisis in Yemen in March 2015, in contrast, saw people fleeing in the opposite direction; some 45,000 refugees left Yemen for Djibouti and Somalia. This is but a small number, however, compared to the figures for African internal migration, where in 2019, 18.9 million people were displaced in their own or neighbouring countries.[10]

Tankers and tonnage

War, violence and expulsion are not the only sources of danger, however. International shipping, a precondition for globalization, also imperils the seas, their ecosystems and ultimately human beings as well.

In the twentieth and early twenty-first centuries, shipping or rather the volume of goods transported by sea rose continuously. This can be attributed primarily to the increase in the size of ships. Between 1880 and 2008, the capacity of merchant ships grew on average from around 700 to more than 24,000 gross registered tonnes, while their speed only quadrupled. Resistance from waves and currents sets limits to the increase in ship speeds. Only the transition from sailing ships to steamers markedly increased the speed and reliability of shipping. Afterwards, acceleration was only gradual. The weight of these steel ships rose along with their size and tonnage. This development began in the 1950s with the construction of large tankers.

One catalyst was the Korean War, which made it necessary to transport oil across the Pacific. The temporary nationalization of the British oil industry in the Persian Gulf altered the demand for transport. Refineries were no longer built near the oilfields, but closer to consumers in Europe and Japan, which led to transports of crude oil across international waters. Since larger tankers are more profitable than small ones, they grew along with their total tonnage. This development was interrupted by the oil crises of the 1970s and 1980s, however. It was not until 2004 that the tonnage of the tanker fleet again reached the level of 1980.

Crude oil transports comprise about one third of total cargo worldwide. For some time now, an additional energy carrier in the form of liquified petroleum gas has been moving across the world's seas. The Covid-19 pandemic as well as the de-carbonization of energy will lead to a reduction in tanker and bulk carrier (coal) traffic. While America was the leading oil transporter during the interwar period, Greek and Norwegian shipping companies took over this business sector after the Second World War. In the tanker business, flagging out became a widespread phenomenon, in which shipping companies operated their tankers under the flag of a lower-tax country. This is how Panama and Liberia but also Singapore became the most important home ports for tankers, although their owners continue to be based mainly in Greece, Japan, China and Germany.[11] Tanker accidents with disastrous consequences for the seas and coastlines, like that involving the Liberian-registered *Amoco Cadiz,* which ran aground off Brittany in 1978, heightened criticisms of the safety standards of the flags of convenience.

The growth of the international economy since 1945 boosted demand for raw materials and freight capacity worldwide. Thus, the transport of industrial raw materials quadrupled between 1960 and 1990: freighters brought iron ore from South America, India and Australia to Europe and Japan, while British coal was replaced by American, South African or Australian coal.[12]

The invention of the shipping container and container ships revolutionized freight transport by sea. The idea came from the American transport entrepreneur Malcolm McLean, who realized that carrying freight in containers made it easier to load ships, since cargo no longer had to be loaded and unloaded manually. Containers could be transported directly to ships by rail or truck. At first, they were used for transport along the American coasts and were stored on the ship's decks. Starting in the late 1960s, ships were constructed to carry the containers in their holds. They were followed by purpose-built container ships, which in the twenty-first century can take up to 24,000 standard containers (so-called 20-foot equivalent units, c. 6 m long), but are too large to dock at many ports in Europe and North America.[13]

Some shipping companies like Mærsk-Sealand of Denmark offer round the world container services, which take cargo from the United States through the Mediterranean, the Suez Canal, Singapore, Hong Kong and Taiwan to the US West Coast and back via Japan. The container revolution changed not just international sea freight, but also the ports. Special terminals arose on the coasts away from the old ports – with consequences for the working lives of crew members, who could scarcely leave the ships anymore because of the shorter lay times.[14] The most important change, however, was the size of crews. While in the early nineteenth century it took thirteen sailors to operate a large, 400-tonne sailing ship, nowadays thirteen sailors can operate the container ship Emma Mærsk with its cargo capacity of 14,000 standard containers.

Overall, the trend towards falling freight prices that began in the nineteenth century continued in the twentieth. Thus between 1950 and 2000, the cost of transporting grain fell by 70 per cent and of coal by 80 per cent, mainly because of the increased size of ships.[15] Cheaper sea transport and the simultaneous drop in the price of raw materials led to a shift in the location of industrial production worldwide. From the Industrial Revolution into the 1950s, production sites had been determined by the local availability of raw materials. The new transport opportunities now made it possible for countries with few natural resources to produce industrially on a grand scale. Global supply chains emerged based on the reliable transport of raw materials, semi-finished and finished goods between producers and consumers in distant corners of the world. This transport is secured by a complex shipping system and a global maritime labour market, in which Filipinos represent one in four members of ship's crews.[16] The sailors on container ships work on a rotation system and are exchanged regularly. During the coronavirus crisis, they waited in vain for replacements to arrive, sometimes for months, because of restrictions in air traffic and quarantine regulations. The crisis also led to the collapse of a segment of world trade and shipping. Ships were put out of commission. The collapse affected container shipping first, which however recovered over the course of 2020. From September 2020, international container transhipment again surpassed the figures for the same months in the previous year. This may be attributed mainly to the strong increase in volume in China, where the container ports with the greatest turnover are located.[17]

Cruise ships and giant hotels

According to a study by NABU, the German Nature and Biodiversity Conservation Union, seventeen of twenty cruise ships built for European shipping companies up to 2016 are especially harmful to health and the environment because the companies have chosen to dispense with catalytic converters to reduce nitrogen oxides as well as with soot particle filters: 'A single modern cruise ship emits about 450 kg of soot particles, 5,250 kg of nitrogen oxides and 7,500 kg of sulphur dioxide every day. Taken together, the air pollution produced by the twenty cruise ships studied thus corresponds to that of 120 million modern cars.'[18] The effects are felt both on the seas and in the port cities.

Cruises are a relatively recent phenomenon. After passenger traffic across the world's oceans was gradually replaced by air traffic beginning in the 1960s, the revival of the old pleasure cruise in the 1980s helped to create a new business opportunity for ocean travel. Since ocean liners could no longer compete with airplanes, shipping companies invested in the leisure industry, which however was initially reserved for very wealthy customers. In the twenty-first century this evolved into an affordable pastime for the masses, as is evident from growing passenger numbers and ship capacities and gigantic profits for the cruise ship industry. Thus in 2015, twenty-three million passengers worldwide travelled on cruise ships, which earned the companies some 40 billion US dollars. The Covid-19 pandemic led to the near-collapse of the cruise industry in 2020, with ships docked in the ports and falling shares for stockholders. With the expected recovery in the cruise industry over time, it is hoped that cruise companies will enact policies and develop new ship models that are less harmful to the environment.[19]

Those who do not go on cruises fly with charter airlines to the Mediterranean, the Canaries or the Caribbean, where giant hotels disfigure the coastal landscapes so beloved in the nineteenth and twentieth centuries. It was only a small step from package tours to the migration of pensioners and retirees from Britain, France, Germany, the Netherlands, Sweden and Switzerland to the Mediterranean coasts. Since the 1980s, this has evolved into a mass movement which shifted local demographics, especially because the migrant retirees have not integrated into local societies. The dividing lines between tourism and migration are fluid, since many Germans or Britons commute back and forth several times a year between their residences.[20]

The ecological consequences are significant, especially since waste disposal is generally not geared towards streams of tourists, and swimming pools and artificial irrigation use so much water that shortages arise. Moreover, rubbish and above all wastewater, 80 per cent of which flows untreated into the sea, contribute significantly to pollution and the deterioration of water quality.[21]

While city folk long sought tranquillity and respite from urban life at the coast with its pristine nature and clean air, mass tourists now bring their urban surroundings, with their novel forms of entertainment, to the seaside, and thereby inexorably destroy this traditional recreational space. Logically enough, tourists now search for previous generations' place of longing in the sinking islands of the Pacific and Indian Oceans, which they can reach relatively quickly by air. But the frigid Arctic and Antarctic regions have also become the sites of a new cruise ship adventure tourism, drawing visitors to two seas, the Arctic Ocean and the Antarctic or Southern Ocean, which only began to attract more attention in the twentieth century.

The recognition of new oceans

The Arctic Ocean and the Southern Ocean are the smallest of the world's oceans and the latest to be recognized as such. Although indigenous peoples – Inuit, Aleut and Native American – have been living in the Arctic region for centuries and whalers ventured into these seas, no one had actually crossed these oceans before the twentieth century. It was only the races to the North and South Poles that brought them wider public attention and eventually scientific recognition.

Beginning in the sixteenth century, various (European) explorers set out to find a northeast or northwest passage through the Arctic that would link Europe with Asia but failed because the potential routes were blocked by white ice. Only in the early twentieth century did the Norwegian Roald Amundsen finally identify the Northwest Passage. In 1893, another Norwegian, Fridtjof Nansen, penetrated Arctic waters with his ship the *Fram* and came close to the North Pole, which Amundsen flew over with the airship *Norge* in 1926. It was also Amundsen who vied with the Britons Robert Falcon Scott and Ernest Shackleton to be the first person to reach the South Pole. Amundsen and his team succeeded on 14 December 1911, followed thirty-three days later by Scott. Scott and his team died of starvation and cold on their way back, while Shackleton passed away from a heart attack while mapping the Antarctic coastline in 1922.[22]

In 1921, the newly founded International Hydrographic Bureau (IHB, known since 1970 as the International Hydrographic Organization) formally recognized the Arctic Ocean as an ocean. The IHB's goal was to develop hydrographic and nautical charting standards. To this end, it produced several editions of the *Limits of Oceans and Seas*, which also identified the Southern Ocean. The member states, however, saw no reason to delimit the Southern Ocean from the Atlantic, Pacific or Indian Oceans. The Southern Ocean was officially recognized in the most recent edition of 2002, but this publication has not yet been ratified by the member states.

The international community nevertheless acknowledged the unique role of the Antarctic environment in the so-called Antarctic Treaty of 1959. This agreement prohibits military activities as well as nuclear testing and encourages scientific research, which is currently being conducted at seventy permanent research stations. In this respect, the Southern Ocean avoided the fate of the Arctic Ocean, which had become a strategic region for the competing superpowers, the United States and the Soviet Union. In 1958, the US submarine *Nautilus* made the first underwater crossing, while the Russian icebreaker *Arktika* reached the North Pole in 1977, crossing the Arctic Ocean and pushing through the sea ice.

In the Declaration announced at the Arctic Ocean conference in Ilulissat, Greenland on 28 May 2008, the five states bordering the Arctic Ocean (United States, Russia, Canada, Norway and Denmark) at least committed to protecting the marine environment, although this does not preclude the exploitation of the rich oil and gas resources as well as metals and mineral mining.

Both oceans are remarkable for their richness of species and unique ecological situation. Thanks to its remote location, the Southern Ocean is home to a large number of endemic marine organisms, especially invertebrates, many of which exist nowhere else.[23] Marine research in the Southern Ocean has focused on whales, for example on whale marking, but also includes the study of krill, 'the food of the whales'.[24] The Arctic Ocean and the ice formations host 102 different mammalian species, the most famous being the polar bear, as well as 200 bird species and 633 species of fish, not to mention 1,300 invertebrates. The melting of the Arctic Ocean icescape and the decreasing formation of sea ice endanger biodiversity and the ecosystem.[25]

One unique threat facing the Arctic and Southern Ocean ecosystem is ozone depletion, the springtime decrease in stratospheric ozone around the polar regions. At the height of ozone depletion, 50 per cent of stratospheric ozone was destroyed by chlorofluorocarbons (CFCs). In recent decades, the influx of CFCs has fortunately been reduced because of the multilateral agreement in the Montreal Protocol of 1987. According to NASA, in 2019, the ozone hole over Antarctica was the smallest since it was first discovered in 1982. The Arctic and Southern Oceans are therefore rightly regarded as bellwethers of global climate and environmental change.[26]

Exploitation and destruction

In April 2010, the BP-operated *Deepwater Horizon* offshore drilling rig exploded in the Gulf of Mexico, spilling some 800 million litres of oil.[27] Oxygen levels in the ocean dropped dramatically, with a lasting effect on sea birds, fish and oyster beds. The US government imposed a moratorium on deep sea drilling, which a Louisiana court however reversed. Oil production in the sea started in the late nineteenth century, when Henry L. Williams began to exploit the oilfields off the coast of Santa Barbara, California. At first, drilling was limited to coastal areas and shallow waters. After the Second World War offshore drilling for natural gas began as well. With time, drilling for oil and gas was extended to depths of more than 1,500 metres, conducted from special offshore drilling rigs. Extensive pipeline systems on the seabed cross the Baltic, the Mediterranean or the Gulf of Mexico, for example, to transport oil and gas over large distances from the point of production to consumers. Another project begun with great hopes in the 1970s, the deep-sea mining of manganese nodules, proved to be unprofitable.

Energy production did not stop at the sea either. Tidal power stations make use of tidal amplitudes and thus the energy from the earth's rotation to produce electricity, but at the expense of coastal flora and fauna. Moreover, there has been a veritable boom in coastal and offshore wind parks in both the North Sea and Baltic regions and the Atlantic, which, however, are in turn connected to new electrical power lines on the seabed.[28]

The use of wind and other renewable energy sources is intended to counteract climate change, which is a major threat to the seas. They are, after all, an integral part of the world's climate, producing approximately half of the oxygen we breathe. At the same time, the seas slow global warming, for example by absorbing one third of the carbon dioxide produced worldwide. Nevertheless, they are endangered to an unprecedented degree: sea levels, temperatures and acidification are rising with the absorption of carbon dioxide. Pollution is increasing, and parts of the sea are dying because the necessary oxygen is disappearing. In many places, the sea is also being exploited beyond all sustainability.

The seas can no longer regenerate on their own – with lasting consequences for biodiversity and the ecosystem. While the seas have absorbed about one third of CO_2 emissions, which have risen sharply in the past 200 years, they are nevertheless subject to continuing acidification, threatening the survival of molluscs, crabs, corals and fish populations as well as the human food chain. Only reduced CO_2 emissions can prevent increasing acidification. The effects of global warming are comparable. Thus, in the past two centuries, the seas have absorbed approximately 80 per cent of the heat released into the atmosphere. While this has mitigated global warming on land, the simultaneous rise in ocean temperatures has multiple consequences. Apart from rising sea levels, these include the emergence of extreme tropical weather conditions. Although the experts are divided on whether the number of tropical storms has gone up, the force of storms will certainly increase. The effects on coral reefs and fish stocks should also not be underestimated. Because of rising ocean temperatures, fish populations are migrating into deeper and colder regions. Coral reefs are bleaching and dying because of warming, which affects more than just their role as a basic food source for various marine animals. The important contribution of coral reefs to protecting islands and coasts from storms and waves is also being lost.[29]

Rising sea levels are closely associated with the warming of land and sea. The water heats up and expands while the melting of glaciers and ice fields increases the amount of water. The consequences, apart from the erosion of beaches and cliffs, are mainly floods and storm surges, which affect low-lying coastal countries such as the Netherlands, Bangladesh or Indonesia as well as islands and island groups. Sea levels rose 25 centimetres between 1850 and 2000, including 1.8 mm annually from 1961 to 2003 alone and 2.5 mm annually thereafter. How far and how quickly sea levels rise depend on the course of climate change. Scientists expect a rise of 0.3–2.5 m up to 2100 in comparison to the year 2000. A rapid melting of the Greenland Ice Sheet, however, would raise sea levels by more than 7 m, and the melting of the Antarctic by 56 m.[30]

However unlikely such a scenario may appear, several hundred million people, especially in South and Southeast Asia, who are not responsible for climate change, will be affected by rising sea levels, because they will have to leave their low-lying homes on the coasts or because saltwater surges will pollute their groundwater and destroy their rice paddies. Island nations like the Maldives or Tuvalu and Kiribati, which lie just a few metres above sea level, will be inundated and consumed by the sea, and cities like Shanghai and Singapore, with populations in the millions, will have to arm themselves with costly protective measures against the rising waters.[31]

Eutrophication and pollution

Another danger to the oceans is so-called eutrophication or over-enrichment with minerals. In this process, water is supplied with minerals, especially phosphates and nitrates. These usually stem from runoff from agricultural fertilizers, which flows into the oceans along with wastewater and river water when it rains. Together with emissions from the air and the warming of the seas, they increase the growth of marine plants, especially algae. High concentrations of algae lead to oxygen depletion, flight reactions by marine animal populations and the death of large oceanic spaces.

There are currently some 500 of these dead zones worldwide, in which no marine life survives. They include New York Bay, the northern Adriatic, the Gulf of Mexico, Montevideo Bay and the Yangtse River estuary as well as large parts of the Baltic Sea. There, because of the reduced exchange of water with the North Sea, the dead zone expanded from 5,000 to 60,000 km² between 1898 and 2012.[32] Several inflows of saltwater from the North Sea in 2014 alone brought new oxygen to the Baltic, so that organisms were able to reclaim their habitat.

Most marine pollution comes from land, and a large portion of that from agriculture. But the introduction of industrial residues and chemicals as well as the disposal of radioactive waste also contaminates the seas. This includes oil spills from tanker accidents and drilling but also the cleaning of oil tanks by ships at sea. The seas are also polluted with heavy metals and industrial waste, including the dumping of metals, chemical fluids and dredged material in the North Sea, for example. Insecticides (DDT) and plasticizers (PCB) also find their way into the oceans and damage fish populations as well as seals and sea birds. Fish and molluscs, which filter the water, store high concentrations of toxins, and people who consume large quantities of fish take in a corresponding amount of PCB. Fish such as Baltic herring often exhibits a far higher concentration of PCB than the EU permits for human and animal consumption.[33]

The pollution of the oceans with plastic debris is a danger that has gained increasing attention of late. Plastic production has doubled every eleven years since it began in the 1950s, and a significant portion ends up in the seas. All of the oceans have a concentration of 580,000 plastic particles per square kilometre, which can take between one and several centuries to break down. Although part of this sinks to the seabed, the plastic debris moves with the ocean currents and is found at even higher concentrations on shorelines and in harbours. This represents an unprecedented threat to marine life. From microorganisms to whales, all animals ingest plastics with their food, poisoning them and permanently damaging their digestive systems. Two-thirds of all sea birds consume plastics, a figure expected to rise to nearly 100 per cent by 2050.[34] The only solution is to reduce plastic production and use, especially by coastal populations and cruise ship passengers.

Overfishing

The pollution and warming of the seas naturally have lasting effects on international fish stocks, which are already endangered by overfishing, since in many parts of the world more fish are being caught than the regeneration rates of fish populations can replace. Overfishing is not a wholly new phenomenon. In the late nineteenth century, for instance, new fishing techniques and practices sharply reduced the cod population in the Atlantic, and Japanese trawlers systematically fished the seas of Southeast Asia. In the Pacific region, too, the demands of the Chinese and American markets nearly decimated the populations of sea otters, whales and seals.[35]

In the period after the Second World War, fishing was revived first in the coastal waters of Europe, North America and Japan, only to spread quickly across the world's oceans. This second fishery revolution was rooted in a further expansion of the radius and fishing depth of the trawlers and the refitting of trawlers to serve as fish factories, where the catch could be filleted, frozen and processed into fish meal. This included the development of market demand for fish oil as well as for fishmeal as animal feed. Spanish, Japanese and Soviet fishing fleets in particular operated worldwide, and it was only the universal establishment of territorial waters for exclusive economic exploitation within a 200-mile zone in 1982 that limited the radius – but not the intensity – of fishing.[36]

The catches reached a highpoint of 86.3 million tonnes in 1996, dropping to around 79.5 million tonnes in 2010. At the moment, around 45 million people worldwide are employed in fisheries, mostly as small-scale fishers, 85 per cent of them in Asia. Estimates of the decline of fish populations vary; some scholars believe they have fallen by around 50 per cent. The *Food and Agriculture Organization of the United Nations* (FAO) estimates that 87 per cent of fish stocks have now been overfished or almost totally exhausted. Similar figures (88 per cent) exist for EU waters, while in 1970 overfishing was still quite limited in Europe. The EU has adopted an accordingly rigorous policy on annual catch quotas, much to the dismay of the fishing industry. The European Commission recommends quotas based on regular expert reports on the stocks of various fish, for example a restriction on allowable catches for twenty-eight fish stocks in 2016, together with the maintenance of or increase in quotas for thirty-five stocks. This increase gives fishers the opportunity to compensate for the lower quotas of some fish with increased catches of others. At the same time, increases in allowable catches indicate that some fish stocks have recovered, while others – such as the cod and sole stocks in the Irish Sea and the Bay of Biscay – continue to be endangered.[37] Only an international fisheries policy along this model could safeguard fish stocks worldwide and a source of protein for the world's population.[38]

Whaling has also experienced heated conflicts between proponents of conservation and exploitation. Until the 1930s, whaling was dominated by Anglo-Norwegian consortia. The British financed the industry and Norwegians manned the factory ships that allowed whales to be taken on board. From the 1930s, Japan regularly sent whaling ships to the Southern Ocean, and not long thereafter the Soviet Union developed its whaling industry. At the same time, the International Council for the Exploration of the Sea (ICES) foresaw the impending over-exploitation of whale stocks, and in 1931 pushed for a convention to regulate whaling. Agreements about the quotas for whales caught and the barrels of oil produced followed, with the aim of maintaining the profitability of the industry. After the Second World War, in 1946, the International Whaling Commission (IWC) was created under US influence. North American marine biologists were convinced that science could guide the international management of the whaling industry, as whale stocks were continuing to decline, and governments were subsidizing the whaling fleets. Hunting blue and humpback whales was prohibited in the 1960s, and in 1972 the US government suggested a moratorium on all commercial whaling, which was finally declared by the IWC in 1982. Nevertheless, the Japanese whaling fleet resumed the hunt 'for scientific purposes' in 1987. They were hindered by Greenpeace activists who brought public attention to Japanese whaling but also to other illegal fishing activities in the Southern Ocean.[39]

It took another twenty years for the governments of Australia and New Zealand to bring Japan's 'scientific whaling' before the International Court of Justice. In 2014, the court prohibited Japan from whaling in the Southern Ocean, having found that the annual whale slaughter was for commercial purposes and therefore illegal. In 2018 Japan redesigned its scientific program, limiting the hunt to an annual quota of 333 minke whales, but also left the IWC that year. As a result, Japan resumed commercial whaling in July 2019, but promised that the whalers would stay within the country's territorial waters and commercial zones. These subsidized whaling activities faced criticism, but also raised the question of profitability, since the demand for whale meat in the Japanese diet has decreased drastically since the 1960s.

Notes

1   The fisherman Mahyuddin on the 2004 tsunami. Quoted by K. Lamb in an article in *The Guardian* (www.theguardian.com/global-development/2014/dec/25/indian-ocean-tsunami-survivors-stories-aceh; accessed 24 November 2020).

2   Bose, *A Hundred Horizons*, 1–4.

3   Matsuda, *Pacific Worlds*, 275–92, 315–34; Buschmann, *Oceans in World History*, 110–1.

4   A. Menzel, *Sailing the Waters of Institutional Complexity. State-to-State Cooperation on the Combat of Piracy*, PhD dissertation University of Greifswald, 2019; A. Menzel and L. Otto 'Connecting the Dots. Implications of the Intertwined Global Challenges to Maritime Security', in L. Otto (ed.). *Global Challenges in Maritime Security. An Introduction* (Wiesbaden, 2020), 229-43; J. E. Wadsworth, *Global Piracy. A Documentary History of Seaborne Banditry* (London and New York, 2019), 215–32, 265–81.

5   The IOM Global Migration Data Analysis Centre: *Missing Migrants Project* tracks incidents involving migrants, including refugees and asylum-seekers, who have died or gone missing in the process of migration towards an international destination (https://missingmigrants.iom.int/, Last update: 9 November 2020).

6   W. Benz, 'Jewish Refugees from Nazi Germany and from German Occupied Europe since 1933', in K. J. Bade et al. (eds.), *The Encyclopedia of European Migration and Minorities: From the Seventeenth Century To The Present* (Cambridge and New York, 2011), 536–40.

7   J.-J. Jordi, *1962. L'arrivée des Pieds-Noirs* (Paris, 2002) and *De l'Exode à l'Exil. Rapatriés et pieds-noirs en France; l'exemple marseillais, 1954–1992* (Paris, 1993), and 'Algerian *Pieds-Noirs* in France since 1954', in Bade et al. (eds.), *Encyclopedia of Migration*, 224–5.

8   P. C. Emmer, 'West Indians in Great Britain, France and the Netherlands since the End of World War II', in Bade et al. (eds.), *Encyclopedia of Migration*, 739–43.

9   S. Rah, *Asylsuchende und Migranten auf See. Staatliche Rechte und Pflichten aus völkerrechtlicher Sicht* (Berlin, 2009), 7–11.

10   2016: 16.3 million people fleeing within Africa; brief dossier by H. Brankamp, 'Die "Flüchtlingskrise": Flucht und Vertreibung in Afrika', *Bundeszentrale für Politische Bildung*, 28 February 2018 (https://www.bpb.de/gesellschaft/ migration/kurzdossiers/265328/flucht-und-vertreibung); 2019: 18.9 million IDPs in Africa (UNHCR. The UN Refugee Agency, *Global Trends. Forced Displacement in 2019*, https://www.unhcr.org/5ee200e37.pdf, p. 82), 7.5 million refugees: not specified whether the borders crossed were 'only' within Africa (Ibid.).

11   United Nations Conference on Trade and Development (UNCTAD), Maritime Transport Statistics 2015 (http://unctadstat.unctad.org/wds/ReportFolders/ reportFolders.aspx; accessed 24 November 2020).

12   Y. Kaukiainen, 'The Role of Shipping in the "Second Stage of Globalisation"', *International Journal of Maritime History* 26 (2014): 64–81.

13   T. Stevenson, 'Raue See. Die Geopolitik des maritimen Welthandels', *Le Monde diplomatique*, 13 August 2020 (https://monde-diplomatique.de/ artikel/!5688408). See also the same author's 'In Ocean Scale. Considering the Most Essential Feature of the Modern Economy', *The Times Literary*

Supplement (TLS), 19 June 2020, no. 6116, https://www.the-tls.co.uk/
articles/sinews-of-war-and-trade-laleh-khalili-book-review/).

In 2018, mega ships were already carrying 31 per cent of the volume
of global container transports. See 'Re-evaluating the risk of mega ships',
Lockton Companies, 27 June 2019. The largest mega ship to date, with a
capacity of about 24,000 TEU, went into service in 2020.

14 Y. Kauklainen, 'The Advantages of Water Carriage. Scale Economies and
Shipping Technology, c. 1870–2000', in Harlaftis, Tenold and Valdaliso (eds.),
The World's Key Industry, 64–87.

15 Y. Kauklainen, 'Growth, Diversification and Globalization. Main Trends in
International Shipping since 1850', in L. R. Fischer and E. Lage (eds.),
*International Merchant Shipping in the Nineteenth and Twentieth Centuries.
The Comparative Dimension* (St John's, 2008), 41–2.

16 E. Ekberg, E. Lange and E. Merok, 'Building the Networks of Trade.
Perspectives on Twentieth-Century Maritime History', in Harlaftis, Tenold and
Valdaliso (eds.), *The World's Key Industry*, 88–105.

17 The Global Container Throughput Index fell to its lowest point in three
years in April 2020 but has been returning to normal (Institut für
Seeverkehrswirtschaft und Logistik, RWI/ISL-Containerumschlag-Index, 26
May 2020: https://www.isl.org/de/containerindex; https://www.isl.org/en/
containerindex/april-2020).

Twenty per cent more total losses were recorded in the shipping industry
compared to the year before. See 'Safety & Shipping Review 2020', Allianz
Global Corporate & Specialty (AGCS), 15 July 2020, Munich (https://www.
agcs.allianz.com/content/dam/onemarketing/agcs/agcs/reports/AGCS-Safety-
Shipping-Review-2020.pdf).

18 D. Rieger, 'Kein Kreuzfahrtschiff empfehlenswert. Fast alle Schiffe fallen bei
NABU-Kreuzfahrt-Check durch', *NABU*, 6 August 2013: https://www.nabu.
de/umwelt-und-ressourcen/verkehr/schifffahrt/kreuzschifffahrt/16042.html,
accessed 24 November 2020).

19 Thirty-two million passengers were expected for 2020 ('State of the Cruise
Industry. Outlook 2020', Report of the Cruise Lines International Association
(CLIA): https://cruising.org/-/media/research-updates/research/state-of-the-
cruise-industry.ashx). Shares in the three largest shipping companies fell
70–80 per cent in April 2020 (M. Giese, 'COVID-19 impacts on global cruise
industry. How is the cruise industry coping with the COVID-19 crisis?' *KPMG
Blog*, 23 July 2020: https://home.kpmg/xx/en/blogs/home/posts/2020/07/
covid-19-impacts-on-global-cruise-industry.html).

In Europe, 94 per cent fewer cruise ships docked between April and July
2020 (European Maritime Safety Agency, EMSA report: 'Covid-19 – Impact
on Shipping', 17 July 2020: http://emsa.europa.eu/newsroom/covid19-impact/
download/6290/3836/23.html).

20 K. O'Reilly, 'British Affluence Migrants in the Costa del Sol in the Late
20th Century', in Bade et al. (eds.), *Encyclopedia of Migration*, 262–4; K.
Schriewer, 'German Affluence Migrants in Spain since the Late 20th Century'
in Ibid., 402–4.

21 'Mittelmeer' (www.wasser-wissen.de/abwasserlexikon/m/mittelmeer.html, accessed 18 November 2015).

22 G. Dilly, 'The Southern Ocean', in R. F. Buschmann and L. Nolde (eds.), *The World's Ocean: Geography, History and Environment* (Santa Barbara, CA, 2018), 80–3.

23 Ibid., 79.

24 A. Antonello, 'The Southern Ocean', in Armitage, Bashford and Sivasundaram (eds.), *Oceanic Histories*, 305.

25 S. N. Edelsohn et al., 'The Arctic Ocean', in Buschmann and Nolde (eds.), *The World's Ocean*, 3–17.

26 S. Sörlin, 'The Arctic Ocean', in Armitage, Bashford and Sivasundaram (eds.), *Oceanic Histories*, 287; N. Wormbs, R. Döscher, A. E. Nilsson and S. Sörlin, 'Bellwether, Exceptionalism, and Other Tropes: Political Coproduction of Arctic Climate Modeling', in M. Heymann, G. Gramelsberger and M. Mahony (eds.), *Cultures of Prediction: Epistemic and Cultural Shifts in Computer-based Atmospheric and Climate Science* (London and New York, 2017), 133–55.

27 T. Schröder (ed.), *World Ocean Review. Living with the Oceans*, no. 3: Marine Resources - Opportunities and Risks (Hamburg, 2014), 10–51. See also www.futureocean.org/de/.

28 *Welt im Wandel. Menschheitserbe Meer*, ed. Wissenschaftlicher Beirat der Bundesregierung Globale Umweltveränderungen (WBGU) (Berlin, 2013), 218–41.

29 T. Schröder (ed.), *World Ocean Review. Living with the Oceans*, no. 1 (Hamburg, 2010).

30 Sea level rose by 15–20 cm between 1993 (when satellite recording began) and 2018. R. Lindsey, 'Climate Change. Global Sea Level'. *National Oceanic and Atmospheric Administration Climate.gov* (https://www.climate.gov/ news-features/understanding-climate/climate-change-global-sea-level).

    An increase of 0.3–2.5m as compared to 2000 is expected by 2100 (Ibid.). The annual increase between 2018 and 2019 was 6.1 mm (Ibid.), and in 2020 it was 3.3mm. NASA, *Sea Level* (https://climate.nasa.gov/vital-signs/sea-level/).

31 K. J. Noone, 'Sea-Level Rise', in K. J. Noone, U. R. Sumaila and R. J. Diaz (eds.), *Managing Ocean Environments in a Changing Climate. Sustainability and Economic Perspectives* (Amsterdam, Boston and Heidelberg, 2013), 97–126; K. M. Wowk, 'Paths to Sustainable Ocean Resources', in Ibid., 312–3.

32 J. Carstensen et al., 'Deoxygenation of the Baltic Sea during the Last Century', *PNAS* 111, no. 15 (2014): 5628–33 (www.pnas.org/ content/111/15/5628.full.pdf, accessed 17 November 2015); 'Meer atmet auf: Neues Salzwasser für die Ostsee' (http://globalmagazin.com/themen/natur/ meer-atmet-auf-salzwassereinbruch-in-der-zentralen-ostsee/, accessed 24 November 2020).

33 H. Eriksson-Hägg et al., 'Marine Pollution', in Noone, Sumaila and Diaz (eds.), *Managing Ocean Environments*, 127–70.

34 C. Wilcox, E. Van Sebille and B. D. Hardesty, 'Threat of Plastic Pollution to Seabirds Is Global, Pervasive, and Increasing', *PNAS* 112, no. 38

(2015): 11899–904 (www.pnas.org/content/112/38/11899.full.pdf, accessed 17 November 2015).

35 See above, part VIII 'Pacific', sub-chapter 'Sandalwood, sea cucumbers and sea otters'.

36 Cushing, *The Provident Sea*, 234–58.

37 European Commission press release of 10 November 2015, 'Commission proposes fishing opportunities in the Atlantic and North Sea for 2016' (https://ec.europa.eu/commission/presscorner/detail/en/IP_15_6016, accessed 24 November 2020).

38 W. W. L. Cheung, A. D. Rogers and U. R. Sumaila, 'The Potential Economic Costs of the Overuse of Marine Fish Stocks', in Noone, Sumaila and Diaz (eds.), *Managing Ocean Environments*, 171–92.

39 Antonello, 'Southern Ocean', 302–14.

Conclusion

Since time immemorial, the seas have connected the world by permitting the transport of goods and people to the most far-flung regions. Without maritime shipping, there would be no globalization, regardless of how we define its beginning. Even today, 90 per cent of freight transport globally is carried by the sea route.

But the seas are no mere transport medium. Exchange shaped the societies involved and helped to create new ones on both sides of the oceans. Historians have been particularly interested in the societies that are linked by one or multiple seas as well as their relationships to each other.

This book cites many examples. Merchants were the first people to cross the ocean voluntarily, and the goods and ideas they carried with them changed cultures, just as the significance of goods within the exchange process also changed. The mentalities of merchants, their trading partners, buyers and consumers also influenced exchange across the seas. New merchant communities with similar economic interests, social origins and shared ways of life arose on the coasts and islands, as illustrated by the Hanseatic merchants on the Baltic, Muslim and Chinese trade in the Indian Ocean region and the Dutch who were active on all the world's seas.

For a long time, the migration of merchants across oceans was linked to the trade in luxury goods, since they at first purchased and distributed the valuable commodities personally and settled in the sites of production and sales. That is why their early presence on the Mediterranean and Baltic Sea and the Indian Ocean is associated with luxury goods and the demand for them among local elites.

Bulk goods such as grain, timber, fish, sugar and tobacco, in contrast, dominated exchange across both the Atlantic and the early modern North and Baltic Seas. The human beings taken across the Atlantic and the Pacific were mostly enslaved people, indentured servants, coolies and of course emigrants. The last group sought to improve their lot by migrating, but like enslaved people and coolies, they brought their ideas and life practices with them to their new homelands.

While coastal dwellers and islanders lived off the natural resources of the sea as well as the treasures that washed up on shore, others utilized the opportunity of maritime shipping. Merchants, fur hunters, pearl divers and beachcombers satisfied elite demand for coral, pearls, sea otter pelts or sea cucumbers. For enslaved people, emigrants and coolies, in contrast, the sea represented a dangerous passage to an uncertain future.

Steamships drew the seas closer together because they lessened the dependence on winds and currents, and their greater speeds shortened ocean voyages. At the same time, they made it easier for people to experience the ocean, which had long been a place of longing. Steamer passages across the English Channel or the Danish Sound were transformed into literature and art and thus into maritime sites of memory.

For all of the people who lived from and crossed the oceans, they were a communicative space. Sailors, islanders and coastal dwellers believed in sea gods or their patron saints, whose favour they sought through a variety of practices. Since the earliest times, merchants and voyagers communicated across the seas and maintained contact with their business partners and families. Ship's logs and travel accounts gave literary form to sea passages, conveying images of the world to those back home or to future travellers. The latest fashions and ideas were also passed on across the seas. At the same time, merchants created maritime spaces by connecting the coasts of one or several seas. This linked together the world's commodities and integrated increasing numbers of people into the often-overlapping networks.

In addition to the seas' abovementioned functions as providers of resources, spaces of transport and communication, places of longing and sites of memory, they have a key role to play as regulators of world climate in the present and the future.

Bibliography

A

Abulafia, David. 'Neolithic Meets Medieval. First Encounters in the Canary Islands'. In *Medieval Frontiers. Concepts and Practices*, edited by D. Abulafia and F. Berend, 255–78. Aldershot: Ashgate, 2002.

Abulafia, David. *The Discovery of Mankind. Atlantic Encounters in the Age of Columbus*. New Haven, London: Yale University Press, 2008.

Abulafia, David. *The Great Sea. A Human History of the Mediterranean*. Oxford: Oxford University Press, 2011.

Abulafia, David. 'Thalassocracies'. In *A Companion to Mediterranean History*, edited by P. Horden and S. Kinoshita, 139–53. Chichester, West Sussex: Whiley, 2014.

Abulafia, David. *The Boundless Sea. A Human History of the Oceans*. London: Allen Lane, 2019.

Adamczyk, Dariusz. 'Od dirhemów do fenigów. Reorientacja bałtyckiego systemu handlowego na przełomie X i XI wieku'. In *Średniowiecze polskie i powszechne 4*, edited by I. Panic and J. Sperka, 15–27. Katowice: Wydawnictwo Uniwersytetu Śląskiego, 2007.

Adamczyk, Dariusz. 'Friesen, Wikinger, Araber. Die Ostseewelt zwischen Dorestad und Samarkand ca. 700–1100'. In *Ostsee 700–2000. Gesellschaft – Wirtschaft – Kultur*, edited by A. Komlosy, H. H. Nolte and I. Sooman, 32–48. Vienna: Promedia, 2008.

Adamczyk, Dariusz. *Silber und Macht. Fernhandel, Tribute und die piastische Herrschaftsbildung in nordosteuropäischer Perspektive (800–1100)*. Wiesbaden: Harrassowitz, 2014.

Ahvenainen, Jorma. *The History of the Caribbean Telegraphs before the First World War*. Helsinki: Suomalainen Tiedeakatemia, 1996.

Ahvenainen, Jorma. 'The Role of Telegraphs in the 19th-Century Revolution of Communications'. In *Kommunikationsrevolutionen. Die neuen Medien des 16. und 19. Jahrhunderts*, edited by M. North, 73–80. 2nd edn. Cologne, Weimar and Vienna: Böhlau, 2001.

Ahvenainen, Jorma. *The European Cable Companies in South America before the First World War*. Helsinki: Academia Scientiarum Fennica, 2004.

Alcuin. 'Alcuini Epistulae'. In *Monumenta Germaniae Historica*, Epp. 4, edited by E. Dümmler. Berlin: Weidmann, 1895.

Alexandrowicz, Charles Henry. *An Introduction to the History of the Law of the Nations in the East Indies (16th, 17th and 18th Centuries)*. Oxford: Clarendon Press, 1967.

Alpers, Edward A. *The Indian Ocean in World History*. Oxford and New York: Oxford University Press, 2014.

Amrith, Sunil S. *Crossing the Bay of Bengal. The Furies of Nature and the Fortunes of Migrants*. Cambridge, MA and London: Harvard University Press, 2013.

Andaya, Leonard Y. *Leaves of the Same Tree. Trade and Ethnicity in the Straits of Melaka*. Honolulu: University of Hawai'i Press, 2008.

Androshchuk, Fedir. 'The Vikings in the East'. In *The Viking World*, edited by S. Brink and N. Price, 517–24. London and New York: Routledge, 2009.

Antonello, Alessandro. 'The Southern Ocean'. In *Oceanic Histories*, edited by D. Armitage, A. Bashford and S. Sivasundaram, 296–318. Cambridge, New York, Melbourne, New Delhi and Singapore: Cambridge University Press, 2018.

Armitage, David and Michael J. Braddick (eds.). *The British Atlantic World, 1500–1800*. 2nd edn. 2002. Basingstoke and New York: Palgrave Macmillan, 2009.

Armitage, David and Alison Bashford (eds.). *Pacific Histories. Ocean, Land, People*. Basingstoke and New York: Palgrave Macmillan, 2014.

Armitage, David, Alison Bashford and Sujit Sivasundaram (eds.). *Oceanic Histories*. Cambridge, New York, Melbourne, New Delhi and Singapore: Cambridge University Press, 2018.

Armstrong, John and David M. Williams. 'An Appraisal of the Progress of the Steamship in the Nineteenth Century'. In *The World's Key Industry. History and Economics of International Shipping*, edited by G. Harlaftis, S. Tenold and M. Valdaliso, 43–63. Basingstoke and New York: Palgrave Macmillan, 2012.

Arrianus, Flavius. *Arrian's Voyage Round the Euxine Sea. Translated, and Accompanied with a Geographical Dissertation, and Maps*. Oxford: Collingwood, 1805.

Ashtor, Eliyahu. *A Social and Economic History of the Near East in the Middle Ages*. Berkeley, Los Angeles, London: University of California Press, 1976.

Ashtor, Eliyahu. *Levant Trade in the Later Middle Ages*. Princeton: Princeton University Press, 1983.

Aslanian, Sebouh David. *From the Indian Ocean to the Mediterranean. The Global Trade Networks of Armenian Merchants from New Julfa*. Berkeley: University of California Press, 2011.

Assadourian, Carlos Sempat. *El sistema de la economía colonial. Mercado internor, regiones y espacio económico*. Lima: Instituto de Estudios Peruanos, 1983.

B

Bade, Klaus J., Pieter C. Emmer, Leo Lucassen and Jochen Oltmer (eds.). *The Encyclopedia of European Migration and Minorities. From the Seventeenth Century to the Present*. Cambridge and New York: Cambridge University Press, 2011.

Bahar, Matthew R. *Storm of the Sea. Indians and Empires in the Atlantic's Age of Sail*. Oxford and New York: Oxford University Press, 2019.

Bailyn, Bernard. *Atlantic History. Concept and Contours*. Cambridge, MA: Harvard University Press, 2005.

Barman, Jean. *Leaving Paradise. Indigenous Hawaiians in the Pacific Northwest, 1787–1898*. Honolulu: University of Hawai'i Press, 2006.

Bayly, Christopher A. *The Birth of the Modern World 1780–1914. Global Connections and Comparisons*. Malden, MA, Oxford and Victoria: Blackwell, 2004.

Beamish, North Ludlow. *The Discovery of America by the Northmen, in the Tenth Century*. London: T. and W. Boone, 1841.

Beaujard, Philippe. *The Worlds of the Indian Ocean. A Global History*. Cambridge and New York: Cambridge University Press, 2019.

Bell, Caryn Cossé. *Revolution, Romanticism, and the Afro-Creole Protest Tradition in Louisiana, 1718–1868*. Baton Rouge: Louisiana State University Press, 1997.

Bellmann, Dagmar. *Von Höllengefährten zu schwimmenden Palästen. Die Passagierschifffahrt auf dem Atlantik (1840–1930)*. Frankfurt a. M. and New York: Campus-Verlag, 2015.

Bentley, Jerry H. and Herbert F. Ziegler. *Traditions and Encounters. A Global Perspective on the Past*. 3rd edn. Boston, MA: McGraw-Hill, 2006.

Bentley, Jerry H., Renate Bridenthal and Karen Wigen. *Seascapes. Maritime Histories, Littoral Cultures, and Transoceanic Exchanges*. Honolulu: University of Hawai'i Press, 2007.

Benz, Wolfgang. 'Jewish Refugees from Nazi Germany and from German-Occupied Europe since 1933'. In *The Encyclopedia of European Migration and Minorities. From the Seventeenth Century to the Present*, edited by Klaus J. Bade et al., 536–40. Cambridge and New York: Cambridge University Press, 2011.

Bérard, Pierre. *Le voyage de La Pérouse. Itinéraires et aspects singuliers*. Albi: Un Autre Reg'Art, 2010.

Berg, Maxine (ed.). *Writing the History of the Global. Challenges for the 21st Century*. Oxford: Oxford University Press, 2013.

Beurdeley, Jean-Michel. *The Chinese Collector through the Centuries. From the Han to the 20th Century*. Fribourg: Office du Livre, 1966.

Bishara, Fahad Ahmad. 'Mapping the Indian Ocean World of Gulf Merchants, c. 1870–1960'. In *The Indian Ocean. Oceanic Connections and the Creation of New Societies*, edited by A. Sheriff and H. Engseng, 69–93. London: Hurst, 2014.

Blockmans, Wim P. 'Der holländische Durchbruch in die Ostsee'. In *Der hansische Sonderweg? Beiträge zur Sozial- und Wirtschaftsgeschichte der Hanse*, edited by S. Jenks and M. North, 49–58. Cologne, Weimar and Vienna: Böhlau, 1993.

Blockmans, Wim. *Metropolen aan de Noordzee. De Geschiedenis van Nederland 1000–1560*. Amsterdam: Bakker, 2010.

Blumenberg, Hans. *Schiffbruch mit Zuschauer. Paradigma einer Daseinsmetapher*. Reprint. Frankfurt a. M.: Suhrkamp, 2011.

Blussé, Léonard. *Visible Cities. Canton, Nagasaki, and Batavia and the Coming of the Americans*. Cambridge, MA and London: Harvard University Press, 2008.

Blussé, Léonard. 'On the Waterfront. Life and Labour around the Batavian Roadstead'. In *Asian Port Cities, 1600–1800. Local and Foreign Cultural Interactions*, edited by Haneda Masashi, 119–38. Singapore: NUS Press, 2009.

Blussé, Léonard. *The Chinese Annals of Batavia, the Kai Ba Lidai Shiji and Other Stories (1610–1795)*. Leiden and Boston: Brill, 2018.

Boccaccio, Giovanni. *The Decameron*, translated by G. H. McWilliam. 2nd edn. London: Penguin, 1995.

Bogucka, Maria. *Gdańskie rzemiosło tekstylne od XVI do połowy XVII wieku*. Wrocław: Zakład im. Ossolińskich Wydawn, 1956.

Bogucka, Maria. 'The Baltic and Amsterdam in the First Half of the 17th Century'. In *The Interactions of Amsterdam and Antwerp with the Baltic Region, 1400–1800: De Nederlanden en het Oostzeegebied, 1400–1800*, edited by W. J. Wieringa, 51–7. Dordrecht: Springer, 1983.

Bogucka, Maria. 'Dutch Merchants' Activities in Gdańsk in the First Half of the 17th Century'. In *Baltic Affairs. Relations between the Netherlands and North-Eastern Europe 1500–1800*, edited by J. P. S. Lemmink and J. S. A. M. Koningsbrugge, 19–32. Nijmegen: Inos, 1990.

Bohn, Robert. *Gotland*. 5th edn. Kronshagen: Stein, 1997.

Bolster, W. Jeffrey. *The Mortal Sea. Fishing the Atlantic in the Age of Sail*. Cambridge, MA and London: Belknap Press of Harvard University Press, 2012.

Bonnet, Corinne. *Melquart. Cultes et mythes de l'Héraclès tyrien en méditerranée*. Louvain: Peeters and Namur; Namur University Press, 1988.

Borgolte, Michael and Nikolas Jaspert (eds.). *Maritimes Mittelalter. Meere als Kommunikationsräume*. Ostfildern: Jan Thorbecke Verlag, 2016.

Borschberg, Peter. 'O comércio da âmbar cinzento asiático na época moderna'. *Revista Oriente* 8 (2004): 3–25.

Borschberg, Peter. 'Der asiatische Ambra-Handel während der frühen Neuzeit'. In *Mirabilia Asiatica II. Seltene Waren im Seehandel*, edited by J. Alves, C. Guillot and R. Ptak, 167–201. Wiesbaden and Lisbon: Harrassowitz, 2004.

Borschberg, Peter. 'Ethnicity, Language and Culture in Melaka after the Transition from Portuguese to Dutch Rule'. *Journal of the Malaysian Branch of the Royal Asiatic Society* 83, no. 2 (2010): 93–117.

Borschberg, Peter. *The Singapore and Melaka Straits. Violence, Security and Diplomacy in the 17th Century*. Singapore: NUS Press, 2010.

Borschberg, Peter and Michael North. 'Transcending Borders. The Sea as Realm of Memory'. *Asia Europe Journal* 8 (2010): 279–92.

Borschberg, Peter. *Hugo Grotius, the Portuguese and Free Trade in the East Indies*. Singapore: NUS Press, 2011.

Borschberg, Peter (ed.). *The Memoirs and Memorials of Jacques de Coutre: Security, Trade and Society in 16th- and 17th-Century South East Asia*. Singapore: NUS Press, 2013.

Borschberg, Peter (ed.). *Jacques de Coutre's Singapore and Johor. 1594–c. 1625*. Singapore: NUS Press, 2015.

Borschberg, Peter (ed.). *Journal, Memorials and Letters of Cornelis Matelieff de Jonge. Security, Diplomacy and Commerce in 17th-Century Southeast Asia*. Singapore: NUS Press, 2015.

Borschberg, Peter. 'Dutch Objections to British Singapore, 1819–1824. Law, Politics, Commerce and a Diplomatic Misstep'. *Journal of Southeast Asian Studies* 50, no. 4 (2019): 540–61.

Bose, Sugata. *A Hundred Horizons. The Indian Ocean in the Age of Global Empire*. Cambridge, MA and London: Harvard University Press, 2006.

Boutet, Guiomar de Carlos (ed.). *España y América. Un oceáno de negocios. Quinto centenario de la Casa de la Contratación, 1503–2003*. Madrid: Sociedad Estatal de Conmemoraciones Culturales, 2003.

Boyce, Robert W. D. 'Submarine Cables as a Factor in Britain's Ascendancy'. In *Kommunikationsrevolutionen. Die neuen Medien des 16. und 19. Jahrhunderts*, edited by M. North, 81–99. 2nd edn. Cologne, Weimar and Vienna: Böhlau, 2001.

Boxer, Charles Ralph. *The Dutch in Brazil, 1625–1654*. Oxford: Clarendon Press, 1957.

Boxer, Charles Ralph. *The Great Ship from Amacon. Annals of Macao and the Old Japan Trade, 1555–1640*. Lisbon: Centro de Estudos Históricos Ultramarinos, 1959.

Boxer, Charles Ralph. *The Portuguese Seaborne Empire 1415–1825*. Harmondsworth: Penguin Books, 1973.

Bracker, Jörgen, Michael North and Peter Tamm. *Maler der See. Marinemalerei in dreihundert Jahren*. Herford: Koehler, 1980.

Bracker, Jörgen, Volker Henn and Rainer Postel (eds.). *Die Hanse. Lebenswirklichkeit und Mythos. Textband zur Hamburger Hanse-Ausstellung von 1989*. 2nd edn. Lübeck: Schmidt-Römhild, 1998.

Brandis, K. G. 'Arrians Periplus Ponti Euxini'. *Rheinisches Museum für Philologie* 51 (1896): 109–26.

Brandt, Klaus, Michael Müller-Wille and Christian Radtke (eds.). *Haithabu und die frühe Stadtentwicklung im nördlichen Europa*. Neumünster: Wachholtz-Verlag, 2002.

Braudel, Fernand. *La Méditerranée et le monde méditeranéen à l'époque de Philippe II*. Paris: Colin, 1949.

Braudel, Fernand. *The Mediterranean and the Mediterranean World in the Age of Philip II*, translated by Sian Reynolds. 2 vols. London: Collins, 1972–3.

Bremen, Adam von. *History of the Archbishops of Hamburg-Bremen*, translated with an Introduction and Notes by Francis J. Tschan. New York: Columbia University Press, 2002.

Brenner, Agathe. '"Wenn jemand eine Reise tut, so kann er was erzählen…". Die Anfänge des Bädertourismus am Beispiel des ersten deutschen Seebades Doberan-Heiligendamm'. State Examination thesis, University of Greifswald, Greifswald 2010.

Brink, Stefan and Neil Price (eds.). *The Viking World*. London and New York: Routledge 2008.

Bronwen, Douglas. 'Religion'. In *Pacific Histories. Ocean, Land, People*, edited by D. Armitage and A. Bashford, 193–215. Basingstoke and New York: Palgrave Macmillan, 2014.

Broodbank, Cyprian. *The Making of the Middle Sea. A History of the Mediterranean from the Beginning to the Emergence of the Classical World*. Oxford and New York: Oxford University Press, 2013.

Brook, Timothy. *Mr. Selden's Map of China. Decoding Secrets of a Vanished Cartographer*. New York: Bloomsbury, 2013.

Bruijn, Jaap R. 'De personeelsbehoefte van de VOC overzee en aan boord, bezien in Aziatisch en Nederlands perspectief'. *Low Countries Historical Review* 91 (1976): 218–48.

Bruijn, Jaap R. *Schippers van de VOC in de achttiende eeuw aan de wal en op zee*. Amsterdam: De Bataafsche Leeuw, 2008.

Bruijn, Max de and Remco Raben (eds.). *The World of Jan Brandes, 1743–1808. Drawings of a Dutch Traveller in Batavia, Ceylon and Southern Africa*. Zwolle: Waanders, 2004.

Buchet, Christian and N.A.M. Rodger (eds). *The Sea in History. The Modern World/La Mer dans l'Histoire. Le période contemporaine*. Woodbridge: The Boydell Press, 2017.

Buchet, Christian and Gérard Le Bouëdec (eds.). *The Sea in History. The Early Modern World /La Mer dans l'Histoire, La Période Moderne*. Woodbridge: The Boydell Press, 2017.

Buchet, Christian, Philip De Souza and Pascal Arnaud (eds.). *The Sea in History. The Ancient World. La Mer dans l'histoire. L'Antiquité*. Woodbridge: The Boydell Press, 2017.

Burkholder, Mark A. and Lyman L. Johnson. *Colonial Latin America*. 8th edn. Oxford and New York: Oxford University Press, 2012.

Buschmann, Rainer F. *Oceans in World History*. Boston, Burr Ridge and Dubuque: McGraw-Hill, 2007.

Buschmann, Rainer F. *Iberian Visions of the Pacific Ocean. 1507–1899*. Basingstoke and New York: Palgrave Macmillan, 2014.

Buschmann, Rainer F., Edward R. Slack and James B. Tueller. *Navigating the Spanish Lake. The Pacific in the Iberian World, 1521–1898*. Honolulu: University of Hawai'i Press, 2014.

Buschmann, Rainer F. and Lance Nolde (eds.). *The World's Oceans. Geography, History, and Environment*. Santa Barbara, CA: ABC-CLIO, 2018.

Butcher, John G. *The Closing of the Frontier. A History of the Marine Fisheries of Southeast Asia c. 1850–2000*. Singapore: Institute of Southeast Asian Studies, 2004.

Butel, Paul. *Histoire de l'Atlantique, de l'Antiquité à nos jours*. Reprint, Paris: Perrin, 2012.

C

Calder, Alex, Bridget Orr and Jonathan Lamb (eds.). *Voyages and Beaches. Pacific Encounters, 1769–1840*. Honolulu: University of Hawai'i Press, 1999.

Campbell, Gwyn. 'Slavery and the Trans-Indian Ocean World Slave Trade'. In *Cross-Currents and Community Networks. The History of the Indian Ocean World*, edited by H. P. Ray and E. A. Alpers, 286–305. Oxford and New Delhi: Oxford University Press, 2007.

Campbell, Gwyn and Alessandro Stanziani (eds.). *Bonded Labour in the Indian Ocean World*. London: Pickering & Chatto, 2013.

Campos, Françozo Mariana de. *De Olinda a Holanda. O gabinete de curiosidades de Nassau*. Campinas: Unicamp, 2014.

Carney, Judith A. 'African Plant and Animal Species in 18th-Century Tropical America'. In *Cultural Exchange and Consumption Patterns in the Age of Enlightenment. Europe and the Atlantic World*, edited by V. Hyden-Hanscho, R. Pieper and W. Stangl, 97–116. Bochum: Winkler, 2013.

Carretta, Vincent. *Equiano the African. Biography of a Self-Made Man*. Athens, GA: University of Georgia Press, 2005.

Carson, Rachel. *The Sea around Us*. New York: Oxford University Press, 1951.

Carstensen, Jacob, Jesper H. Andersen, Bo G. Gustafsson and Daniel J. Conley. 'Deoxygenation of the Baltic Sea during the Last Century'. *Proceedings of the National Academy of Sciences of the United States of America* 111, no. 15 (2014): 5628–33.

Casale, Giancarlo. *The Ottoman Age of Exploration*. Oxford and New York: Oxford University Press, 2010.

Casson, Lionel (ed.). *The Periplus Maris Erythraei*. Princeton: University Press, 1989.

Casson, Lionel. 'New Light on Maritime Loans. P. Vindob. G 40822'. In *Trade in Early India*, edited by R. Chakravarti, 228–43. New Delhi: Oxford University Press, 2001.

Chaffee, John W. *The Muslim Merchants of Premodern China. The History of a Maritime Asian Trade Diaspora, 750–1400*. Cambridge and New York: Cambridge University Press, 2018.

Chakravarti, Ranabir. 'Nakhudas and Nauvittakas. Ship-Owning-Merchants in the West Coast of India (AD 1000–1500)'. *Journal of the Economic and Social History of the Orient* 43 (2000): 34–64.

Chakravarti, Ranabir. 'Seafaring, Ships and Ship Owners. India and the Indian Ocean (AD 700–1500)'. In *Ships and the Development of Maritime Technology in the Indian Ocean*, edited by D. Parkin and R. Barnes, 28–61. London: Routledge Curzon, 2002.

Chakravarti, Ranabir. 'Merchants, Merchandise and Merchantmen in the Western Sea-board of India (c. 500 BCE–1500 CE)'. In *The Trading World of the Indian Ocean, 1500–1800*, edited by O. Prakash, 53–116. Delhi, Chennai and Chandigarh: Pearson, 2012.

Chakravarti, Ranabir. *India and the Indian Ocean. Issues in Trade and Politics (up to c. 1500 CE)*. Mumbai: Maritime History Society, 2014.

Chakravarti, Ranabir. *The Pull towards the Coast and Other Essays. The Indian Ocean History and the Subcontinent before 1500*. New Delhi: Primus Books, 2020.

Chakravarti, Ranabir. *Trade and Traders in Early Indian Society*. 3rd edn. London and New York: Routledge, 2021.

Chamberlin, J. Edward. *Island. How Islands Transform the World*. Katonah, NY: BlueBridge, 2013.

Chamisso, Adelbert von. *A Voyage around the World with the Romanzov Exploring Expedition in the Years 1815–1818 in the Brig Rurik, Captain Otto von Kotzebue*. Honolulu: University of Hawaii Press, 1986.

Chamisso, Adelbert von. *Reise um die Welt*. 2nd edn. Berlin: Rütten & Loening, 1978.

Chandler, Robert J. and Stephen J. Potash. *Gold, Silk, Pioneers and Mail. The Story of the Pacific Mail Steamship Company*. San Francisco: Glencannon Press, 2007.

Chaplin, Joyce E. *The First Scientific American. Benjamin Franklin and the Pursuit of Genius*. New York: Basic Books, 2006.

Chaplin, Joyce E. 'The Atlantic Ocean and Its Contemporary Meanings, 1492–1808'. In *Atlantic History. A Critical Appraisal*, edited by J. P. Greene and P. D. Morgan, 35–51. Oxford and New York: Oxford University Press, 2009.

Chappell, David. *Double Ghosts. Oceanian Voyagers on Euroamerican Ships*. Armonk, NY: Sharpe, 1997.

Chappell, David A. 'Ahab's Boat. Non-European Seamen in Western Ships of Exploration and Commerce'. In *Sea Changes. Historicizing the Ocean*, edited by B. Klein and G. Mackenthun, 75–90. New York and London: Routledge, 2004.

Chaudhuri, Kirti Narayan. *Asia before Europe. Economy and Civilisation of the Indian Ocean from the Rise of Islam to 1750*. Cambridge, New York and Melbourne: Cambridge University Press, 1990.

Chaudhuri, Kirti Narayan. *The Trading World of Asia and the English East India Company 1660–1760*. Cambridge, New York and Melbourne: Cambridge University Press, 2006.

Chaudhury, Sushil. 'Trading Networks in a Traditional Diaspora. Armenians in India, c. 1600–1800'. In *Diaspora Entrepreneurial Networks. Four Centuries of History*, edited by I. Baghdiantz McCabe, G. Harlaftis and I. P. Minoglou, 51–72. Oxford and New York: Berg, 2005.

Chaunu, Pierre. *Sevilla y América siglos XVI y XVII*. Seville: Secretariado de Publicaciones de la Universidad de Sevilla, 1983.

Cheung, William W. L., A. D. Rogers and Ussif Rashid Sumaila. 'The Potential Economic Costs of the Overuse of Marine Fish Stocks'. In *Managing Ocean Environments in a Changing Climate. Sustainability and Economic Perspectives*, edited by K. J. Noone, U. R. Sumaila and R. J. Diaz, 171–92. Amsterdam, Boston and Heidelberg: Elsevier, 2013.

Chin, James K. 'The Hokkien Merchants in the South China Sea, 1500–1800'. In *The Trading World of the Indian Ocean, 1500–1800*, edited by O. Prakash, 433–61. Delhi, Chennai and Chandigarh: Pearson, 2012.

Ciéslak, Edmund. *Historia Gdańska*, vol. 2: *1454–1655*. Gdańsk: Wydawnitctwo Morskie, 1982.

Ciriacono, Salvatore. 'Industria e artigianato'. In *Storia di Venezia. Il Rinascimento società ed economia*, edited by A. Tenenti and U. Tucci, 523–92. Rome: Istituto dell'Enciclopedia Italiana, 1996.

Ciriacono, Salvatore. *Building on Water. Venice, Holland and the Construction of the European Landscape in Early Modern Times*. Oxford: Berghahn, 2006.

Coclanis, Peter A. *The Atlantic Economy during the Seventeenth and Eighteenth Centuries. Organization, Operation, Practice, and Personnel*. Columbia: University of South Carolina Press, 2005.

Conermann, Stephan. 'South Asia and the Indian Ocean'. In *Empires and Encounters 1350–1750*, edited by W. Reinhard, 391–554, 983–1002 and 1078–90. Cambridge, MA: Harvard University Press, 2015.

Cook, Harold. *Matters of Exchange. Commerce, Medicine, and Science in the Dutch Golden Age*. New Haven and London: Yale University Press, 2007.

Cook, James, Joseph Banks and John Hawkesworth. 'The Unfortunate Compiler'. In *Exploration and Exchange. A South Sea Anthology 1680–1900*, edited by J. Lamb, V. Smith and N. Thomas, 73–92. Chicago and London: University of Chicago Press, 2000.

Corbin, Alain. *The Lure of the Sea. The Discovery of the Seaside in the Western World, 1750–1840*, translated by Jocelyn Phelps. Berkeley and Los Angeles: University of California Press, 1994.

Crosby, Alfred W. *The Columbian Exchange. Biological and Cultural Consequences of 1492*. Westport, CT and London: Praeger, 2003.

Cunliffe, Barry W. *The Extraordinary Voyage of Pytheas the Greek*. London: Penguin, 2002.

Cunliffe, Barry W. *Facing the Ocean. The Atlantic and Its Peoples, 8000 BC–AD 1500*. Oxford and New York: Oxford University Press, 2004.

Cunliffe, Barry W. *Europe between the Oceans. 9000 BC–AD 1000*. New Haven and London: Yale University Press, 2011.

Curtin, Philip D. *Cross-Cultural Trade in World History*. Cambridge, New York and Melbourne: Cambridge University Press, 1984.

Cushing, David H. *The Provident Sea*. Cambridge, New York and Melbourne: Cambridge University Press, 1988.

D

D'Arcy, Paul. *The People of the Sea. Environment, Identity, and History in Oceania*. Honolulu: University of Hawai'i Press, 2006.

Dampier, William. *A New Voyage Round the World*. London: Knapton, 1697.

Dana, Richard Henry. *Two Years before the Mast. A Personal Narrative*. New York: Harper, 1840. London: Dutton, 1969.

Das Gupta, Ashin. *The World of the Indian Ocean Merchant, 1500–1800*. New Delhi and New York: Oxford University Press, 2004.

David, Karel. *Global Ocean of Knowledge, 1600–1860. Globalization and Maritime Knowledge in the Atlantic World*. London: Bloomsbury Academic, 2020.

De Souza, Philip. *Seafaring and Civilization. Maritime Perspectives on World History*. London: Profile Books, 2001.

Defoe, Daniel. *A Plan of the English Commerce*. London: Rivington, 1728.

Denzel, Markus A. 'Die Errichtung der Hamburger Bank 1619. Ausbreitung einer stabilen Währung und Ausdehnung des bargeldlosen Zahlungsverkehrs'. In *Schlüsselereignisse der deutschen Bankengeschichte*, edited by C. Burhop, D. Lindenlaub and J. Scholtyseck, 38–50. Stuttgart: Franz Steiner Verlag, 2013.

Denzel, Markus A. 'Hamburg-Swedish Connections. Exchange Rates and Maritime Insurance from the Late Seventeenth to the Mid-Nineteenth Century'. In *Preindustrial Commercial History. Flows and Contacts between Cities in Scandinavia and North Western Europe*, edited by Markus A. Denzel and C. Dalhede, 199–230. Stuttgart: Franz Steiner Verlag, 2014.

Dewulf, Jeroen. *The Pinkster King and the King of Kongo. The Forgotten History of America's Dutch-owned Slaves*. Jackson: University Press of Mississippi, 2017.

Dewulf, Jeroen. 'From Papiamentu to Afro-Catholic Brotherhoods: An Interdisciplinary Analysis of Iberian Elements in Curaçaoan Popular Culture'. *Studies in Latin American Popular Culture* 36 (2018): 69–94.

Diffie, Bailey Wallys and George Davidson Winius. *Foundations of the Portuguese Empire, 1415–1580*. Minneapolis: University of Minnesota Press, 1977.

Dilly, Geoff. 'The Southern Ocean'. In *The World's Oceans. Geography, History, and Environment*, edited by Rainer F. Buschmann and L. Nolde, 72–89. Santa Barbara: ABC-CLIO, 2018.

Dini, Bruno. 'Seeversicherung'. *Lexikon des Mittelalters* 7 (1995): 1691–2.

Diouf, Sylviane A. (ed.). *Fighting the Slave Trade. West African Strategies*. Athens, OH: Ohio University Press.

Dodds, Klaus and Mark Nuttall. *The Scramble for the Poles. The Geopolitics of the Arctic and Antarctic*. Cambridge: Polity Books, 2015.

Doe, Erik van der, Perry Moree and Dirk J. Tang (eds.). *De dominee met het stenen hart en andere overzeese briefgeheimen*. Zutphen: Walburg Pers, 2008.

Dollinger, Philippe. *Die Hanse*. 4th edn. Stuttgart: Kröner, 1989.

Dreher, Martin. *Hegemon und Symmachoi. Untersuchungen zum Zweiten Athenischen Seebund*. Berlin and New York: de Gruyter, 1995.

Dreyer, Edward L. *Zheng He. China and the Oceans in the Early Ming Dynasty, 1405–1433*. New York and London: Pearson Longman, 2007.

Dubois, Laurent. 'The French Atlantic'. In *Atlantic History. A Critical Appraisal*, edited by J. P. Greene and P. D. Morgan, 137–61. Oxford and New York: Oxford University Press, 2009.

Dunsch, Boris. '"Why Do We Violate Strange Seas and Sacred Waters?" The Sea as Bridge and Boundary in Greek and Roman Poetry'. In *Beyond the Sea. Reviewing the Manifold Dimensions of Water as Barrier and Bridge*, edited by M. Grzechnik and H. Hurskainen, 17–42. Cologne, Weimar and Vienna: Böhlau, 2015.

Durstel, Eric R. *Renegade Women. Gender, Identity and Boundaries in the Early Modern Mediterranean*. Baltimore: Johns Hopkins University Press, 2011.

Dyke, Paul A. van. *The Canton Trade. Life and Enterprise on the China Coast 1700–1845*. Hong Kong: Hong Kong University Press, 2005.

E

Earle, Peter. *Sailors. English Merchant Seamen 1650–1775*. London: Methuen, 2007.

Edelsohn, Sarah Nicole, Juliet Glennon, Dylan Jarvis, Andrew Vierra and Rainer F. Buschmann. 'The Arctic Ocean'. In *The World's Oceans. Geography, History, and Environment*, edited by R. F. Buschmann and L. Nolde, 3–17. Santa Barbara: ABC-CLIO, 2018.

Ekberg, Espen, Even Lange and Eivind Merok. 'Building the Networks of Trade. Perspectives on Twentieth-Century Maritime History'. In *The World's Key Industry. History and Economics of International Shipping*, edited by G. Harlaftis, S. Tenold, J. M. Valdaliso Gago and T. Charlautē, 88–105. Basingstoke and New York: Palgrave Macmillan, 2012.

Eklöf Amirell, Stefan and Leos Müller (eds.). *Persistent Piracy. Maritime Violence and State-Formation in Global Historical Perspective*. Basingstoke and New York: Palgrave Macmillan, 2014.

Elliott, John H. 'Atlantic History. A Circumnavigation'. In *The British Atlantic World, 1500–1800*, edited by D. Armitage and M. J. Braddick, 253–70. 2nd edn., Basingstoke and New York: Palgrave Macmillan, 2009.

Eltis, David. 'Precolonial Western Africa and the Atlantic Economy'. In *Slavery and the Rise of the Atlantic System*, edited by B. L. Solow, 97–119. Cambridge, New York and Melbourne: Cambridge University Press, 1991.

Elvert, Jürgen. *Europa, das Meer und die Welt. Eine maritime Geschichte der Neuzeit*. Munich: Deutsche Verlags-Anstalt, 2018.

Elvert, Jürgen, Sigurd Hess and Heinrich Walle (eds.). *Maritime Wirtschaft in Deutschland. Schifffahrt – Werften – Handel – Seemacht im 19. und 20. Jahrhundert*. Stuttgart: Franz Steiner Verlag, 2012.

Emmer, Pieter C. 'West Indians in Great Britain, France, and the Netherlands since the End of World War II'. In *The Encyclopedia of European Migration and Minorities: From the Seventeenth Century to the Present*, edited by K. J. Bade et al., 739–43. Cambridge and New York: Cambridge University Press, 2011.

Emmer, Pieter C. and Jos J. L. Gommans. *The Dutch Overseas Empire, 1600–1800*. Cambridge and New York: Cambridge University Press, 2021.

Epkenhans, Michael. *Die wilhelminische Flottenrüstung 1908–1914*. Munich: Oldenbourg, 1991.

Epkenhans, Michael. 'Flotten und Flottenrüstung im 20. Jahrhundert'. In *Maritime Wirtschaft in Deutschland. Schifffahrt – Werften – Handel – Seemacht im 19. und 20. Jahrhundert*, edited by J. Elvert, S. Hess and H. Walle, 176–89. Stuttgart: Franz Steiner Verlag, 2012.

Epstein, Steven A. 'Hybridity'. In *A Companion to Mediterranean History*, edited by P. Horden and S. Kinoshita, 345–58. Chichester, West Sussex: Whiley, 2014.

Eriksson-Hägg, Hanna, Dan Wilhelmsson, Richard C. Thompson, Katrin Holmström and Olof Linden. 'Marine Pollution'. In *Managing Ocean Environments in a Changing Climate. Sustainability and Economic Perspectives*, edited by K. J. Noone, U. R. Sumaila and R. J. Diaz, 127–70. Amsterdam, Boston and Heidelberg: Elsevier, 2013.

Evans, James and J. Lennart Berggren (eds.). *Gemino's Introduction to the Phenomena. A Translation and Study of a Hellenistic Survey of Astronomy*. Princeton and Oxford: Princeton University Press, 2006.

F

Fagan, Brian M. *Beyond the Blue Horizon. How the Earliest Mariners Unlocked the Secrets of the Oceans*. London and New York: Bloomsbury Press, 2012.

Fatah-Black, Karwan. *White Lies and Black Markets. Evading Metropolitan Authority in Colonial Suriname, 1650–1800*. Leiden and Boston: Brill, 2015.

Feldbæk, Ole. *Dansk Søfarts Historie*, vol. 3: *1720–1814. Storhandelens tid*. Copenhagen: Gyldenhall, 1997.

Fernández-Armesto, Felipe. *Before Columbus. Exploration and Colonisation from the Mediterranean to the Atlantic, 1229–1492*. London and Basingstoke: Macmillan Education, 1987.

Fernando, M. R. 'Commerce in the Malay Archipelago, 1400–1800'. In *The Trading World of the Indian Ocean, 1500–1800*, edited by O. Prakash, 387–431. Delhi, Chennai and Chandigarh: Pearson, 2012.

Ferrão, Cristina and José Paulo Monteiro Soares (eds.). *The 'Thierbuch' and 'Autobiography' of Zacharias Wagener*. Rio de Janeiro: Editora Index, 1997.

Fischer, Lewis R. and Helge W. Nordvik. 'Maritime Transport and the Integration of the North Atlantic Economy, 1850–1914'. In *The Emergence of a World Economy 1500–1914. Papers of the IX. International Congress of Economic History*, edited by W. Fischer, 519–46. Stuttgart: Franz Steiner Verlag, 1986.

Fischer, Steven Roger. *A History of the Pacific Islands*. Basingstoke and New York: Palgrave Macmillan, 2002.

Flaig, Egon. *Weltgeschichte der Sklaverei*. Munich: Beck, 2009.

Forrer, Matthi. *Hokusai. Prints and Drawings*. Munich, Berlin, London and New York: Prestel, 2010.

Forster, John Reinhold. *Observations Made during a Voyage round the World on Physical Geography, Natural History, and Ethic Philosophy*. London: Printed for G. Robinson, 1778.

Fouquet, Gerhard and Gabriel Zeilinger. *Katastrophen im Spätmittelalter*. Darmstadt and Mainz: Wissenschaftliche Buchgesellschaft, 2011.

Frank, Caroline. *Objectifying China. Imagining America. Chinese Commodities in Early America*. Chicago and London: University of Chicago Press, 2011.

Franzoi, Alessandro. 'Sagezza di mercante (CLE 1533)'. *Rivista di Cultura Classica e Medievale* 463 (2004): 257–63.

Freitag, Ulrike and William G. Clarence-Smith. *Hadhrami Traders, Scholars and Statesmen in the Indian Ocean. 1750s–1960s*. Leiden and Boston: Brill, 1997.

Fritze, Konrad. *Am Wendepunkt der Hanse. Untersuchungen zur Wirtschafts- und Sozialgeschichte wendischer Hansestädte in der ersten Hälfte des 15. Jahrhunderts*. Berlin: Deutscher Verlag der Wissenschaften, 1967.

Fudge, John D. *Cargoes, Embargoes and Emissaries. The Commercial and Political Interaction of England and the German Hanse, 1450–1510*. Toronto: University of Toronto Press, 1995.

Fusaro, Maria. 'Les Anglais et les Grecs. Un réseau de coopération commercial en Méditerranée vénitienne'. *Annales. Histoire, Sciences Sociales* 58, no. 3 (2003): 605–25.

Fusaro, Maria, Colin Heywood and Mohamed Salah Omri. *Trade and Cultural Exchange in the Early Modern Mediterranean. Braudel's Maritime Legacy*. London and New York: Tauris Academic Studies, 2010.

G

Gaastra, Femme S. 'Die Vereinigte Ostindische Compagnie der Niederlande – ein Abriss ihrer Geschichte'. In *Kaufleute als Kolonialherren. Die Handelswelt der Niederländer vom Kap der Guten Hoffnung bis Nagasaki 1600–1800*, edited by E. Schmitt, T. Schleich and T. Beck, 1–89. Bamberg: Buchners, 1988.

Gaastra, Femme S. *The Dutch East India Company. Expansion and Decline*. Zutphen: Walburg Pers, 2003.

Gabaccia, Donna R. and Dirk Hoerder (eds.). *Connecting Seas and Connected Ocean Rims. Indian, Atlantic, and Pacific Oceans and China Seas Migrations from the 1830s to the 1930s*. Leiden and Boston: Brill, 2011.

Games, Alison. *Migration and the Origins of the English Atlantic World*. Cambridge, MA and London: Harvard University Press, 1999.

Games, Alison. 'Atlantic History. Definitions, Challenges, Opportunities'. *American Historical Review* 111 (2006): 741–57.

Games, Alison. 'Beyond the Atlantic. English Globetrotters and Transoceanic Connections'. *The William and Mary Quarterly* 63, no. 4 (2006): 675–92.

Games, Alison. 'Migration'. In *The British Atlantic World, 1500–1800*, edited by D. Armitage and M. J. Braddick, 33–52. 2nd edn. Basingstoke and New York: Palgrave Macmillan, 2009.

Gardiner, Tudor. 'Terms for Thalassocracy in Thucydides'. *Rheinisches Museum für Philologie* NF 112, no. 1 (1969): 16–22.

Gascoigne, John. *Encountering the Pacific in the Age of Enlightenment.* Cambridge and New York: Cambridge University Press, 2014.

Gause, Fritz. *Die Geschichte der Stadt Königsberg*, vol. 1. Cologne and Graz: Böhlau, 1965.

Geertz, Clifford. *The Interpretation of Cultures. Selected Essays.* New York: Basic Books, 1973.

Gelder, Maartje van. *Trading Places. The Netherlandish Merchants in Early Modern Venice.* Leiden and Boston: Brill, 2009.

Gertwagen, Ruthy. 'Nautical Technology'. In *A Companion to Mediterranean History*, edited by P. Horden and S. Kinoshita, 154–69. Chichester, West Sussex: Whiley, 2014.

Giet, Stanislas. *Basile de Césarée, Homélies sur l'Hexaéméron.* Paris: Editions du Cerf, 1950.

Gillis, John. *Islands of the Mind. How the Human Imagination Created the Atlantic World.* Houndmills: Palgrave Macmillan, 2004.

Gillis, John R. *The Human Shore. Seacoasts in History.* Chicago and London: The University of Chicago Press, 2012.

Gilroy, Paul. *The Black Atlantic. Modernity and Double-Consciousness.* Cambridge, MA and London: Harvard University Press, 1993.

Gipouloux, François. *La Mediterranée asiatique. Villes portuaires et réseaux marchands en Chine, au Japon et en Asie du Sud-Est, XVIe–XXIe siecle.* Paris: CNRS Éditions, 2009.

Gipouloux, François. *The Asian Mediterranean. Port Cities and Trading Networks in China, Japan and Southeast Asia. 13th–21st century*, translated by J. Hall and D. Martin. Cheltenham and Northampton: Elgar, 2011.

Giráldez, Arturo. *The Age of Trade.* Lanham, Boulder, New York and London: Rowman & Littlefield, 2015.

Glamann, Kristof. *Dutch-Asiatic Trade 1620–1740.* Copenhagen: Danish Science Press, 1958.

Goitein, Shlomo Dov (ed.). *Letters of Medieval Jewish Traders.* Princeton: Princeton University Press, 1973.

Goldberg, Jessica L. *Trade and Institutions in the Medieval Mediterranean. The Geniza Merchants and Their Business World.* Cambridge and New York: Cambridge University Press, 2012.

Gorski, Richard. 'Roles of the Sea. Views from the Shore'. In *Roles of the Sea in Medieval England*, edited by R. Gorski. Woodbridge and Rochester. New York: Boydell Press, 2012.

Greene, Jack P. and Philip D. Morgan (eds.). *Atlantic History. A Critical Appraisal.* Oxford and New York: Oxford University Press, 2009.

Greene, Jack P. and Philip D. Morgan. 'Introduction: The Present State of Atlantic History', in *Atlantic History. A Critical Appraisal*, edited by J. P. Greene and P. D. Morgan, 5–7. Oxford and New York: Oxford University Press, 2009.

Greene, Molly. *Catholic Pirates and Greek Merchants. A Maritime History of the Mediterranean.* Princeton and Woodstock: Princeton University Press, 2010.

Greene, Molly. 'The Early Modern Mediterranean'. In *A Companion to Mediterranean History*, edited by P. Horden and S. Kinoshita, 91–106. Chichester, West Sussex: Whiley, 2014.

Greif, Avner. *Institutions and the Path to the Modern Economy. Lessons from Medieval Trade*. Cambridge, New York and Melbourne: Cambridge University Press, 2006.

Groth, Eckhard. *Das Verhältnis der livländischen Städte zum Novgoroder Hansekontor im 14. Jahrhundert*. Hamburg: Baltische Gesellschaft, 1999.

Gründer, Horst. *Eine Geschichte der europäischen Expansion. Von Entdeckern und Eroberern zum Kolonialismus*. Darmstadt: Wissenschaftliche Buchgesellschaft, 2003.

Grzechnik, Marta and Heta Hurskainen (eds.). *Beyond the Sea. Reviewing the Manifold Dimensions of Water as Barrier and Bridge*. Cologne, Weimar and Vienna: Böhlau, 2015.

Guest, Harriet. *Empire, Barbarism, and Civilization. James Cook, William Hodges, and the Return to the Pacific*. Cambridge, New York and Melbourne: Cambridge University Press, 2007.

Gunn, Geoffrey C. *History without Borders. The Making of an Asian World Region 1000–1800*. Hong Kong: Hong Kong University Press, 2011.

H

Hakluyt, Richard. *Divers Voyages Touching the Discovery of America and the Islands Adjacent*. London: Hakluyt Society, 1850.

Hall, Joseph M. *Zamumo's Gifts. Indian-European Exchange in the Colonial Southeast*. Philadelphia: University of Pennsylvania Press, 2009.

Hall, Kenneth R. *A History of Early Southeast Asia. Maritime Trade and Societal Development, 100–1500*. Lanham and Plymouth: Rowman & Littlefield, 2011.

Hämäläinen, Pekka. *The Comanche Empire*. New Haven and London: Yale University Press, 2008.

Hämäläinen, Pekka. *Lakota America. A New History of Indigenous Power*. New Haven and London: Yale University Press, 2019.

Hammel-Kiesow, Rolf. 'Novgorod und Lübeck. Siedlungsgefüge zweier Handelsstädte im Vergleich'. In *Novgorod. Markt und Kontor der Hanse*, edited by N. Angermann and K. Friedland, 25–68. Cologne, Weimar and Vienna: Böhlau, 2002.

Hammel-Kiesow, Rolf. *Die Hanse*. 5th edn. Munich: Beck, 2014.

Haneda, Masashi (ed.). *Asian Port Cities, 1600–1800. Local and Foreign Cultural Interactions*. Singapore: NUS Press, 2009.

Harlaftis, Gelina. 'The "Eastern Invasion". Greeks in Mediterranean Trade and Shipping in the Eighteenth and Early Nineteenth Centuries'. In *Trade and Cultural Exchange in the Early Modern Mediterranean. Braudel's Maritime Legacy*, edited by M. Fusaro, C. Heywood and M. S. Omri, 223–52. London and New York: Tauris Academic Studies, 2010.

Harlaftis, Gelina, Stig Tenold and Jesús M. Valdaliso (eds.). *The World's Key Industry. History and Economics of International Shipping*. Basingstoke and New York: Palgrave Macmillan, 2012.

Harreld, Donald J. (ed.). *A Companion to the Hanseatic League*. Leiden and Boston: Brill, 2015.

Hart, Peter. *Gallipoli*. London: Profile, 2011.

Hatz, Gerd. *Handel und Verkehr zwischen dem Deutschen Reich und Schweden in der späten Wikingerzeit. Die Deutschen Münzen des 10. und 11. Jahrhunderts in Schweden.* Stockholm: Almqvist och Wiksell, 1974.

Hatz, Gerd. 'Der Handel in der späten Wikingerzeit zwischen Nordeuropa (insbesondere Schweden) und dem Deutschen Reich nach numismatischen Quellen'. In *Untersuchungen zu Handel und Verkehr der vor- und frühgeschichtlichen Zeit in Mittel- und Nordeuropa*, vol. 4: *Der Handel der Karolinger- und Wikingerzeit*, edited by K. Düwel, 86–122. Göttingen: Vandenhoeck & Ruprecht, 1987.

Hatz, Gerd. 'Danegeld'. In *Von Aktie bis Zoll. Ein historisches Lexikon des Geldes*, edited by M. North, 78. Munich: Beck, 1995.

Hatz, Gerd. 'Die Münzen von Alt-Lübeck', *Offa* 21/22 (1964/65): 262.

Hausberger, Bernd. *Die Verknüpfung der Welt. Geschichte der frühen Globalisierung vom 16. bis zum 18. Jahrhundert.* Vienna: Mandelbaum Verlag, 2015.

Havard, Gilles and Cécile Vidal. *Histoire de L'Amérique Française.* 2nd edn. Paris: Flammarion, 2008.

Heijer, Henk den. *De geschiedenis van de WIC.* 2nd edn. Zutphen: Walburg Pers, 2002.

Heinsen, Johan. *Mutiny in the Danish Atlantic World. Convicts, Sailors and a Dissonant Empire.* London and New York: Bloomsbury Academic, 2017.

Henn, Volker. 'Was war die Hanse?' In *Die Hanse. Lebenswirklichkeit und Mythos*, edited by J. Bracker, V. Henn and R. Postel, 14–23. 2nd edn. Lübeck: Schmidt-Römhild, 1998.

Hensel, Silke. 'Latin American Perspectives on Migration in the Atlantic World'. In *Connecting Seas and Connected Ocean Rims. Indian, Atlantic, and Pacific Oceans and China Seas Migrations from the 1830s to the 1930s*, edited by D. R. Gabaccia and D. Hoerder, 281–301. Leiden and Boston: Brill, 2011.

Hermann, Joachim. *Zwischen Hradschin und Vineta. Frühe Kulturen der Westslawen.* 2nd edn. Leipzig: Urania, 1976.

Hermann, Joachim. *Wikinger und Slawen. Zur Frühgeschichte der Ostseevölker.* Neumünster: Wachholtz, 1982.

Hershenzon, Daniel. *The Captive Sea. Slavery, Communication, and Commerce in Early Modern Spain and the Mediterranean.* Philadelphia: University of Pennsylvania Press, 2018.

Hochstrasser, Julie B. 'The Butterfly Effect. Embodied Cognition and Perceptual Knowledge in Maria Sibylla Merian's *Metamorphosis Insectorum Surinamensium*'. In *The Dutch Trading Companies as Knowledge Networks*, edited by S. Huigen, J. de Jong and E. Kolfin, 59–101. Leiden and Boston: Brill, 2010.

Hocquet, Jean-Claude. *Venise et la mer. XIIe–XVIIIe siècle.* Paris: Fajard, 2006.

Hoffmann, Erich. 'Lübeck im Hoch- und Spätmittelalter. Die große Zeit Lübecks'. In *Lübeckische Geschichte*, edited by A. Graßmann, 79–340. Lübeck: Schmidt-Römhild, 1988.

Homer. *The Odyssey*, translated by Augustus Taber Murray. 2 vols. Cambridge, MA: Harvard University Press and London: William Heinemann, 1919.

Hoogervorst, Tom. 'Sailors, Tailors, Cooks and Crooks. On Loanwords and Neglected Lives in Indian Ocean Ports'. *Itinerario* 42, no. 3 (2012): 516–48.

Horden, Peregrine and Nicholas Purcell. *The Corrupting Sea. A Study of Mediterranean History.* Oxford: Blackwell, 2000.

Horden, Peregrine and Nicholas Purcell. 'The Mediterranean and "the New Thalassology"'. *American Historical Review* 111 (2006): 722–40.

Howkins, Adrian. *The Polar Regions. An Environmental History*. Cambridge: Polity Books, 2015.

Hu-Dehart, Evelyn. 'Chinese Coolie Labor in Cuba in the Nineteenth Century. Free Labor of Neoslavery'. *Contributions in Black Studies* 12 (1994): 38–54.

Hunter, Phyllis W. *Purchasing Identity in the Atlantic World, Massachusetts Merchants, 1670–1780*. Ithaca, NY: Cornell University Press, 2001.

I

Ibn Battuta. *Travels in Asia and Africa, 1325–1354*, edited and translated by H. A.R. Gibb. London: George Routledge [and] Sons, 1929.

Ibn Battuta. *Die Wunder des Morgenlandes. Reisen durch Afrika und Asien*. Nach der arabischen Ausgabe von Muhammad al-Bailuni ins Deutsche übertragen, kommentiert und mit einem Nachweis versehen von Ralf Elger. Munich: Beck, 2010.

Ibn Majid al-Najdi, Ahman and Gerald Randall Tibbetts (eds.). *Arab Navigation in the Indian Ocean before the Coming of the Portuguese. Being a Translation of Kitab al-Fawa'id fi usul al-bahr*. London: Royal Asiatic Society of Great Britain and Ireland, 1971.

Igler, David. *The Great Ocean. Pacific Worlds from Captain Cook to the Gold Rush*. Oxford, New York and Auckland: Oxford University Press, 2013.

Ingstad, Anne Stine and Helge Ingstad. *The Norse Discovery of America*, vol. 1: *Excavations of a Norse Settlement at L'Anse aux Meadows, Newfoundland 1961–1968*. Oslo, Bergen, Stavanger and Tromsø: Norwegian University Press, 1985.

Iradiel Murugarren, Paulino. 'El comercio en el Mediterráneo catalano-aragonés. Espacios y redes'. In *Comercio y hombres de negocios en Castilla y Europa en tiempos de Isabel la Católica*, edited by H. Casado Alonso and A. García-Baquero, 123–50. Madrid: Sociedad Estatal de Conmemoraciones Culturales, 2007.

Israel, Jonathan I. *Dutch Primacy in World Trade, 1585–1740*. Oxford: Clarendon Press, 1989.

J

Jacobs, Els M. *Varem om Peper en Thee. Korte geschiedenis van de Verenigde Oostindische Compagnie*. Zutphen: Walburg Pers and Amsterdam: Rijksmuseum 'Nederlands Scheepvaart Museum', 1991.

Jaffer, Aaron. *Lascars and Indian Ocean Seafaring. 1780–1860. Shipboard Life, Unrest and Mutiny*. Woodbridge and Rochester, NY: Boydell Press, 2015.

Jakubowski-Tiessen, Manfred. *Sturmflut 1717. Die Bewältigung einer Naturkatastrophe in der frühen Neuzeit*. Munich: Oldenbourg, 1992.

Janson, Henrik. 'Pagani and Cristiani. Cultural Identity and Exclusion around the Baltic in the Early Middle Ages'. In *The Reception of Medieval Europe in the Baltic Sea Region. Papers of the XIIth Visby Symposium, held at Gotland University Visby*, edited by J. Staecker, 171–91. Visby: Gotland University Press, 2009.

Jaspert, Nikolas and Sebastian Kolditz (eds.). *Seeraub im Mittelmeerraum. Piraterie, Korsarentum und maritime Gewalt von der Antike bis zur Neuzeit.* Munich: Fink and Paderborn: Schöningh, 2013.

Jenks, Stuart. 'Die "Carta mercatoria". Ein "Hansisches" Privileg'. *Hansische Geschichtsblätter* 108 (1990): 45–86.

Jenks, Stuart. *England, die Hanse und Preußen. Handel und Diplomatie, 1377–1474.* Cologne and Vienna: Böhlau, 1992.

Johnson, Donald S. and Juha Nurminen. *The History of Seafaring. Navigating the World's Oceans.* London: Conway, 2008.

Johnson, Michael. 'Whales and Whaling'. In *The World's Oceans. Geography, History, and Environment*, edited by R. F. Buschmann and L. Nolde, 399–402. Santa Barbara: ABC-CLIO, 2018.

Jordi, Jean-Jacques. *De l'Exode à l'Exil. Rapatriés et pieds-noirs en France; l'exemple marseillais, 1954–1992.* Paris: L'Harmattan, 1993.

Jordi, Jean-Jacques. *1962. L'arrivée des Pieds-Noirs.* Paris: Éd. Autrement, 1995.

Jordi, Jean-Jacques. 'Algerian *Pieds-Noirs* in France since 1954'. In *The Encyclopedia of European Migration and Minorities. From the Seventeenth Century to the Present*, edited by K. J. Bade et al., 224–5. Cambridge and New York: Cambridge University Press, 2011.

Jörn, Nils, Ralf-Gunnar Werlich and Horst Wernicke (eds.). *Der Stralsunder Frieden von 1370. Prosopographische Studien.* Cologne, Weimar and Vienna: Böhlau, 1998.

K

Kaiser, Wolfgang. 'Frictions profitables. L'économie de la rançon en Méditerranée occidentale (XVIe–XVIIe siècles)'. In *Ricchezza del Mare, Ricchezza dal Mare Secc. XIII–XVIII. Atti della 'Trentasettesima Settimana di studi', 11–15 April 2005*, Vol. 2, edited by S. Cavaciocchi, 689–701. Florence: Le Monnier, 2006.

Kaiser, Wolfgang and Guillaume Calafat. 'The Economy of Ransoming in the Early Modern Mediterranean. A Form of Cross-Cultural Trade between Southern Europe and the Maghreb (Sixteenth to Eighteenth Centuries)'. In *Religion and Trade. Cross-Cultural Exchanges in World History, 1000–1900*, edited by F. Trivellato, L. Halevi and C. Antunes, 108–30. Oxford and New York: Oxford University Press, 2014.

Karge, Wolf. *Heiligendamm. Erstes deutsches Seebad. Gegründet 1793.* Schwerin: Demmler, 1993.

Kaufmann, Thomas DaCosta and Michael North (eds.). *Mediating Netherlandish Art and Material Culture in Asia.* Amsterdam: Amsterdam University Press, 2014.

Kaukiainen, Yrjo. 'Growth, Diversification and Globalization. Main Trends in International Shipping since 1850'. In *International Merchant Shipping in the Nineteenth and Twentieth Centuries. The Comparative Dimension*, edited by L. R. Fischer and E. Lange, 1–56. St John's, Newfoundland: International Maritime Economic History Association, 2008.

Kaukianen, Yrjo. 'Overseas Migration and the Development of Ocean Navigation. A Europe-Outward Perspective'. In *Connecting Seas and Connected Ocean Rims. Indian, Atlantic, and Pacific Oceans and China Seas Migrations from the*

1830s to the 1930s, edited by D. R. Gabaccia and D. Hoerder, 371–87. Leiden and Boston: Brill, 2011.

Kaukianen, Yrjo. 'The Advantages of Water Carriage. Scale Economies and Shipping Technology, c. 1870–2000'. In *The World's Key Industry. History and Economics of International Shipping*, edited by G. Harlaftis, S. Tenold and M. Valdaliso, 64–87. Basingstoke and New York: Palgrave Macmillan, 2012.

Kaukiainen, Yrjo. 'The Role of Shipping in the "Second Stage of Globalisation"'. *International Journal of Maritime History* 26 (2014): 64–81.

Keong, Ng Chin. 'At the Crossroads of the Maritime Silk Route'. In *Maritime Heritage of Singapore*, edited by T. Y. Tan and A. Lau, 60–79. Singapore: Suntree Media, 2005.

Keong, Ng Chin. *Trade and Society. The Amoy Network on the China Coast, 1683–1735*. 2nd edn. Singapore: NUS Press, 2015.

Ketting, Herman. *Leven, werk en rebellie aan boord van Oost-Indiëvaarders (1595–1650)*. Amsterdam and Leiden: Aksant, 2002.

Kikuchi, Yuta. *Hamburgs Ostsee- und Mitteleuropahandel 1600–1800. Warenaustausch und Hinterlandnetzwerke*. Cologne, Weimar and Vienna: Böhlau, 2018.

King, Charles. *The Black Sea. A History*. Oxford and New York: Oxford University Press, 2004.

Kirby, David G. and Merja-Liisa Hinkkanen. *The Baltic and the North Seas*. London and New York: Routledge, 2000.

Kizik, Edmund. *Mennonici w Gdańsku, Elblągu i na Żuławach wiślanych w drugiej połowie XVII i w XVIII wieku*. Gdańsk: Gdańskie Towarzystwo Naukowe, 1994.

Klein, Bernhard and Gesa Mackenthun (eds.). *Sea Changes. Historicizing the Ocean*. New York and London: Routledge, 2004.

Klein, Herbert S. *The Atlantic Slave Trade*. 2nd edn. Cambridge, New York and Melbourne: Cambridge University Press, 2010.

Klinge, Matti. *Die Ostseewelt*. Helsinki: Otava, 1995.

Klinge, Matti. *The Baltic World*. Revised, expanded edn. Helsinki: Otava-Publishing, 2010.

Klooster, Wim. *The Dutch Moment. War, Trade, and Settlement in the Seventeenth-Century Atlantic World*. Ithaca and London: Cornell University Press, 2016.

Knick, Harley C. 'Late Nineteenth Century Transportation, Trade and Settlement'. In *The Emergence of a World Economy 1500–1914. Papers of the IX. International Congress of Economic History*, edited by W. Fischer, 593–618. Stuttgart: Franz Steiner Verlag, 1986.

Knick, Harley C. 'Shipping and Stable Economies in the Periphery'. In *The World's Key Industry. History and Economics of International Shipping*, edited by G. Harlaftis, S. Tenold and M. Valdaliso, 29–42. Basingstoke and New York: Palgrave Macmillan, 2012.

Kotzebue, Otto von. *Entdeckungsreise in die Südsee und nach der Berings-Straße zur Erforschung einer nordöstlichen Durchfahrt. Unternommen in den Jahren 1815, 1816, 1817 und 1818, auf Kosten Sr. Erlaucht des Herrn Reichs-Kanzlers Grafen Rumanzoff auf dem Schiffe Rurick unter dem Befehle des Lieutenants der Russisch-Kaiserlichen Marine Otto von Kotzebue*. 3 vols. Weimar: Hoffmann, 1821.

Kotzebue, Otto von. *Voyage of Discovery in the South Sea, and to Behring's Straits, in Search of a North-East Passage: Undertaken in the Years 1815, 16, 17, and 18, in the Ship Rurick*. London: Sir R. Phillips, 1821.

Kotzebue, Otto von. *Neue Reise um die Welt in den Jahren 1823, 24, 25 und 26. Mit 2 Kupferstichen und 3 Charten*, edited by Wilhelm Hoffmann. Weimar: Hoffmann, 1830.

Kotzebue, Otto von. *A New Voyage round the World in the Years 1823–1826*. London 1830. Reprint, Amsterdam: Israel, 1967.

Krabbendam, Hans, Cornelis A. van Minnen and Giles Scott-Smith (eds.). *Four Centuries of Dutch-American Relations 1609–2009*. Albany, NY: State University of New York Press, 2009.

Kraus, Alexander and Martina Winkler (eds.). *Weltmeere. Wissen und Wahrnehmung im langen 19. Jahrhundert*. Göttingen: Vandenhoeck & Ruprecht, 2014.

Kresse, Walter. *Die Fahrtgebiete der Hamburger Handelsflotte 1824–1888*. Hamburg: Museum für Hamburgische Geschichte, 1972.

Krieger, Martin. *Kaufleute, Seeräuber und Diplomaten. Der dänische Handel auf dem Indischen Ozean (1620–1868)*. Cologne, Weimar and Vienna: Böhlau, 1998.

Krieger, Martin and Michael North (eds.). *Land und Meer. Kultureller Austausch zwischen Westeuropa und dem Ostseeraum in der Frühen Neuzeit*. Cologne, Weimar and Vienna: Böhlau, 2004.

Kriger, Colleen E. 'Mapping the History of Cotton Textile Production in Precolonial West Africa'. *African Economic History* 33 (2005): 87–116.

Kriger, Colleen E. 'The Importance of Mande Textiles in the African Side of the Atlantic Trade, ca. 1680–1710'. *Mande Studies* 11 (2011): 1–21.

Krohn, Deborah L., Marybeth De Filippis and Peter N. Miller (eds.). *Dutch New York between East and West. The World of Margrieta van Varick*. New Haven: Bard Graduate Center Decorative Arts, Design History, Material Culture, 2009.

Krusenstern, Adam Johann von. *Reise um die Welt 1803–06*. 3 vols. Petersburg: Schnoor, 1810–12.

Krusenstern, Adam Johann von. *Atlas de l'Océan Pacifique*. 2 vols. Petersburg: Impr. du Département de l'instruction publique, 1824–7.

Krusenstern, Ivan F. *Voyage round the World, in the Years 1803,1804,1805 & 1806 by Order of His Imperial Majesty Alexander I., on board the Ships Nadesha and Neva, under the Command of A[dam] J[ohann] von Krusenstern*, translated by Richard Belgrave Hoppner. London: Murray, 1813.

Kupperman, Karen Ordahl. *The Jamestown Project*. Cambridge, MA: Belknap Press of Harvard University Press, 2007.

Kupperman, Karen Ordahl. *The Atlantic in World History*. Oxford, New York: Oxford University Press, 2012.

Kurilo, Olga (ed.). *Seebäder an der Ostsee im 19. und 20. Jahrhundert*. Munich: Meidenbauer, 2009.

Kwa, Chong Guan, Derek Heng, Peter Borschberg and Tai Yong Tan. *Seven Hundred Years. A History of Singapore*. Singapore: National Library Board, 2019.

L

Landwehr, Götz. 'Seerecht (Seehandelsrecht)'. In *Handwörterbuch zur deutschen Rechtsgeschichte*, vol. 4: *Protonotarius Apostolicus – Strafprozessordnung*, edited by A. Erler and E. Kaufmann, 1596–614. Berlin: Erich Schmidt Verlag, 1990.

Landwehr, Götz. 'Das Seerecht im Ostseeraum vom Mittelalter bis zum Ausgang des 18. Jahrhunderts'. In *Geschichte und Perspektiven des Rechts im*

Ostseeraum, edited by J. Eckert and K. Å. Modéer, 275–304. Frankfurt a. M., Berlin, Bern and Vienna: Lang, 2002.

Lane, Frederic C. *Venice. A Maritime Republic*. Baltimore and London: Johns Hopkins University Press, 1973.

Lane, Kris E. *Colour of Paradise. The Emerald in the Age of Gunpowder Empires*. New Haven and London: Yale University Press, 2010.

Larsen, Svend Erik. 'Sea, Identity and Literature'. *1616. Anuario de Literatura Comparada* 2 (2012): 171–88.

Latham, Anthony J. H. 'The International Trade in Rice and Wheat since 1868. A Study in Market Integration'. In *The Emergence of a World Economy 1500–1914. Papers of the IX. International Congress of Economic History*, edited by W. Fischer, 645–64. Stuttgart: Franz Steiner Verlag, 1986.

Latham, Anthony J. H. and Larry Neal. 'The International Market in Rice and Wheat, 1868–1914'. *Economic History Review* 36, no. 2 (1983): 260–80.

Lee, Peter, Leonard Y. Andaya, Barbara Watson Andaya, Gael Newton and Alan Chong. *Port Cities. Multicultural Emporiums of Asia, 1500–1900*. Singapore: Asian Civilisations Museum, 2016.

Leibsohn, Dana. 'Made in China, Made in Mexico'. In *At the Crossroads. The Arts of Spanish America and Early Global Trade, 1492–1850. Papers from the 2010 Mayer Center Symposium at the Denver Art Museum*, edited by D. Pierce, R. Y. Otsuka and M. Bonta de la Pezuela, 11–40. Denver: Frederick & Jan Mayer Center for Pre-Columbian and Spanish Colonial Art, Denver Art Museum, 2012.

Leimus, Ivar. 'Millennium Breakthrough. North Goes West'. *Ajalookultuuri ajakiri TUNA*, Special Issue (2009): 7–34.

Lesger, Clé. 'De wereld als horizon. De economie tussen 1578 en 1650'. In *Geschiedenis van Amsterdam*, vol. 2/1: *Centrum van de wereld, 1578–1650*, edited by W. Frijhoff and B. Bakker, 103–87. Amsterdam: SUN, 2004.

Letts, Malcolm (ed.). *Pero Tafu. Travels and Adventures, 1435–1439*. London: Routledge, 1926.

Liebersohn, Harry. *The Traveller's World. Europe to the Pacific*. Cambridge, MA and London: Harvard University Press, 2006.

Lindblad, Jan Thomas. 'Foreign Trade of the Dutch Republic in the Seventeenth Century'. In *The Dutch Economy in the Golden Age. Nine Studies*, edited by K. Davids and L. Noordegraaf, 219–49. Amsterdam: Nederlandsch Economisch-Historisch Archief, 1993.

Lindblad, Jan Thomas. 'Louis de Geer (1587–1652). Dutch Entrepreneur and the Father of Swedish Industry'. In *Entrepreneurs and Entrepreneurship in Early Modern Times. Merchants and Industrialists within the Orbit of the Dutch Staple Market*, edited by C. Lesger and L. Noordegraaf, 77–84. The Hague: Stichting Hollandse Historische Reeks, 1995.

Lipman, Andrew. *The Saltwater Frontier. Indians and the Contest for the American Coast*. New Haven and London: Yale University Press, 2015.

Lloyd, Terrence Henry. *England and the German Hanse, 1157–1611. A Study of Their Trade and Commercial Diplomacy*. Cambridge and New York: Cambridge University Press, 1991.

Lockhart, James and Enrique Otte (eds.), *Letters and Peoples of the Indies*. Westport, 1976.

Lombard, Denys. 'Une autre "Méditerranée" dans le Sud-est Asiatique'. *Hérodote* 28 (1998): 184–93.

Lubbock, Basil (ed.). *Barlow's Journal of His Life at Sea in King's Ships, East and West Indiamen and Other Ships from 1659 to 1703*. London: Hurst & Blackett, 1934.

Lübke, Christian. *Das östliche Europa*. Munich: Siedler, 2004.

Lucassen, Jan. 'Zeevarenden'. In *Maritieme geschiedenis der Nederlanden*, vol. 2: *Zeventiende eeuw, van 1585 tot ca 1680*, edited by L. M. Akveld, S. Hart and W. J. van Hoboken, 126–58. Bussum: de Boer, 1977.

Lucassen, Jan. 'A Multinational and Its Labor Force. The Dutch East India Company, 1595–1795'. *International Labor and Working-Class History* 66 (2004): 12–39.

Lunsford, Virginia West. *Piracy and Privateering in the Golden Age Netherlands*. Basingstoke and New York: Palgrave Macmillan, 2005.

M

Mack, John. *The Sea. A Cultural History*. London: Reaktion Books, 2011.

Maddison, Ben. *Class and Colonialism in Antarctic Exploration, 1750–1920*. London: Pickering & Chatto, 2014.

Mahan, Alfred T. *The Influence of Sea Power upon History 1660–1783*. 2nd edn. Bremen: Salzwasser-Verlag, 2010.

Malan, Antonia. 'Furniture at the Cape in the Eighteenth Century. An Archaeological Approach'. In *Domestic Interiors at the Cape and in Batavia 1602–1795*, edited by T. M. Eliëns and M. Geijn-Verhoeven, 139–59. Zwolle: Waanders, 2002.

Mancall, Peter. *Hakluyt's Promise. An Elizabethan's Obsession for an English America*. New Haven and London: Yale University Press, 2007.

Manitius, Carolus. *Gemini Elementa Astronomiae*. Leipzig: Teubner, 1898.

Marques, António Henrique R. de Oliveira (ed.). *História dos Portugueses no Extremo Oriente*, 3 vols. Lisbon: Fundação Oriente, 1995–2000.

Martín-Merás, María Luisa. 'Fabricando la imagen del mundo. Los trabajos cartográficos de la Casa de la Contratación'. In *España y América. Un océano de negocios. Quinto centenario de la Casa de la Contratación, 1503–2003*, edited by G. de C. Boutet, 89–102. Madrid: Sociedad Estatal de Conmemoraciones Culturales, 2003.

Matar, Nabil I. *Europe through Arab Eyes, 1578–1727*. New York and Chichester: Columbia University Press, 2009.

Matsuda, Matt K. 'The Pacific'. *American Historical Review* 111 (2006): 758–80.

Matsuda, Matt K. *Pacific Worlds. A History of Seas, Peoples, and Cultures*. 2nd edn. Cambridge and New York: Cambridge University Press, 2014.

Mauro, Frédéric. *Die europäische Expansion*. Wiesbaden: Steiner, 1984.

McCormick, E. H. *Omai. Pacific Envoy*. Auckland: Auckland University Press, 1977.

McDougall, Walter A. *Let the Sea Make a Noise. A History of the North Pacific from Magellan to MacArthur*. New York: Basic Books, 1993.

McGhee, Robert. *The Last Imaginary Place. A Human History of the Arctic World*. Oxford: Oxford University Press, 2005.

McKee, Sally. 'Gli schiavi'. In *Commercio e cultura mercantile*, edited by F. Franceschi, R. A. Goldthwaite and R. C. Mueller, 339–68. Vicenza: Colla, 2007.

McKeown, Adam. 'Movement'. In *Pacific Histories. Ocean, Land, People*, edited by D. Armitage and A. Bashford, 143–65. Basingstoke and New York: Palgrave Macmillan, 2014.

Melis, Federigo. *Origini e sviluppi delle assicurazioni in Italia (sec. XIV–XVI)*. Rome: Istituto Nazionale delle Assicurazioni, 1975.

Menzel, Anja. *Sailing the Waters of Institutional Complexity. State-to-State Cooperation on the Combat of Piracy*. PhD diss. University of Greifswald 2019.

Menzel, Anja and Lisa Otto. 'Connecting the Dots. Implications of the Intertwined Global Challenges to Maritime Security'. In *Global Challenges in Maritime Security. An Introduction*, edited by L. Otto, 229–43. Wiesbaden: Springer, 2020.

Metcalf, Thomas. *Imperial Connections. India in the Indian Ocean Arena, 1869–1920*. Berkeley: University of California Press, 2008.

Miller, Michael B. *Europe and the Maritime World*. Cambridge and New York: Cambridge University Press, 2013.

Miller, Peter N. (ed.). *The Sea. Thalassography and Historiography*. Ann Arbor: University of Michigan Press, 2013.

Miller, Peter N. 'The Mediterranean and the Mediterranean World in the Age of Peiresc'. In *The Sea. Thalassography and Historiography*, edited by P. N. Miller, 251–76. Ann Arbor: University of Michigan Press, 2013.

Miller, Peter N. *Peiresc's Mediterranean World*. Cambridge, MA: Harvard University Press, 2015.

Mollat, Michel. *Jacques Coeur ou l'esprit de l'enterprise*. Paris: Aubier, 1988.

Monson, William. 'Advice How to Plant the Island of Madagascar, or St. Lawrence, the Greatest Island in the World, and a Part of Africa'. In *The Naval Tracts of Sir William Monson in Six Books Edited with a Commentary Drawn from the State Papers and Other Original Sources*, edited by M. Oppenheim, 434–9. London: Navy Records Society, 1913.

Moore, Anneliese. 'Harry Maitey. From Polynesia to Prussia'. *Hawaiian Journal of History* 2 (1977): 125–61.

Morgan, Philip D. 'Africa and the Atlantic, c. 1450 to c. 1820'. In *Atlantic History. A Critical Appraisal*, edited by J. P. Greene and P. D. Morgan, 223–48. Oxford and New York: Oxford University Press, 2009.

Mörke, Olaf. *Die Geschwistermeere. Eine Geschichte des Nord- und Ostseeraums*. Stuttgart: Kohlhammer Verlag, 2015.

Morosini, Roberta. 'Penelopi in viaggio "fuori rotta" nel Decameron e altrove. "Metamorfosi" et scambi nel Mediterraneo medievale'. *California Italian Studies Journal* 1 (2010): 1–32.

N

Nadri, Ghulam. 'Sailing in Hazardous Waters. Maritime Merchants of Gujarat in the Second Half of the Eighteenth Century'. In *The Trading World of the Indian Ocean, 1500–1800*, edited by O. Prakash, 255–84. Delhi, Chennai and Chandigarh: Pearson, 2012.

Nehlsen-von Stryk, Karin. *Die venezianische Seeversicherung im 15. Jahrhundert*. Ebelsbach: Gremer, 1986.

Neutsch, Cornelius. 'Briefverkehr als Medium internationaler
   Kommunikation im ausgehenden 19. und beginnenden 20. Jahrhundert'.
   In *Kommunikationsrevolutionen. Die neuen Medien des 16. und 19.
   Jahrhunderts*, edited by M. North, 129–55. 2nd edn. Cologne, Weimar and
   Vienna: Böhlau, 2001.
Niedner, Felix (ed.). *Grönländer und Färinger Geschichten*, translated by E. von
   Mendelssohn. Jena: Diederichs, 1912.
Niemeijer, Hendrik E. *Calvinisme en koloniale stadscultuur, Batavia 1619–1725*.
   Amsterdam: Vrije Universiteit Amsterdam, 1996.
Niemeijer, Hendrik E. *Batavia. Een koloniale samenleving in de zeventiende eeuw*.
   Amsterdam: Uitgeverij Balans, 2005.
Nierstrasz, Chris. *Rivalry for Trade in Tea and Textiles. The English and Dutch East
   India Companies (1700–1800)*. Basingstoke and New York: Palgrave MacMillan,
   2015.
Nieuwenhuize, Hielke van. '*Die privat organisierte niederländische Hilfsflotte in
   schwedischem Dienst im Torstenssonkrieg (1643–1645). Aufstellung, Einsatz
   und ihre Bedeutung für den Export niederländischer Seefahrtstechnologie*'.
   PhD diss. University of Greifswald, 2016.
Nieuwenhuize, Hielke van. *Niederländische Seefahrer in schwedischen Diensten.
   Seeschifffahrt und Technologietransfer im 17. Jahrhundert*. Cologne, Weimar
   and Vienna: Böhlau, 2021.
Noone, Kevin J. 'Sea-Level Rise'. In *Managing Ocean Environments in a Changing
   Climate. Sustainability and Economic Perspectives*, edited by K. J. Noone,
   U. R. Sumaila and R. J. Diaz, 97–126. Amsterdam, Boston and Heidelberg:
   Elsevier, 2013.
Noone, Kevin J., Ussif Rashid Sumaila and Robert J. Diaz (eds.). *Managing
   Ocean Environments in a Changing Climate. Sustainability and Economic
   Perspectives*. Amsterdam, Boston and Heidelberg: Elsevier, 2013.
North, Michael. *Art and Commerce in the Dutch Golden Age*. New Haven and
   London: Yale University Press, 1997.
North, Michael. 'German Sailors, 1650–1900'. In *'Those Emblems of Hell?'
   European Sailors and the Maritime Labour Market, 1570–1870*, edited by J.
   R. Bruijn, J. Lucassen and P. C. van Royen, 253–66. St John's, Newfoundland:
   International Maritime Economic History Association, 1997.
North, Michael. *Art and Commerce in the Dutch Golden Age*. New Haven and
   London: Yale University Press, 1999.
North, Michael. 'Modell Niederlande. Wissenstransfer und Strukturanpassung
   in Zeiten der Globalisierung'. In *Deutsch-Niederländische Beziehungen in
   Vergangenheit, Gegenwart und Zukunft. IV. Symposium, 27./28. November
   1998*, ed. by the Deutsch-Niederländische Gesellschaft e.V., 165–76. Berlin:
   Vorstand der DNG, 1999.
North, Michael. 'Das Bild des Kaufmanns'. In *Der neue Mensch. Perspektiven der
   Renaissance*, edited by M. Schwarze, 233–57. Regensburg: Pustet, 2000.
North, Michael. 'Einleitung'. In *Kommunikationsrevolutionen. Die neuen Medien
   des 16. und 19. Jahrhunderts*, edited by M. North, IX–XIX. 2nd edn. Cologne,
   Weimar, Vienna: Böhlau, 2001.
North, Michael. 'The Long Way of Professionalisation in the Early Modern
   German Art Trade'. In *Economia e arte, secc. XIII.–XVIII.*, edited by S.
   Cabaciocchi, 459–71. Florence: Le Monnier, 2002.

North, Michael. 'The Hamburg Art Market and Influences on Northern and Central Europe'. *Scandinavian Journal of History* 28 (2003): 253–61.

North, Michael. 'Koloniale Kunstwelten in Ostindien. Kulturelle Kommunikation im Umkreis der Handelskompanien'. *Jahrbuch für Europäische Überseegeschichte* 5 (2005): 55–72.

North, Michael. *Kleine Geschichte des Geldes*. Munich: Beck, 2009.

North, Michael (ed.). *Artistic and Cultural Exchanges between Europe and Asia, 1400–1900. Rethinking Markets, Workshops and Collections*. Farnham, Surrey: Ashgate, 2010.

North, Michael. *The Expansion of Europe, 1250–1500*, translated by P. E. Selwyn. Manchester: Manchester University Press, 2012.

North, Michael. *Geschichte der Niederlande*. 4th edn. Munich: Beck, 2013.

North, Michael. 'Towards a Global Material Culture. Domestic Interiors in the Atlantic and Other Worlds'. In *Cultural Exchange and Consumption Patterns in the Age of Enlightenment. Europe and the Atlantic World*, edited by V. Hyden-Hanscho, R. Pieper and W. Stangl, 81–96. Bochum: Winkler, 2013.

North, Michael. 'Art and Material Culture in the Cape Colony and Batavia in the Seventeenth and Eighteenth Centuries'. In *Mediating Netherlandish Art and Material Culture in Asia*, edited by Thomas DaCosta Kaufmann and Michael North, 111–28. Amsterdam: Amsterdam University Press, 2014.

North, Michael. *Kommunikation, Handel, Geld und Banken in der Frühen Neuzeit*. 2nd edn. Munich, Berlin and Boston: de Gruyter Oldenbourg, 2014.

North, Michael. *The Baltic. A History*, translated by Kenneth Kronenberg. Cambridge, MA: Harvard University Press, 2015.

North, Michael. 'The Atlantic Ocean'. In *The World's Oceans. Geography, History, and Environment*, edited by R. F. Buschmann and L. Nolde, 18–34. Santa Barbara: ABC-CLIO, 2018.

North, Michael. 'The Baltic Sea'. In *Oceanic Histories*, edited by D. R. Armitage, A. Bashford and S. Sivasundaram, 209–33. Cambridge, New York, Melbourne, New Delhi and Singapore: Cambridge University Press, 2018.

North, Michael. 'Europe Meets Asia. Between Missionary Work and Cultural Exchange'. In *Europe and the Sea. Exhibition catalogue, Deutsches Historisches Museum*, edited by D. Blume, C. Brennecke, U. Breymayer and T. Eisentraut, 53–61. Munich: Hirmer, 2018.

North, Michael. 'Connected Seas I'. *History Compass* (2018), e12503 (https://doi.org/10.1111/hic3.12503).

North, Michael. 'Connected Seas II. The Perception and Memory of the Seas'. *History Compass* (2018), e12502 (https://doi.org/10.1111/hic3.12502).

Northrup, David. *Africa's Discovery of Europe, 1450–1850*. Oxford and New York: Oxford University Press, 2002.

Nurminen, Juha and Matti Lainema. *A History of Arctic Exploration: Discovery, Adventure, and Endurance at the Top of the World*. London: Conway, 2010.

O

O'Brien, Patrick. 'Historiographical Traditions and Modern Imperatives for the Restoration of Global History'. *Journal of Global History* 1 (2006): 3–39.

O'Reilly, Karen. 'British Affluence Migrants in the Costa del Sol in the Late 20th Century'. In *The Encyclopedia of European Migration and Minorities: From the Seventeenth Century to the Present*, edited by K. J. Bade et al., 262–4. Cambridge and New York: Cambridge University Press, 2011.

Ogborn, Miles. *Global Lives. Britain and the World 1550–1800*. Cambridge and New York: Cambridge University Press, 2008.

Ojala, Jari and Antti Räihä. 'Navigation Acts and the Integration of North Baltic Shipping in the Early Nineteenth Century', *International Journal of Maritime History* 29 (2017): 1–18.

Ojala, Jari, Jaakko Pehkonen and Jari Eloranta. 'Deskilling and Decline in Skill Premiums during the Age of Sail. Swedish and Finnish Seamen, 1751–1913'. *Explorations in Economic History* 61 (2016): 85–94.

Orlandi, Angela. *Mercaderies i diners. La correspondència datiniana entre València i Mallorca (1395–1398)*. Valencia: Universidad de Valencia, 2008.

Orlandi, Angela. 'The Catalonia Company. An Almost Unexpected Success'. In *Francesco di Marco Datini. The Man, the Merchant*, edited by G. Nigro, 347–76. Florence: Firenze University Press and Prato: Fondazione Istituto Internazionale di Storia Economica F. Datini, 2010.

Ormrod, David. *The Rise of Commercial Empires. England and the Netherlands in the Age of Mercantilism, 1650–1770*. Cambridge, New York and Melbourne: Cambridge University Press, 2003.

Ortelius, Abraham. *Theatrum Orbis Terrarum*. Gedruckt zu Nuernberg durch Johann Koler Anno MDLXXII, Nuremberg 1572. Darmstadt: Primus, 2006.

Osterhammel, Jürgen. *Transformation of the World. A Global History of the Nineteenth Century*. Princeton and Oxford: Princeton and University Press, 2014.

P

Paine, Lincoln P. *The Sea and Civilization. A Maritime History of the World*. London: Atlantic Books, 2013.

Palmer, Sarah. 'The British Shipping Industry 1850–1914'. In *Change and Adaptation in Maritime History. The North Atlantic Fleets in the Nineteenth Century*, edited by L. R. Fischer and G. E. Panting, 87–115. St John's, Newfoundland: Memorial University of Newfoundland Maritime History Group, 1984.

Parry, John Horace. *The Discovery of the Sea*. New York: Dial Press, 1974.

Parthasarathi, Prasannan. 'Cotton Textiles in the Indian Subcontinent, 1200–1800'. In *The Spinning World. A Global History of Cotton Textiles, 1200–1850*, edited by G. Riello and P. Parthasarathi, 17–42. Oxford and New York: Oxford University Press, 2009.

Pearsall, Sarah M. S. *Atlantic Families. Lives and Letters in the Later Eighteenth Century*. Oxford and New York: Oxford University Press, 2010.

Pearson, Michael N. *The Indian Ocean*. London and New York: Routledge, 2006.

Peets, Jüri. *The Power of Iron. Iron Production and Blacksmithy in Estonia and Neighbouring Areas in Prehistoric Period and the Middle Ages*. Tallinn: Ajaloo Instituut, 2003.

Pezzolo, Luciano. 'The Venetian Economy'. In *A Companion to Venetian History, 1400–1797*, edited by E. R. Dursteler, 255–90. Leiden and Boston: Brill, 2013.

Phillips, Carla Rahn. 'The Organization of Oceanic Empires. The Iberian World in the Habsburg Period'. In *Seascapes. Maritime Histories, Littoral Cultures, and Transoceanic Exchanges*, edited by J. H. Bentley, R. Bridenthal and K. Wigen, 71–86. Honolulu: University of Hawai'i Press, 2007.

Picard, Christophe. *Sea of the Caliphs. The Mediterranean in the Medieval Islamic World*, translated by Nicholas Elliott. Cambridge and London: The Belknap Press of Harvard University Press, 2018.

Pieper, Renate. *Die Vermittlung einer neuen Welt. Amerika im Kommunikationsnetz des habsburgischen Imperiums (1493–1598)*. Mainz: von Zabern, 2000.

Pieper, Renate. 'From Cultural Exchange to Cultural Memory. Spanish American Objects in Spanish and Austrian Households of the Early 18th Century'. In *Cultural Exchange and Consumption Patterns in the Age of Enlightenment. Europe and the Atlantic World*, edited by V. Hyden-Hanscho, R. Pieper and W. Stangl, 213–34. Bochum: Winkler, 2013.

Pierce, Donna (ed.). *Asia and Spanish America. Trans-Pacific Artistic and Cultural Exchange, 1500–1800*. Denver: Denver Art Museum, 2009.

Pigafetta, Antonio. *Magellan's Voyage around the World*, translated by J. A. Robertson. Cleveland: Clark, 1906.

Po, Ronald C. *The Blue Frontier. Maritime Vision and Power in the Qing Empire*. Cambridge and New York: Cambridge University Press, 2018.

Pohl, Hans. 'Die Consulados im spanischen Amerika'. *Jahrbuch für Geschichte von Staat, Wirtschaft und Gesellschaft Lateinamerikas* 3 (1966): 402–15.

Prakash, Om. 'The Trading World of the Indian Ocean. Some Defining Features'. In *The Trading World of the Indian Ocean, 1500–1800*, edited by O. Prakash, 3–52. Delhi, Chennai and Chandigarh: Pearson, 2012.

Prakash, Om (ed.). *The Trading World of the Indian Ocean, 1500–1800*. Delhi, Chennai and Chandigarh: Pearson, 2012.

Prange, Sebastian R. *Monsoon Islam. Trade and Faith on the Medieval Malabar Coast*. Cambridge and New York: Cambridge University Press, 2018.

Price, Neil. 'Dying and the Dead. Viking Age Mortuary Behaviour'. In *The Viking World*, edited by S. Brink and N. Price, 257–73. London and New York: Routledge, 2009.

Ptak, Roderich. 'Ming Maritime Trade to Southeast Asia, 1368–1567. Visions of a "System"'. In *From the Mediterranean to the China Sea. Miscellaneous Notes*, edited by C. Guillot, D. Lombard and R. Ptak, 157–91. Wiesbaden: Harrassowitz, 1998.

Ptak, Roderich. *Die maritime Seidenstraße. Küstenräume, Seefahrt und Handel in vorkolonialer Zeit*. Munich: Beck, 2007.

R

Rah, Sicco. *Asylsuchende und Migranten auf See. Staatliche Rechte und Pflichten aus völkerrechtlicher Sicht*. Berlin and Heidelberg: Springer, 2009.

Rauh, Nicholas Kregotis. *Merchants, Sailors and Pirates in the Roman World*. Stroud: Tempus, 2003.

Ravenstein, Ernst Georg (ed.). *A Journal of the First Voyage of Vasco da Gama 1497–1499*. London: Hakluyt Society, 1898.

Rediker, Marcus. 'The Pirate and the Gallows. An Atlantic Theater of Terror and Resistance'. In *Seascapes. Maritime Histories, Littoral Cultures, and Transoceanic Exchanges*, edited by J. H. Bentley, R. Bridenthal and K. Wigen, 239–50. Honolulu: University of Hawai'i Press, 2007.

Rediker, Marcus. *Outlaws of the Atlantic. Sailors, Pirates and Motley Crews in the Age of Sail*. Boston: Beacon Press, 2014.

Reichert, Folker. *Die Erfahrung der Welt. Reisen und Kulturbegegnung im späten Mittelalter*. Stuttgart, Berlin and Cologne: Kohlhammer, 2001.

Reid, Anthony. *Southeast Asia in the Age of Commerce, 1450–1680*. 2 vols. New Haven and London: Yale University Press, 1988–1995.

Reinhard, Wolfgang. *Geschichte der europäischen Expansion*, vol. 1: *Die Alte Welt bis 1818*. Stuttgart, Berlin and Cologne: Kohlhammer, 1983.

Reinhard, Wolfgang. *Geschichte der europäischen Expansion*, vol. 2: *Die Neue Welt*. Stuttgart, Berlin and Cologne: Kohlhammer, 1985.

Reinhard, Wolfgang. *Geschichte der europäischen Expansion*, vol. 3: *Die Alte Welt seit 1918*. Stuttgart, Berlin and Cologne: Kohlhammer, 1988.

Reinhard, Wolfgang. *Geschichte der europäischen Expansion*, vol. 4: *Dritte Welt Afrika*. Stuttgart, Berlin and Cologne: Kohlhammer, 1990.

Reinhard, Wolfgang (ed.). *Geschichte der Welt. Weltreiche und Weltmeere, 1350–1750*. Munich: C. H. Beck, 2014.

Reinhard, Wolfgang (ed.). *Empires and Encounters. 1350–1750*. Cambridge, MA: Belknap Press of Harvard University Press, 2015.

Reinhard, Wolfgang. *Die Unterwerfung der Welt. Globalgeschichte der europäischen Expansion 1415–2015*. Munich: Beck, 2016.

Ressel, Magnus. *Zwischen Sklavenkassen und Türkenpässen. Nordeuropa und die Barbaresken in der Frühen Neuzeit*. Berlin and Boston: de Gruyter, 2012.

Ressel, Magnus. 'Protestant Slaves in Northern Africa during the Early Modern Age'. In *Serfdom and Slavery in the European Economy 11th–18th Centuries*, edited by S. Cavaciocchi, 523–36. Florence: Firenze University Press, 2014.

Richter, Dieter. *Das Meer. Geschichte der ältesten Landschaft*. Berlin: Wagenbach, 2014.

Rink, Oliver A. 'Seafarers and Businessmen. The Growth of Dutch Commerce in the Lower Hudson River Valley'. In *Dutch New York. The Roots of Hudson Valley Culture*, edited by R. Panetta, 7–34. New York: Hudson River Museum and Fordham University Press, 2009.

Roding, Juliette. 'The Myth of the Dutch Renaissance in Denmark. Dutch Influence on Danish Architecture in the 17th Century'. In *Baltic Affairs. Relations between the Netherlands and North-Eastern Europe 1500–1800*, edited by J. P. S. Lemmink and J. S. A. M., Koningsbrugge, 343–53. Nijmegen: Inos, 1990.

Roding, Juliette. 'The North Sea Coasts, an Architectural Unity?' In *The North Sea and Culture (1550–1800), Proceedings of the International Conference Held at Leiden, 21–22 April 1995*, edited by J. Roding and L. Heerma van Voss, 95–106. Hilversum: Verloren, 1996.

Rosenstein, Nathan Stewart. *Rome at War: Farms, Families, and Death in the Middle Republic. Studies in the History of Greece and Rome*. Chapel Hill, NC: University of North Carolina Press, 2004.

Rossum, Matthias van. 'A "Moorish World" within the Company. The VOC, Maritime Logistics and Subaltern Networks of Asian Sailors'. *Itinerario* 36, no. 3 (2012): 39–60.

Rossum, Matthias van. *Werkers van de wereld. Globalisering, arbeid en interculturele ontmoetingen tussen Aziatische en Europese zeelieden in dienst van de VOC, 1600–1800*. Hilversum: Verloren, 2014.

Rozwadowski, Helen M. *The Sea Knows No Boundaries. A Century of Marine Science under ICES*. Copenhagen: International Council for the Exploration of the Sea, 2002.

Rozwadowski, Helen M. *Vast Expanses. A History of the Oceans*. London: Reaction Books, 2018.

Rubiés, Joan-Pau. 'The Worlds of Europeans, Africans, and Americans, c. 1490'. In *The Oxford Handbook of the Atlantic World c. 1450–c. 1850*, edited by N. Canny and P. Morgan, 21–37. Oxford and New York: Oxford University Press, 2011.

Rumphius, George Everhard. *D'Amboinsche Rariteitkamer*. Amsterdam: Halma, 1705.

Rupert, Linda M. *Creolization and Contraband. Curaçao in the Early Modern Atlantic World*. Athens and London: University of Georgia Press, 2012.

Russell, Peter Edward. 'Prince Henry the Navigator'. In *Portugal, Spain and the African Atlantic. 1343–1490. Chivalry and Crusade from John of Gaunt to Henry the Navigator*, edited by P. E. Russell, 3–30. Aldershot: Variorum, 1995.

Russell-Wood, Anthony John R. 'The Portuguese Atlantic, 1415–1808'. In *Atlantic History. A Critical Appraisal*, edited by J. P. Greene and P. D. Morgan, 81–109. Oxford and New York: Oxford University Press, 2009.

S

Saldanha, Arun. 'The Itineraries of Geography, Jan Huygen van Linschoten's Itinerario and Dutch Expedition to the Indian Ocean. 1594–1602'. *Annals of the Association of American Geographers* 101 (2011): 149–77.

Salesa, Damon. 'The Pacific in Indigenous Times'. In *Pacific Histories. Ocean, Land, People*, edited by D. Armitage and A. Bashford, 31–52. Basingstoke and New York: Palgrave Macmillan, 2014.

Samsonowicz, Henryk. 'Die Handelsstraße Ostsee-Schwarzes Meer im 13. und 14. Jahrhundert'. In *Der hansische Sonderweg? Beiträge zur Sozial- und Wirtschaftsgeschichte der Hanse*, edited by S. Jenks and M. North, 23–30. Cologne, Weimar and Vienna: Böhlau, 1993.

Sánchez-Albornoz, Nicolás. *La población de América latina. Desde los tiempos precolombinos al año 2025*. Madrid: Ed Alianza, 1994.

Sarnowsky, Jürgen. *Die Erkundung der Welt. Die großen Entdeckungsreisen von Marco Polo bis Humboldt*. Munich: Beck, 2015.

Sawyer, Birgit. *The Viking-Age Rune-Stones. Custom and Commemoration in Early Medieval Scandinavia*. Oxford and New York: Oxford University Press, 2000.

Sawyer, Peter. *The Oxford Illustrated History of the Vikings*. Oxford and New York: Oxford University Press, 1997.

Schaff, Philip and Henry Wace (eds.). *A Select Library of the Nicene and Post-Nicene Fathers of the Christian Church*, 2nd series, vol. VIII: *St. Basil. Letters and Select Works*. New York: The Christian literature Company, 1895.

Schama, Simon. *The Embarrassment of Riches. An Interpretation of Dutch Culture*. New York: Knopf, 1987.

Scheltjens, Werner. *Dutch Deltas. Emergence, Functions and Structure of the Low Countries' Maritime Transport System, ca. 1300–1850.* Leiden and Boston: Brill, 2015.

Schildhauer, Johannes. 'Zur Verlagerung des See- und Handelsverkehrs im nordeuropäischen Raum während des 15. und 16. Jahrhunderts. Eine Untersuchung auf der Grundlage der Danziger Pfalkammerbücher'. *Jahrbuch für Wirtschaftsgeschichte* 9, no. 4 (1968): 187–211.

Schmeidler, Bernhard (ed.). *Magistri Adam Bremensis Gesta Hammaburgensis ecclesiae pontificum.* Hannover and Leipzig: Hahn, 1917.

Schmidt, Benjamin. *Innocence Abroad. The Dutch Imagination and the New World, 1570–1670.* Cambridge, New York and Melbourne: Cambridge University Press, 2001.

Schmidt, Benjamin. 'The Dutch Atlantic. From Provincialism to Globalism'. In *Atlantic History. A Critical Appraisal*, edited by J. P. Greene and P. D. Morgan, 163–87. Oxford and New York: Oxford University Press, 2009.

Schmidt, Benjamin. *Inventing Exoticism. Geography, Globalism, and Europe's Early Modern World.* Philadelphia: University of Pennsylvania Press, 2015.

Schmitt, Carl. *Land und Meer. Eine weltgeschichtliche Betrachtung.* Leipzig: Reclam, 1942.

Schmitt, Eberhard and Charles Verlinden (eds.). *Die mittelalterlichen Ursprünge der europäischen Expansion.* Munich: Beck, 1986.

Schmitt, Eberhard et al. (eds.). *Dokumente zur Geschichte der europäischen Expansion*, vol. 4: *Wirtschaft und Handel der Kolonialreiche.* Munich: Beck, 1988.

Schnurmann, Claudia. *Atlantische Welten. Engländer und Niederländer im amerikanisch-atlantischen Raum 1648–1713.* Cologne, Weimar and Vienna: Böhlau, 1998.

Schöffer, Ivo and F. S. Gaastra. 'The Import of Bullion and Coin into Asia by the Dutch East India Company in the Seventeenth and Eighteenth Centuries'. In *Dutch Capitalism and World Capitalism*, edited by M. Aymard, 215–33. Cambridge, New York and Melbourne: Cambridge University Press, 1982.

Schottenhammer, Angela (ed.). *The East Asian 'Mediterranean'. Maritime Crossroads of Culture, Commerce and Human Migration.* Wiesbaden: Harrassowitz, 2008.

Schriewer, Klaus. 'German Affluence Migrants in Spain since the Late 20th Century'. In *The Encyclopedia of European Migration and Minorities: From the Seventeenth Century to the Present*, edited by K. Bade et al., 402–4. Cambridge and New York: Cambridge University Press, 2011.

Schröder, Tim (ed.). *World Ocean Review. Living with the Oceans*, no. 1. Hamburg: maribus gGmbH, 2010.

Schröder, Tim (ed.). *World Ocean Review. Living with the Oceans*, no. 3: *Marine Resources - Opportunities and Risks.* Hamburg: Maribus gGmbH, 2014.

Schuller, Wolfgang. *Die Herrschaft der Athener im Ersten Attischen Seebund.* Berlin and New York: de Gruyter, 1974.

Schuller, Wolfgang. *Das erste Europa 1000 v. Chr.–500 n. Chr.* Stuttgart: Ulmer, 2004.

Schumpeter, Elizabeth Boody. *English Overseas Trade Statistics, 1697–1808.* Oxford: Clarendon Press, 1960.

Seifert, Dieter. *Kompagnons und Konkurrenten. Holland und die Hanse im späten Mittelalter.* Cologne, Weimar and Vienna: Böhlau, 1997.

Serrera, Ramón María. 'La Casa de la Contratación en Sevilla (1503–1717)'. In *España y América. Un océano de negocios. Quinto centenario de la Casa de la Contratación, 1503–2003*, edited by G. de C. Boutet, 47–64. Madrid: Sociedad Estatal de Conmemoraciones Culturales, 2003.

Sheriff, Abdul. 'Globalisation with a Difference. An Overview'. In *The Indian Ocean. Oceanic Connections and the Creation of New Societies*, edited by A. Sheriff and H. Engseng, 11–44. London: Hurst, 2014.

Sicking, Louis. 'A Wider Spread of Risk. A Key to Understanding Holland's Domination of Eastward and Westward Seafaring from the Low Countries in the Sixteenth Century'. In *The Dynamics of Economic Culture in the North Sea and Baltic Region in the Late Middle Ages and Early Modern Period*, edited by H. Brand and L. Müller, 122–35. Hilversum: Verloren, 2007.

Sigurðsson, Gísli. 'Introduction'. In *The Vinland Sagas. The Icelandic Sagas about the First Documented Voyages across the North Atlantic*, edited by G. Sigurðsson, ix–xxxix. London: Penguin Books, 2008.

Sigurðsson, Gísli. 'The North Atlantic Expansion'. In *The Viking World*, edited by Stefan Brink and Neil Price, 562–70. London and New York: Routledge, 2009.

Sigurðsson, Jón Viðar. 'Iceland'. In *The Viking World*, edited by Stefan Brink and Neil Price, 571–8. London and New York: Routledge, 2009.

Sinn, Elizabeth. *Pacific Crossing. California Gold, Chinese Migration, and the Making of Hong Kong*. Hong Kong: Hong Kong University Press, 2013.

Skwiot, Christine. 'Migration and the Politics of Sovereignty, Settlement, and Belonging in Hawai'i'. In *Connecting Seas and Connected Ocean Rims. Indian, Atlantic, and Pacific Oceans and China Seas Migrations from the 1830s to the 1930s*, edited by D. R. Gabaccia and D. Hoerder, 440–63. Leiden and Boston: Brill, 2011.

Smith, Adam. *An Inquiry into the Nature and Causes of the Wealth of Nations*. Books I, II, III, IV and VI. Digital edn. Amsterdam: Meta Libri, 2007.

Smith, Clinton F. 'Native Borderlands. Colonialism and the Development of Native Power'. In *Globalizing Borderlands Studies in Europe and North America*, edited by J. W. I. Lee and M. North, 193–207. Lincoln and London: University of Nebraska Press, 2016.

Smith, Vanessa. 'Falling from Grace. George Vason'. In *Exploration and Exchange. A South Sea Anthology 1680–1900*, edited by J. Lamb, V. Smith and N. Thomas, 156–69. Chicago and London: University of Chicago Press, 2000.

Sobel, Dava. *Longitude. The True Story of a Lone Genius Who Solved the Greatest Scientific Problem of His Time*. New York: Bloomsbury, 2007.

Sörlin, Sverker. 'The Arctic Ocean'. In *Oceanic Histories*, edited by D. Armitage, A. Bashford and S. Sivasundaram, 269–95. Cambridge, New York, Melbourne, New Delhi and Singapore: Cambridge University Press, 2018.

Stangl, Werner. *Zwischen Authentizität und Fiktion. Die private Korrespondenz spanischer Emigranten aus Amerika, 1492–1824*. Cologne, Weimar and Vienna: Böhlau, 2012.

Steele, Ian Kenneth. *The English Atlantic, 1675–1740. An Exploration of Communication and Community*. Oxford and New York: Oxford University Press, 1986.

Steinberg, Philip E. *The Social Construction of the Ocean*. Cambridge, New York and Melbourne: Cambridge University Press, 2001.

Stein-Hölkeskamp, Elke. *Das archaische Griechenland. Die Stadt und das Meer.* Munich: Beck, 2015.

Stern, Philip J. *The Company-State. Corporate Sovereignty and the Early Modern Foundations of the British Empire in India.* Oxford and New York: Oxford University Press, 2011.

Steuer, Heiko. 'Geldgeschäfte und Hoheitsrechte zwischen Ostseeländern und islamischer Welt'. *Zeitschrift für Archäologie* 12 (1978): 255–60.

Steuer, Heiko. 'Gewichtsgeldwirtschaft im frühgeschichtlichen Europa – Feinwaagen und Gewichte als Quellen zur Währungsgeschichte'. In *Untersuchungen zu Handel und Verkehr der vor- und frühgeschichtlichen Zeit in Mittel- und Nordeuropa,* vol. 4: *Der Handel der Karolinger- und Wikingerzeit,* edited by K. Düwel, 405–527. Göttingen: Vandenhoeck & Ruprecht, 1987.

Stieda, Wilhelm (ed.). *Hildebrand Veckinchusen. Briefwechsel eines deutschen Kaufmanns im 15. Jahrhundert.* Leipzig: Verlag von S. Hirzel, 1921.

Strabo. *The Geography of Strabo,* translated by Horace White, vol. II. Cambridge, MA: Harvard University Press, 1988.

Strasser, Ulrike. 'Die Kartierung der Palaosinseln. Geographische Imagination und Wissenstransfer zwischen europäischen Jesuiten und mikronesischen Insulanern um 1700'. *Geschichte und Gesellschaft* 362 (2010): 197–230.

Subrahmanyam, Sanjay. *The Portuguese Empire in Asia 1500–1700. A Political and Economic History.* 2nd edn. Chichester: Willey-Blackwell, 2012.

Subrahmanyam, Sanjay. *Europe's India. Words, People, Empires, 1500–1800.* Cambridge, MA: Harvard University Press, 2017.

Subrahmanyam, Sanjay. *Empires between Islam and Christianity, 1500–1800.* Albany: SUNY Press, 2019.

Subramanian, Lakshmi. 'Commerce, Circulation, and Consumption. Indian Ocean Communities in Historical Perspective'. In *Indian Ocean Studies. Cultural, Social, and Political Perspectives,* edited by S. Moorthy and A. Jamal, 136–57. New York and Abingdon: Routledge, 2010.

Sugiyama, Akiko. 'The Transmission and Circulation of Western Opera in the Netherlands East Indies, 1835–1869. Preliminary Observations'. *SEJARAH: Journal of the Department of History* 26, no. 2 (2017): 98–105.

Sugiyama, Akiko. 'Maritime Journeys of European Opera in the Indonesian Archipelago, 1835–1869'. *International Journal of Maritime History* 31, no. 2 (2019): 248–62.

Sutherland, Heather. 'Southeast Asian History and the Mediterranean Analogy'. *Journal of Southeast Asian Studies,* 34, no. 1 (2003): 1–20.

T

Tagliacozzo, Eric, Helen F. Siu and Peter C. Perdue (eds.). *Asia Inside Out. Changing Times.* Cambridge, MA and London: Harvard University Press, 2019.

Tan, Tai Yong and Aileen Lau (eds.). *Maritime Heritage of Singapore.* Singapore: Suntree Media, 2005.

Tate, E. Mowbray. *Transpacific Steam. The Story of Steam Navigation from the Pacific Coast of North America to the Far East and the Antipodes, 1867–1941.* New York: Cornwall Books, 1986.

Taylor, Jean Gelman. *The Social World of Batavia. European and Eurasian in Dutch Asia.* 2nd edn. Madison: University of Wisconsin Press, 2009.

Tenenti, Alberto and Ugo Tucci. *Storia di Venezia*, vol xii: *Il mare.* Rome: Istituto della Enciclopedia Italiana, 1991.

Thomas, Nicholas. *Islanders. The Pacific in the Age of Empire.* New Haven and London: Yale University Press, 2010.

Thomas, Nicholas. 'The Age of Empire in the Pacific'. In *Pacific Histories. Ocean, Land, People*, edited by D. Armitage and A. Bashford, 75–96. Basingstoke and New York: Palgrave Macmillan, 2014.

Thornton, John K. *Africa and Africans in the Making of the Atlantic World. 1400–1800.* 2nd edn. Cambridge and New York: Cambridge University Press, 2006.

Thornton, John. *A Cultural History of the Atlantic World 1250–1820.* Cambridge, New York and Melbourne: Cambridge University Press, 2012.

Tielhof, Milja van. *The 'Mother of All Trades'. The Baltic Grain Trade in Amsterdam from the Late 16th to the 19th Century.* Leiden, Boston and Cologne: Brill, 2002.

Tolbert, Jane. 'Ambiguity and Conversion in the Correspondence of Nicolas-Claude Fabri de Peiresc and Thomas D'Arcos, 1630–1637'. *Journal of Modern History* 13 (2009): 1–24.

Tomber, Roberta. 'From the Roman Red Sea to beyond the Empire. Egyptian Ports and Their Trading Partners'. *British Museum Studies in Ancient Egypt and Sudan* 18 (2012): 201–15.

Trivellato, Francesca. *The Familiarity of Strangers. The Sephardic Diaspora, Livorno, and Cross-Cultural Trade in the Early Modern Period.* New Haven and London: Yale University Press, 2009.

Tucci, Ugo. 'Traffici e navi nel Mediterraneo in età moderna'. In *La penisola italiana e il mare. Costruzioni navali, trasporti e commerci tra xv e xx secolo*, edited by T. Fanfani, 57–70. Naples: Edizioni Scientifische Italiane, 1993.

Tucci, Ugo. *Venezia e dintorni. Evoluzioni e trasformazioni.* Rome: Viella, 2014.

Tung, Jaime C. '"The Sea Is History". Reading Derek Walcott through a Melancholic Lens'. BA thesis, Mount Holyoke College, 2006.

Turner Bushnell, Amy. 'Indigenous America and the Limits of the Atlantic World, 1493–1825'. In *Atlantic History. A Critical Appraisal*, edited by J. P. Greene and P. D. Morgan, 191–221. Oxford and New York: Oxford University Press, 2009.

U

Unger, Richard W. *Dutch Shipbuilding before 1800.* Assen: Van Gorcum, 1978.

Unger, Richard W. *The Ship in the Medieval Economy, 600–1600.* London: Croom Helm and Montreal: McGill-Queen's University Press, 1980.

Unger, Richard W. (ed.). *Shipping and Economic Growth 1350–1850.* Leiden and Boston: Brill, 2011.

V

Valentyn, François. *Oud en Nieuw Oost-Indiën*. Dordrecht: van Braam, 1724–6.

Vason, George. 'Falling from Grace'. In *Exploration and Exchange. A South Sea Anthology 1680–1900*, edited by J. Lamb, V. Smith and N. Thomas, 156–69. Chicago and London: University of Chicago Press, 2000.

Ven, Gerard P. van de. *Man-made Lowlands. History of Water Management and Land Reclamation in the Netherlands*. 4th edn. Utrecht: Uitgeverij Matrijs, 2004.

Verhulst, Adriaan E. 'Der frühmittelalterliche Handel der Niederlande und der Friesenhandel'. In *Untersuchungen zu Handel und Verkehr der vor- und frühgeschichtlichen Zeit*, vol. 3: *Der Handel des frühen Mittelalters. Bericht über die Kolloquien der Kommission für die Altertumskunde Mittel- und Nordeuropas in den Jahren 1980 bis 1983*, edited by K. Düwel and H. Jankuhn, 381–91. Göttingen: Vandenhoeck & Ruprecht, 1985.

Villamar, Cuauhtémoc. *Portuguese Merchants in the Manila Galleon System. 1565–1600*. Milton Park: Taylor & Francis Group, 2021.

Villiers, John. 'The Estado da India in South East Asia'. In *South East Asia. Colonial History*, vol. 1: *Imperialism before 1800*, edited by P. Kratoska and P. Borschberg, 151–78. London and New York: Routledge, 2001.

Vitkus, Daniel J. (ed.). *Piracy, Slavery, and Redemption. Barbary Captivity Narratives from Early Modern England*. New York and Chichester: Columbia University Press, 2001.

Vries, Jan de. 'The Dutch Atlantic Economies'. In *The Atlantic Economy during the Seventeenth and Eighteenth Centuries. Organization, Operation, Practice, and Personnel*, edited by P. Coclanis, 1–29. Columbia: University of South Carolina Press, 2005.

Vries, Jan de and Ad van der Woude. *The First Modern Economy. Success, Failure, and Perseverance of the Dutch Economy, 1500–1815*. Cambridge, New York and Melbourne: Cambridge University Press, 1997.

W

Wadsworth, James E. *Global Piracy. A Documentary History of Seaborne Banditry*. London and New York: Bloomsbury Academic, 2019.

Waghenaer, Lucas Jansz. *T'eerste deel vande Spieghel der zeevaerdt, van de navigatie der Westersche zee [...] in diversche zee caerten begrepen*, Leiden 1584. Facsimile edn. Amsterdam: Meridian Publ. Co., 1964.

Walcott, Derek. *The Star-Apple Kingdom*. 4th edn. New York: Farrar, Straus and Giroux, 1986.

Wardzyński, Michał. 'Zwischen den Niederlanden und Polen-Litauen. Danzig als Mittler niederländischer Kunst und Musterbücher'. In *Land und Meer. Kultureller Austausch zwischen Westeuropa und dem Ostseeraum in der Frühen Neuzeit*, edited by M. Krieger and M. North, 23–50. Cologne, Weimar and Vienna: Böhlau, 2004.

Ware, Rudolph T. *The Walking Qu'ran. Islamic Education, Embodied Knowledge, and History in West Africa*. Chapel Hill: University of North Carolina Press, 2014.

Watson Andaya, Barbara. '"A People That Range into All the Kingdoms of Asia". The Chulia Trading Network in the Malay World in the Seventeenth and Eighteenth Centuries'. In *The Trading World of the Indian Ocean, 1500–1800*, edited by O. Prakash, 353–86. Delhi, Chennai and Chandigarh: Pearson, 2012.

Watson Andaya, Barbara. 'Rivers, Oceans, and Spirits. Water Cosmologies, Gender, and Religious Change in Southeast Asia'. *TRaNS Trans-Regional and -National Studies of Southeast Asia* 1, no. 2 (2016): 1–25.

Watson Andaya, Barbara. 'Oceans Unbounded. Traversing Asia across "Area Studies"'. *Journal of Asian Studies* 65, no. 4 (2006): 669–90.

Watson Andaya, Barbara. 'Seas, Oceans and Cosmologies in Southeast Asia'. *Journal of Southeast Asian Studies* 48, no. 3 (2017): 349–71.

Watson Andaya, Barbara and Leonard Y. Andaya. *A History of Early Modern Southeast Asia, 1400–1830*. Cambridge, New York and Melbourne: Cambridge University Press, 2015.

Wee, Herman van der. *The Growth of the Antwerp Market and the European Economy (Fourteenth–Sixteenth Centuries)*. Louvain: Publications universitaires, 1963.

Wee, Herman van der. 'Structural Changes in European Long-Distance Trade, and Particularly in the Re-Export Trade from South to North, 1350–1750'. In *The Rise of Merchant Empires. Long Distance Trade in the Early Modern World 1350–1750*, edited by J. D. Tracy, 13–33. Cambridge, New York and Melbourne: Cambridge University Press, 1990.

Wendt, Reinhard. 'Einleitung. Der Pazifische Ozean und die Europäer. Ambitionen, Erfahrungen und Transfers'. *Saeculum* 64, no. 1 (2014): 1–7.

Wendt, Reinhard. *Vom Kolonialismus zur Globalisierung. Europa und die Welt seit 1500*. 2nd edn. Paderborn: Schönigh, 2016.

Wenzlhuemer, Roland. *Connecting the Nineteenth-Century World. The Telegraph and Globalization*. Cambridge, New York and Melbourne: Cambridge University Press, 2013.

Wernicke, Horst. *Die Städtehanse 1280–1418. Genesis – Strukturen – Funktionen*. Weimar: Böhlau, 1983.

White, Richard. *The Middle Ground. Indians, Empires, and Republics in the Great Lakes Region, 1650–1815*. Cambridge, New York and Melbourne: Cambridge University Press, 1991.

Whitelock, Dorothy (ed.). *English Historical Documents*, vol. I, *c. 500–1042*. 2nd ed. London: Routledge, 1979.

Wilcox, Chris, Erik van Sebille and Britta Denise Hardesty. 'Threat of Plastic Pollution to Seabirds Is Global, Pervasive, and Increasing'. *PNAS* 112, no. 38 (2015): 11899–904.

Wilson, Charles. *Profit and Power. A Study of England and the Dutch Wars*. London: Longmans, Green, and Co., 1957.

Wilson, Charles Henry. 'The Decline of the Netherlands'. In *Economic History and the Historian. Collected Essays*, edited by C. H. Wilson. London: Weidenfeld & Nicolson, 1969.

Wissenschaftlicher Beirat der Bundesregierung Globale Umweltveränderungen [WBGU]. *Welt im Wandel. Menschheitserbe Meer*. Berlin: WBGU, 2013.

Wolf, Burkhardt. *Fortuna di mare. Literatur und Seefahrt*. Zurich and Berlin: Diaphanes, 2013.

Wolfschmidt, Gudrun (ed.). *'Navigare necesse est.' Geschichte der Navigation*. Norderstedt: Books on Demand, 2008.

Wolfschmidt, Gudrun. 'Von Kompaß und Sextant zu Radar und GPS – Geschichte der Navigation', in *'Navigare necesse est'. Geschichte der Navigation*, edited by Gudrun Wolfschmidt, 17–143. Norderstedt: Books on Demand, 2008.

Wong, Roy Bin. 'Entre monde et nation: les régions braudeliénnes en Asie'. *Annales* 66, no. 1 (2001): 9–16.

Wormbs, Nina, Ralf Döscher, Annika E. Nilsson and Sverker Sörlin. 'Bellwether, Exceptionalism, and Other Tropes: Political Coproduction of Arctic Climate Modeling'. In *Cultures of Prediction: Epistemic and Cultural Shifts in Computer-based Atmospheric and Climate Science*, edited by M. Heymann, G. Gramelsberger and M. Mahony, 133–55. London and New York: Routledge, 2017.

Wowk, Kateryna M. 'Paths to Sustainable Ocean Resources'. In *Managing Ocean Environments in a Changing Climate. Sustainability and Economic Perspectives*, edited by K. J. Noone, U. R. Sumaila and R. J. Diaz, 301–48. Amsterdam, Boston and Heidelberg: Elsevier, 2013.

Z

Zahedieh, Nuala. 'Economy'. In *The British Atlantic World, 1500–1800*, edited by D. Armitage and M. J. Braddick, 53–70. 2nd edn. Basingstoke and New York: Palgrave Macmillan, 2009.

Zakharov, Victor N., Gelina Harlaftis and Olga Katsiardi-Hering. *Merchant Colonies in the Early Modern Period*. London: Pickering & Chatto, 2012.

Zandvliet, Kees. *Mapping for Money. Maps, Plans and Topographic Paintings and Their Role in Dutch Overseas Expansion during the Sixteenth and Seventeenth Centuries*. Amsterdam: Batavian Lion International, 1998.

Zandvliet, Kees. *De Nederlandse ontmoeting met Azië 1600–1950*. Zwolle: Waanders, 2002.

Zeuske, Michael. *Sklavenhändler, Negreros und Atlantikkreolen. Eine Weltgeschichte des Sklavenhandels im atlantischen Raum*. Berlin and Boston: de Gruyter Oldenbourg, 2015.

Zimmerman Munn, Mary Lou. 'Corinthian Trade with the Punic West in the Classical Period'. *Corinth. The Centenary 1896–1996* 20 (2003): 195–217.

Web addresses

Allianz Global Corporate & Specialty. *Allianz. Totalverluste in der Schifffahrt auf Rekordtief, aber Pandemie und politische Spannungen trüben die Aussichten*. Munich: Press Release, 15 July 2020. Available online: https://www.agcs. allianz.com/news-and-insights/news/safety-shipping-review-2020-de.html (accessed 12.12.2020).

Allianz Global Corporate & Specialty. *Safety and Shipping Review 2020*. Available online: https://www.agcs.allianz.com/content/dam/onemarketing/agcs/agcs/ reports/AGCS-Safety-Shipping-Review-2020.pdf (accessed 12.12.2020).

Brankamp, Hanno. 'Die "Flüchtlingskrise". Flucht und Vertreibung in Afrika'. *Bundeszentrale für politische Bildung*, 28 February 2018. Available online: https://www.bpb.de/gesellschaft/migration/kurzdossiers/265328/flucht-und-vertreibung (accessed 12.12.2020).

Cruise Lines International Association (CLIA). *State of the Cruise Industry Outlook*, 2020. Available online: https://cruising.org/-/media/research-updates/research/state-of-the-cruise-industry.ashx (accessed 12.12.2020).

European Commission. *Commission proposes fishing opportunities in the Atlantic and North Sea for 2016*. Brussels: Press Release 10 November 2015. Available online: https://ec.europa.eu/commission/presscorner/detail/en/IP_15_6016 (accessed 24.11.2020).

European Maritime Safety Agency. *COVID-19. Impact on Shipping*. 17 July 2020. Available online: http://www.emsa.europa.eu/newsroom/covid19-impact/item/3836-july-2020-covid-19-impact-on-shipping-report.html (accessed 13.12.2020).

Francisco de Escobar, Letter from Escobar in Sevilla to his junior partner Diego de Ribera in Lima, 1553. Quoted in: http://faculty.smu.edu/bakewell/ bake well/texts/sevillemerchant.html.

Future Oceans Network. Christian-Albrechts-Universität zu Kiel. Available online: https://www.futureocean.org/en/index.php (accessed 09.06.2021).

Giese, Monique. 'COVID-19 impacts on global cruise industry. How is the cruise industry coping with the COVID-19 crisis?' *KPMG Blog* 23 July 2020. Available online: https://home.kpmg/xx/en/blogs/home/posts/2020/07/covid-19-impacts-on-global-cruise-industry.html (accessed 13.12.2020).

Institut für Seeverkehrswirtschaft und Logistik. *RWI/ISL-Containerumschlag-Index. 6,5 Prozent unter Vorjahreswert*, 26 May 2020. Available online: https://www.isl.org/en/containerindex/april-2020 (accessed 09.06.2021)

International Organization for Migration (IOM). *Missing Migrants Project*. Available online: https://missingmigrants.iom.int/ (accessed 09.11.2020).

Lamb, Kate. 'Indian Ocean tsunami. Survivor's Stories from Aceh'. *The Guardian*, 25 December 2014. Available online: https://www.theguardian.com/global-development/2014/dec/25/indian-ocean-tsunami-survivors-stories-aceh (accessed 24.11.2020).

Lindsey, Rebecca. 'Climate Change. Global Sea Level'. *National Oceanic and Atmospheric Administration Climate.gov*, 14 August 2020. Available online: https://www.climate.gov/news-features/understanding-climate/climate-change-global-sea-level (accessed 13.12.2020).

Lockton Companies LLP, *Re-evaluating the risk of mega ships*, 27 June 2019. Available online: https://www.locktoninternational.com/gb/articles/re-evaluating-risk-mega-ships (accessed 12.12.2020).

Maribus gGmbH. *World Ocean Review. Living with the Oceans* no. 1. Hamburg, 2010. Available online: https://worldoceanreview.com/wp-content/downloads/wor1/WOR1_en.pdf (accessed 09.06.2021).

Maribus gGmbH. *World Ocean Review. Living with the Oceans*, no. 3: *Marine Resources - Opportunities and Risks*. Hamburg, 2014. Available online: https://worldoceanreview.com/wp-content/downloads/wor3/WOR3_en.pdf (accessed 09.06.2021).

'Meer atmet auf: Neues Salzwasser für die Ostsee'. *Global Magazin für nachhaltige Zukunft* 2014/2018. Available online: https://globalmagazin.eu/themen/natur/meer-atmet-auf-salzwassereinbruch-in-der-zentralen-ostsee/ (accessed 24.11.2020).

'Mittelmeer', available online:http://www.wasser-wissen.de/abwasserlexikon/m/
mittelmeer.html (accessed 18.11.2015).

NASA. *Sea Level*, August 2020. Available online: https://climate.nasa.gov/vital-
signs/sea-level/ (accessed 13.12.2020).

Rieger, Daniel. 'Kein Kreuzfahrtschiff empfehlenswert. Fast alle Schiffe
fallen bei NABU-Kreuzfahrt-Check durch'. *NABU*, 6 August 2013. Available
online: https://www.nabu.de/umwelt-und-ressourcen/verkehr/schifffahrt/
kreuzschifffahrt/16042.html (accessed 24.11.2020).

Stevenson, Tom. 'In Ocean Scale. Considering the Most Essential Feature of
Modern Economy'. *TLS*, 19 June 2020. Available online: https://www.the-tls.
co.uk/articles/sinews-of-war-and-trade-laleh-khalili-book-review/ (accessed
12.12.2020).

Stevenson, Tom. 'Raue See. Die Geopolitik des maritimen Welthandels'. *Le
Monde diplomatique*, 13 August 2020. Available online: https://monde-
diplomatique.de/artikel/!5688408 (accessed 12.12.2020).

United Nations Conference of Trade and Development, Geneva. Maritime
Transport Statistics (UNCTAD). Available online: http://unctadstat.unctad.org/
wds/ReportFolders/reportFolders.aspx (accessed 24.11.2020).

UNHCR. The UN Refugee Agency, *Global Trends. Forced Displacement in 2019*,
Copenhagen: UNHCR Global Data Service, 2020. Available online: https://
www.unhcr.org/5ee200e37.pdf (accessed 12.12.2020).

Picture Credits

Fig. 1   © Wikipedia Commons

Fig. 2   © Wikipedia Commons

Fig. 3   © Wikipedia Commons

Fig. 4   © Wikimedia Commons

Fig. 5   © Wikipedia Commons

Fig. 6   © Wikipedia Commons

Fig. 7   National Portrait Gallery, London (NPG 538)

Fig. 8   From Adelbert von Chamisso, *Reise um die Welt* (Berlin, 1978), p. 280

Fig. 9   Courtesy of NUS Museum Collection. Singapore (S1970-0052-039-0)

Fig. 10 © Picture alliance/REUTERS/Yannis Behrakis

Index